The paradise on the hill

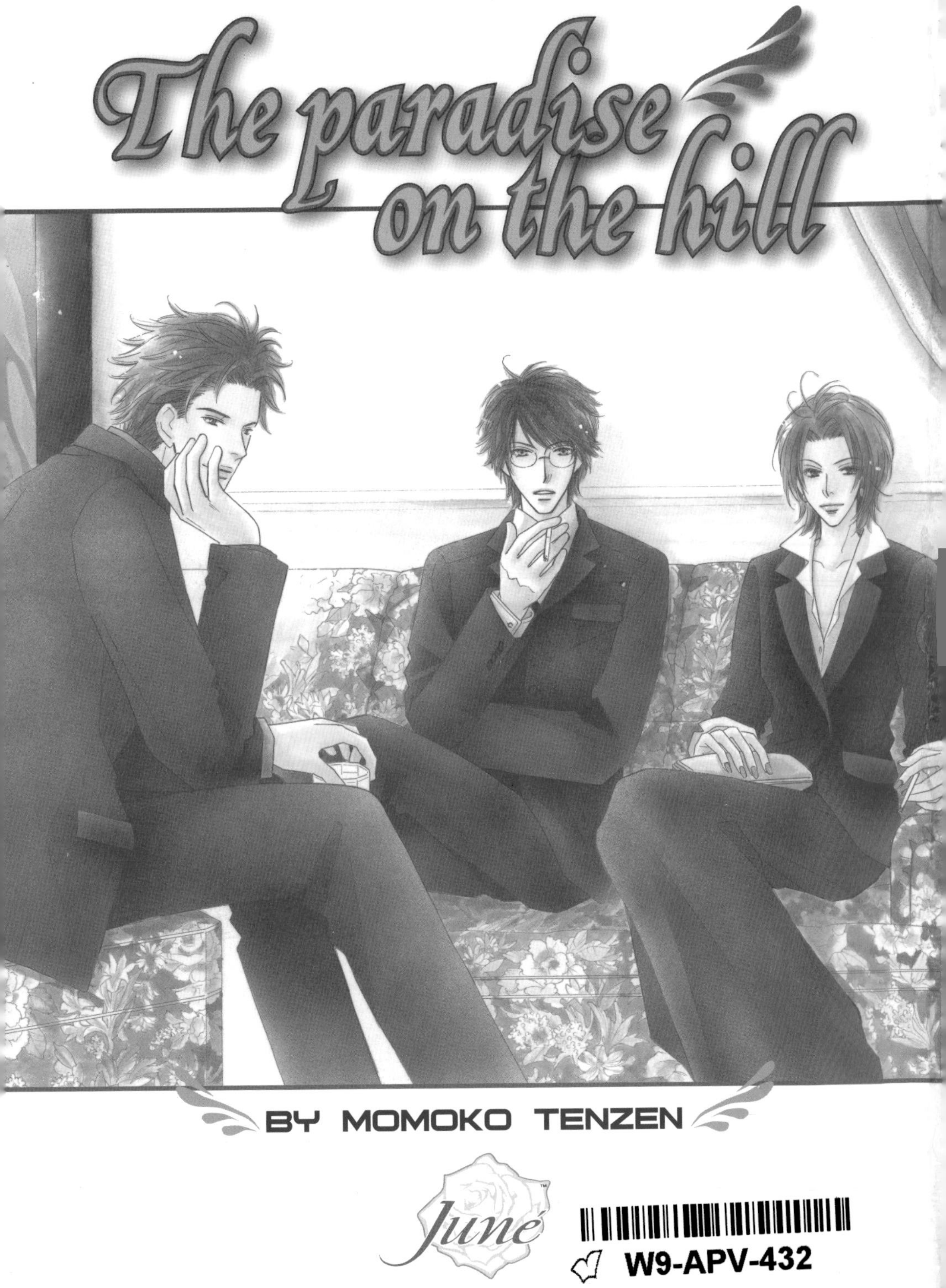

BY MOMOKO TENZEN

June™

The paradise on the hill

CONTENTS

Translation	Earl Gertwagen
Lettering	Tawnie Wilson
Graphic Design	Daryl Kuxhouse/Fred Lui
Editing	Daryl Kuxhouse
Editor in Chief	Fred Lui
Publisher	Hikaru Sasahara

English Edition Published by
DIGITAL MANGA PUBLISHING
A division of DIGITAL MANGA, Inc.
1487 W 178th Street, Suite 300
Gardena, CA 90248

www.dmpbooks.com

First Edition: May 2007
ISBN-10: 1-56970-835-5
ISBN-13: 978-1-56970-835-4

1 3 5 7 9 10 8 6 4 2

Printed in China

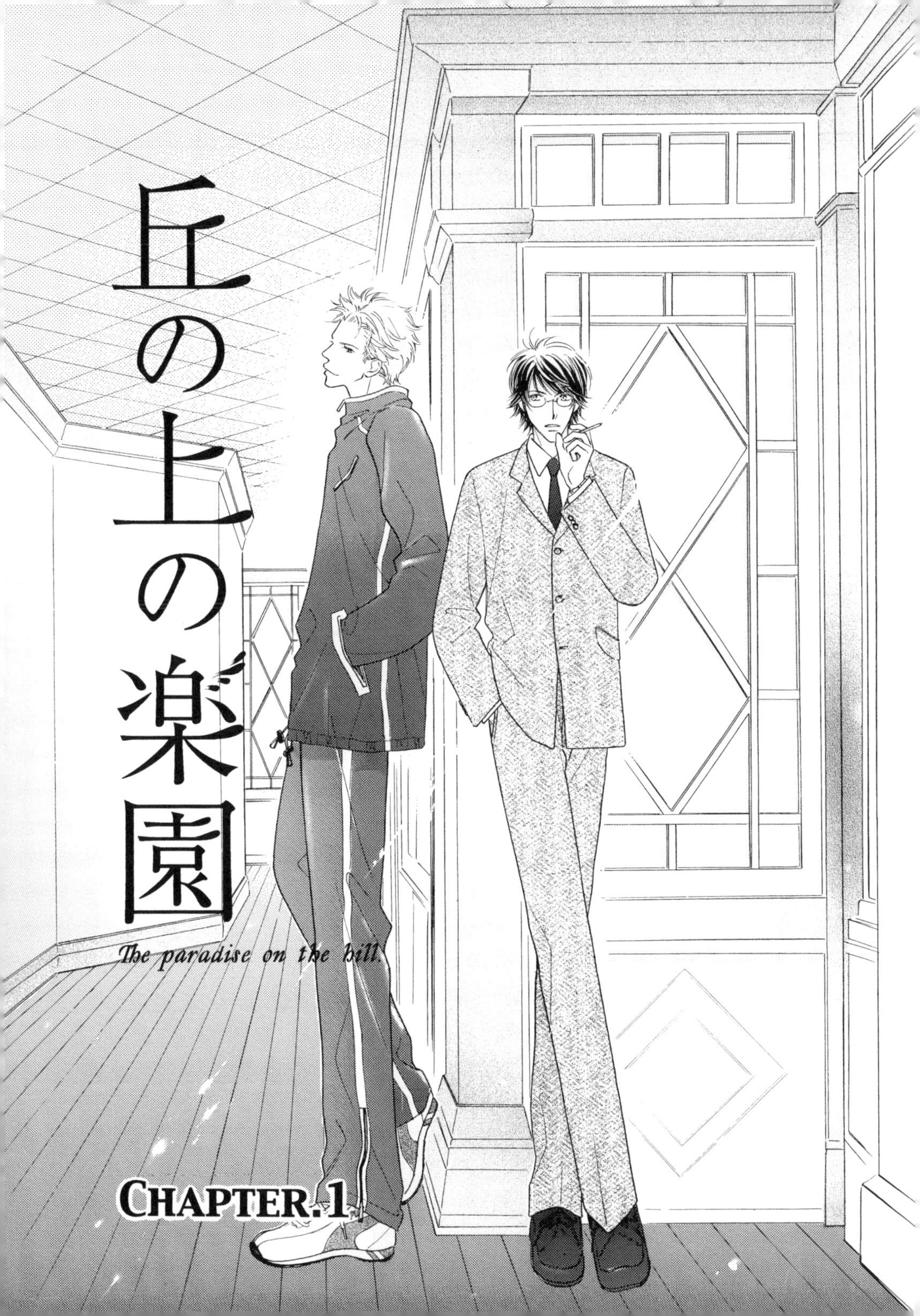
丘の上の楽園
The paradise on the hill.
CHAPTER.1

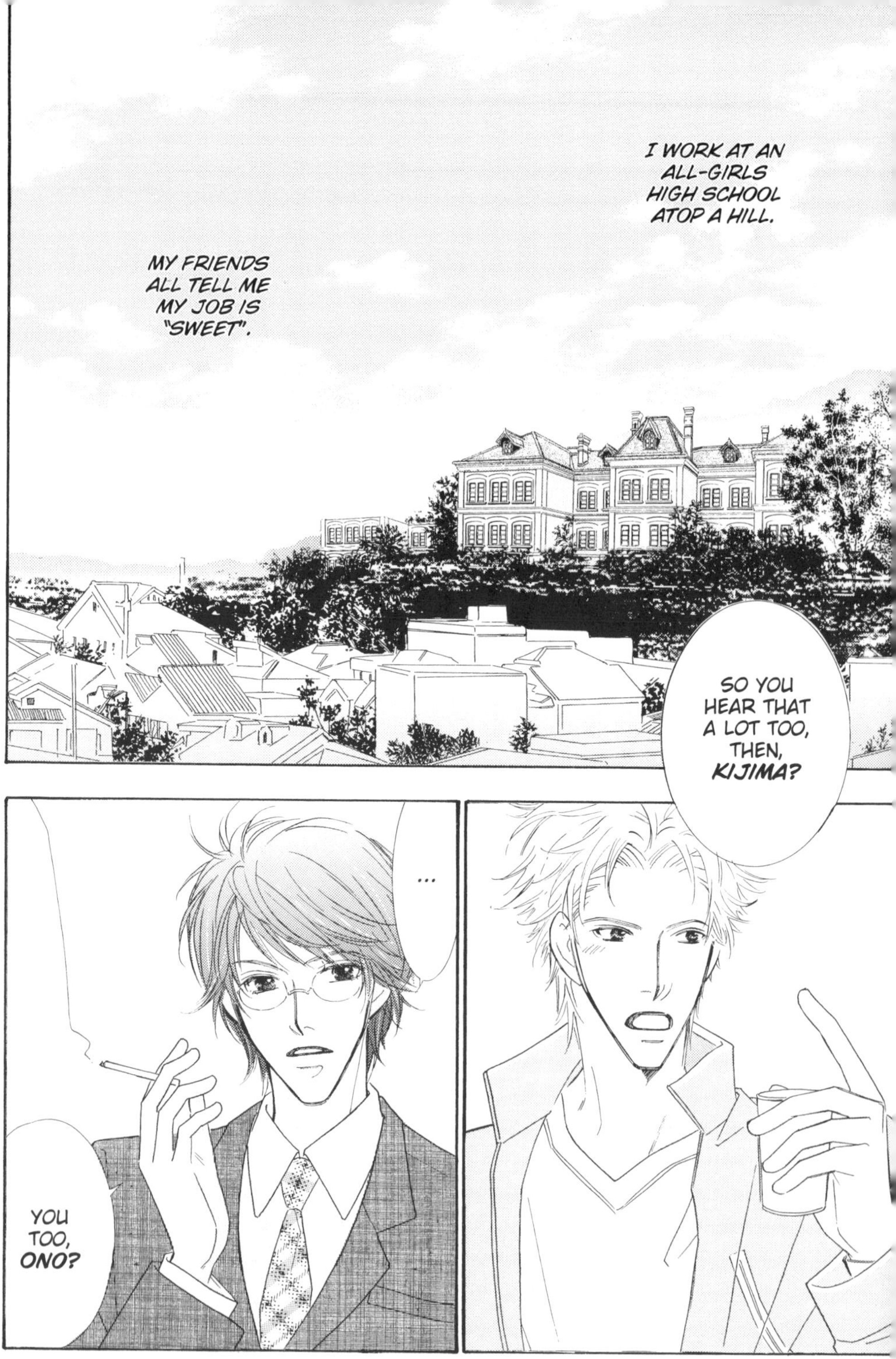
I WORK AT AN ALL-GIRLS HIGH SCHOOL ATOP A HILL.
MY FRIENDS ALL TELL ME MY JOB IS "SWEET".
SO YOU HEAR THAT A LOT TOO, THEN, KIJIMA?
...
YOU TOO, ONO?

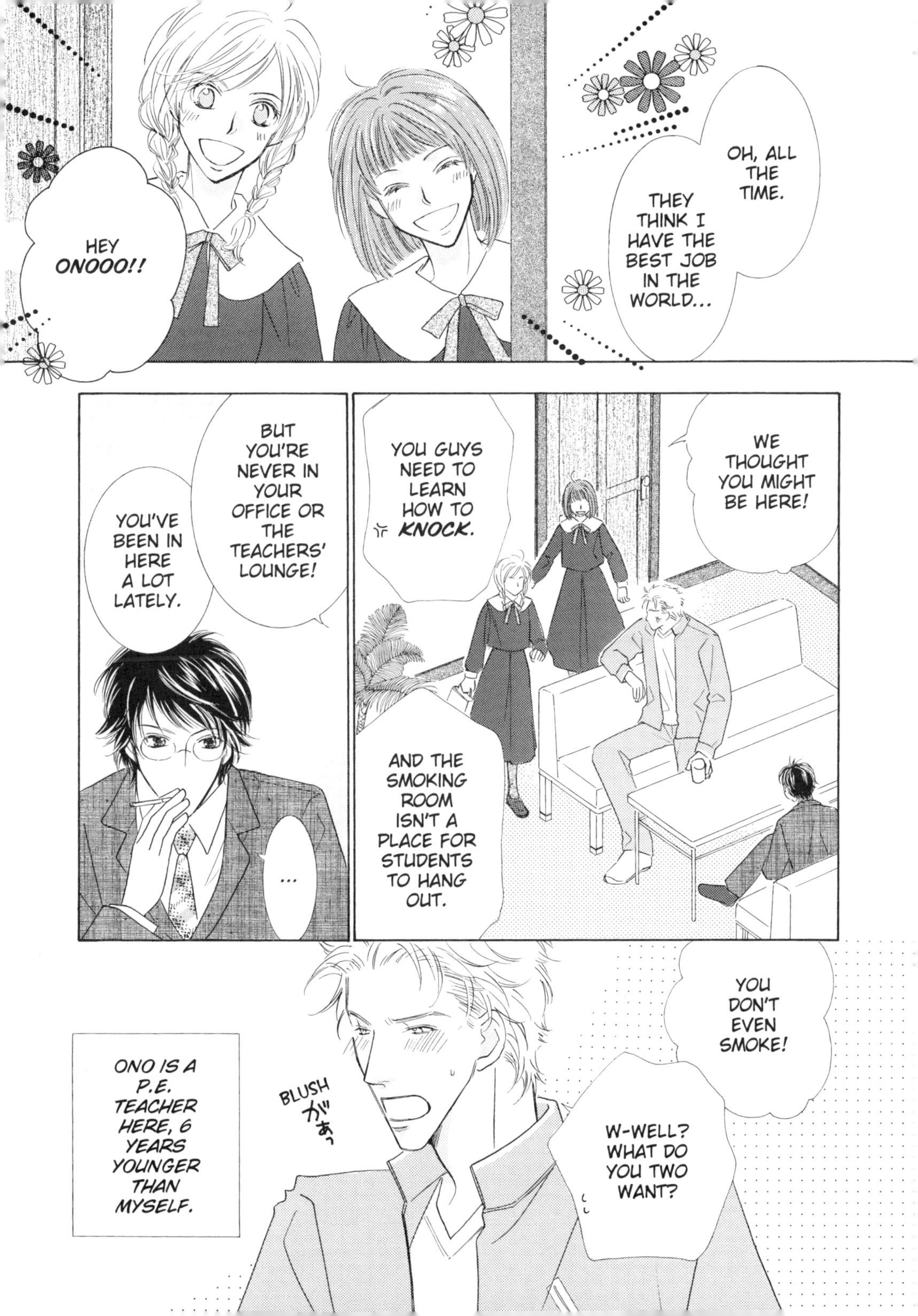
OH, ALL THE TIME.
THEY THINK I HAVE THE BEST JOB IN THE WORLD...
HEY ONOOO!!
WE THOUGHT YOU MIGHT BE HERE!
YOU GUYS NEED TO LEARN HOW TO KNOCK.
AND THE SMOKING ROOM ISN'T A PLACE FOR STUDENTS TO HANG OUT.
BUT YOU'RE NEVER IN YOUR OFFICE OR THE TEACHERS' LOUNGE!
YOU'VE BEEN IN HERE A LOT LATELY.
...
YOU DON'T EVEN SMOKE!
W-WELL? WHAT DO YOU TWO WANT?
BLUSH がぁっ
ONO IS A P.E. TEACHER HERE, 6 YEARS YOUNGER THAN MYSELF.

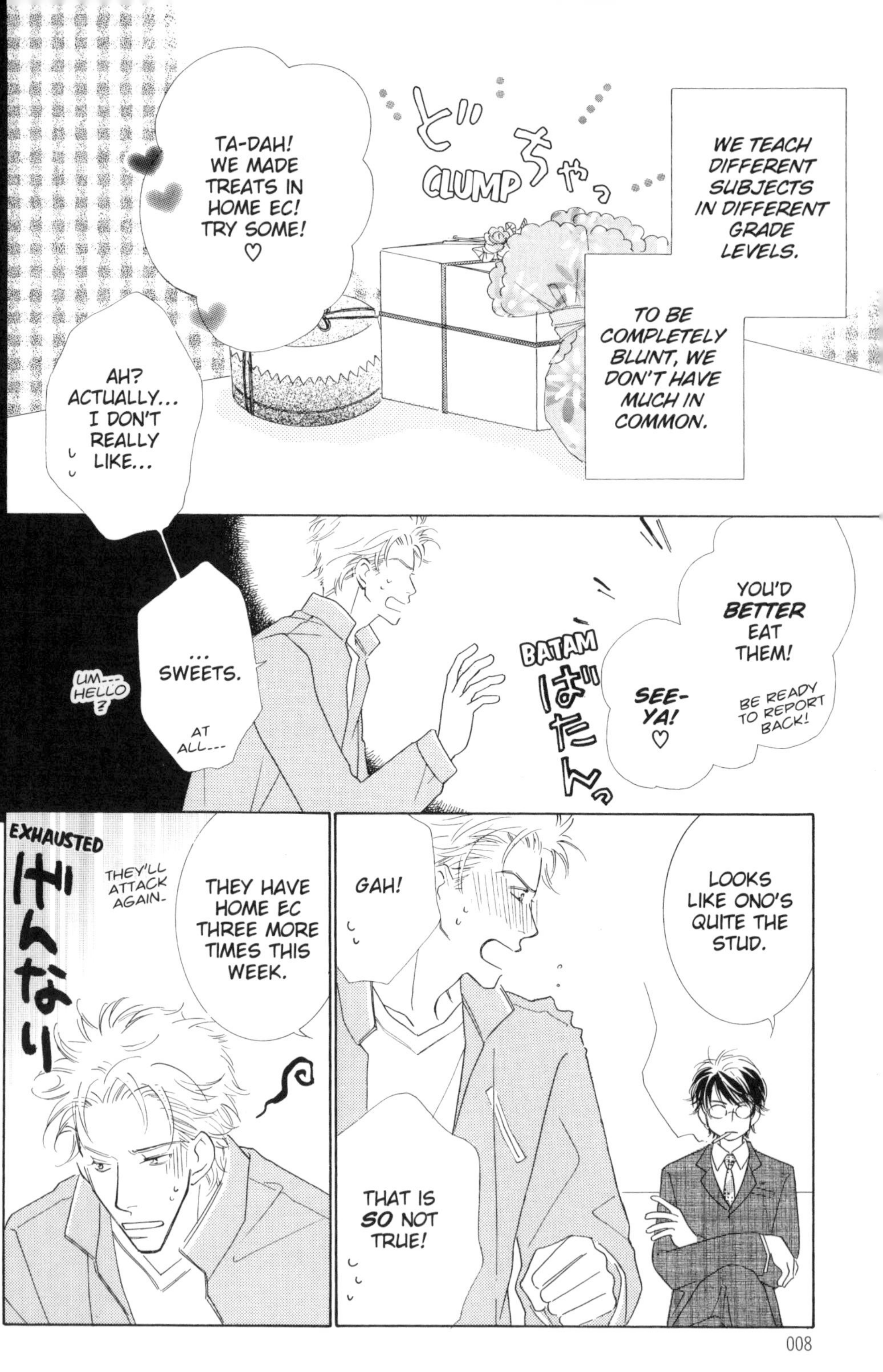
WE TEACH DIFFERENT SUBJECTS IN DIFFERENT GRADE LEVELS.
TO BE COMPLETELY BLUNT, WE DON'T HAVE MUCH IN COMMON.
どちゃっ
CLUMP
TA-DAH! WE MADE TREATS IN HOME EC! TRY SOME! ♡
AH? ACTUALLY... I DON'T REALLY LIKE...
YOU'D BETTER EAT THEM!
BE READY TO REPORT BACK!
SEE-YA! ♡
BATAM
ばたんっ
...SWEETS.
AT ALL...
UM... HELLO?
LOOKS LIKE ONO'S QUITE THE STUD.
GAH!
THAT IS SO NOT TRUE!
THEY HAVE HOME EC THREE MORE TIMES THIS WEEK.
THEY'LL ATTACK AGAIN.
EXHAUSTED
げんなり

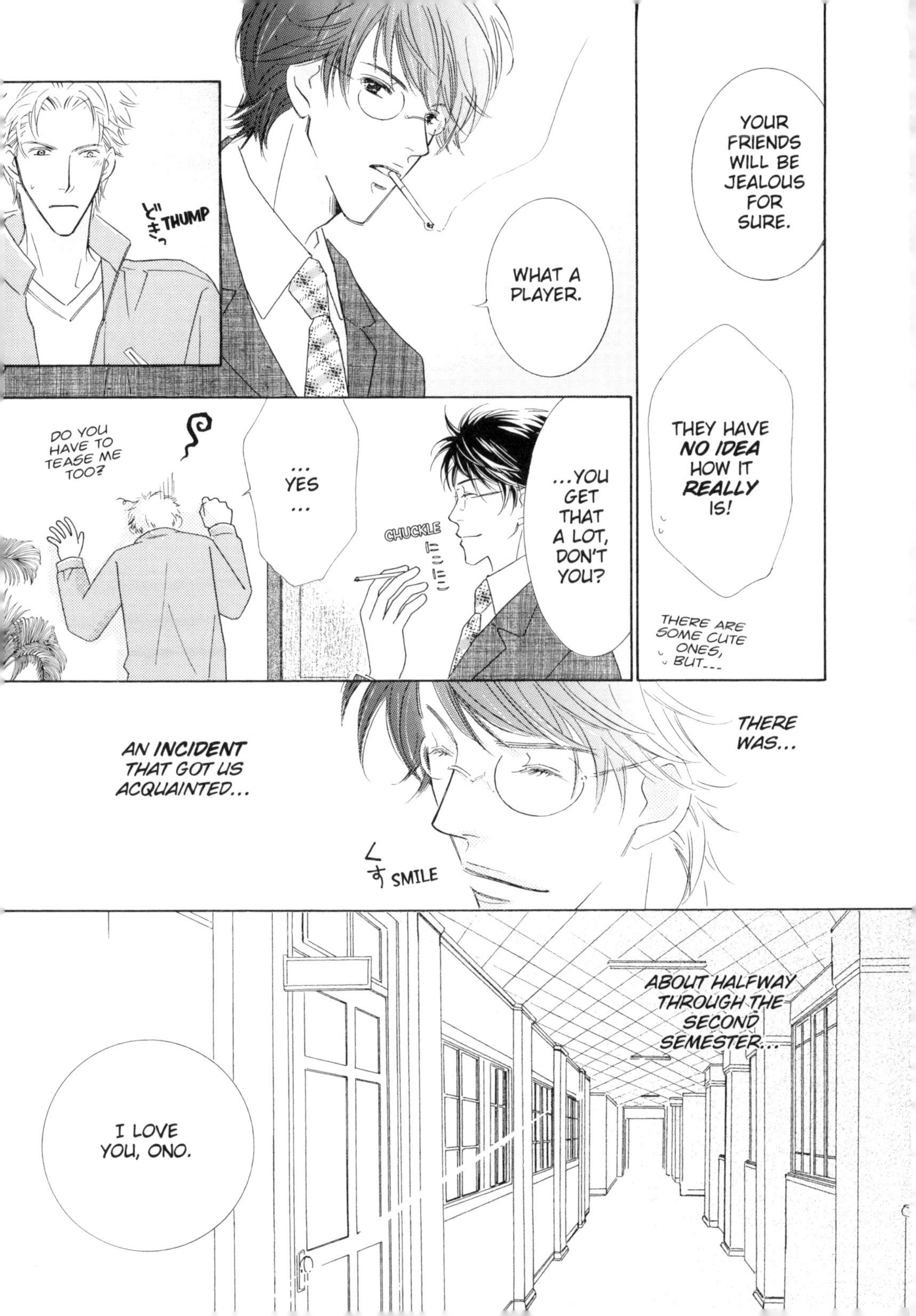
YOUR FRIENDS WILL BE JEALOUS FOR SURE.
THEY HAVE **NO IDEA** HOW IT **REALLY** IS!
THERE ARE SOME CUTE ONES, BUT...
WHAT A PLAYER.
THUMP
...YOU GET THAT A LOT, DON'T YOU?
CHUCKLE
...YES...
DO YOU HAVE TO TEASE ME TOO?
THERE WAS...
AN **INCIDENT** THAT GOT US ACQUAINTED...
SMILE
ABOUT HALFWAY THROUGH THE SECOND SEMESTER...
I LOVE YOU, ONO.

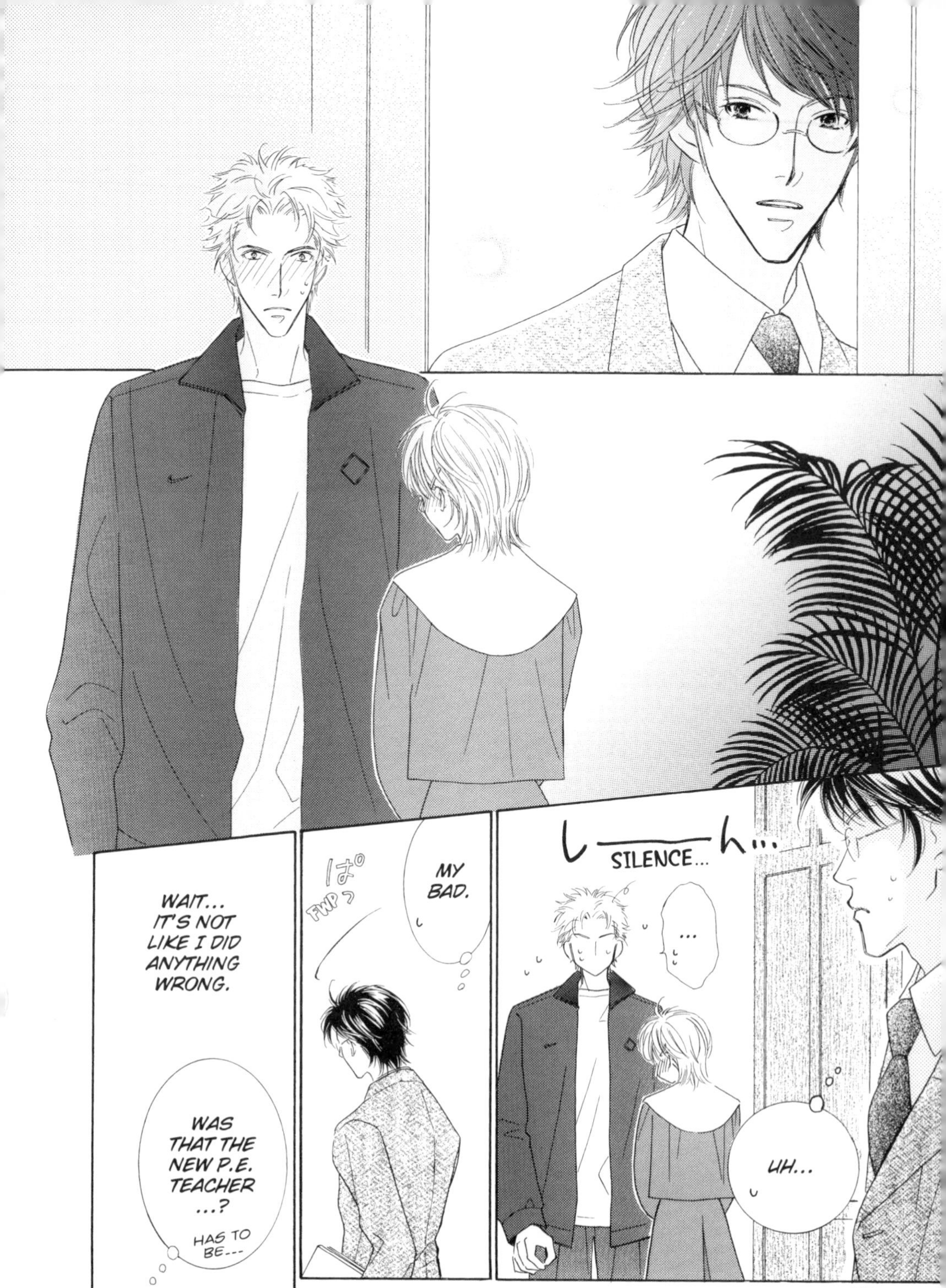
しーーん…
SILENCE…
…
UH…
ぱっ
FWP
MY BAD.
WAIT… IT'S NOT LIKE I DID ANYTHING WRONG.
WAS THAT THE NEW P.E. TEACHER …?
HAS TO BE---

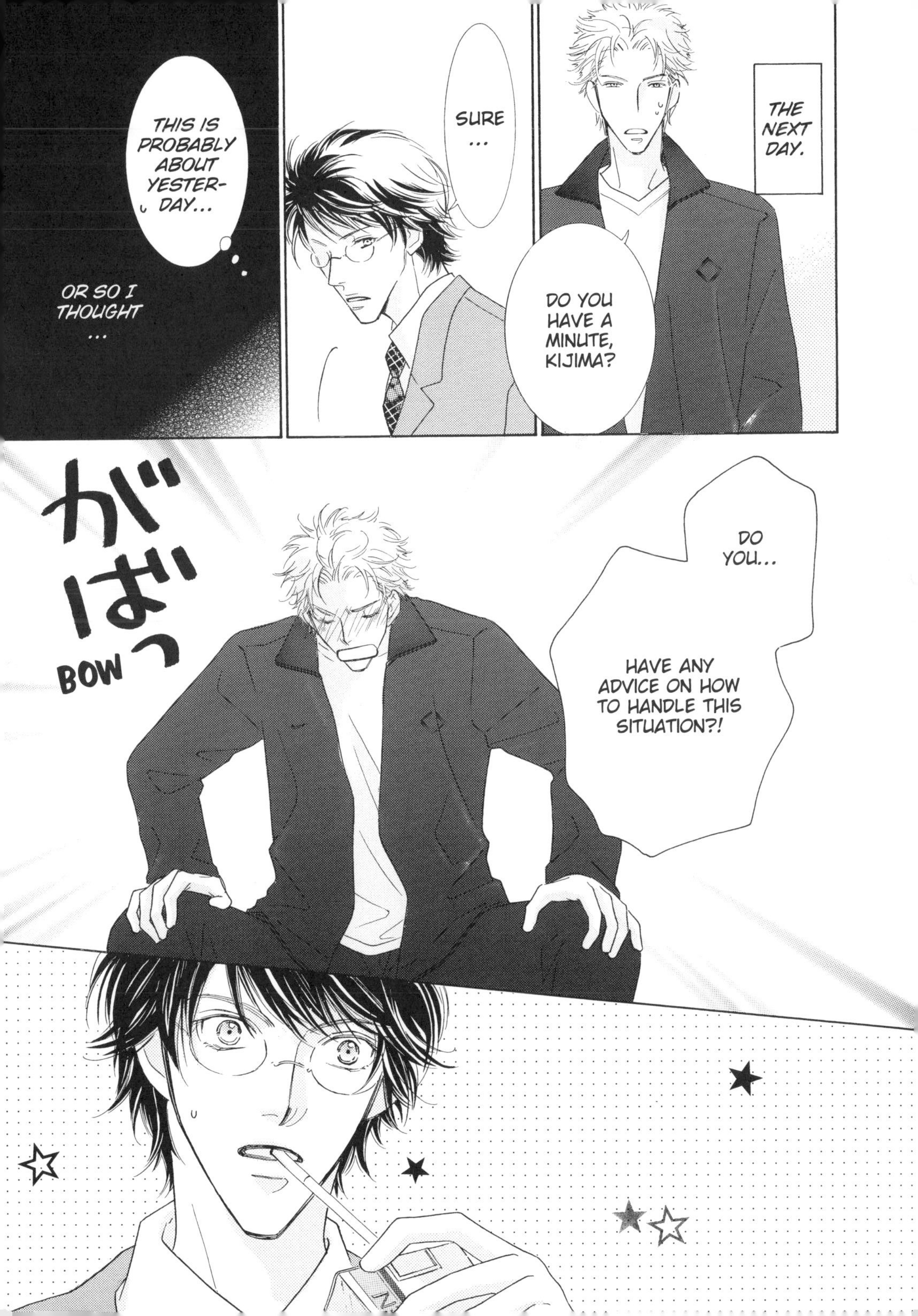
THE NEXT DAY.
DO YOU HAVE A MINUTE, KIJIMA?
SURE ...
THIS IS PROBABLY ABOUT YESTER-DAY...
OR SO I THOUGHT ...
DO YOU...
HAVE ANY ADVICE ON HOW TO HANDLE THIS SITUATION?!
がばっ
BOW

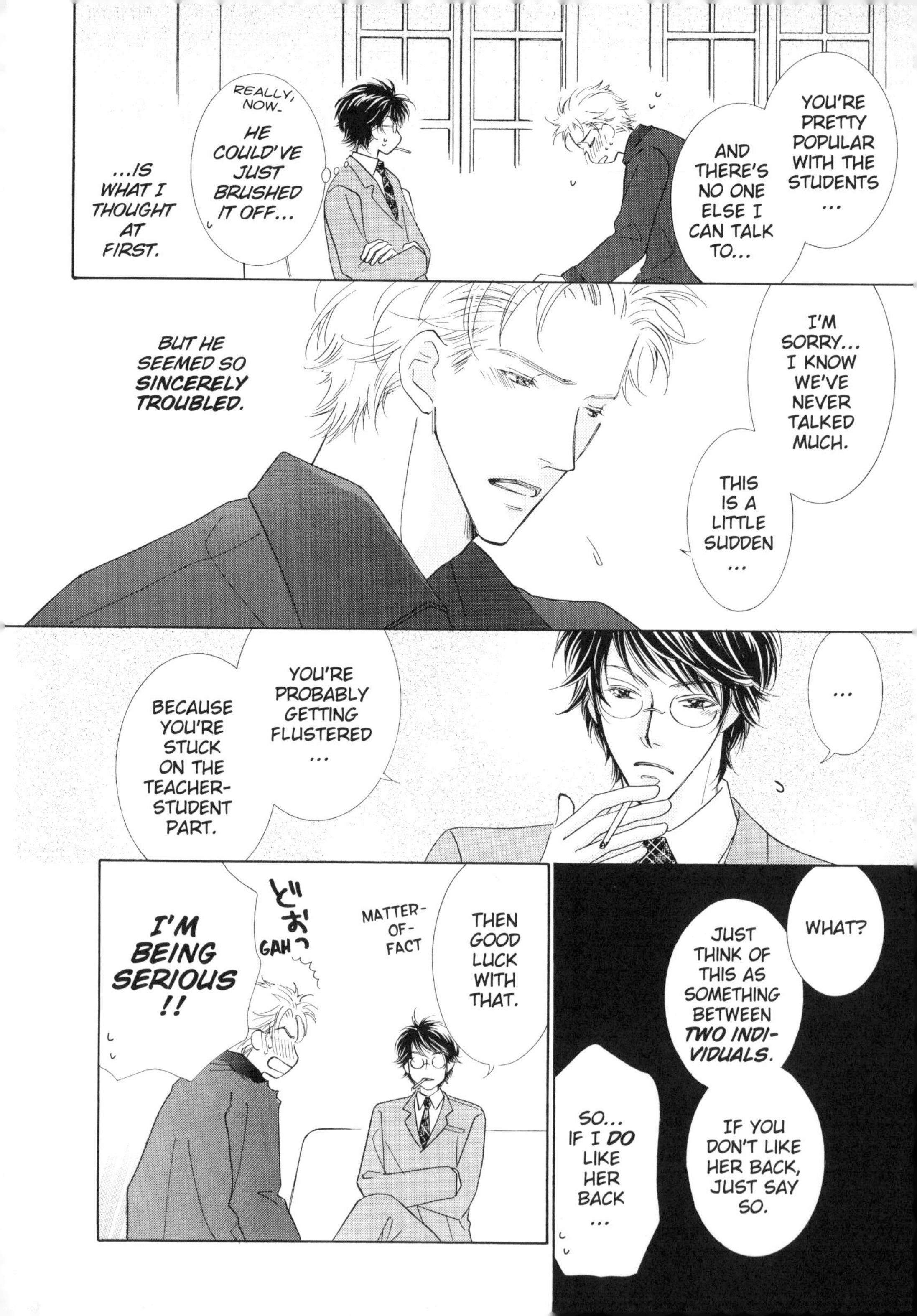
YOU'RE PRETTY POPULAR WITH THE STUDENTS...
AND THERE'S NO ONE ELSE I CAN TALK TO...
REALLY, NOW-
HE COULD'VE JUST BRUSHED IT OFF...
...IS WHAT I THOUGHT AT FIRST.
I'M SORRY... I KNOW WE'VE NEVER TALKED MUCH.
THIS IS A LITTLE SUDDEN...
BUT HE SEEMED SO SINCERELY TROUBLED.
...
YOU'RE PROBABLY GETTING FLUSTERED...
BECAUSE YOU'RE STUCK ON THE TEACHER-STUDENT PART.
WHAT?
JUST THINK OF THIS AS SOMETHING BETWEEN TWO INDIVIDUALS.
IF YOU DON'T LIKE HER BACK, JUST SAY SO.
SO... IF I DO LIKE HER BACK...
THEN GOOD LUCK WITH THAT.
MATTER-OF-FACT
どぉっ
GAH
I'M BEING SERIOUS!!

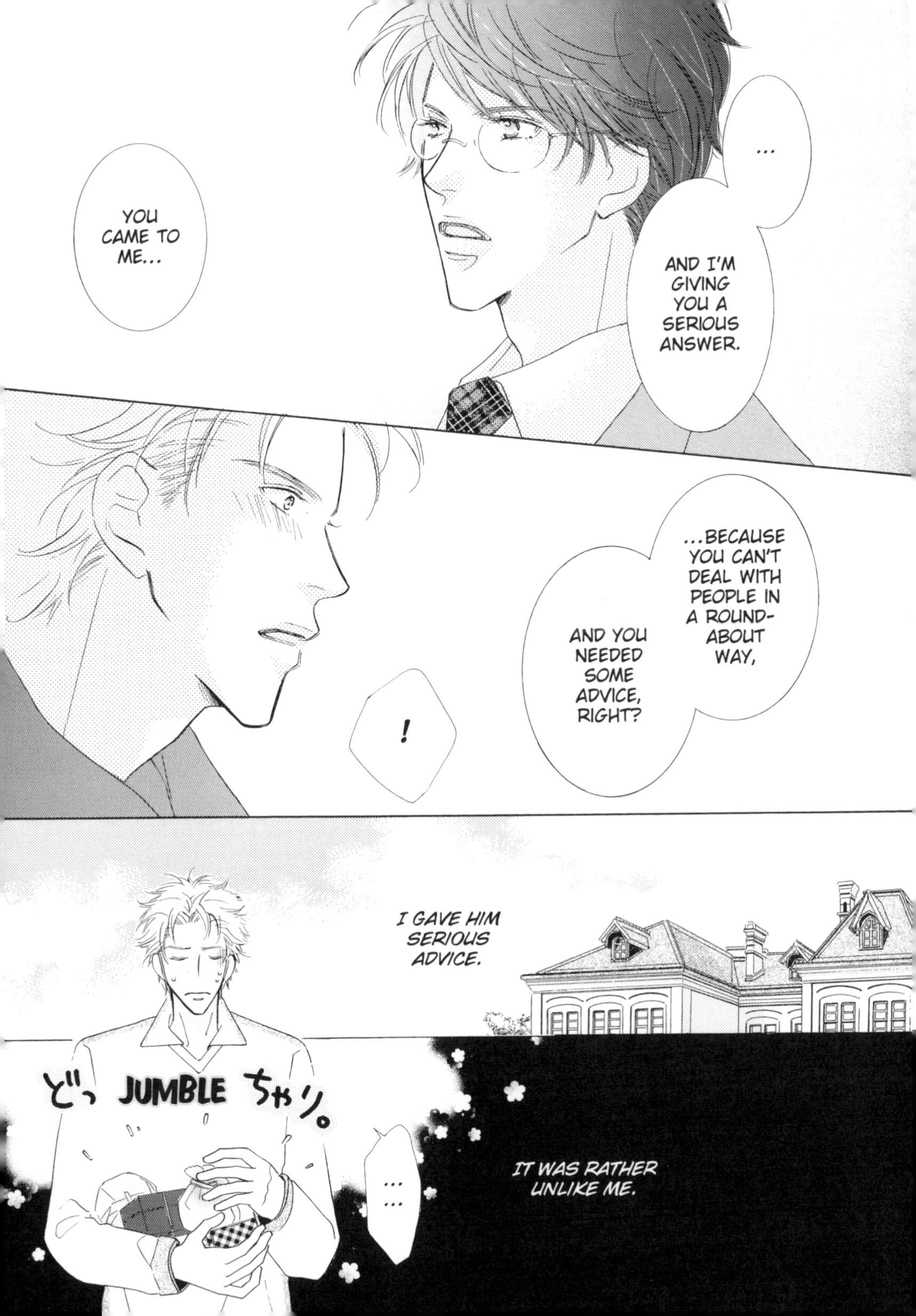
...
YOU CAME TO ME...
AND I'M GIVING YOU A SERIOUS ANSWER.
...BECAUSE YOU CAN'T DEAL WITH PEOPLE IN A ROUND-ABOUT WAY,
AND YOU NEEDED SOME ADVICE, RIGHT?
!
I GAVE HIM SERIOUS ADVICE.
IT WAS RATHER UNLIKE ME.
... ...
どっ JUMBLE ちゃり。

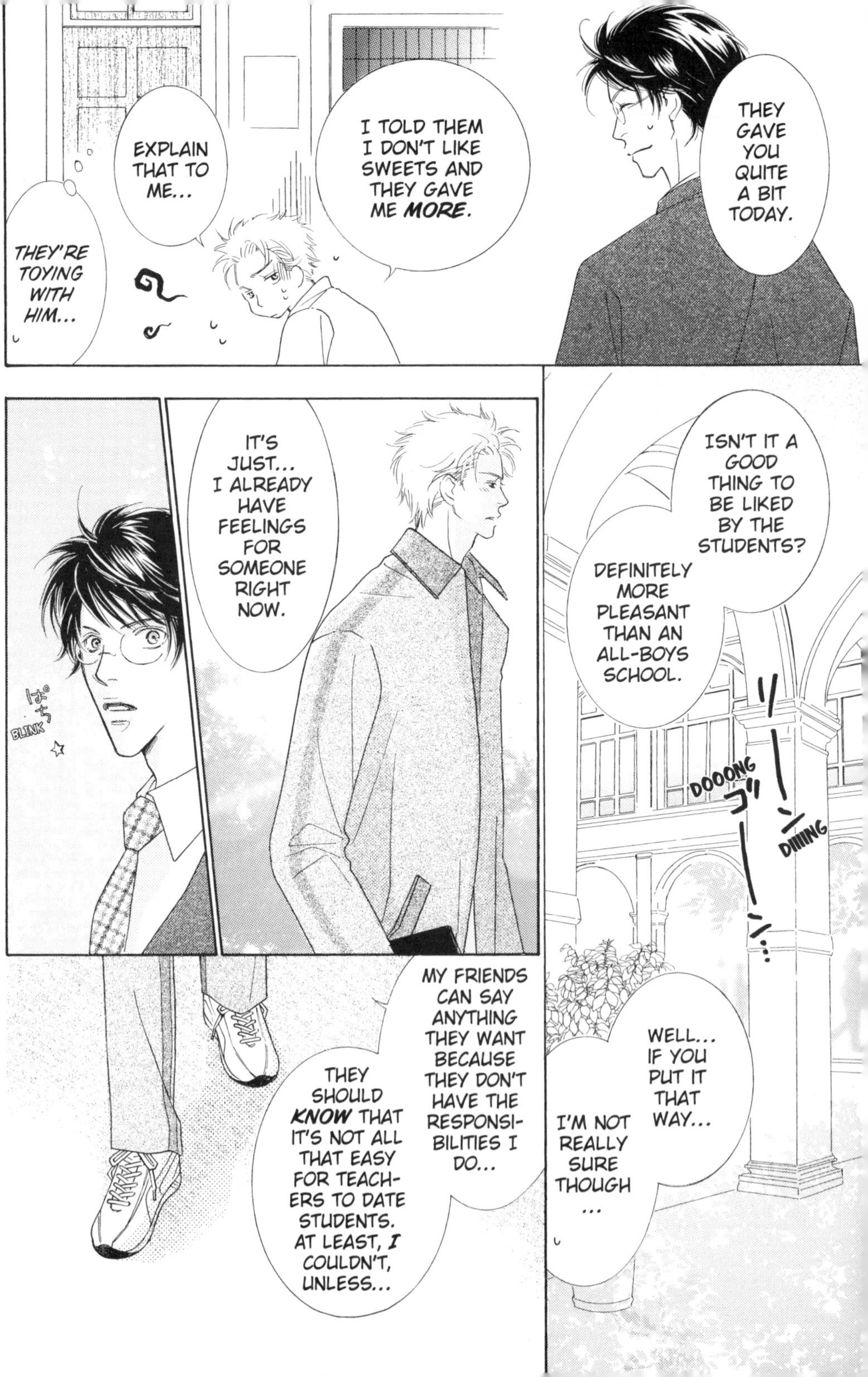
THEY GAVE YOU QUITE A BIT TODAY.
I TOLD THEM I DON'T LIKE SWEETS AND THEY GAVE ME MORE.
EXPLAIN THAT TO ME...
THEY'RE TOYING WITH HIM...
ISN'T IT A GOOD THING TO BE LIKED BY THE STUDENTS?
DEFINITELY MORE PLEASANT THAN AN ALL-BOYS SCHOOL.
DIIIING
DOOONG
WELL... IF YOU PUT IT THAT WAY...
I'M NOT REALLY SURE THOUGH...
IT'S JUST... I ALREADY HAVE FEELINGS FOR SOMEONE RIGHT NOW.
BLINK
MY FRIENDS CAN SAY ANYTHING THEY WANT BECAUSE THEY DON'T HAVE THE RESPONSIBILITIES I DO...
THEY SHOULD KNOW THAT IT'S NOT ALL THAT EASY FOR TEACHERS TO DATE STUDENTS. AT LEAST, I COULDN'T, UNLESS...

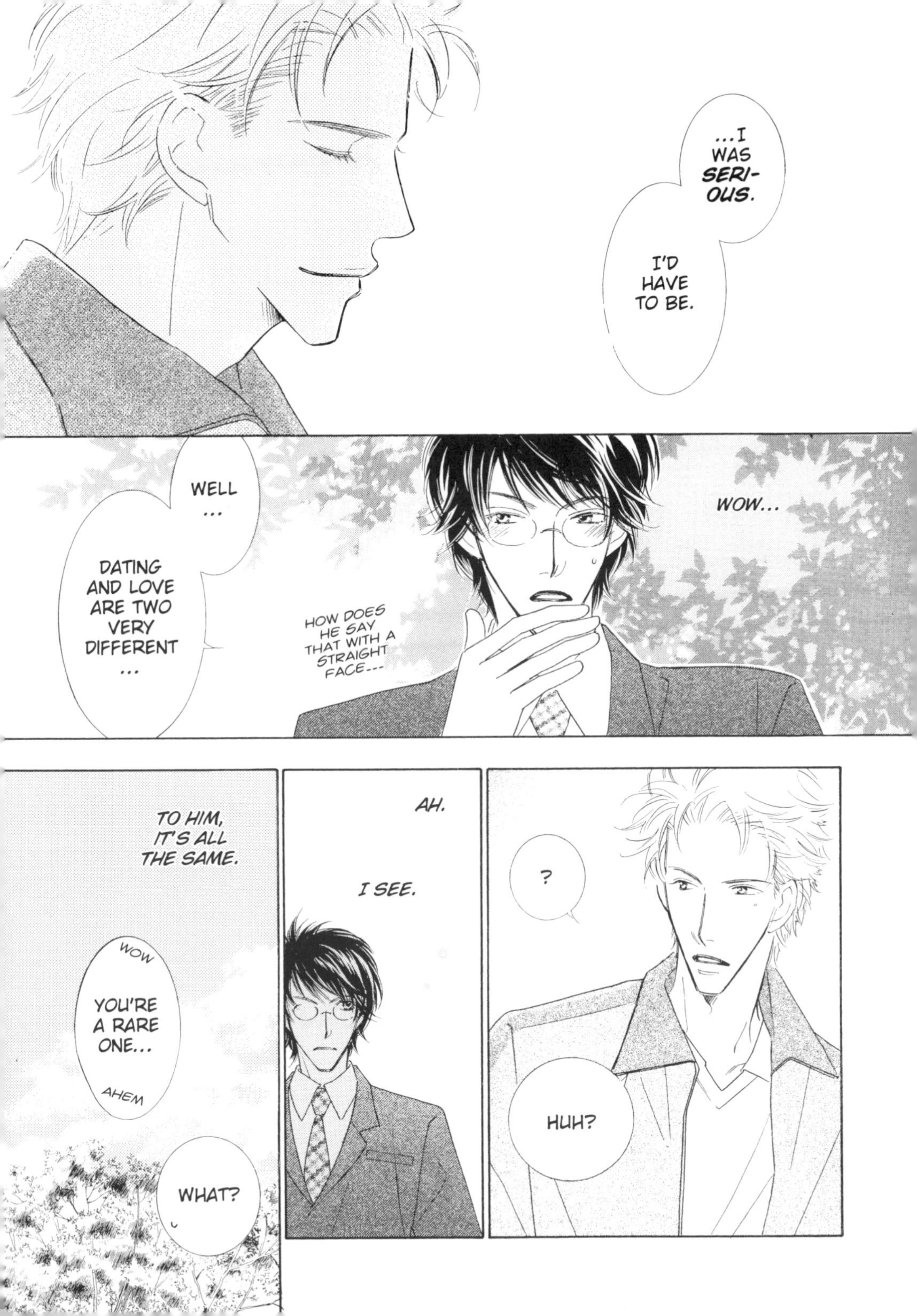
...I WAS SERIOUS.
I'D HAVE TO BE.
WOW...
HOW DOES HE SAY THAT WITH A STRAIGHT FACE...
WELL...
DATING AND LOVE ARE TWO VERY DIFFERENT...
?
HUH?
AH.
I SEE.
TO HIM, IT'S ALL THE SAME.
WOW
YOU'RE A RARE ONE...
AHEM
WHAT?

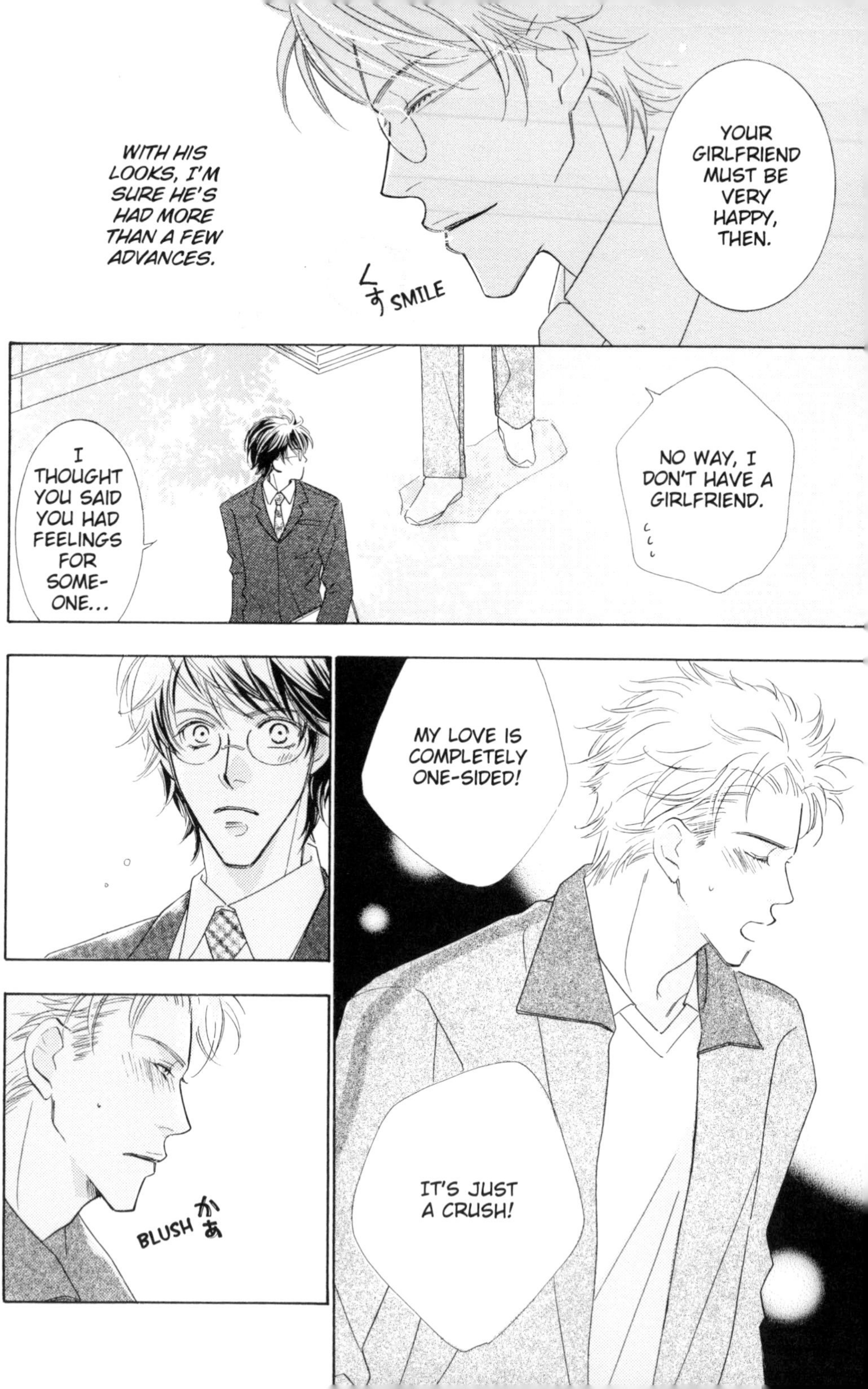

YOUR GIRLFRIEND MUST BE VERY HAPPY, THEN.
WITH HIS LOOKS, I'M SURE HE'S HAD MORE THAN A FEW ADVANCES.
くす SMILE
NO WAY, I DON'T HAVE A GIRLFRIEND.
I THOUGHT YOU SAID YOU HAD FEELINGS FOR SOME-ONE...
MY LOVE IS COMPLETELY ONE-SIDED!
IT'S JUST A CRUSH!
かあ BLUSH

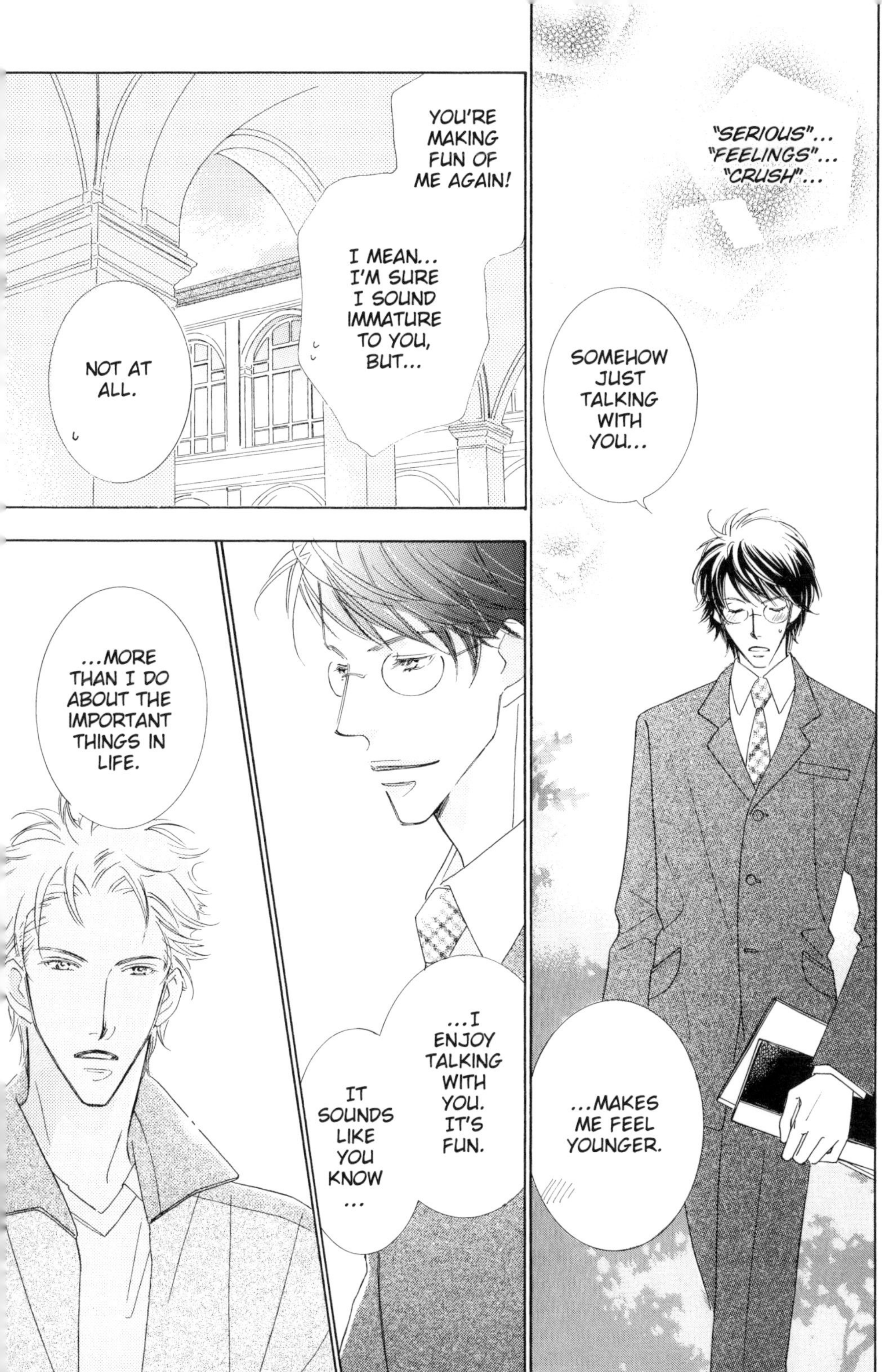
"SERIOUS"... "FEELINGS"... "CRUSH"...
SOMEHOW JUST TALKING WITH YOU...
...MAKES ME FEEL YOUNGER.
YOU'RE MAKING FUN OF ME AGAIN!
I MEAN... I'M SURE I SOUND IMMATURE TO YOU, BUT...
NOT AT ALL.
...I ENJOY TALKING WITH YOU. IT'S FUN.
IT SOUNDS LIKE YOU KNOW...
...MORE THAN I DO ABOUT THE IMPORTANT THINGS IN LIFE.

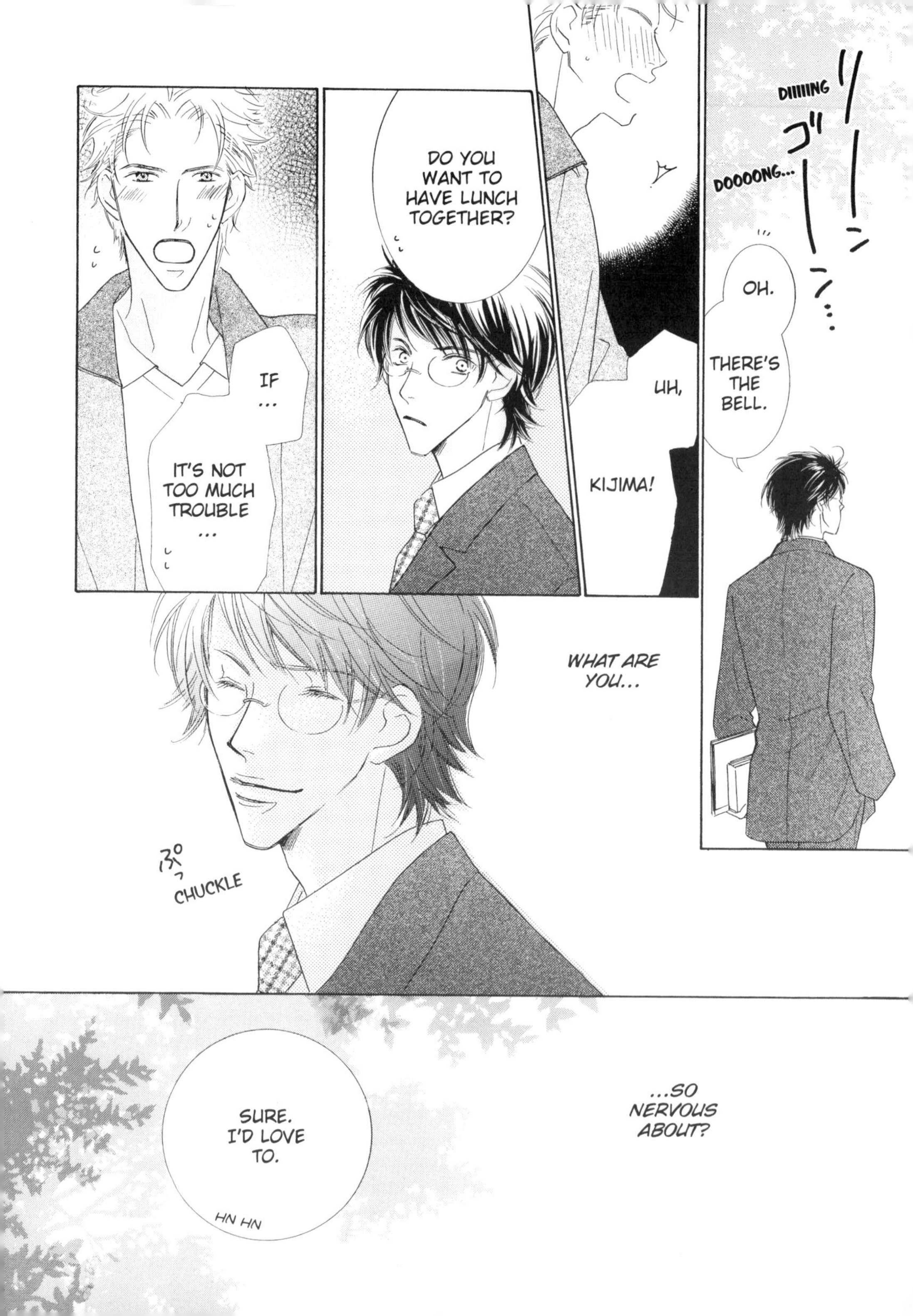
DIIIIING
DOOOONG...
OH.
THERE'S THE BELL.
UH,
KIJIMA!
DO YOU WANT TO HAVE LUNCH TOGETHER?
IF...
IT'S NOT TOO MUCH TROUBLE...
WHAT ARE YOU...
ぷっ
CHUCKLE
...SO NERVOUS ABOUT?
SURE. I'D LOVE TO.
HN HN

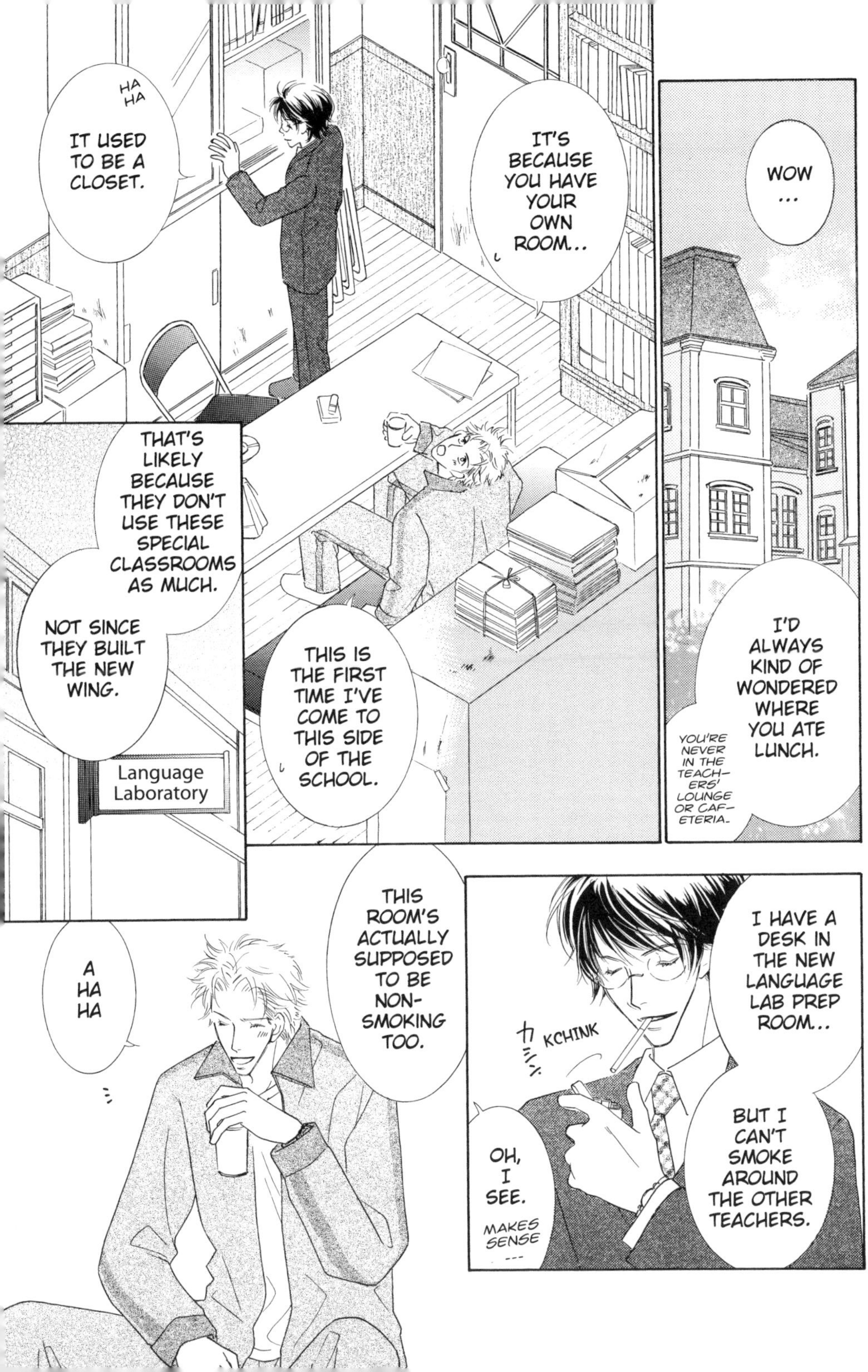
WOW ...
I'D ALWAYS KIND OF WONDERED WHERE YOU ATE LUNCH.
YOU'RE NEVER IN THE TEACH-ERS' LOUNGE OR CAF-ETERIA.
IT'S BECAUSE YOU HAVE YOUR OWN ROOM...
HA HA
IT USED TO BE A CLOSET.
THIS IS THE FIRST TIME I'VE COME TO THIS SIDE OF THE SCHOOL.
THAT'S LIKELY BECAUSE THEY DON'T USE THESE SPECIAL CLASSROOMS AS MUCH.
NOT SINCE THEY BUILT THE NEW WING.
Language Laboratory
I HAVE A DESK IN THE NEW LANGUAGE LAB PREP ROOM...
KCHINK
BUT I CAN'T SMOKE AROUND THE OTHER TEACHERS.
OH, I SEE.
MAKES SENSE ...
THIS ROOM'S ACTUALLY SUPPOSED TO BE NON-SMOKING TOO.
A HA HA

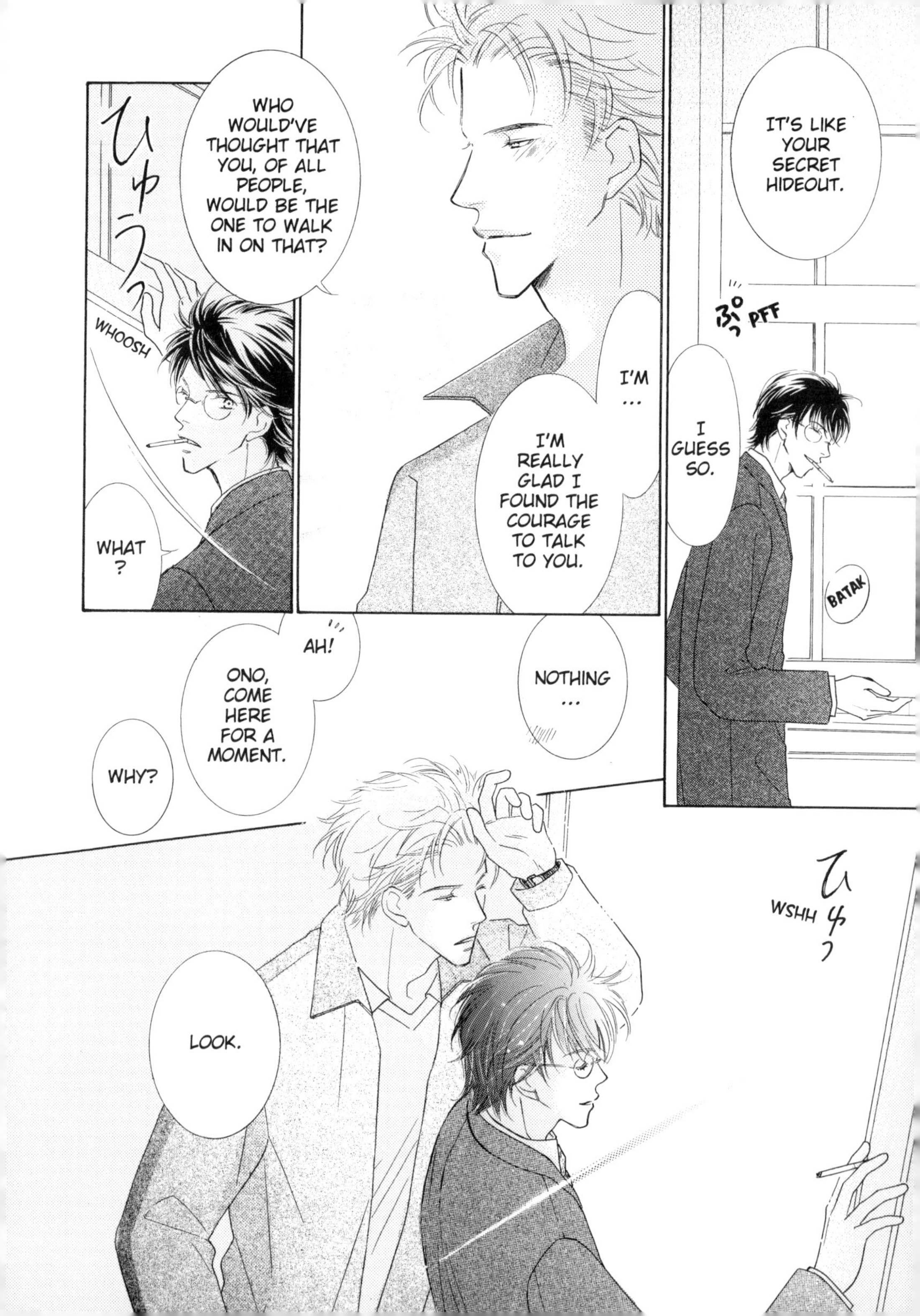
IT'S LIKE YOUR SECRET HIDEOUT.
ぷっ PFF
I GUESS SO.
BATAK
I'M ...
I'M REALLY GLAD I FOUND THE COURAGE TO TALK TO YOU.
WHO WOULD'VE THOUGHT THAT YOU, OF ALL PEOPLE, WOULD BE THE ONE TO WALK IN ON THAT?
ひゅうっ
WHOOSH
WHAT?
NOTHING ...
AH!
ONO, COME HERE FOR A MOMENT.
WHY?
ひゅっ
WSHH
LOOK.

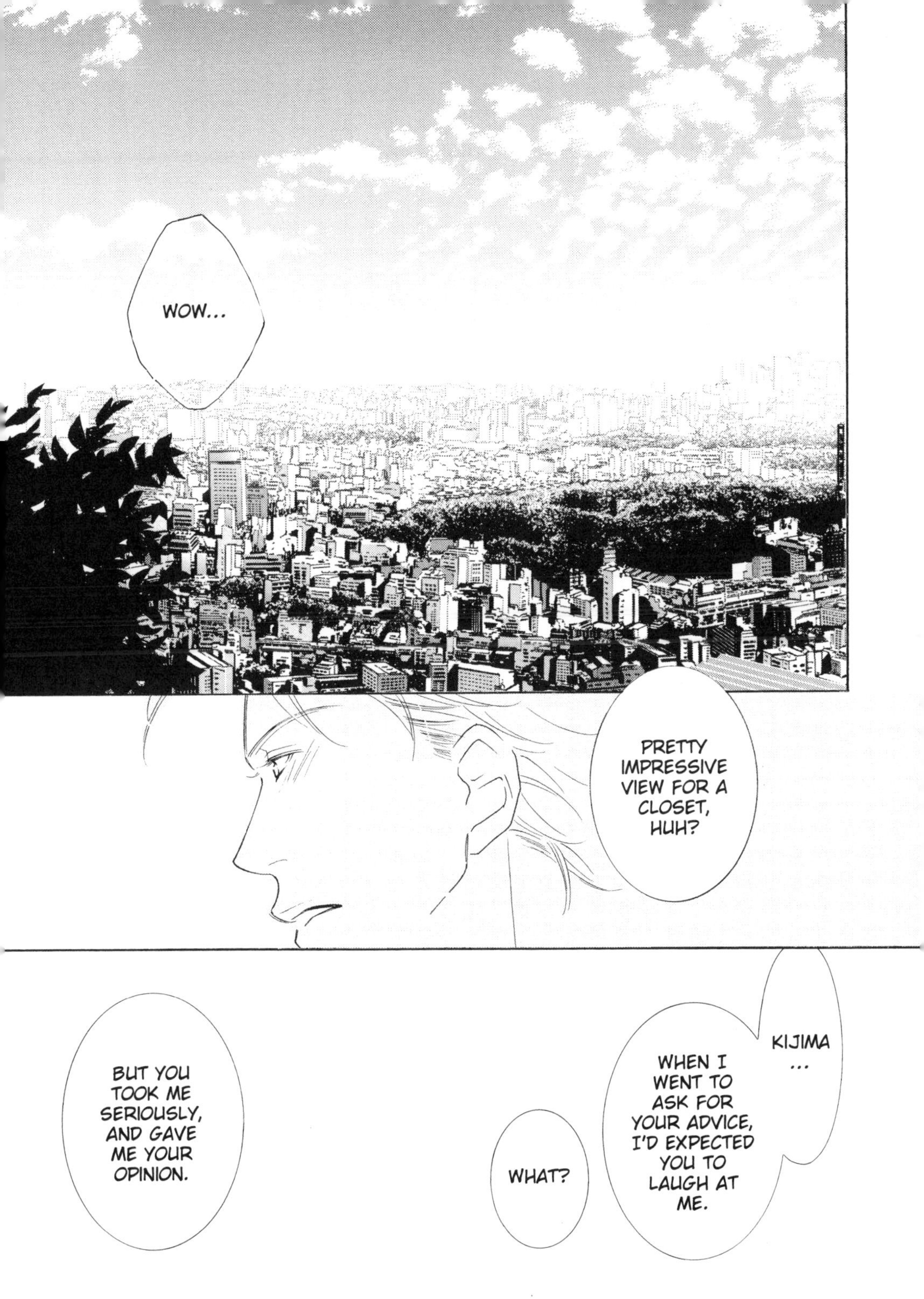
WOW...
PRETTY IMPRESSIVE VIEW FOR A CLOSET, HUH?
KIJIMA...
WHEN I WENT TO ASK FOR YOUR ADVICE, I'D EXPECTED YOU TO LAUGH AT ME.
WHAT?
BUT YOU TOOK ME SERIOUSLY, AND GAVE ME YOUR OPINION.

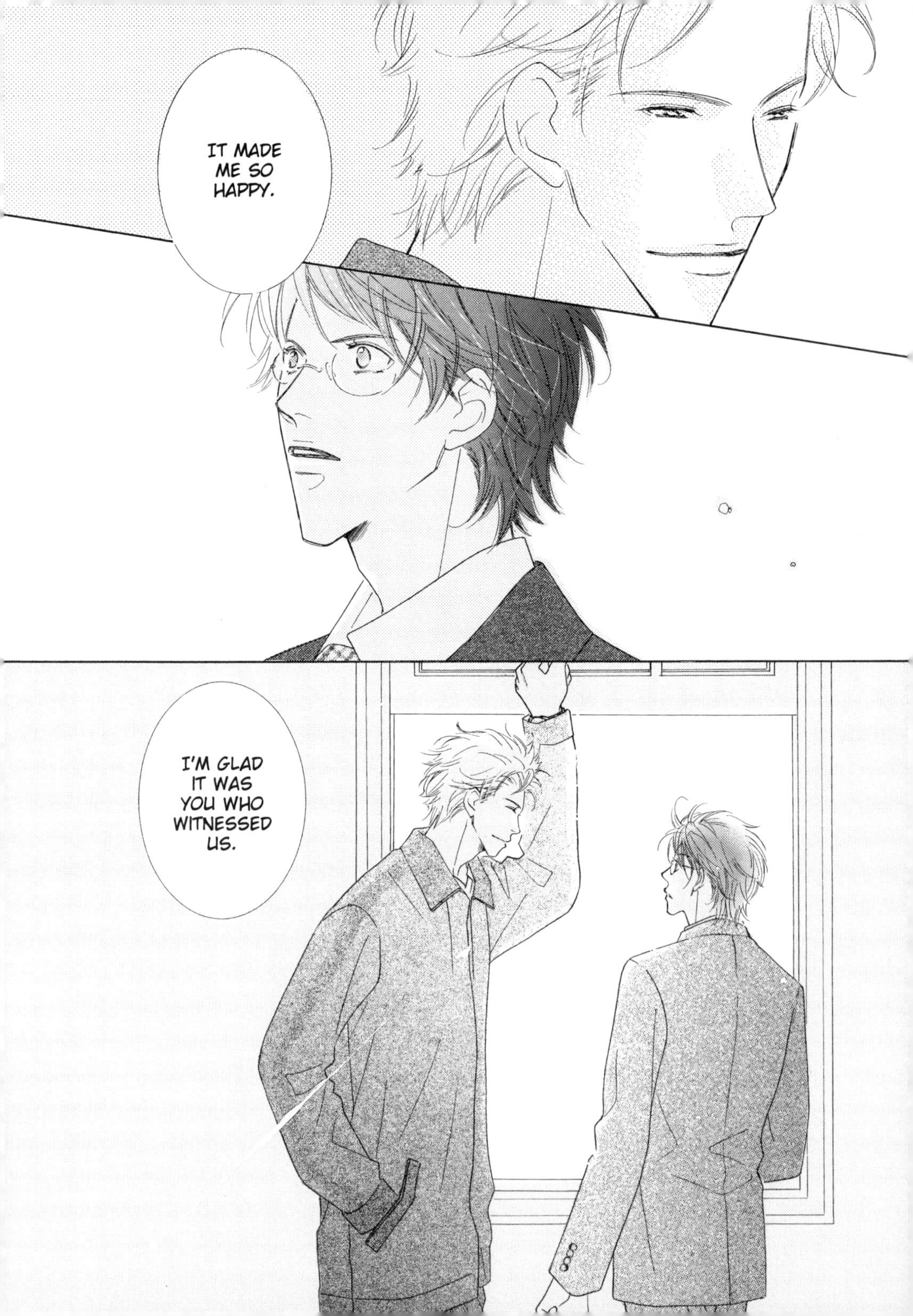
IT MADE ME SO HAPPY.
I'M GLAD IT WAS YOU WHO WITNESSED US.

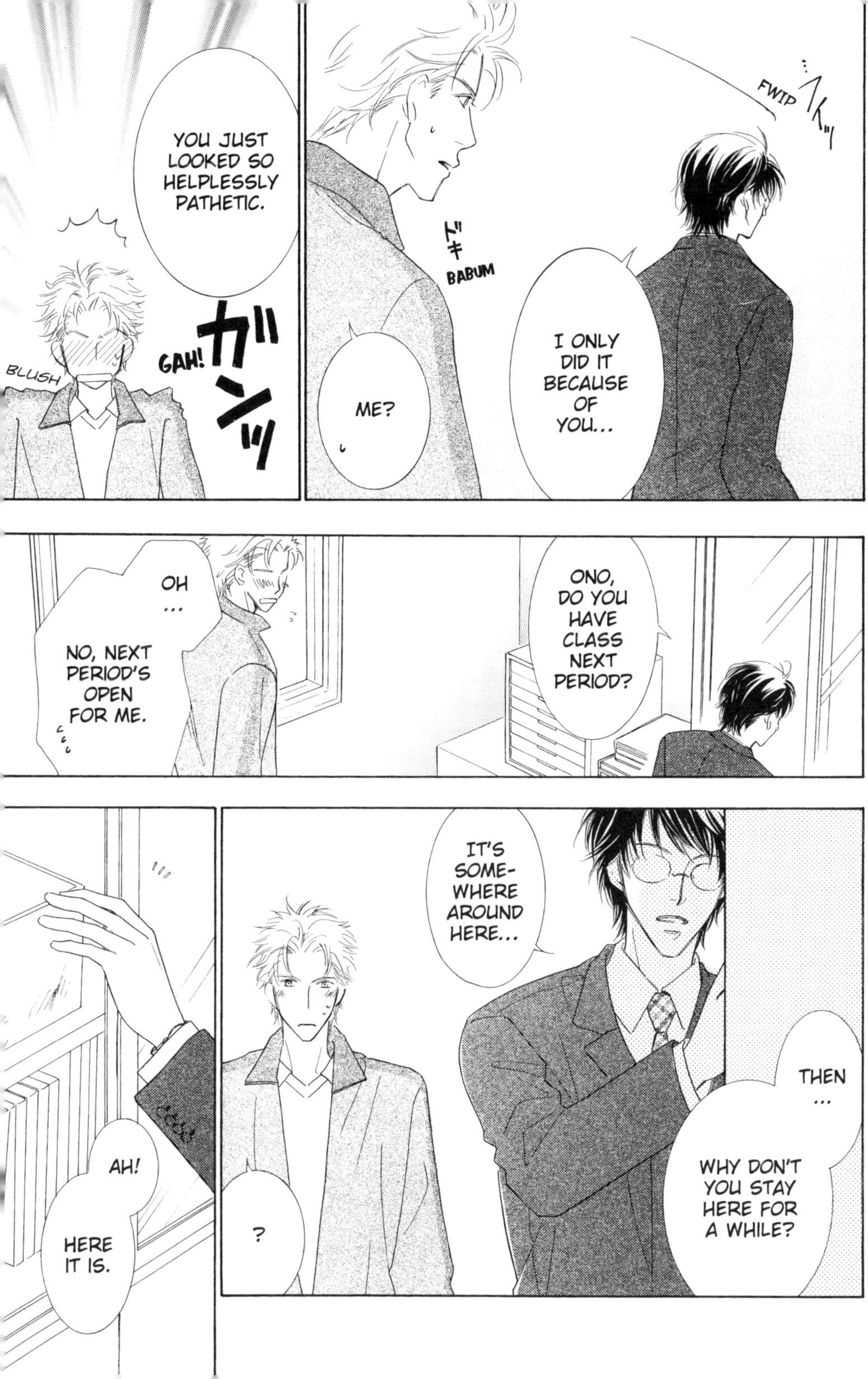
FWIP
I ONLY DID IT BECAUSE OF YOU...
ドキ
BABUM
ME?
YOU JUST LOOKED SO HELPLESSLY PATHETIC.
GAH!
ガンッ
BLUSH
ONO, DO YOU HAVE CLASS NEXT PERIOD?
OH ...
NO, NEXT PERIOD'S OPEN FOR ME.
IT'S SOME-WHERE AROUND HERE...
THEN ...
WHY DON'T YOU STAY HERE FOR A WHILE?
?
AH!
HERE IT IS.

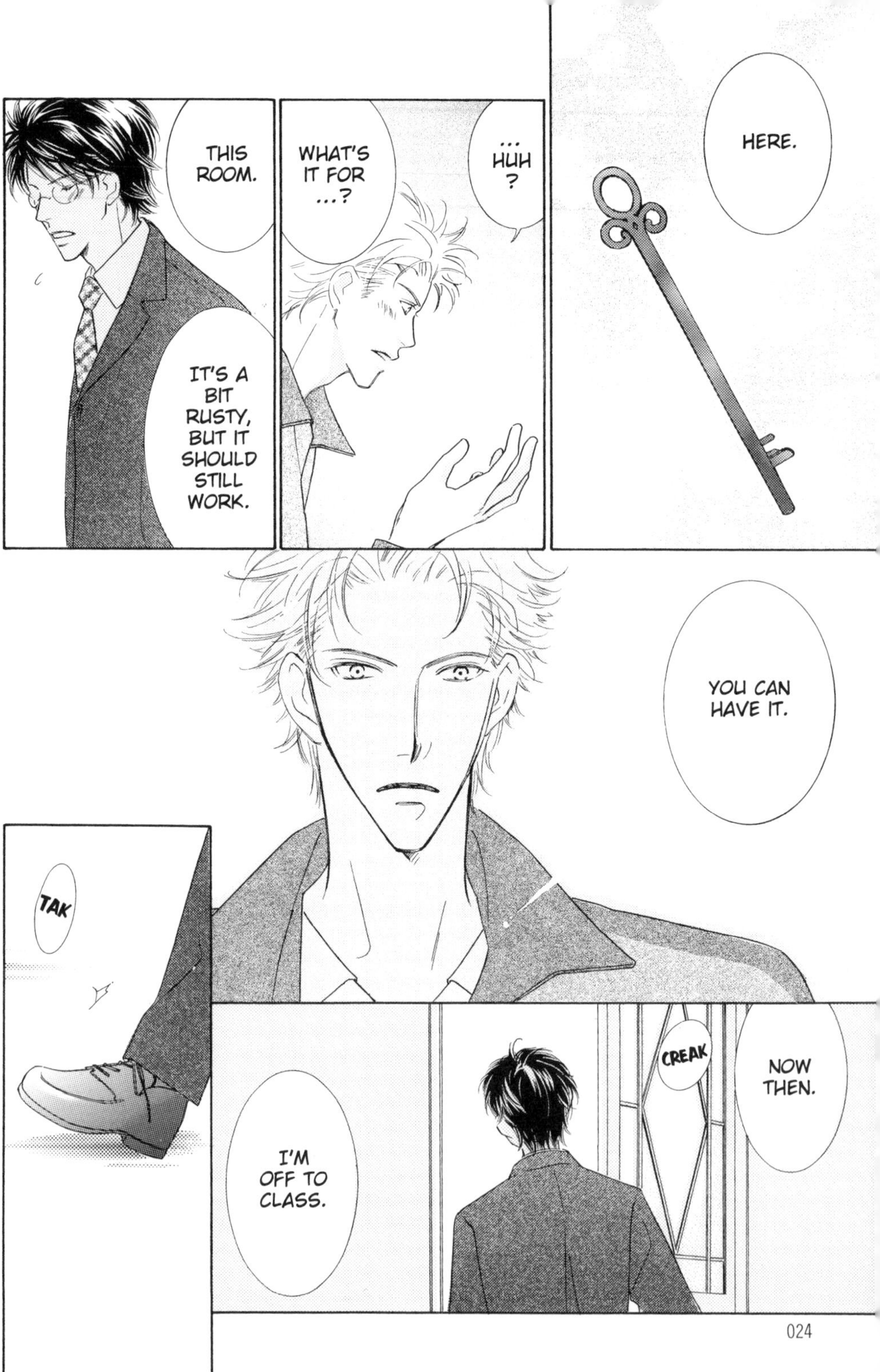
HERE.
...HUH?
WHAT'S IT FOR ...?
THIS ROOM.
IT'S A BIT RUSTY, BUT IT SHOULD STILL WORK.
YOU CAN HAVE IT.
NOW THEN.
CREAK
I'M OFF TO CLASS.
TAK

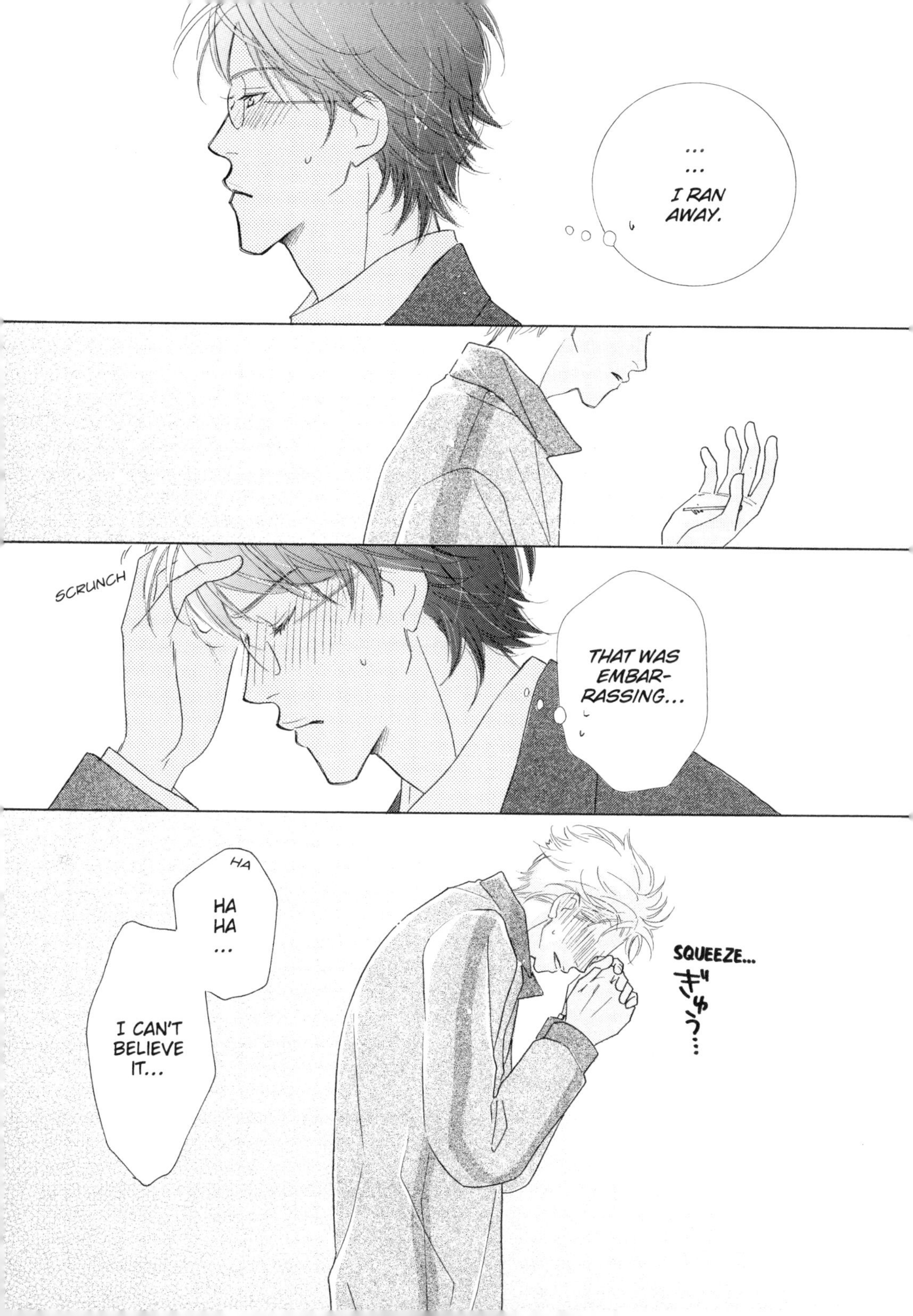
...
...
I RAN AWAY.
THAT WAS EMBAR-RASSING...
SCRUNCH
SQUEEZE...
ぎゅう...
HA
HA HA ...
I CAN'T BELIEVE IT...

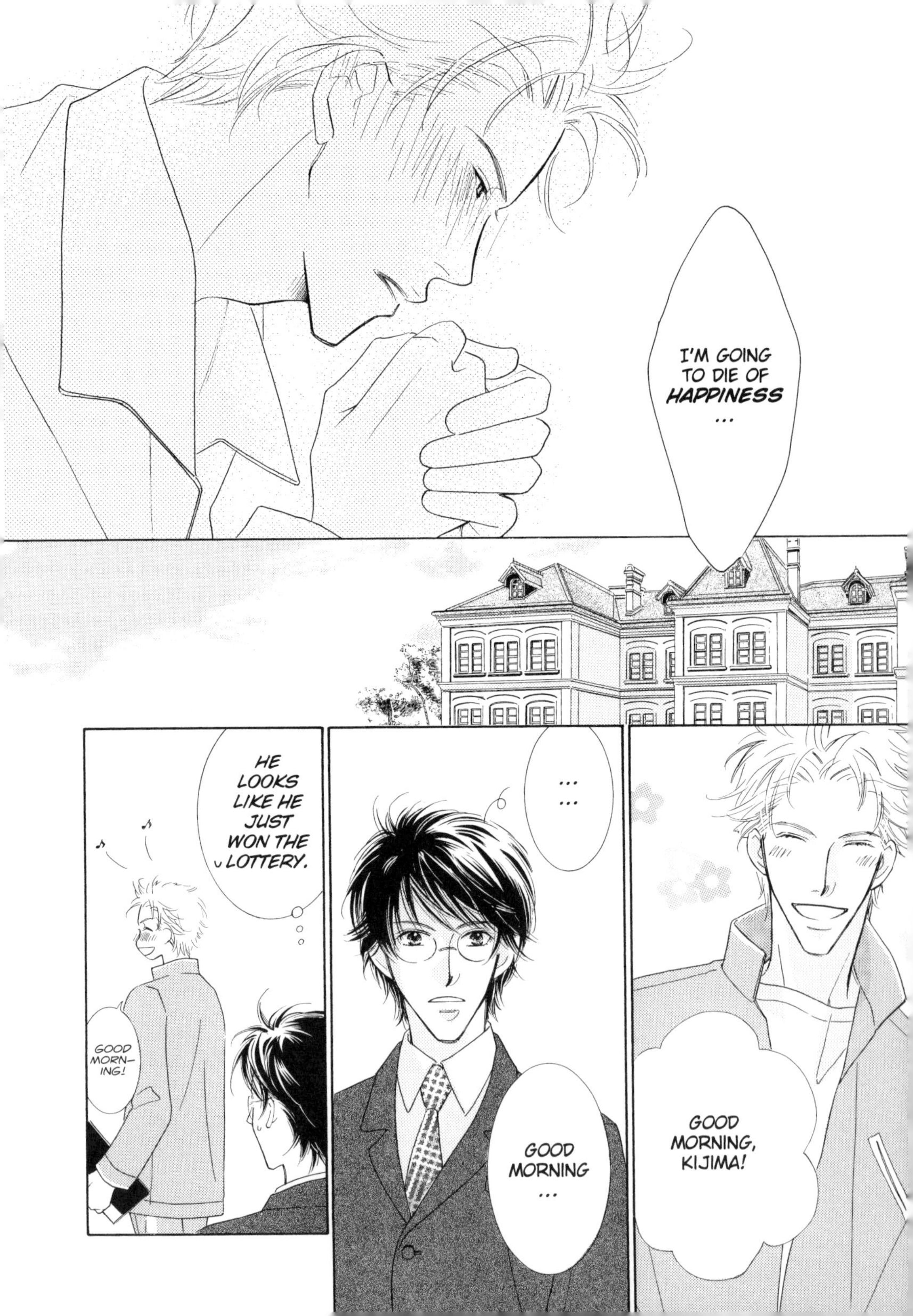
I'M GOING TO DIE OF HAPPINESS ...
GOOD MORNING, KIJIMA!
... ...
GOOD MORNING ...
HE LOOKS LIKE HE JUST WON THE LOTTERY.
GOOD MORNING!

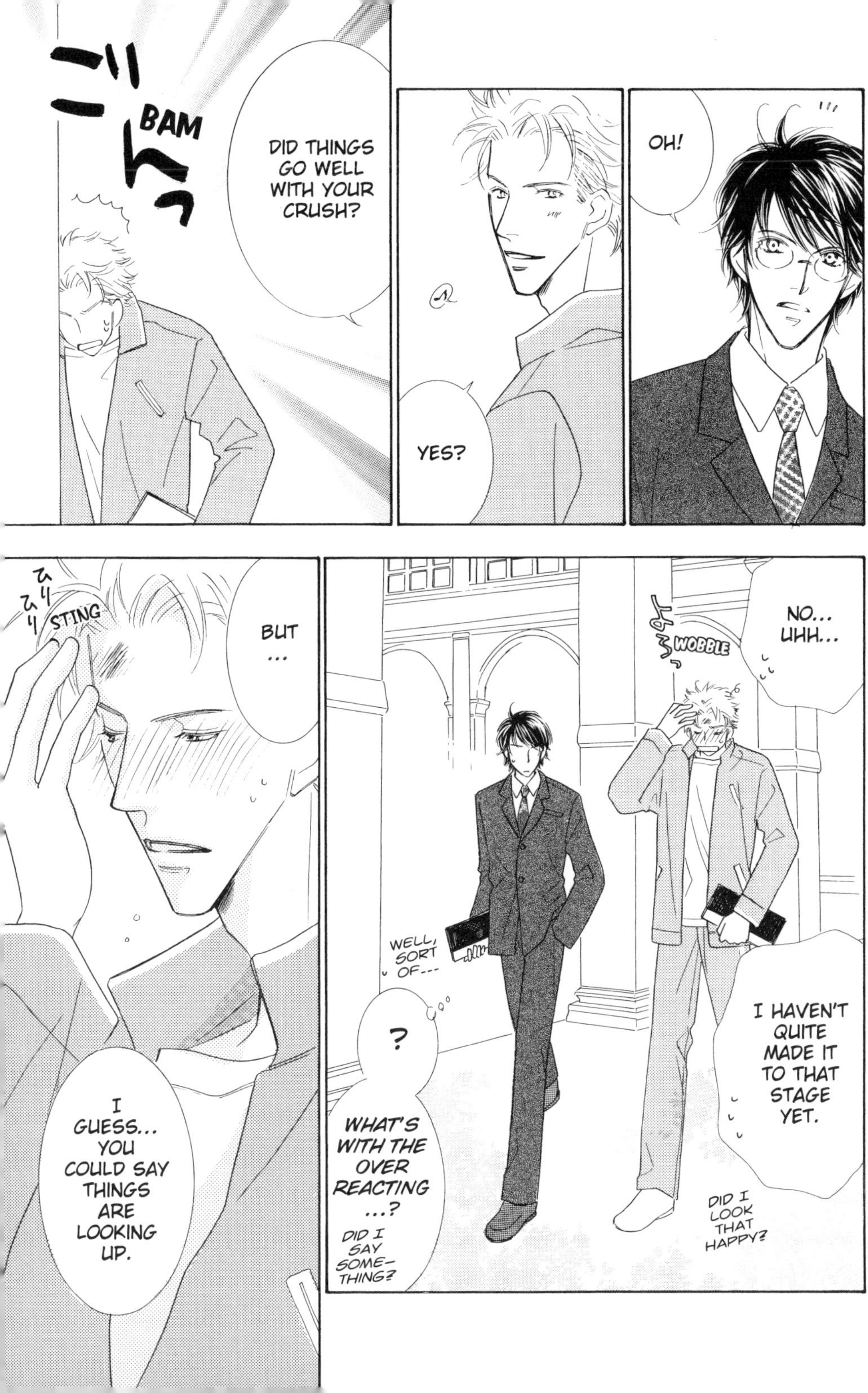
OH!
YES?
BAM
DID THINGS GO WELL WITH YOUR CRUSH?
WOBBLE
NO... UHH...
I HAVEN'T QUITE MADE IT TO THAT STAGE YET.
DID I LOOK THAT HAPPY?
WELL, SORT OF---
?
WHAT'S WITH THE OVER REACTING ...?
DID I SAY SOME-THING?
STING
BUT ...
I GUESS... YOU COULD SAY THINGS ARE LOOKING UP.

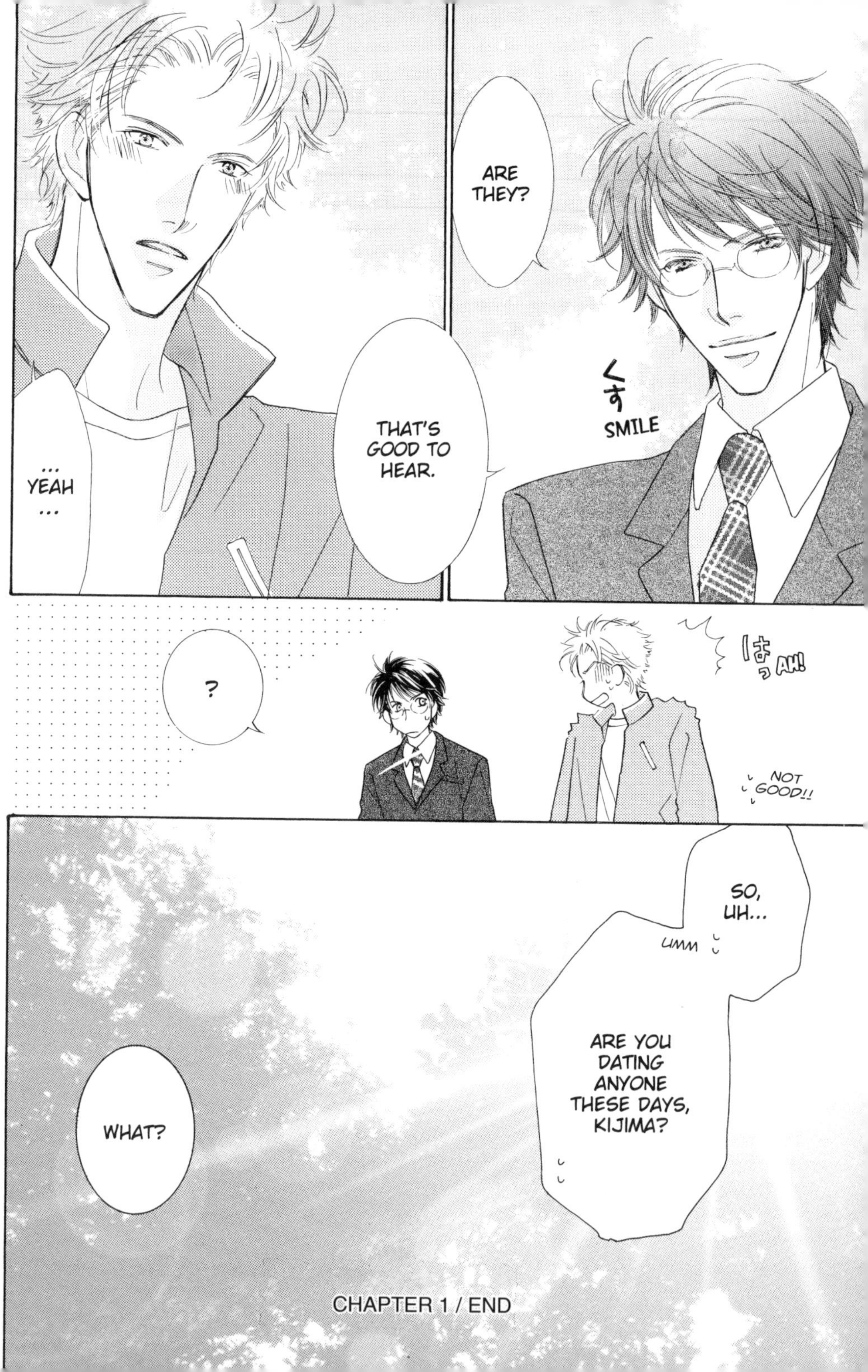
ARE THEY?
くす
SMILE
THAT'S GOOD TO HEAR.
... YEAH ...
はっ
AH!
NOT GOOD!!
?
SO, UH...
UMM
ARE YOU DATING ANYONE THESE DAYS, KIJIMA?
WHAT?
CHAPTER 1 / END

CHAPTER.2

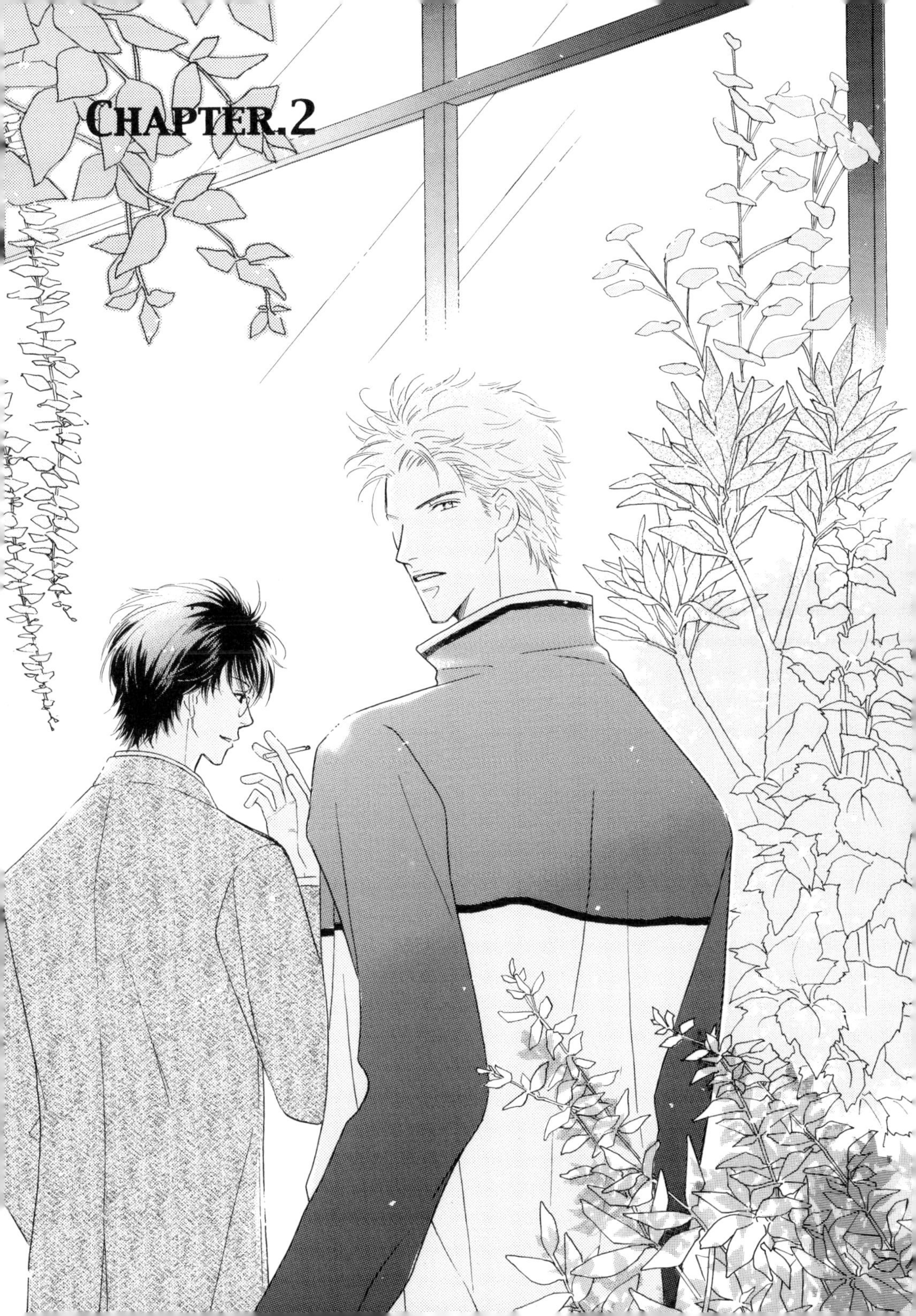

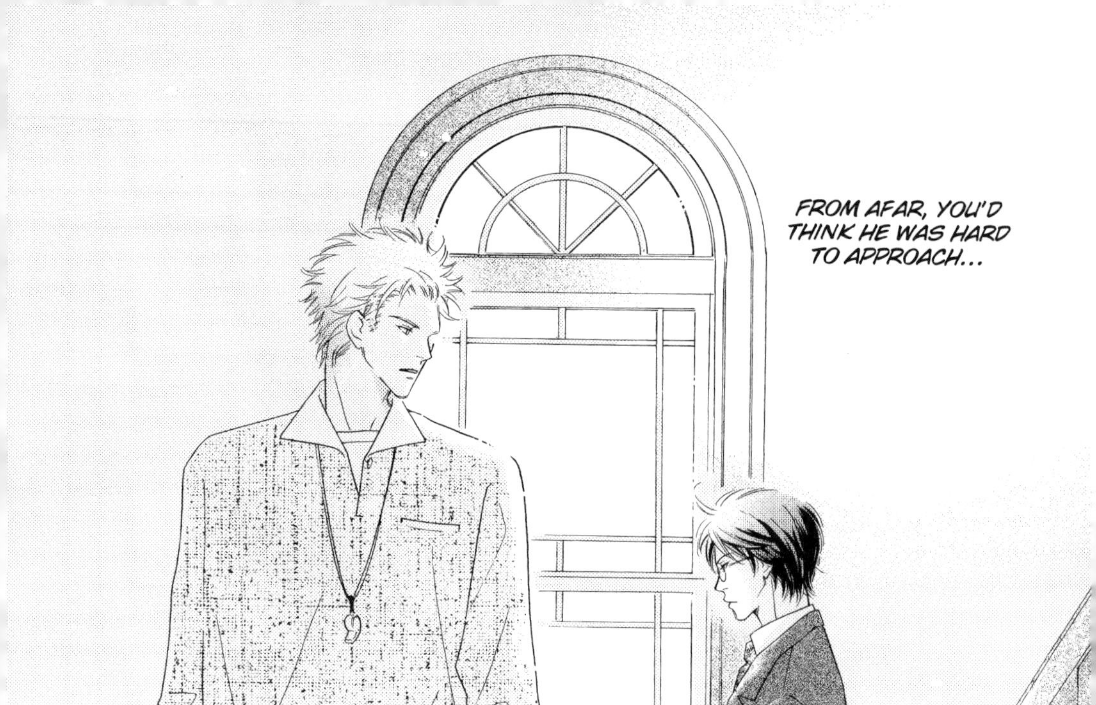
FROM AFAR, YOU'D THINK HE WAS HARD TO APPROACH...
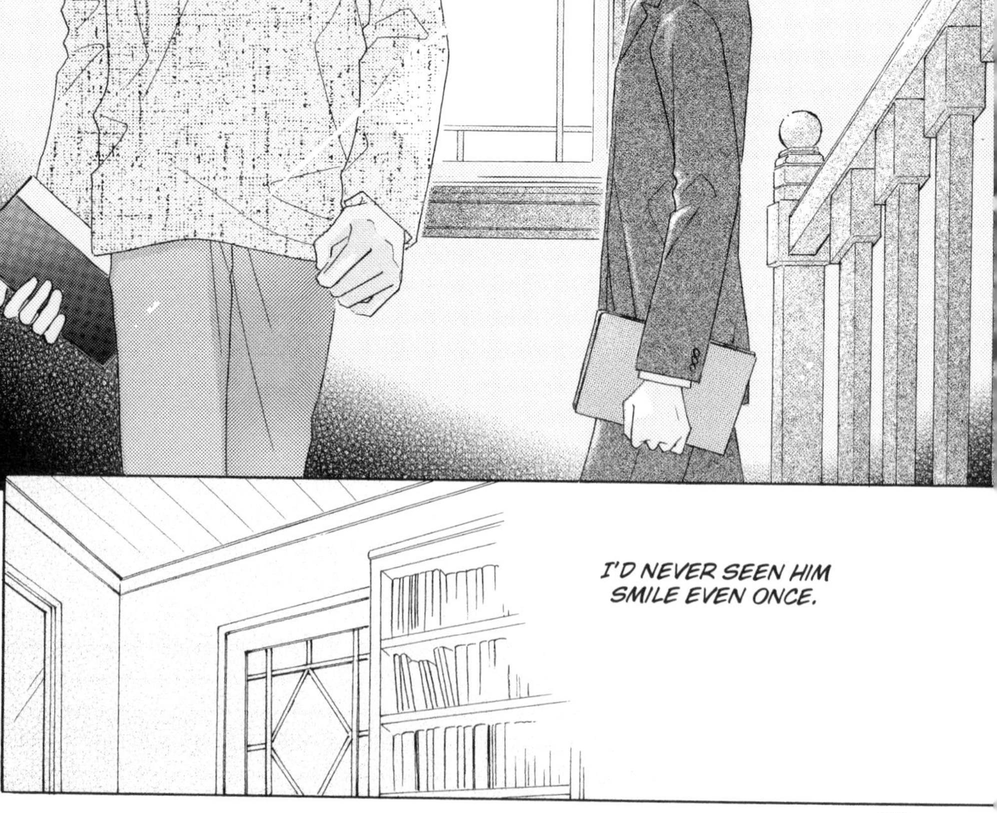
I'D NEVER SEEN HIM SMILE EVEN ONCE.

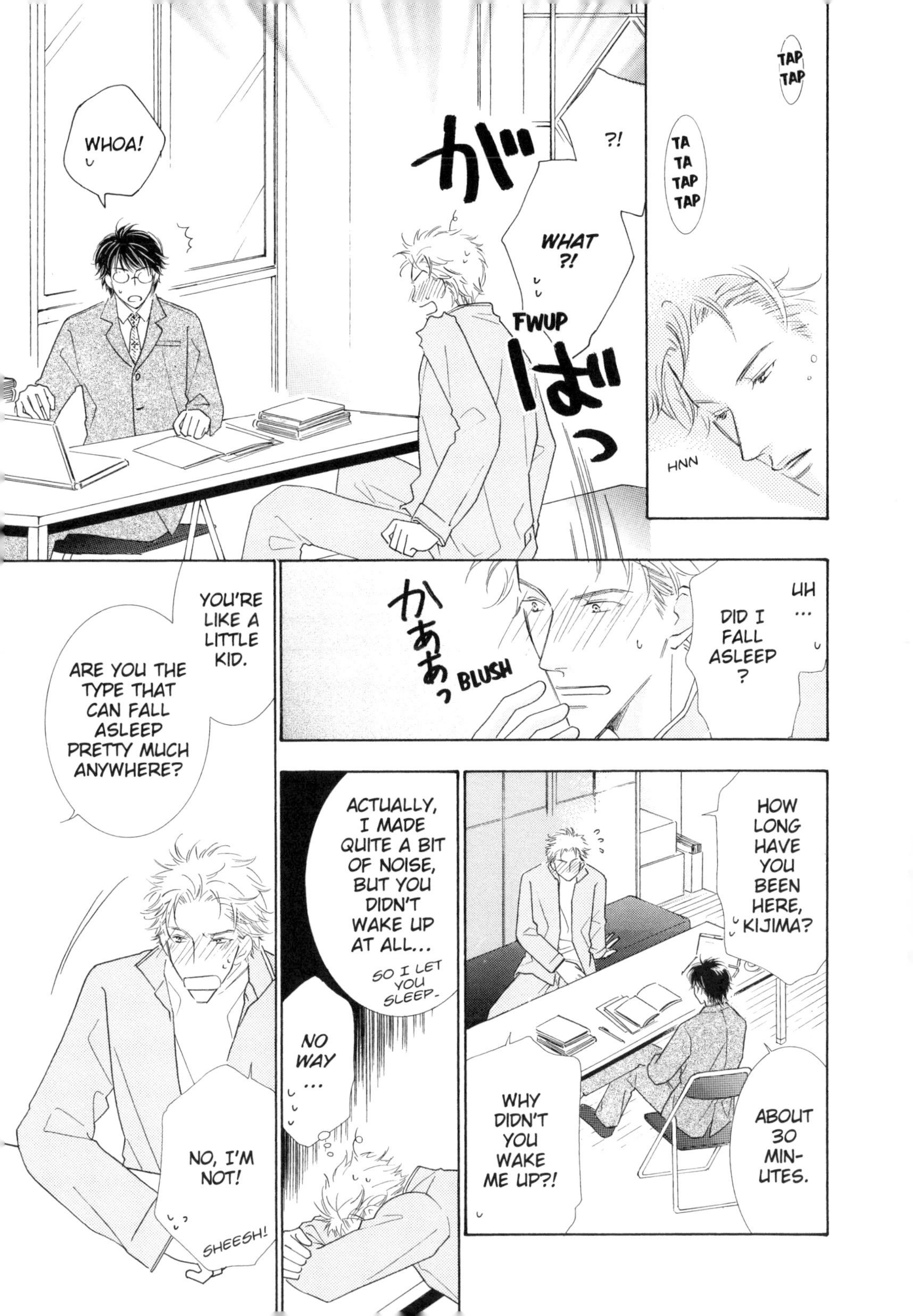
TAP TAP
TA TA TAP TAP
HNN
がっ
?!
WHAT ?!
FWUP
ばっ
WHOA!
UH ...
DID I FALL ASLEEP ?
かあぁっ
BLUSH
HOW LONG HAVE YOU BEEN HERE, KIJIMA?
ABOUT 30 MIN-UTES.
WHY DIDN'T YOU WAKE ME UP?!
ACTUALLY, I MADE QUITE A BIT OF NOISE, BUT YOU DIDN'T WAKE UP AT ALL...
SO I LET YOU SLEEP.
NO WAY ...
YOU'RE LIKE A LITTLE KID.
ARE YOU THE TYPE THAT CAN FALL ASLEEP PRETTY MUCH ANYWHERE?
NO, I'M NOT!
SHEESH!

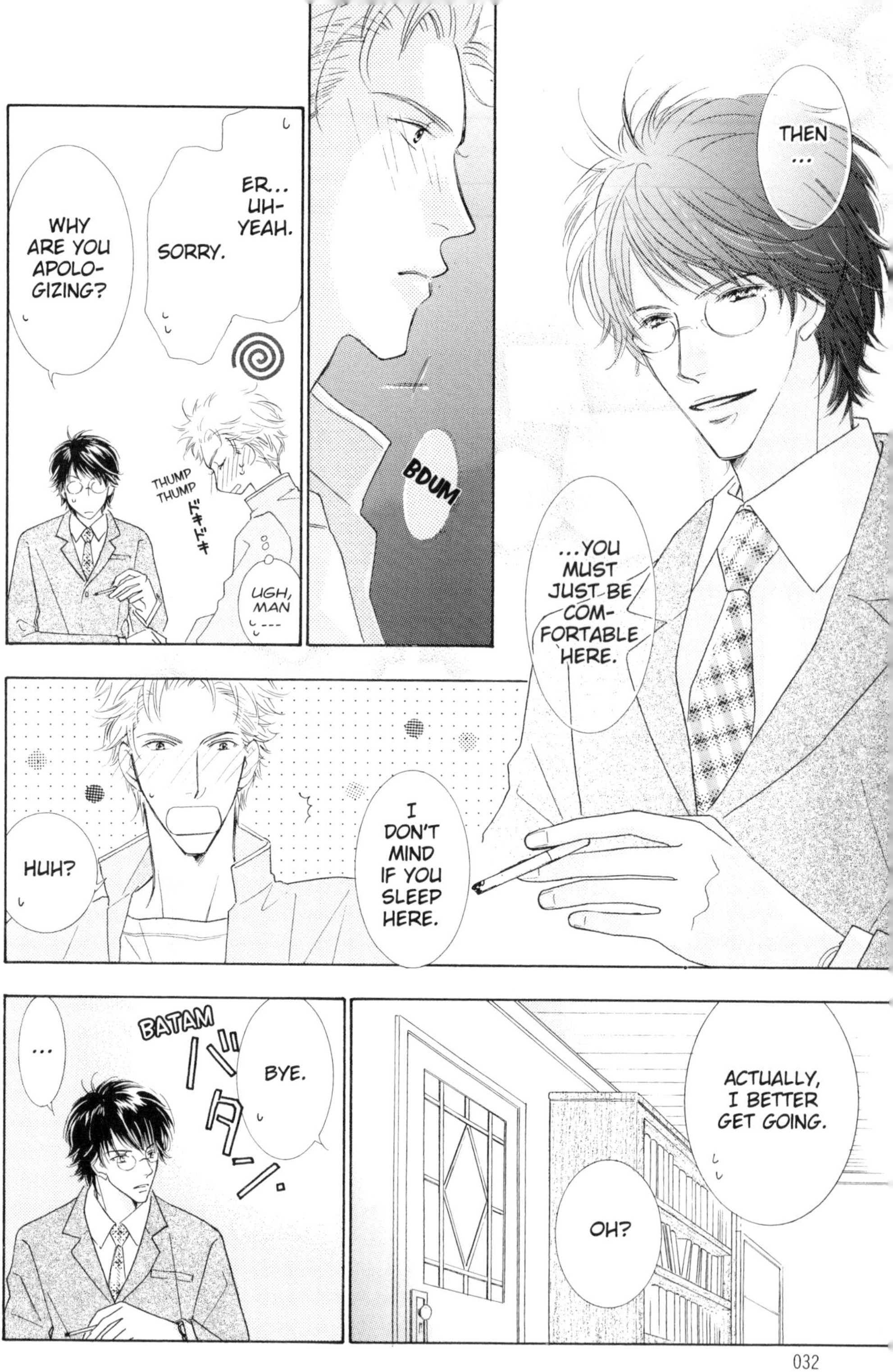
THEN ...
...YOU MUST JUST BE COM-FORTABLE HERE.
BDUM
ER... UH-YEAH.
SORRY.
WHY ARE YOU APOLO-GIZING?
THUMP THUMP
ドキドキ
UGH, MAN
I DON'T MIND IF YOU SLEEP HERE.
HUH?
ACTUALLY, I BETTER GET GOING.
OH?
BATAM
バタン!
BYE.
...

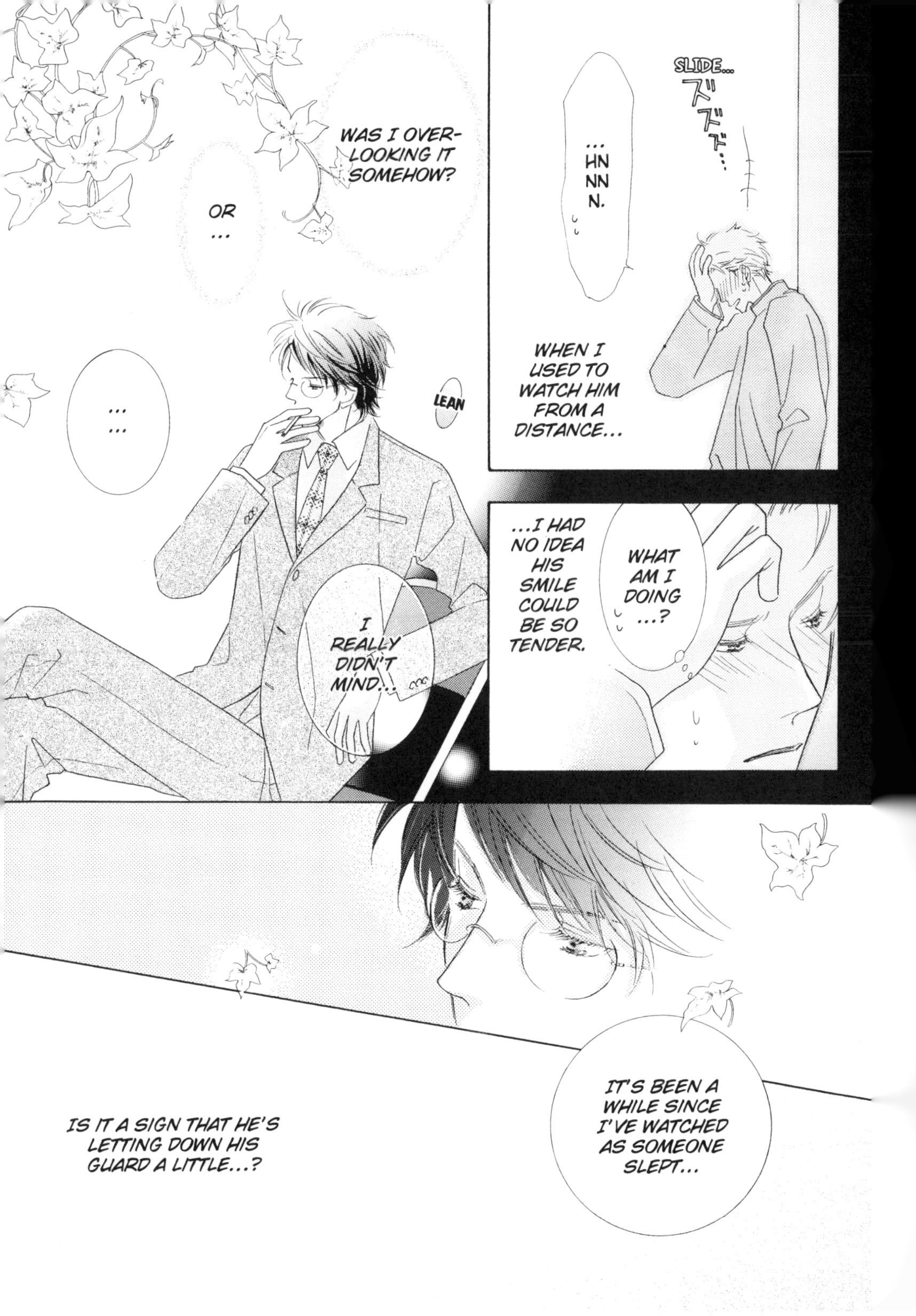
SLIDE...
ズズズ...
...HNNNN.
WHEN I USED TO WATCH HIM FROM A DISTANCE...
...I HAD NO IDEA HIS SMILE COULD BE SO TENDER.
WHAT AM I DOING...?
WAS I OVER-LOOKING IT SOMEHOW?
OR...
LEAN
......
I REALLY DIDN'T MIND...
IT'S BEEN A WHILE SINCE I'VE WATCHED AS SOMEONE SLEPT...
IS IT A SIGN THAT HE'S LETTING DOWN HIS GUARD A LITTLE...?

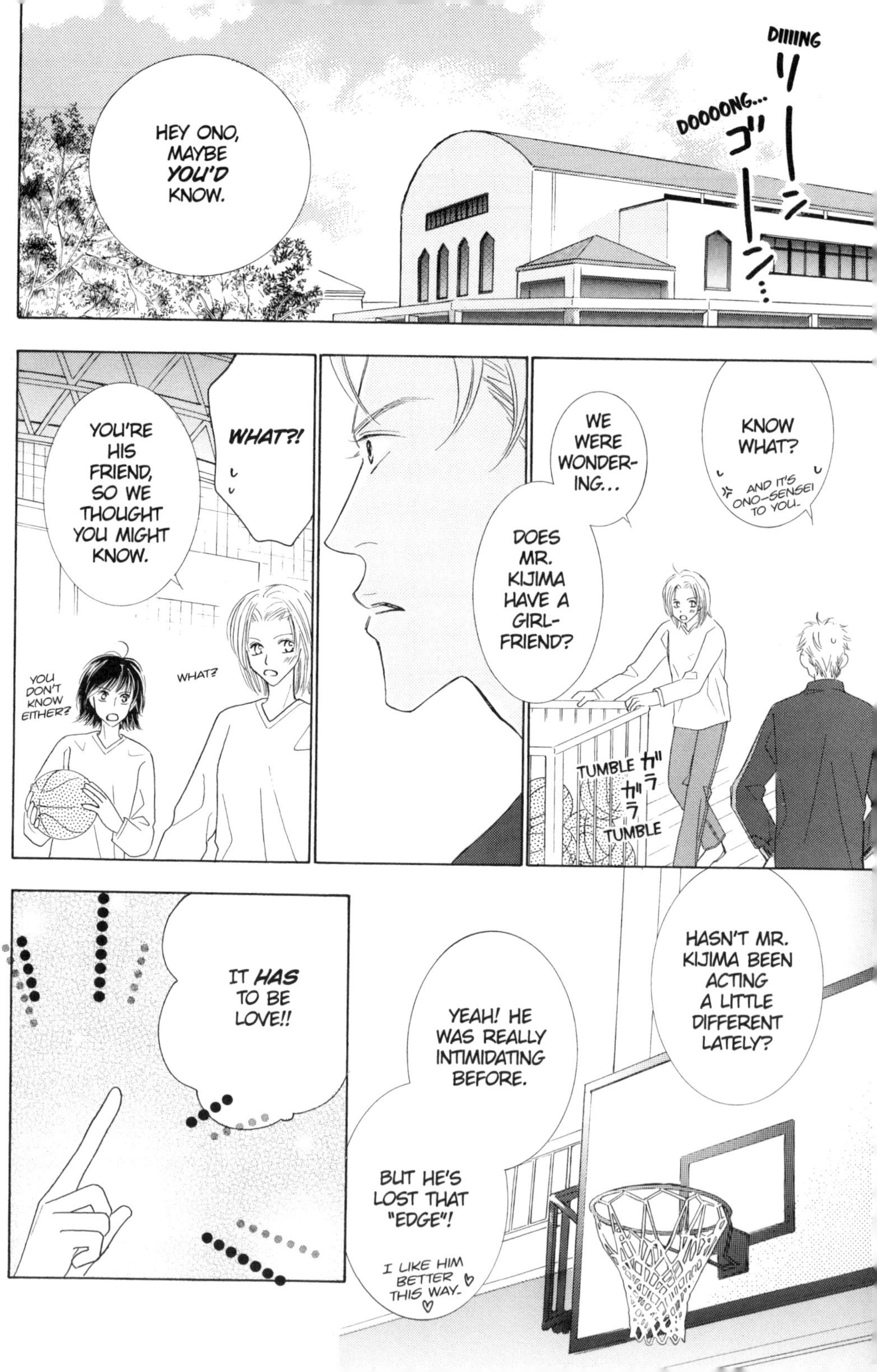
DIIIING
リーン
DOOOONG...
ゴーン…
HEY ONO, MAYBE YOU'D KNOW.
KNOW WHAT?
AND IT'S ONO-SENSEI TO YOU.
WE WERE WONDERING...
DOES MR. KIJIMA HAVE A GIRLFRIEND?
TUMBLE ガラ
ガラ TUMBLE
WHAT?!
YOU'RE HIS FRIEND, SO WE THOUGHT YOU MIGHT KNOW.
WHAT?
YOU DON'T KNOW EITHER?
HASN'T MR. KIJIMA BEEN ACTING A LITTLE DIFFERENT LATELY?
YEAH! HE WAS REALLY INTIMIDATING BEFORE.
BUT HE'S LOST THAT "EDGE"!
I LIKE HIM BETTER THIS WAY.
IT HAS TO BE LOVE!!

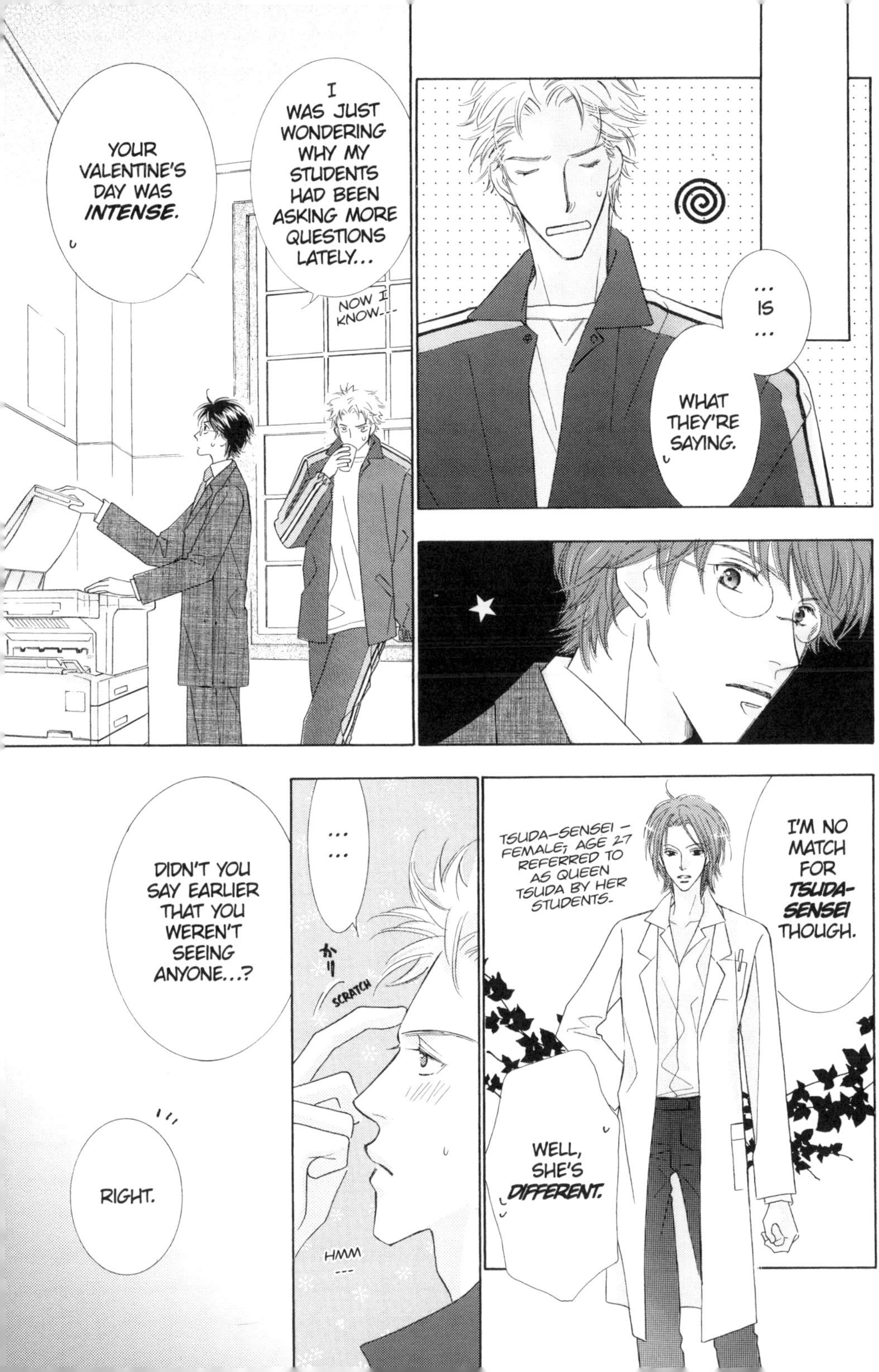

... IS ...
WHAT THEY'RE SAYING.
I WAS JUST WONDERING WHY MY STUDENTS HAD BEEN ASKING MORE QUESTIONS LATELY...
NOW I KNOW...
YOUR VALENTINE'S DAY WAS INTENSE.
I'M NO MATCH FOR TSUDA-SENSEI THOUGH.
TSUDA-SENSEI — FEMALE; AGE 27 REFERRED TO AS QUEEN TSUDA BY HER STUDENTS.
WELL, SHE'S DIFFERENT.
... ...
カリ
SCRATCH
HMM ---
DIDN'T YOU SAY EARLIER THAT YOU WEREN'T SEEING ANYONE...?
RIGHT.

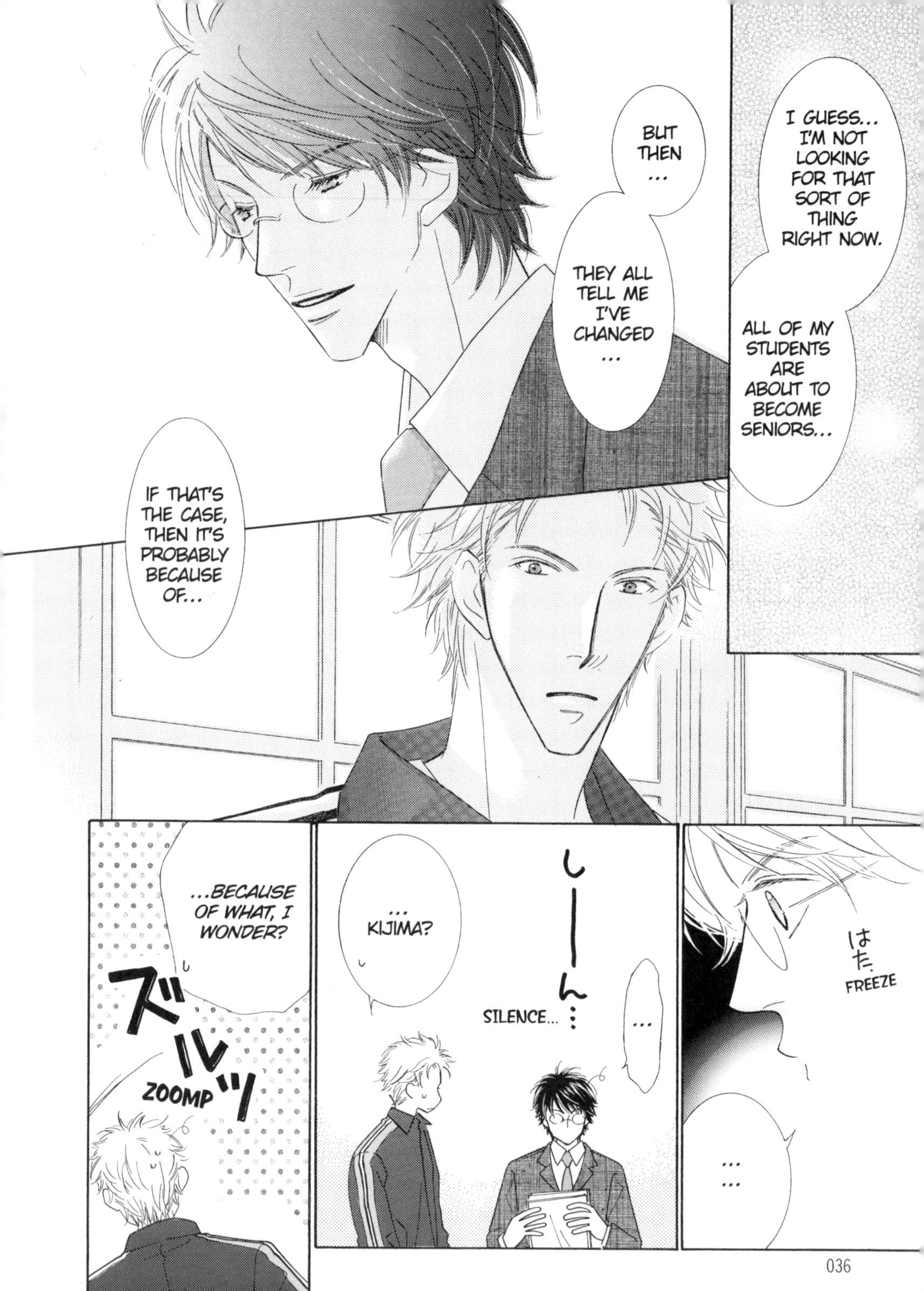

I GUESS... I'M NOT LOOKING FOR THAT SORT OF THING RIGHT NOW.
ALL OF MY STUDENTS ARE ABOUT TO BECOME SENIORS...
BUT THEN ...
THEY ALL TELL ME I'VE CHANGED ...
IF THAT'S THE CASE, THEN IT'S PROBABLY BECAUSE OF...
はた
FREEZE
... ...
しーん…
SILENCE...
...
... KIJIMA?
...BECAUSE OF WHAT, I WONDER?
ズルッ
ZOOMP

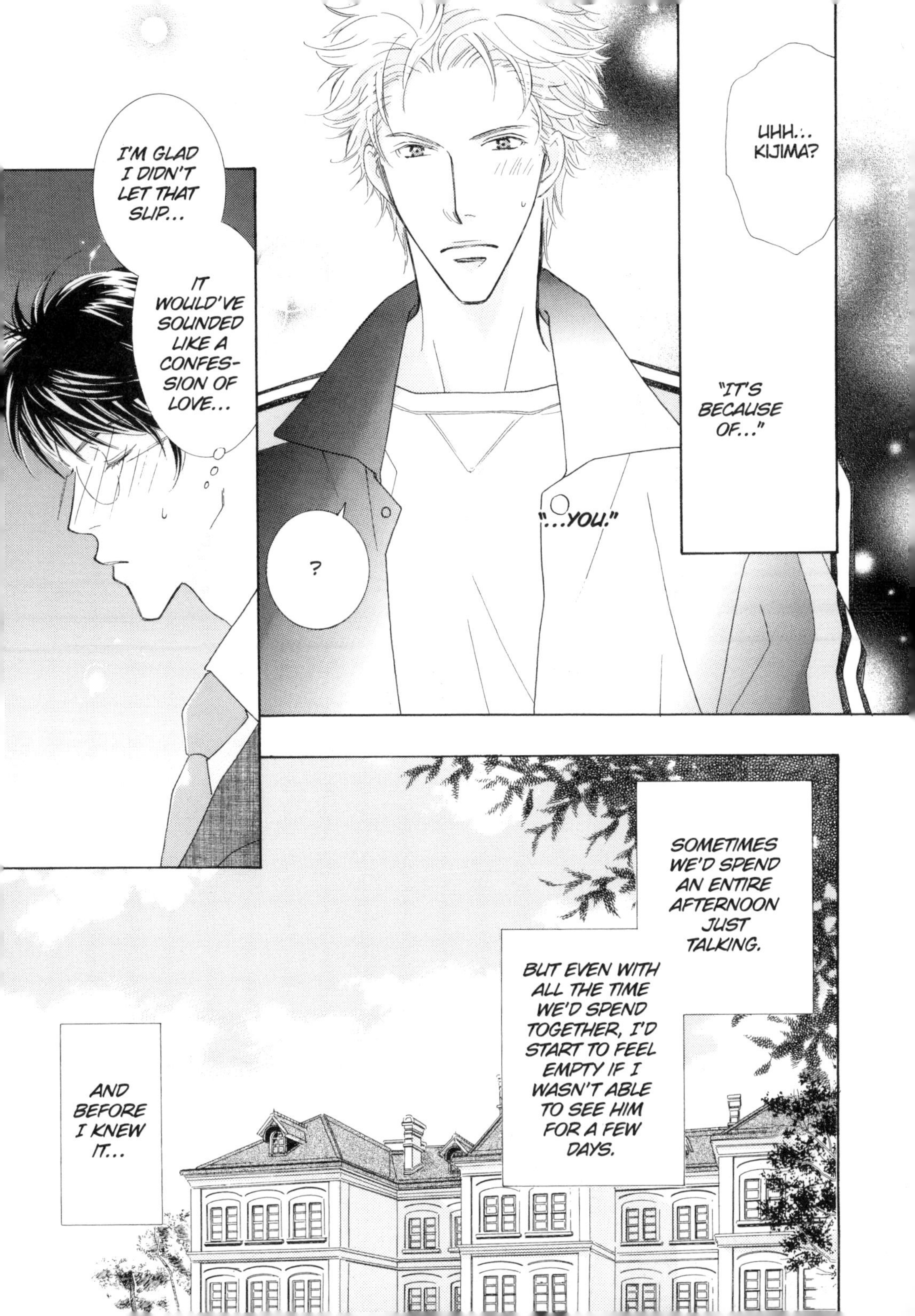
UHH... KIJIMA?
"IT'S BECAUSE OF..."
"...YOU."
?
I'M GLAD I DIDN'T LET THAT SLIP...
IT WOULD'VE SOUNDED LIKE A CONFESSION OF LOVE...
SOMETIMES WE'D SPEND AN ENTIRE AFTERNOON JUST TALKING.
BUT EVEN WITH ALL THE TIME WE'D SPEND TOGETHER, I'D START TO FEEL EMPTY IF I WASN'T ABLE TO SEE HIM FOR A FEW DAYS.
AND BEFORE I KNEW IT...

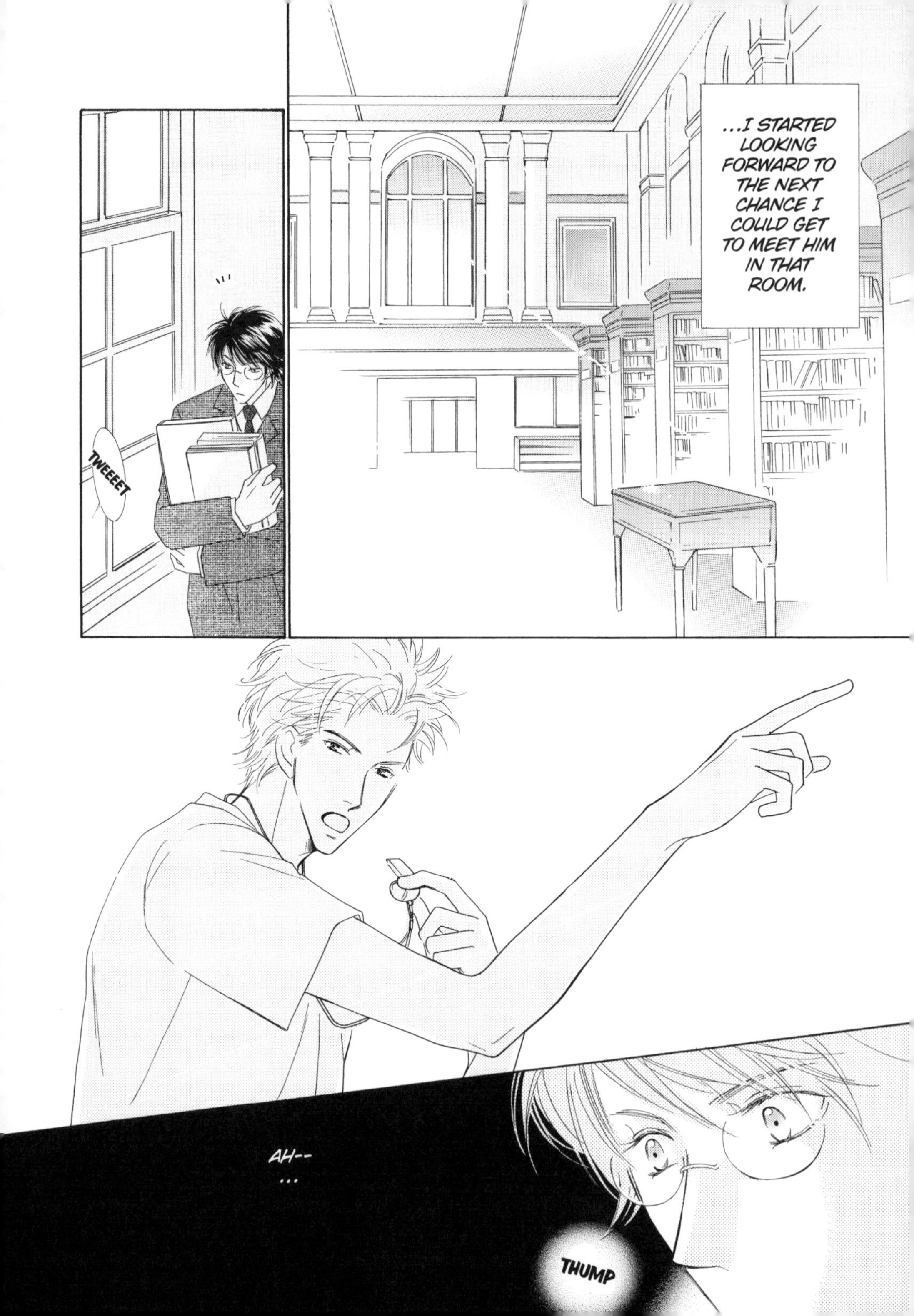
...I STARTED LOOKING FORWARD TO THE NEXT CHANCE I COULD GET TO MEET HIM IN THAT ROOM.
TWEEEET
AH-- ...
THUMP

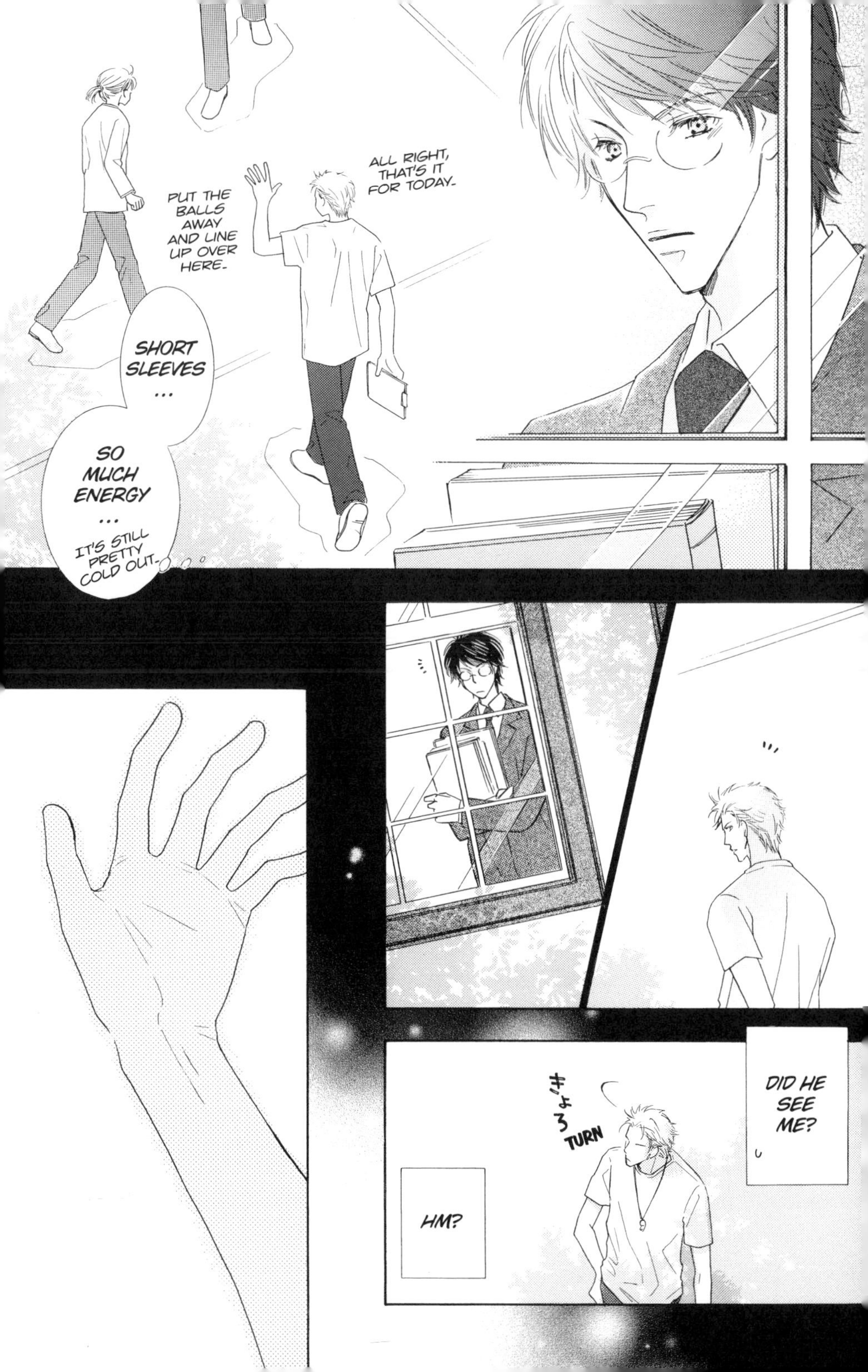
ALL RIGHT, THAT'S IT FOR TODAY.
PUT THE BALLS AWAY AND LINE UP OVER HERE.
SHORT SLEEVES...
SO MUCH ENERGY...
IT'S STILL PRETTY COLD OUT.
DID HE SEE ME?
きょろ TURN
HM?

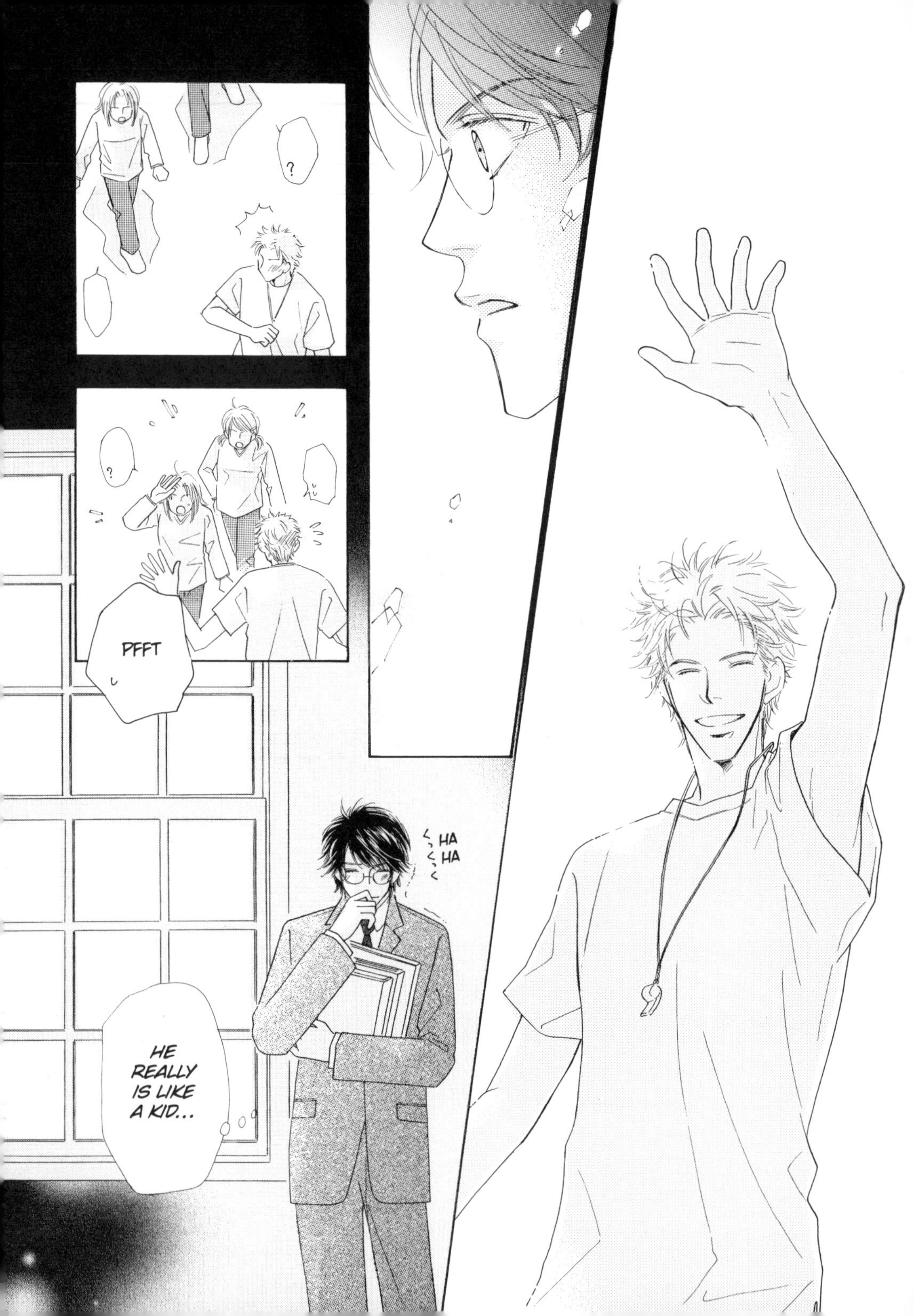
?
?
PFFT
HA HA
HE REALLY IS LIKE A KID...

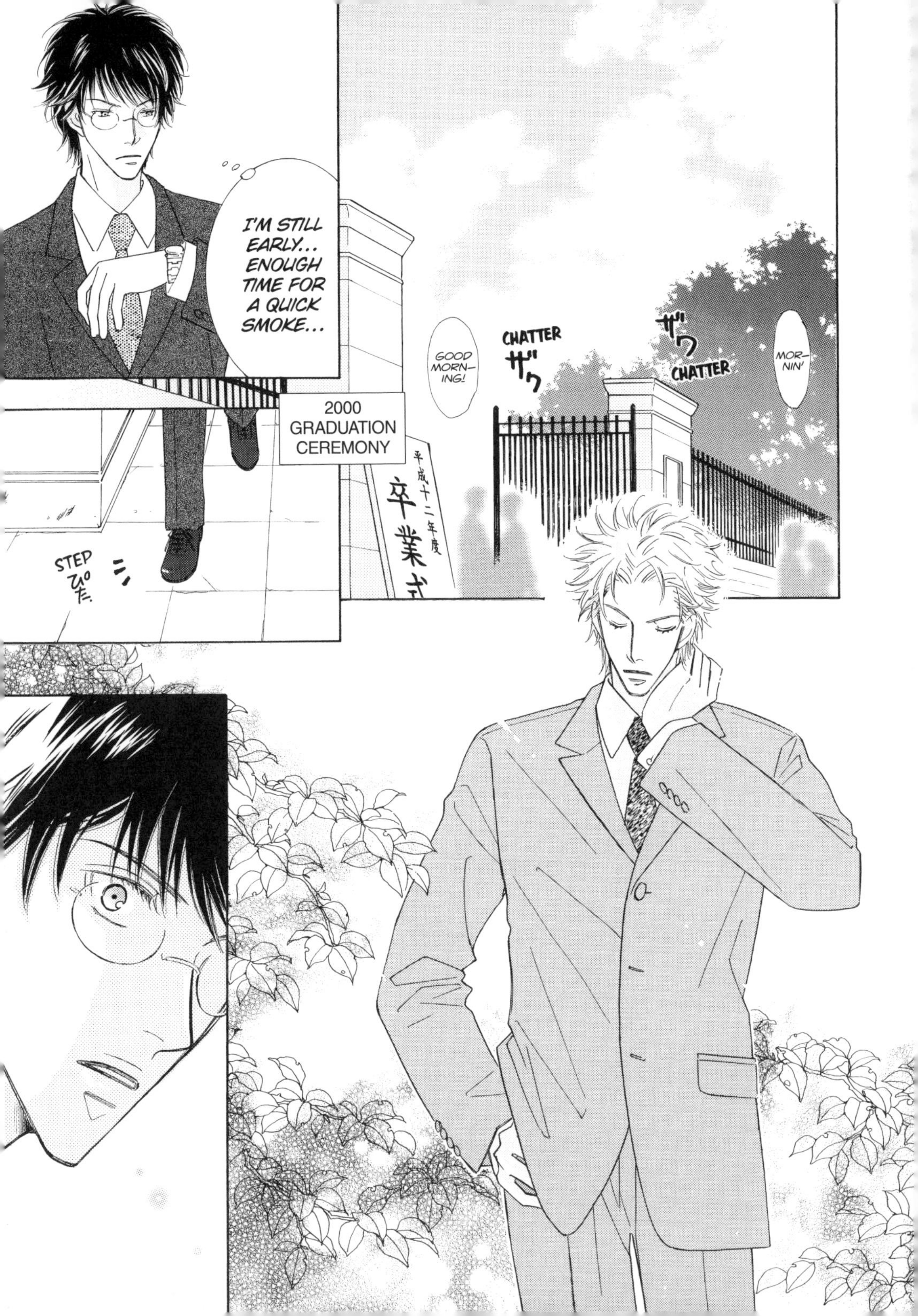

MOR-NIN'
ザワ
CHATTER
CHATTER
GOOD MORN-ING!
平成十二年度
卒業式
2000 GRADUATION CEREMONY
I'M STILL EARLY... ENOUGH TIME FOR A QUICK SMOKE...
STEP
ぴた

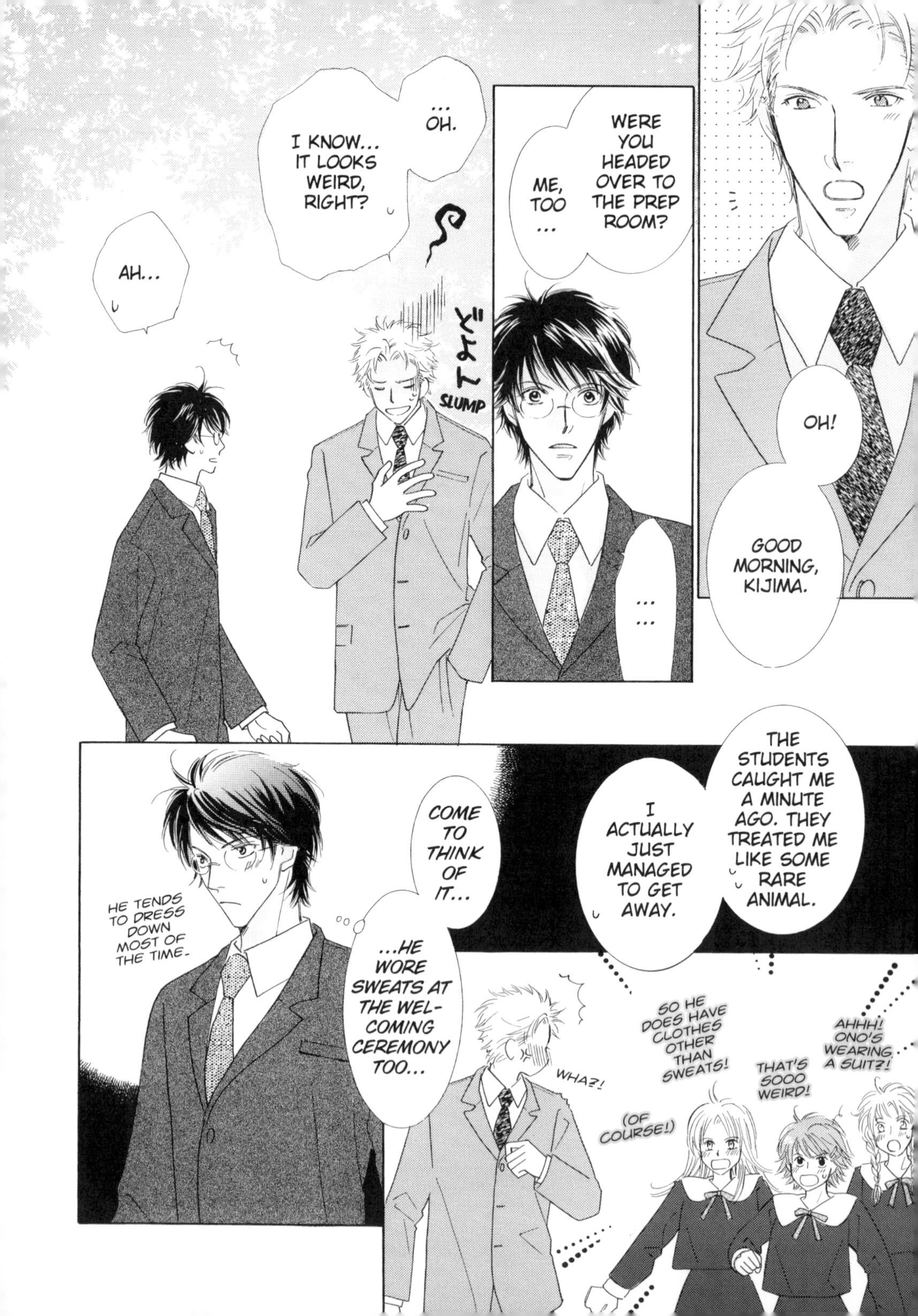
OH!
GOOD MORNING, KIJIMA.
WERE YOU HEADED OVER TO THE PREP ROOM?
ME, TOO...
......
...OH.
I KNOW... IT LOOKS WEIRD, RIGHT?
どよん
SLUMP
AH...
THE STUDENTS CAUGHT ME A MINUTE AGO. THEY TREATED ME LIKE SOME RARE ANIMAL.
I ACTUALLY JUST MANAGED TO GET AWAY.
AHHH! ONO'S WEARING A SUIT?!
THAT'S SOOO WEIRD!
SO HE DOES HAVE CLOTHES OTHER THAN SWEATS!
(OF COURSE!)
WHA?!
COME TO THINK OF IT...
...HE WORE SWEATS AT THE WEL-COMING CEREMONY TOO...
HE TENDS TO DRESS DOWN MOST OF THE TIME.

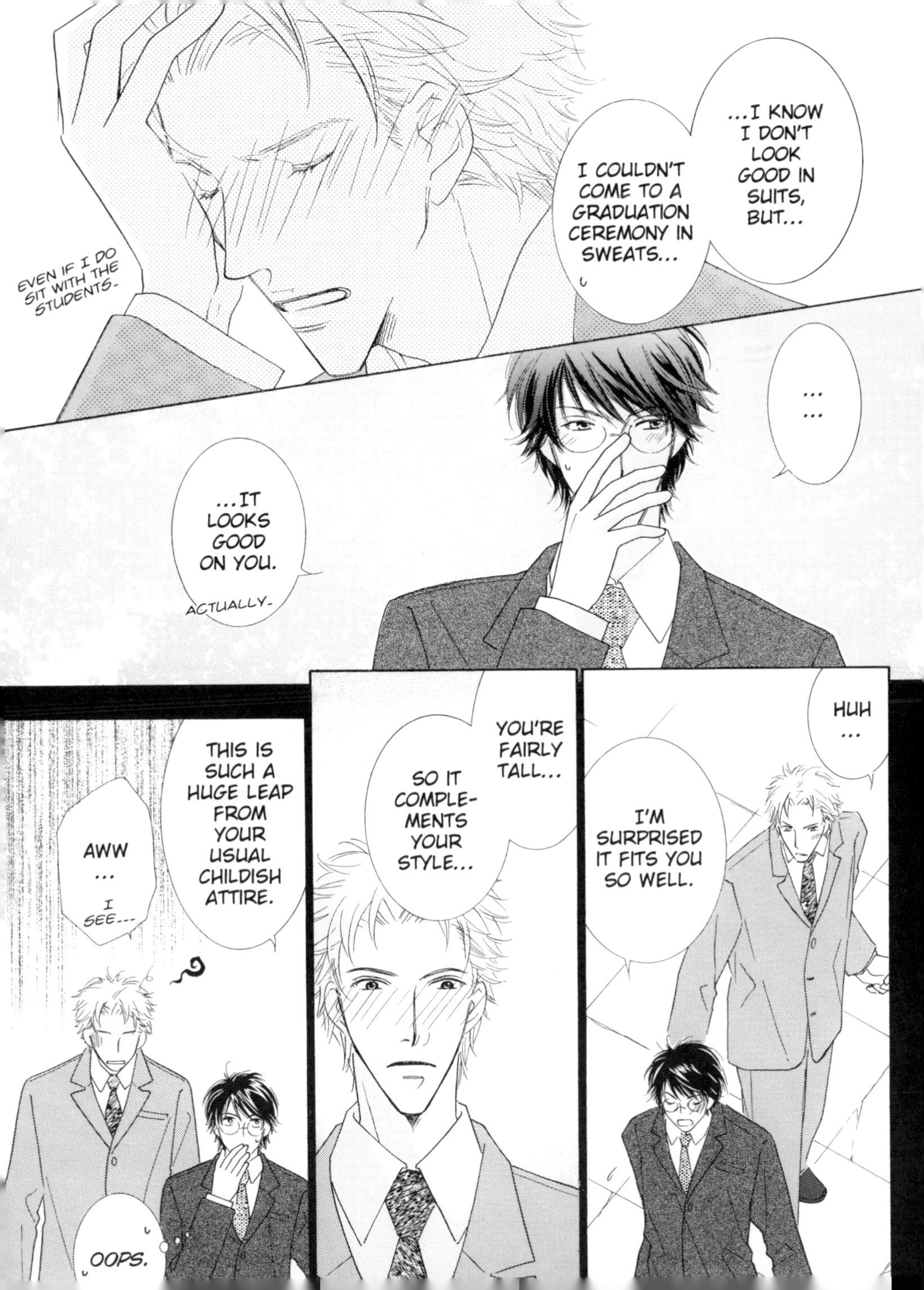
...I KNOW I DON'T LOOK GOOD IN SUITS, BUT...
I COULDN'T COME TO A GRADUATION CEREMONY IN SWEATS...
EVEN IF I DO SIT WITH THE STUDENTS.
... ...
...IT LOOKS GOOD ON YOU.
ACTUALLY.
HUH...
I'M SURPRISED IT FITS YOU SO WELL.
YOU'RE FAIRLY TALL...
SO IT COMPLEMENTS YOUR STYLE...
THIS IS SUCH A HUGE LEAP FROM YOUR USUAL CHILDISH ATTIRE.
AWW...
I SEE...
OOPS.

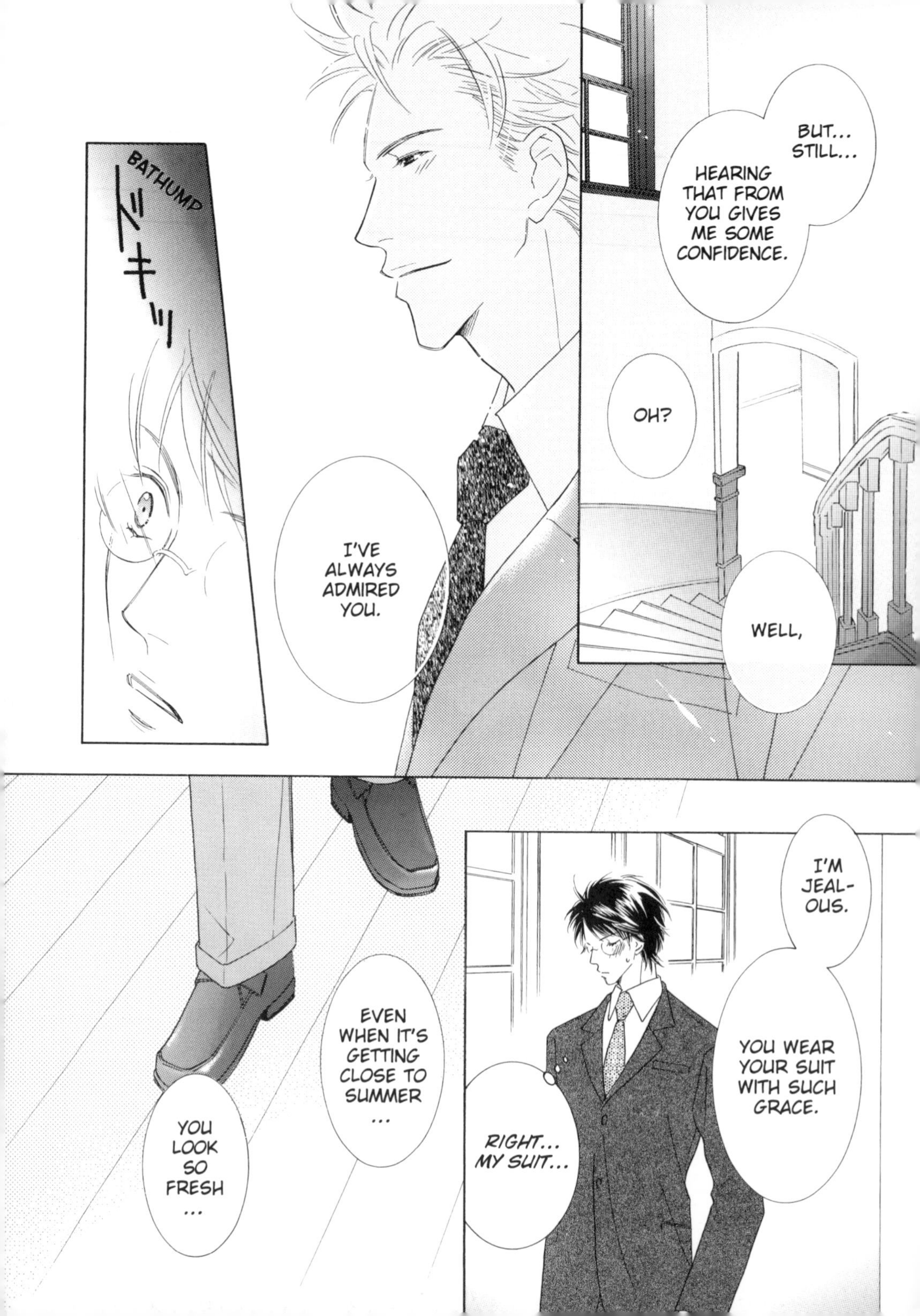
BUT... STILL...
HEARING THAT FROM YOU GIVES ME SOME CONFIDENCE.
OH?
WELL,
I'VE ALWAYS ADMIRED YOU.
BATHUMP
ドキッ
I'M JEAL-OUS.
YOU WEAR YOUR SUIT WITH SUCH GRACE.
RIGHT... MY SUIT...
EVEN WHEN IT'S GETTING CLOSE TO SUMMER...
YOU LOOK SO FRESH...

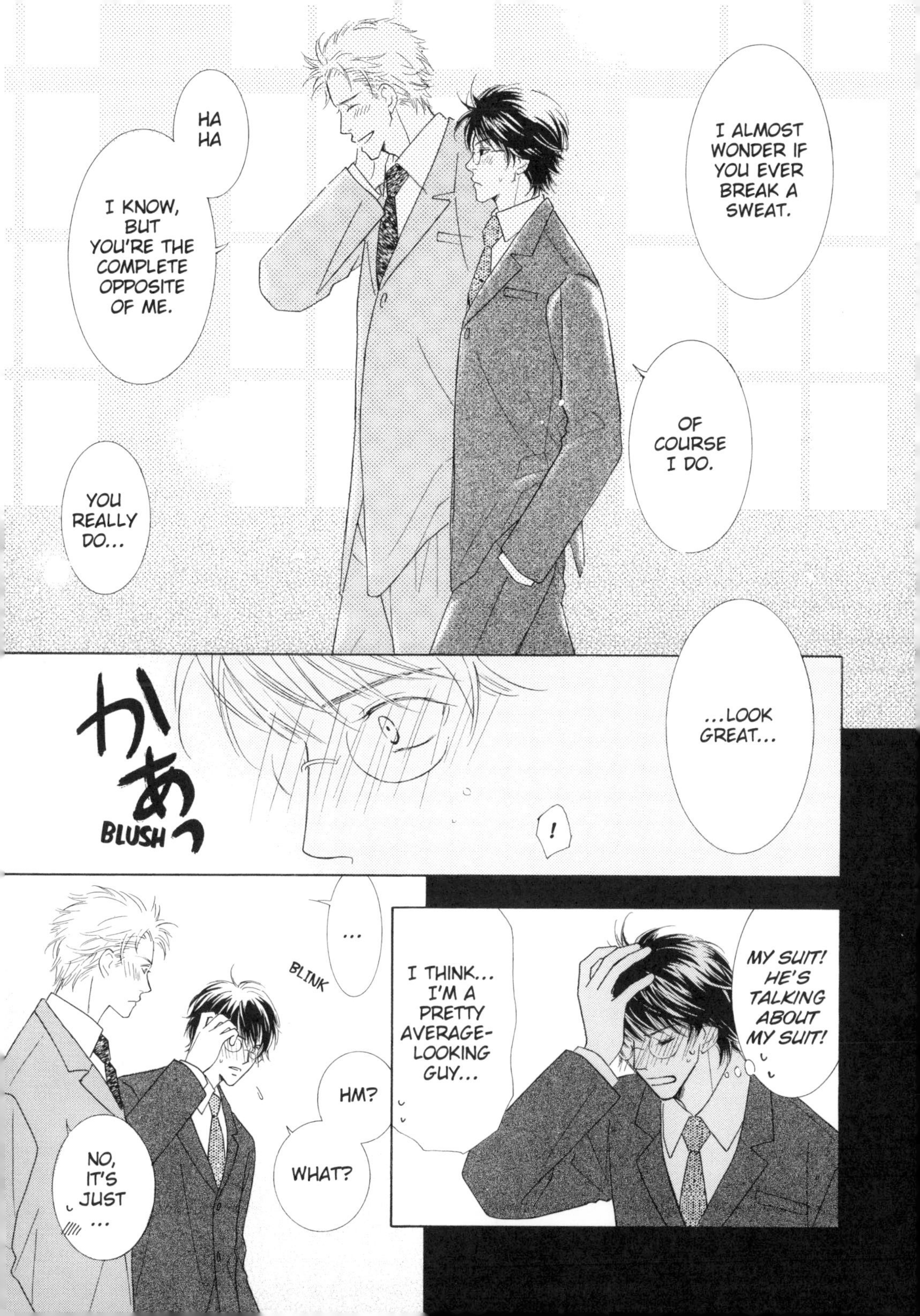
I ALMOST WONDER IF YOU EVER BREAK A SWEAT.
HA HA
I KNOW, BUT YOU'RE THE COMPLETE OPPOSITE OF ME.
OF COURSE I DO.
YOU REALLY DO...
...LOOK GREAT...
!
かあっ
BLUSH
MY SUIT! HE'S TALKING ABOUT MY SUIT!
I THINK... I'M A PRETTY AVERAGE-LOOKING GUY...
...
BLINK
HM?
WHAT?
NO, IT'S JUST ...

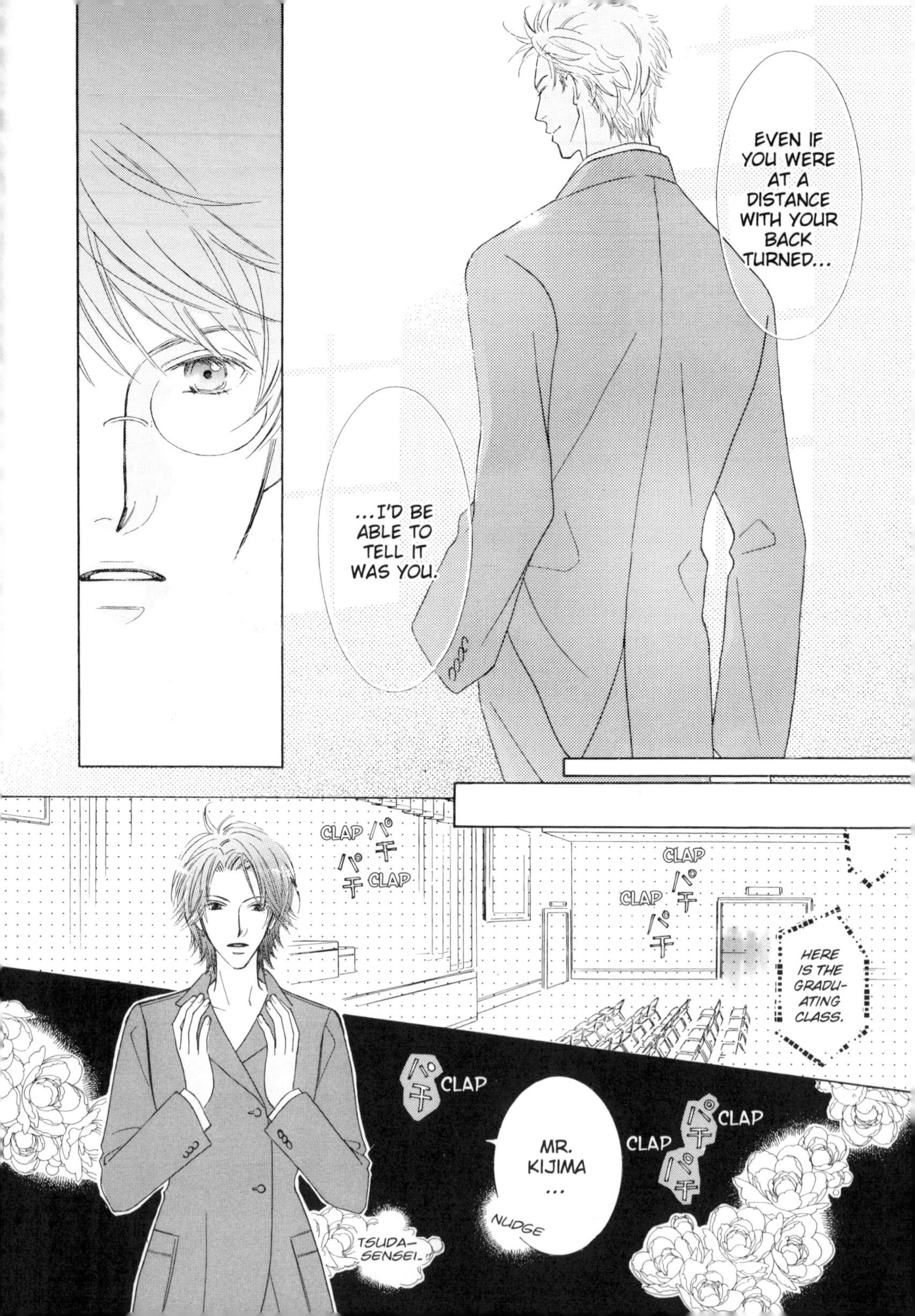
EVEN IF YOU WERE AT A DISTANCE WITH YOUR BACK TURNED...
...I'D BE ABLE TO TELL IT WAS YOU.
HERE IS THE GRADUATING CLASS.
CLAP パチ CLAP パチ
CLAP パチ CLAP パチ
CLAP パチ CLAP パチ
CLAP パチ
MR. KIJIMA ...
NUDGE
TSUDA-SENSEI...

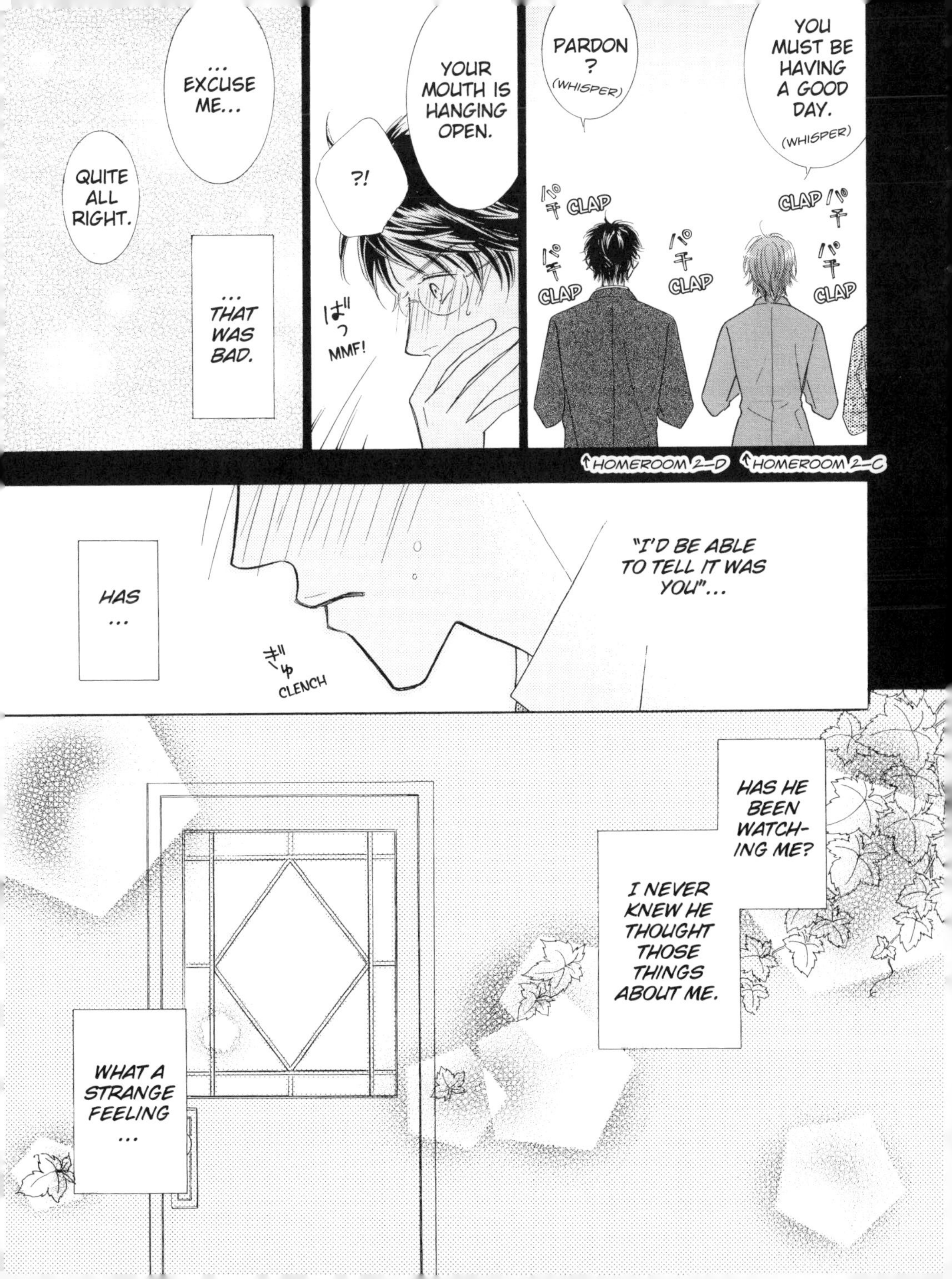
YOU MUST BE HAVING A GOOD DAY.
(WHISPER)
PARDON?
(WHISPER)
CLAP パチ
パチ CLAP
パチ CLAP
パチ CLAP
パチ CLAP
HOMEROOM 2-C
HOMEROOM 2-D
YOUR MOUTH IS HANGING OPEN.
?!
ばっ MMF!
... EXCUSE ME...
QUITE ALL RIGHT.
... THAT WAS BAD.
"I'D BE ABLE TO TELL IT WAS YOU"...
ぎゅ CLENCH
HAS ...
HAS HE BEEN WATCHING ME?
I NEVER KNEW HE THOUGHT THOSE THINGS ABOUT ME.
WHAT A STRANGE FEELING ...

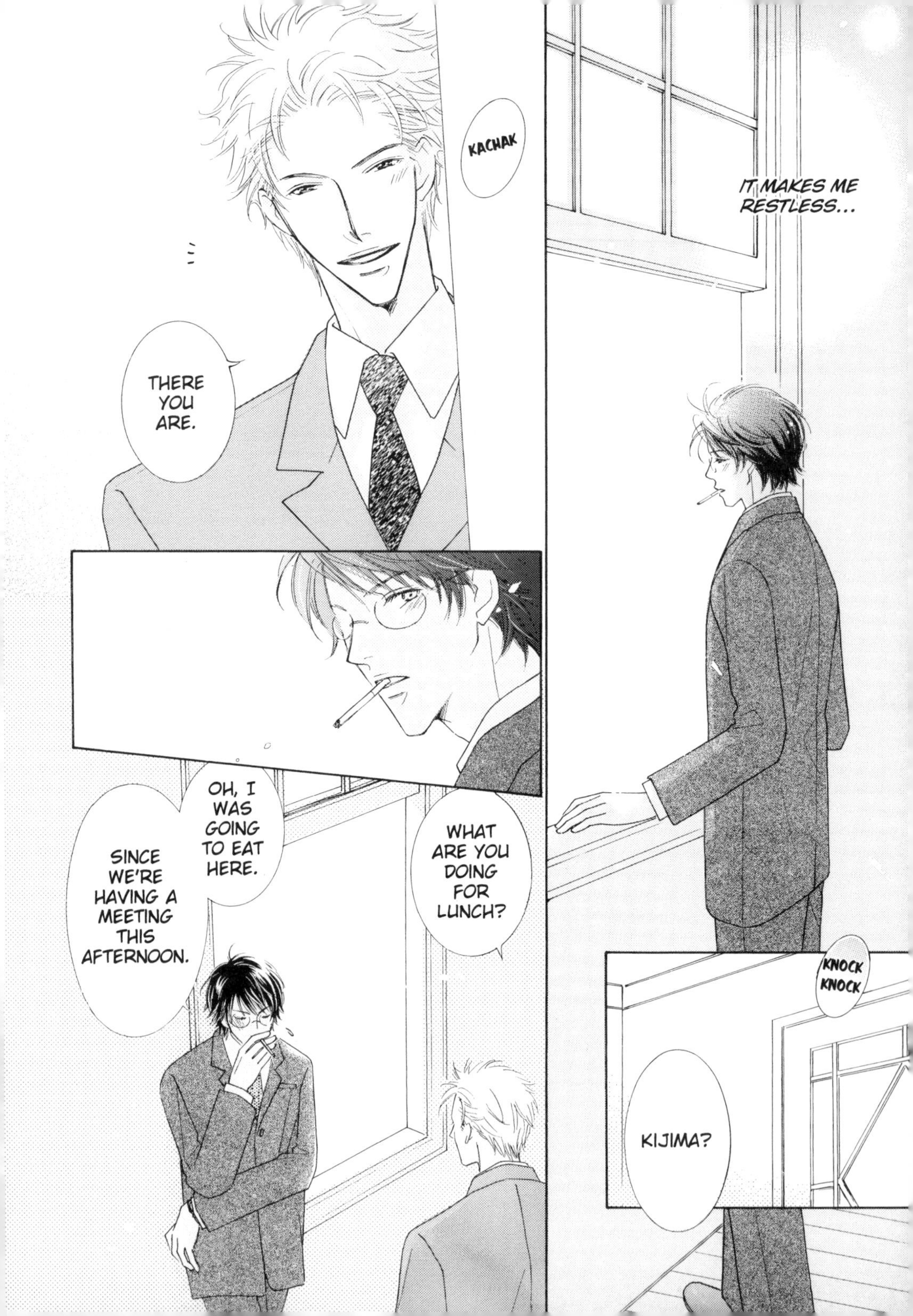
IT MAKES ME RESTLESS...
KNOCK KNOCK
KIJIMA?
KACHAK
THERE YOU ARE.
WHAT ARE YOU DOING FOR LUNCH?
OH, I WAS GOING TO EAT HERE.
SINCE WE'RE HAVING A MEETING THIS AFTERNOON.

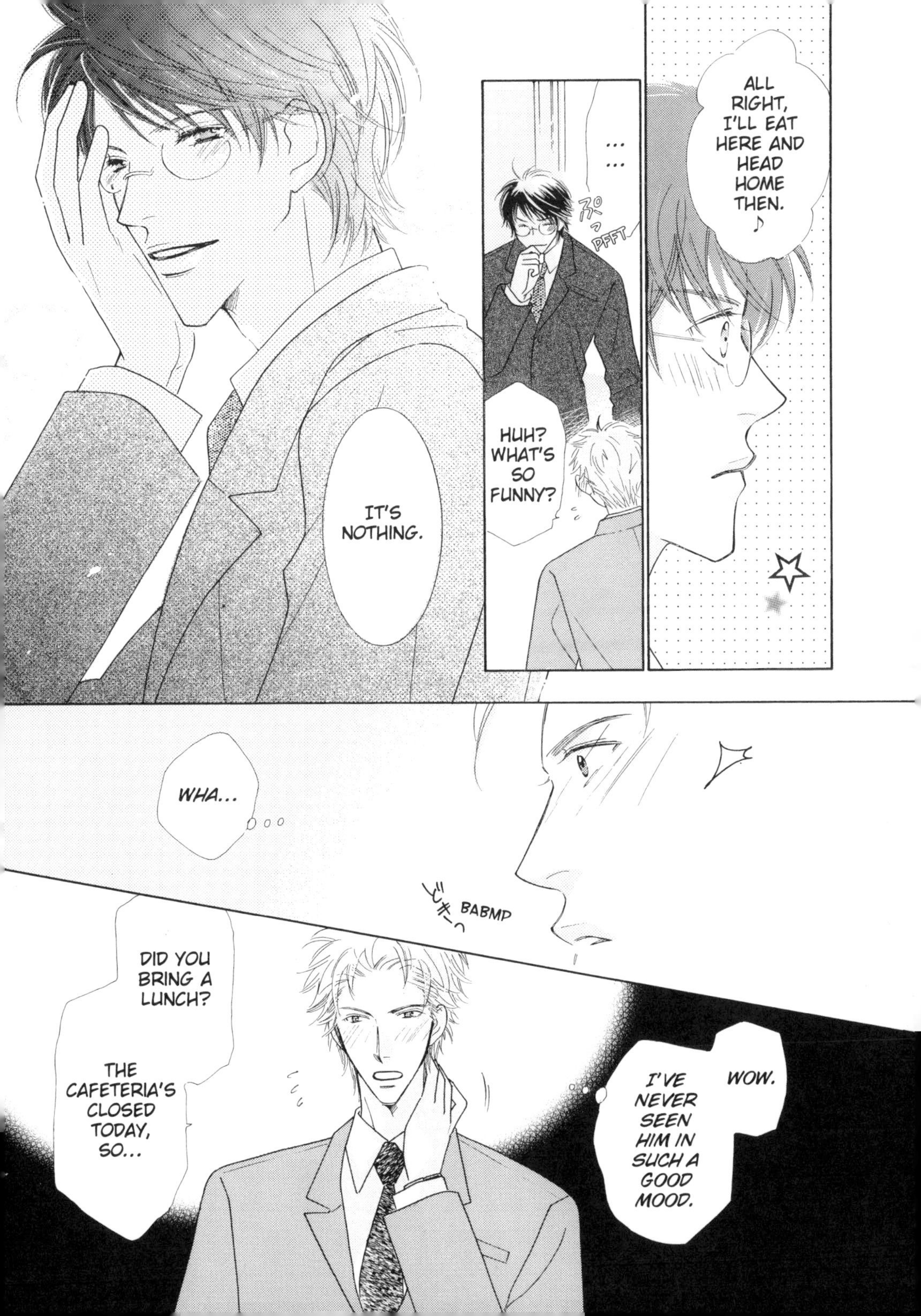
ALL RIGHT, I'LL EAT HERE AND HEAD HOME THEN. ♪
... ...
PFFT
HUH? WHAT'S SO FUNNY?
IT'S NOTHING.
WHA...
BABMP
WOW.
I'VE NEVER SEEN HIM IN SUCH A GOOD MOOD.
DID YOU BRING A LUNCH?
THE CAFETERIA'S CLOSED TODAY, SO...

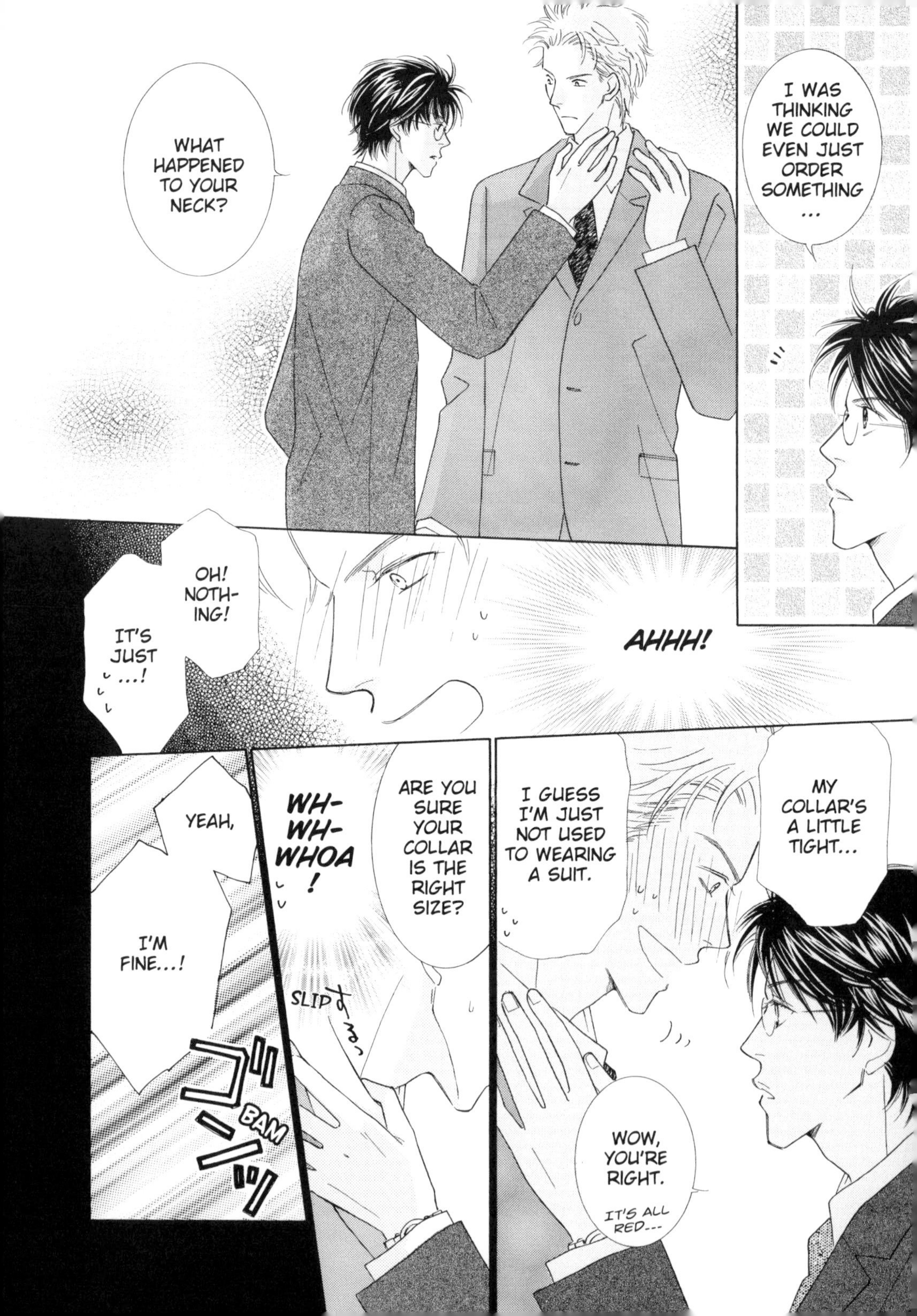
I WAS THINKING WE COULD EVEN JUST ORDER SOMETHING ...
WHAT HAPPENED TO YOUR NECK?
AHHH!
OH! NOTHING!
IT'S JUST ...!
MY COLLAR'S A LITTLE TIGHT...
I GUESS I'M JUST NOT USED TO WEARING A SUIT.
WOW, YOU'RE RIGHT.
IT'S ALL RED---
ARE YOU SURE YOUR COLLAR IS THE RIGHT SIZE?
WH-WH-WHOA!
SLIP
YEAH,
I'M FINE...!
BAM

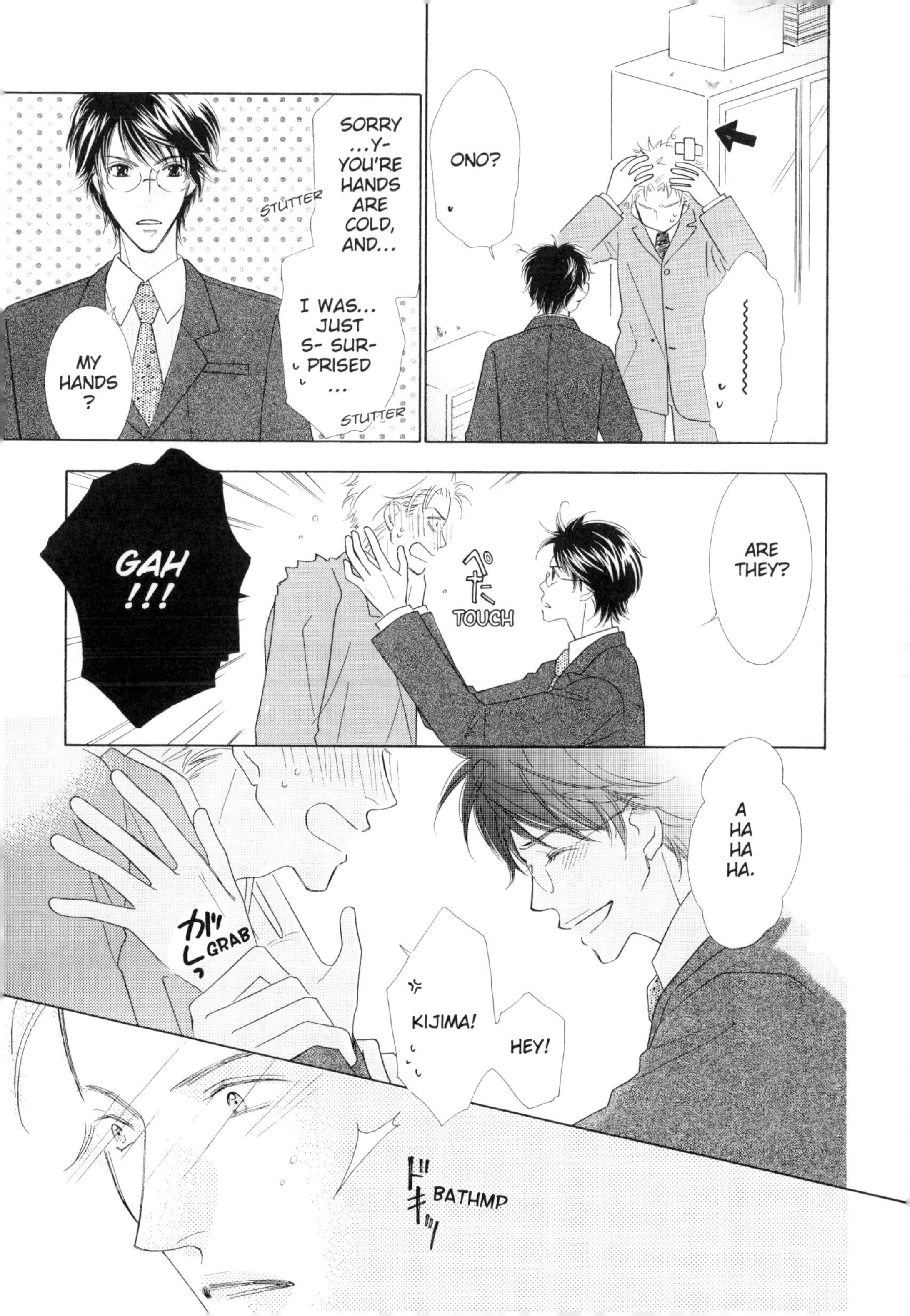
ONO?
SORRY ...Y- YOU'RE HANDS ARE COLD, AND...
STUTTER
I WAS... JUST S- SUR-PRISED ...
STUTTER
MY HANDS ?
ARE THEY?
ぺた
TOUCH
GAH !!!
A HA HA HA.
HEY!
KIJIMA!
ガッ
GRAB
ドキッ
BATHMP

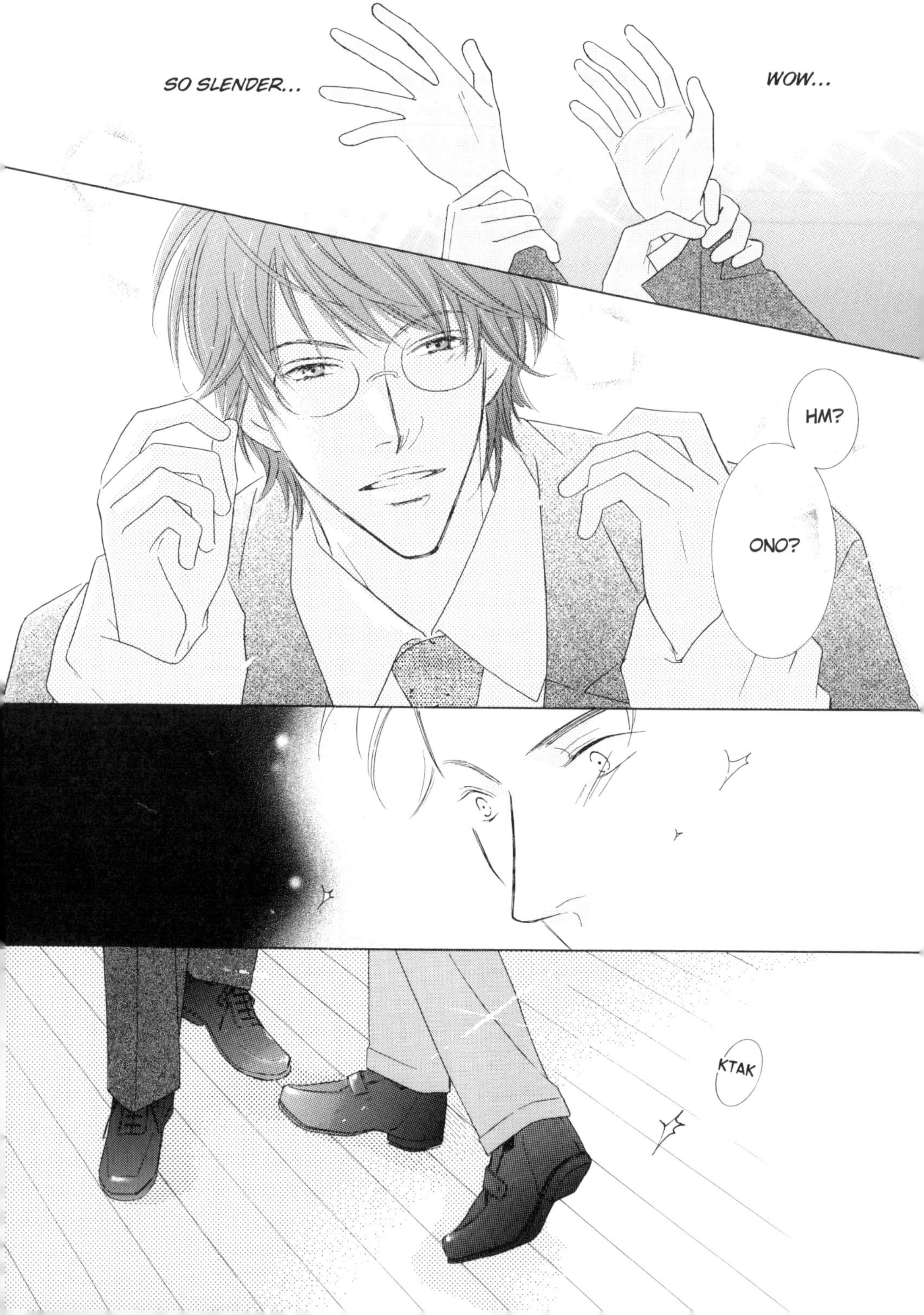
WOW...
SO SLENDER...
HM?
ONO?
KTAK

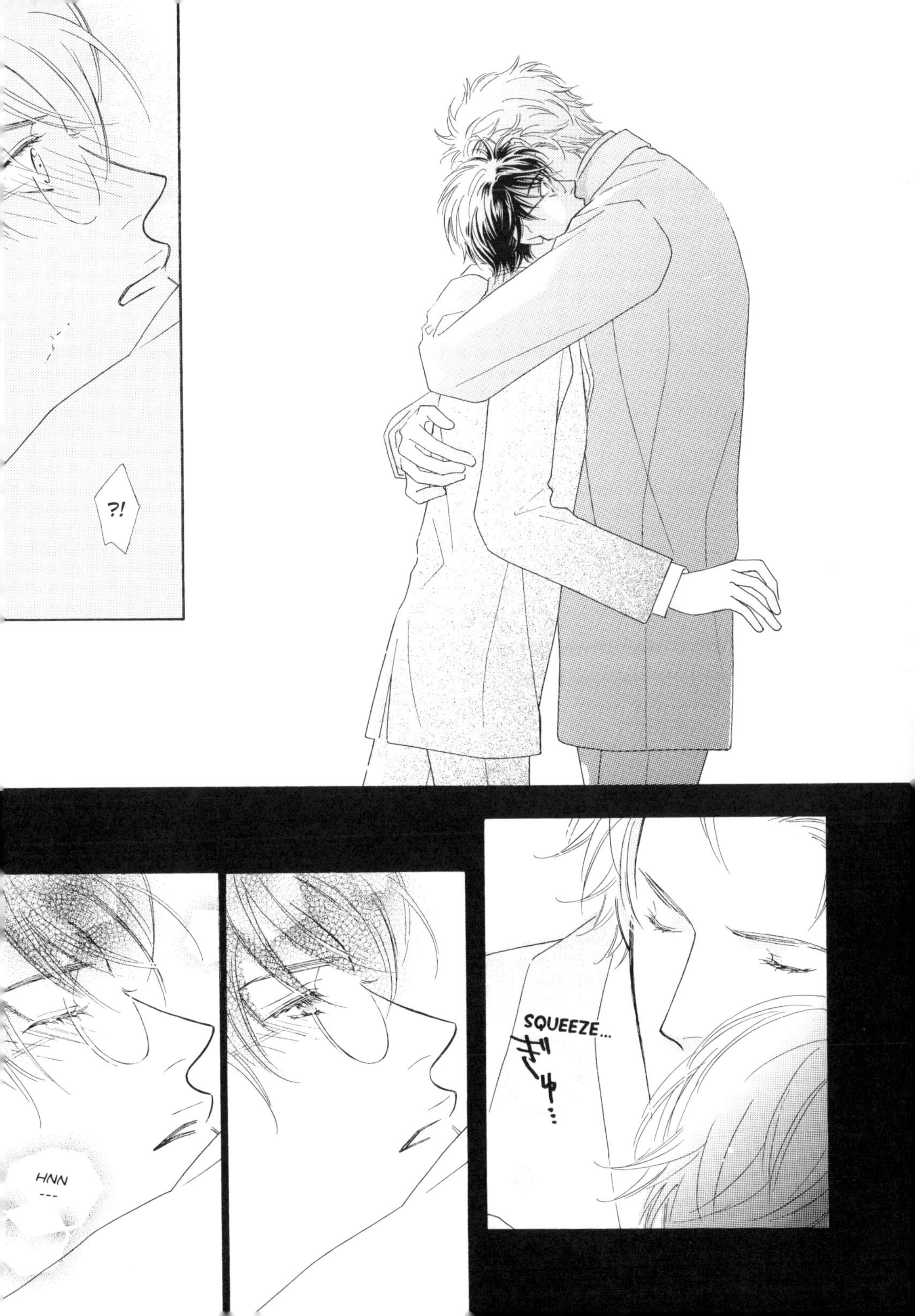
?!
SQUEEZE...
ぎゅ…
HNN

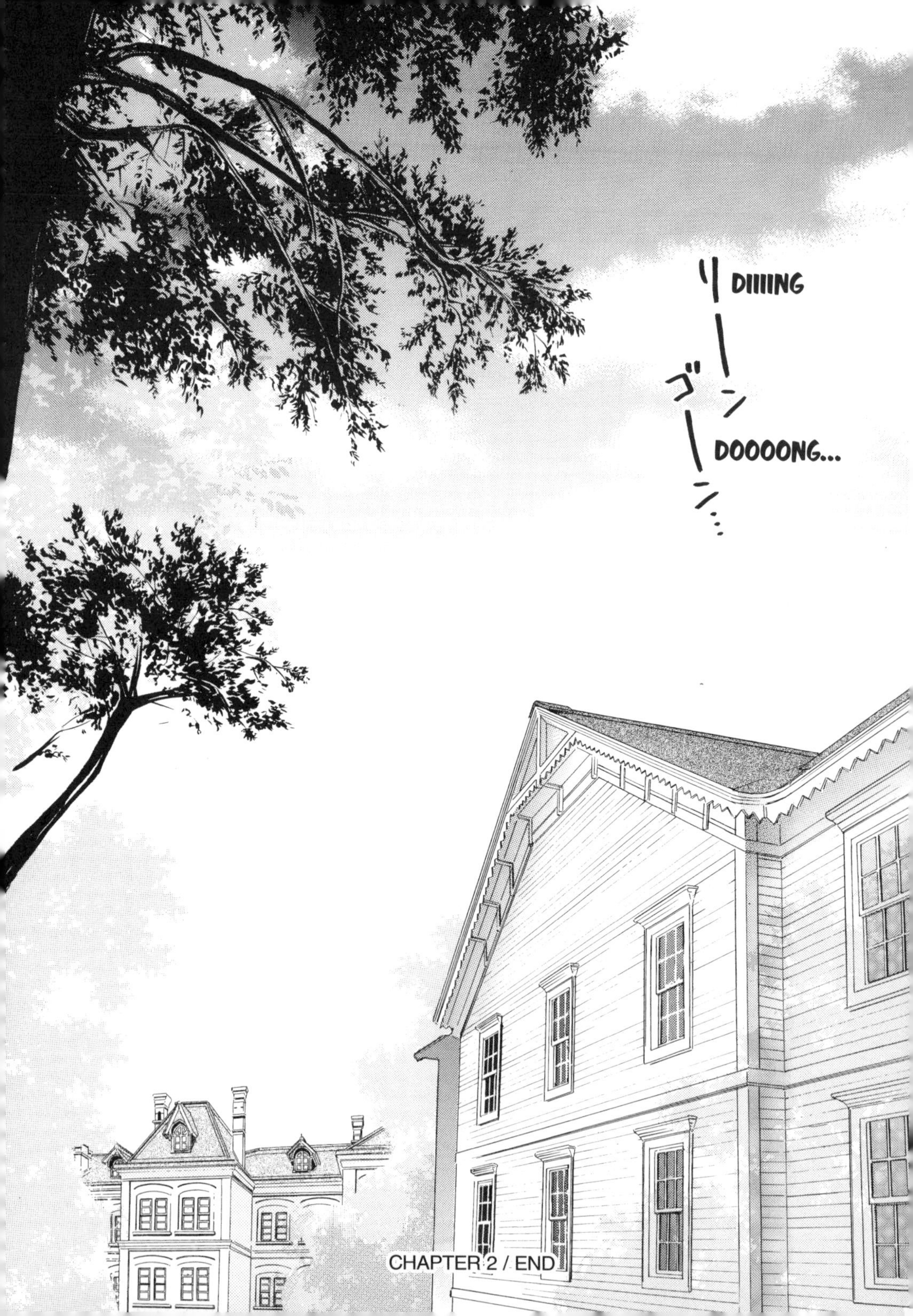
リーン
DIIIING
ゴーン…
DOOOONG...
CHAPTER 2 / END

CHAPTER.3

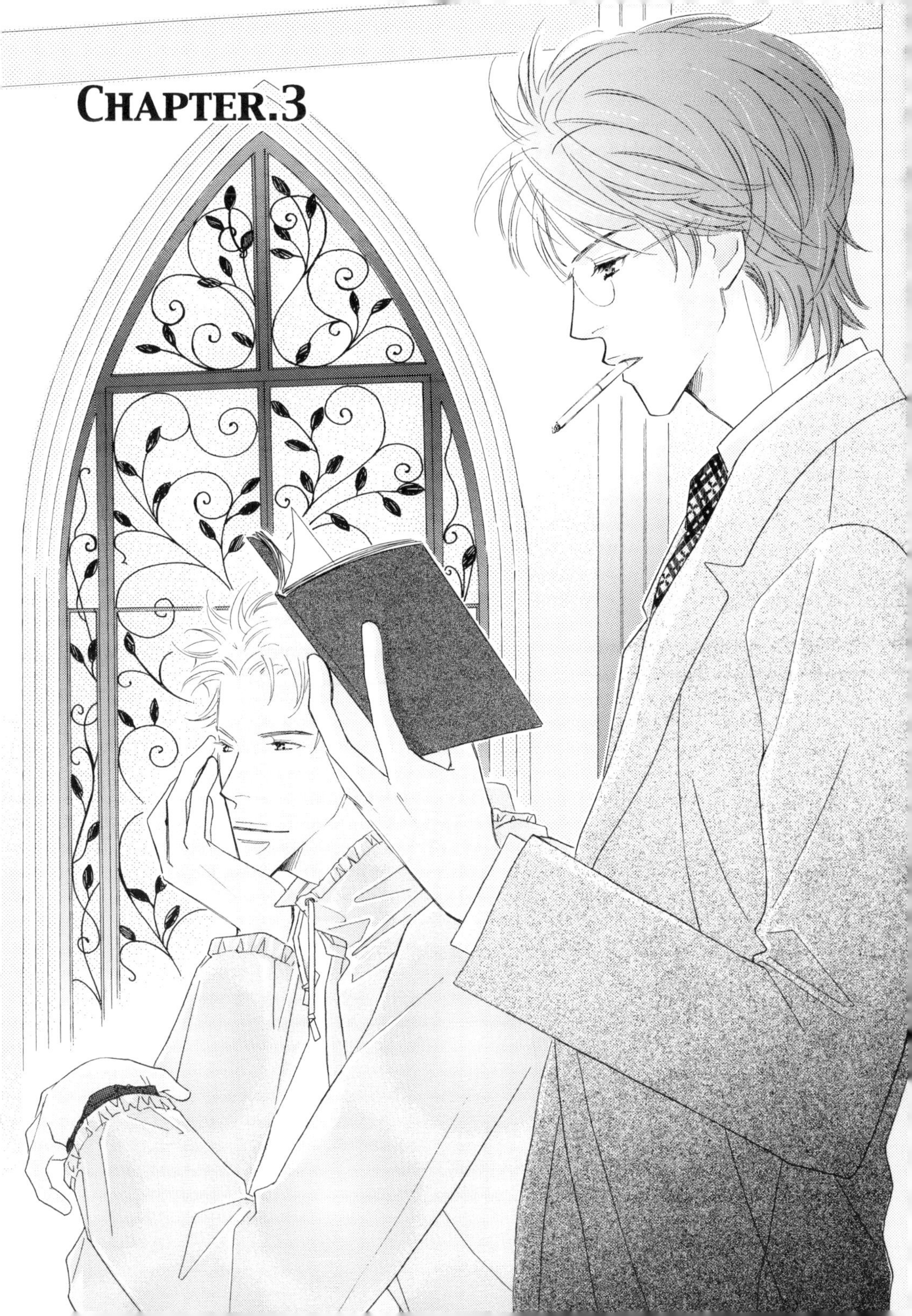

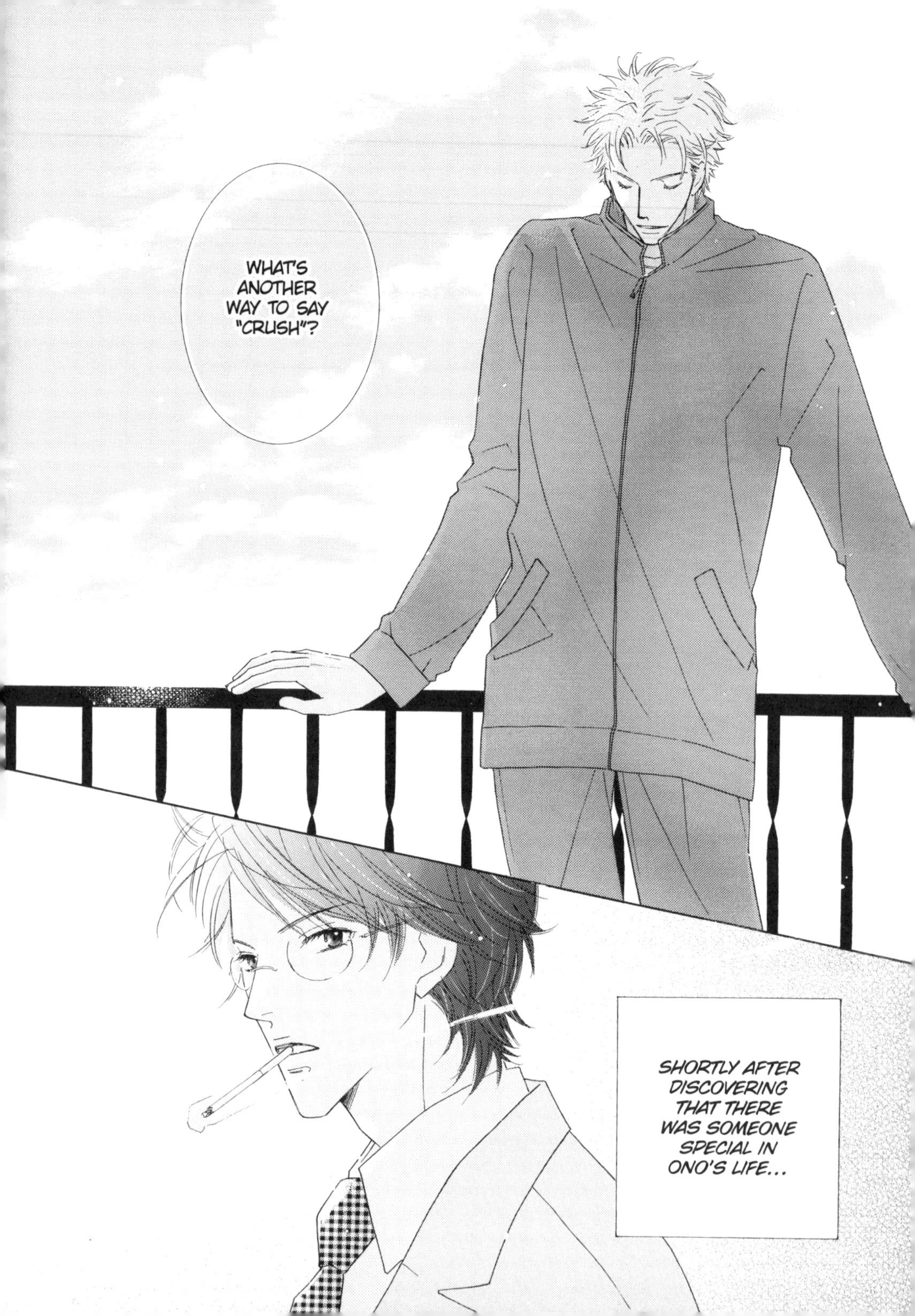
WHAT'S ANOTHER WAY TO SAY "CRUSH"?
SHORTLY AFTER DISCOVERING THAT THERE WAS SOMEONE SPECIAL IN ONO'S LIFE...

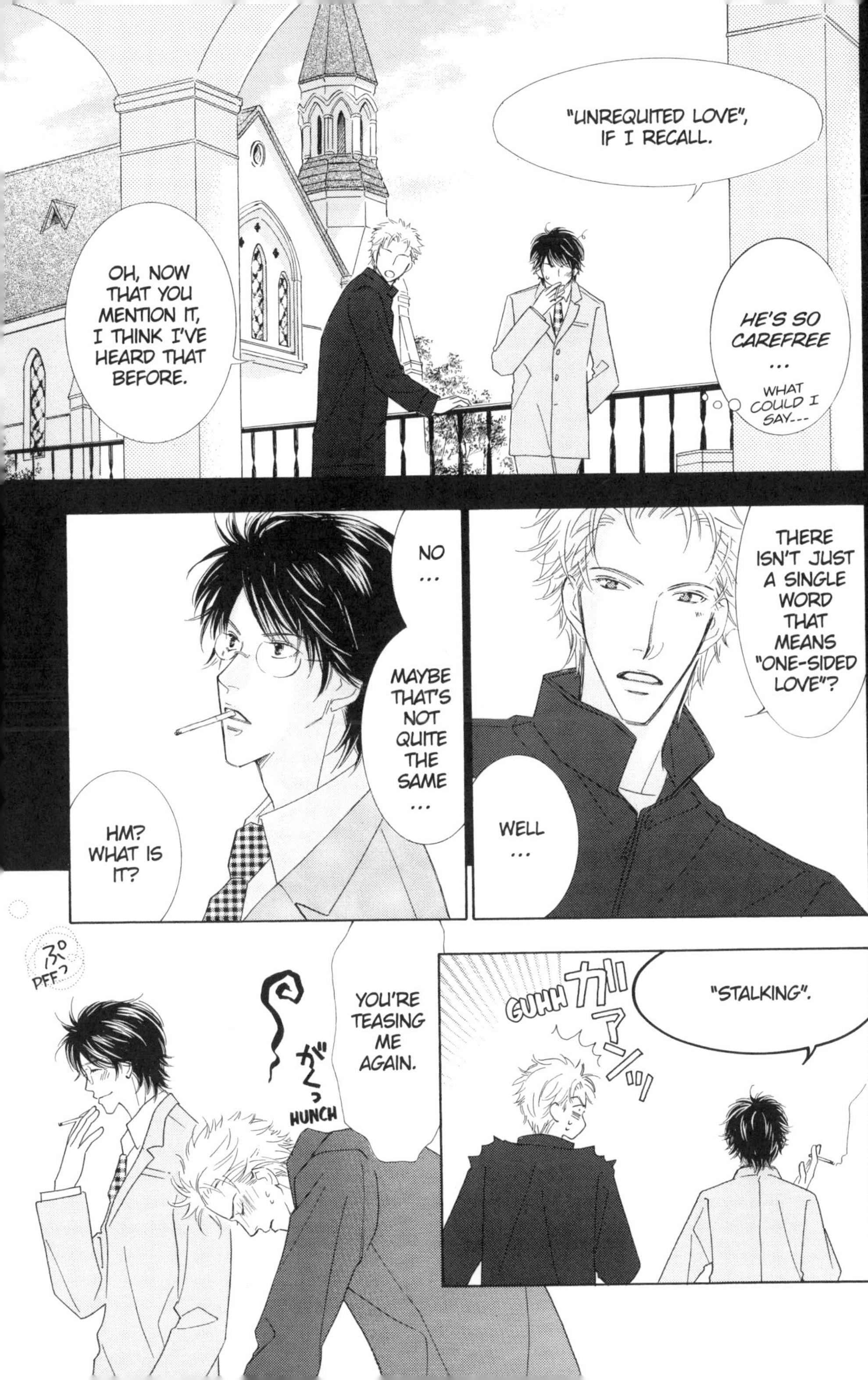
"UNREQUITED LOVE", IF I RECALL.
HE'S SO CAREFREE...
WHAT COULD I SAY---
OH, NOW THAT YOU MENTION IT, I THINK I'VE HEARD THAT BEFORE.
THERE ISN'T JUST A SINGLE WORD THAT MEANS "ONE-SIDED LOVE"?
WELL...
NO...
MAYBE THAT'S NOT QUITE THE SAME...
HM? WHAT IS IT?
"STALKING".
カーンッッ
GUHH
YOU'RE TEASING ME AGAIN.
がくっ
HUNCH
ぷっ
PFF

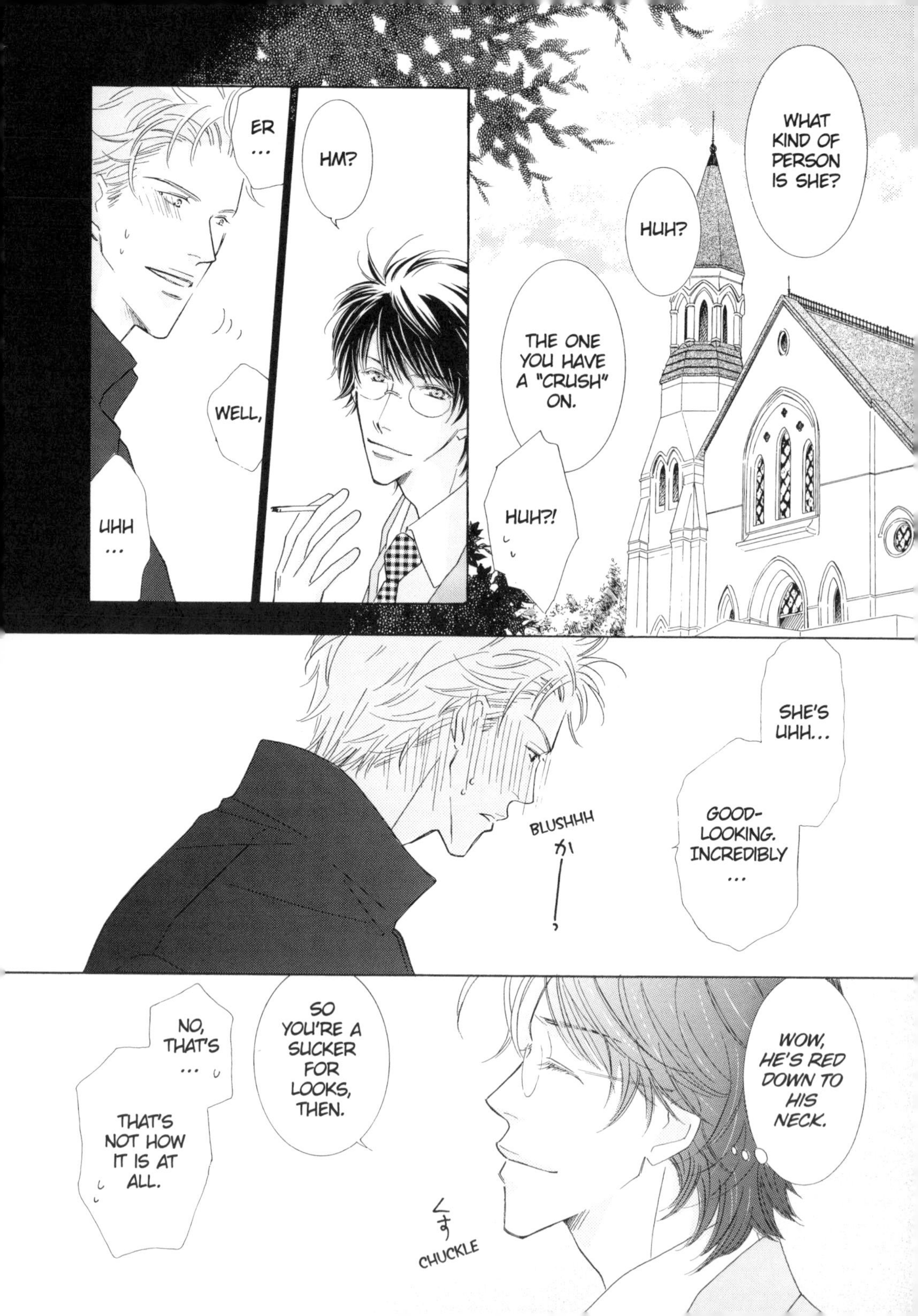
WHAT KIND OF PERSON IS SHE?
HUH?
THE ONE YOU HAVE A "CRUSH" ON.
HUH?!
HM?
ER...
WELL,
UHH...
SHE'S UHH...
GOOD-LOOKING. INCREDIBLY...
BLUSHHH
かー!
WOW, HE'S RED DOWN TO HIS NECK.
くす
CHUCKLE
SO YOU'RE A SUCKER FOR LOOKS, THEN.
NO, THAT'S...
THAT'S NOT HOW IT IS AT ALL.

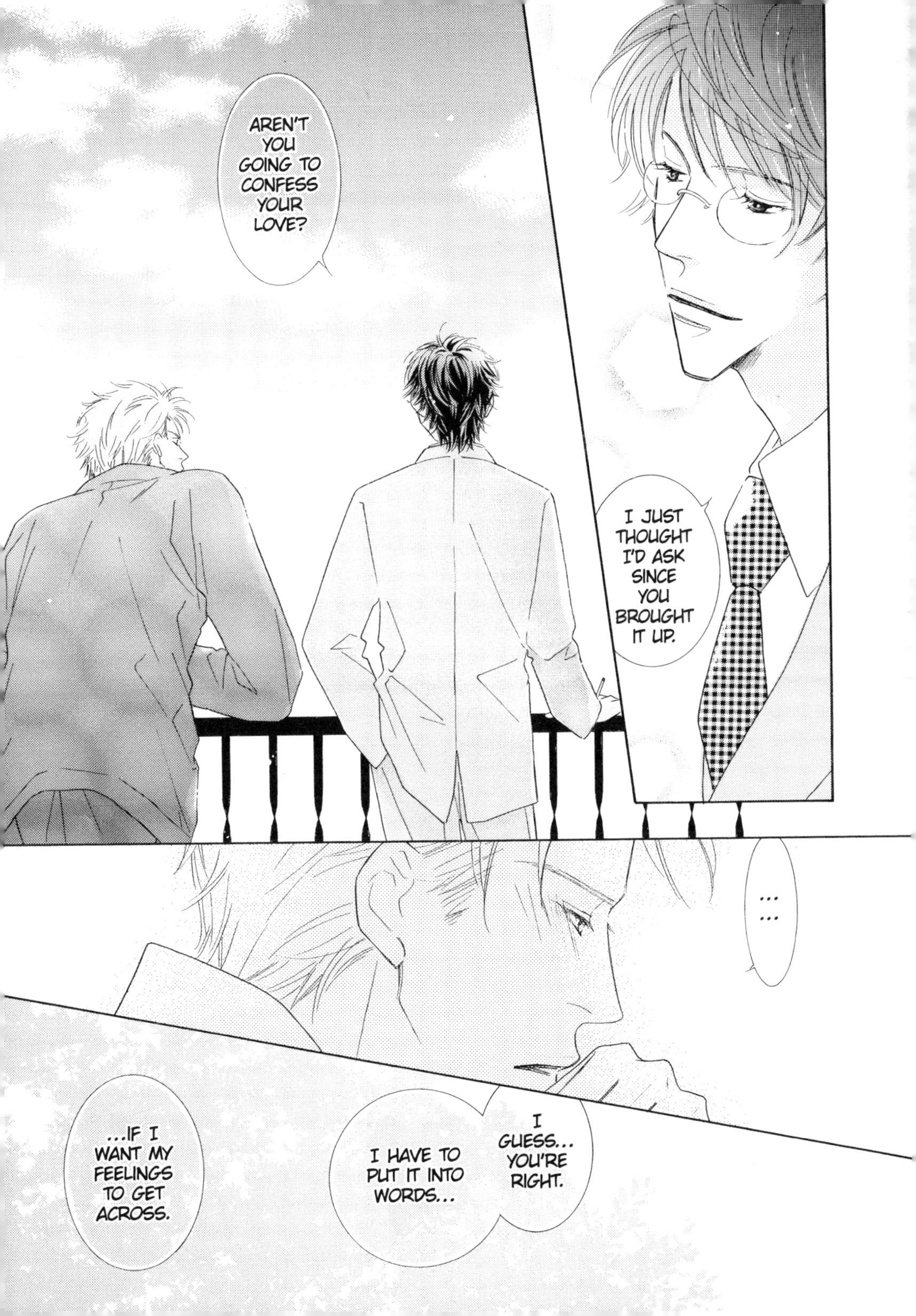
I JUST THOUGHT I'D ASK SINCE YOU BROUGHT IT UP.
AREN'T YOU GOING TO CONFESS YOUR LOVE?
……
I GUESS... YOU'RE RIGHT.
I HAVE TO PUT IT INTO WORDS...
...IF I WANT MY FEELINGS TO GET ACROSS.

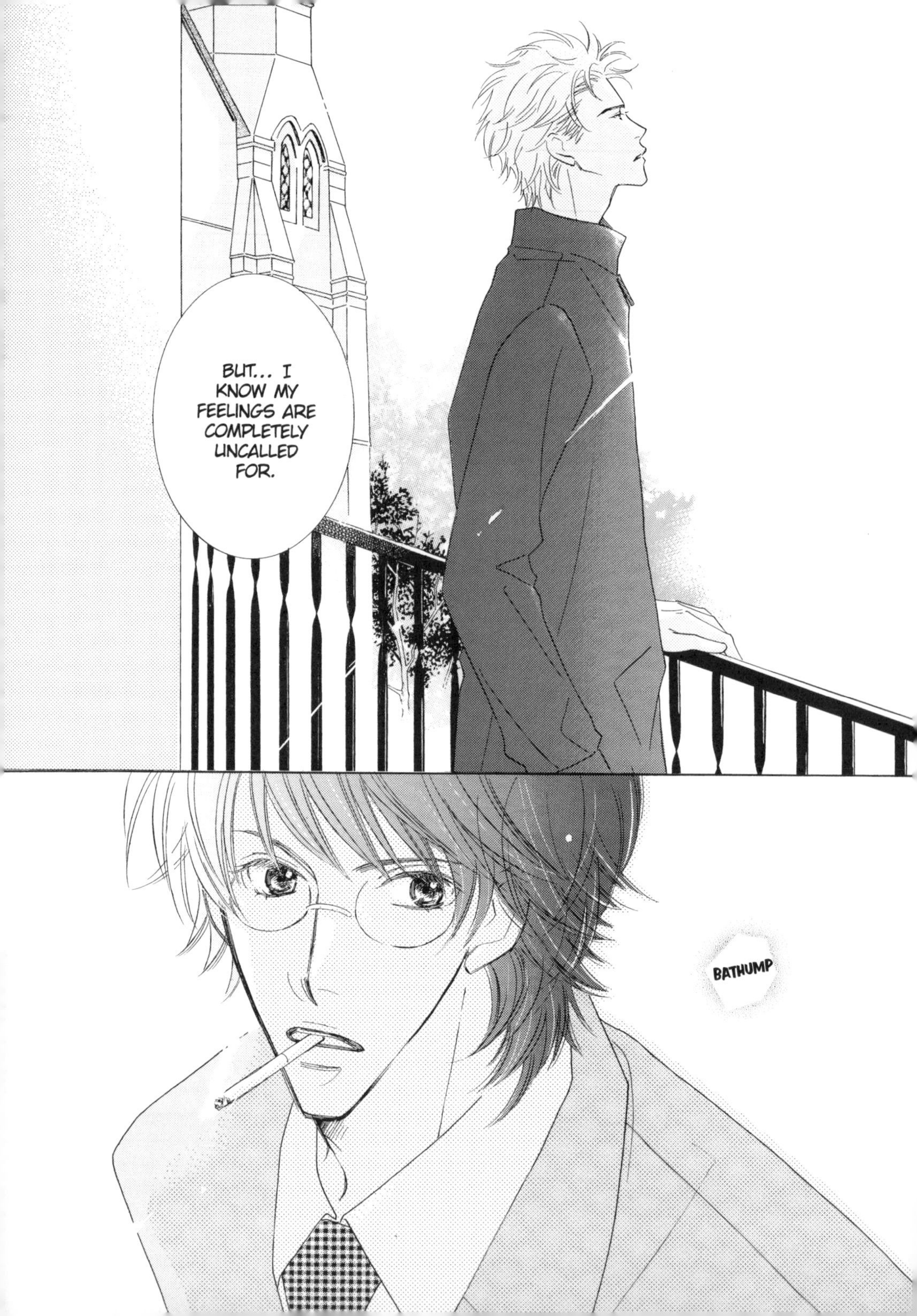
BUT... I KNOW MY FEELINGS ARE COMPLETELY UNCALLED FOR.
BATHUMP

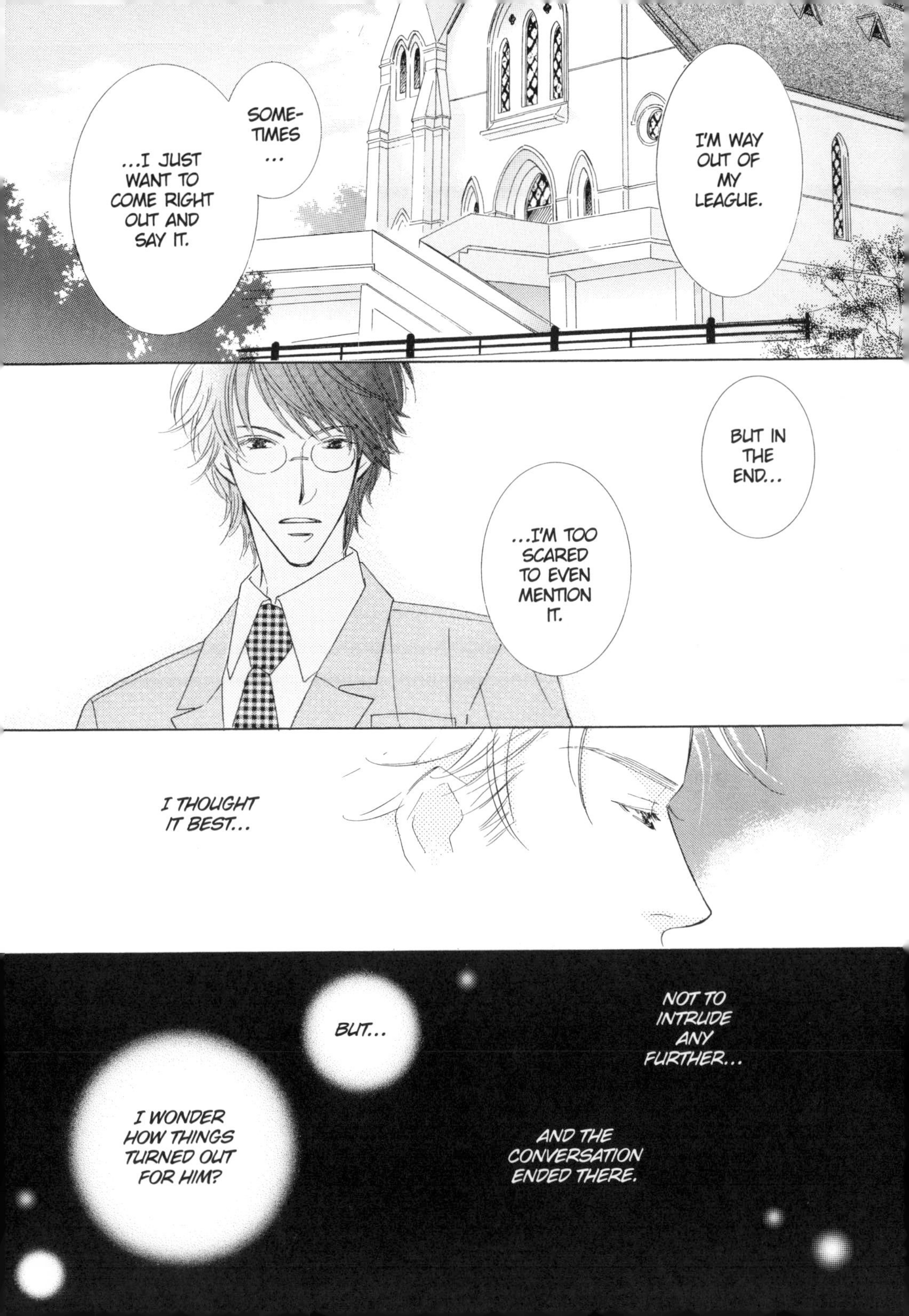
I'M WAY OUT OF MY LEAGUE.
SOME-TIMES...
...I JUST WANT TO COME RIGHT OUT AND SAY IT.
BUT IN THE END...
...I'M TOO SCARED TO EVEN MENTION IT.
I THOUGHT IT BEST...
NOT TO INTRUDE ANY FURTHER...
BUT...
AND THE CONVERSATION ENDED THERE.
I WONDER HOW THINGS TURNED OUT FOR HIM?

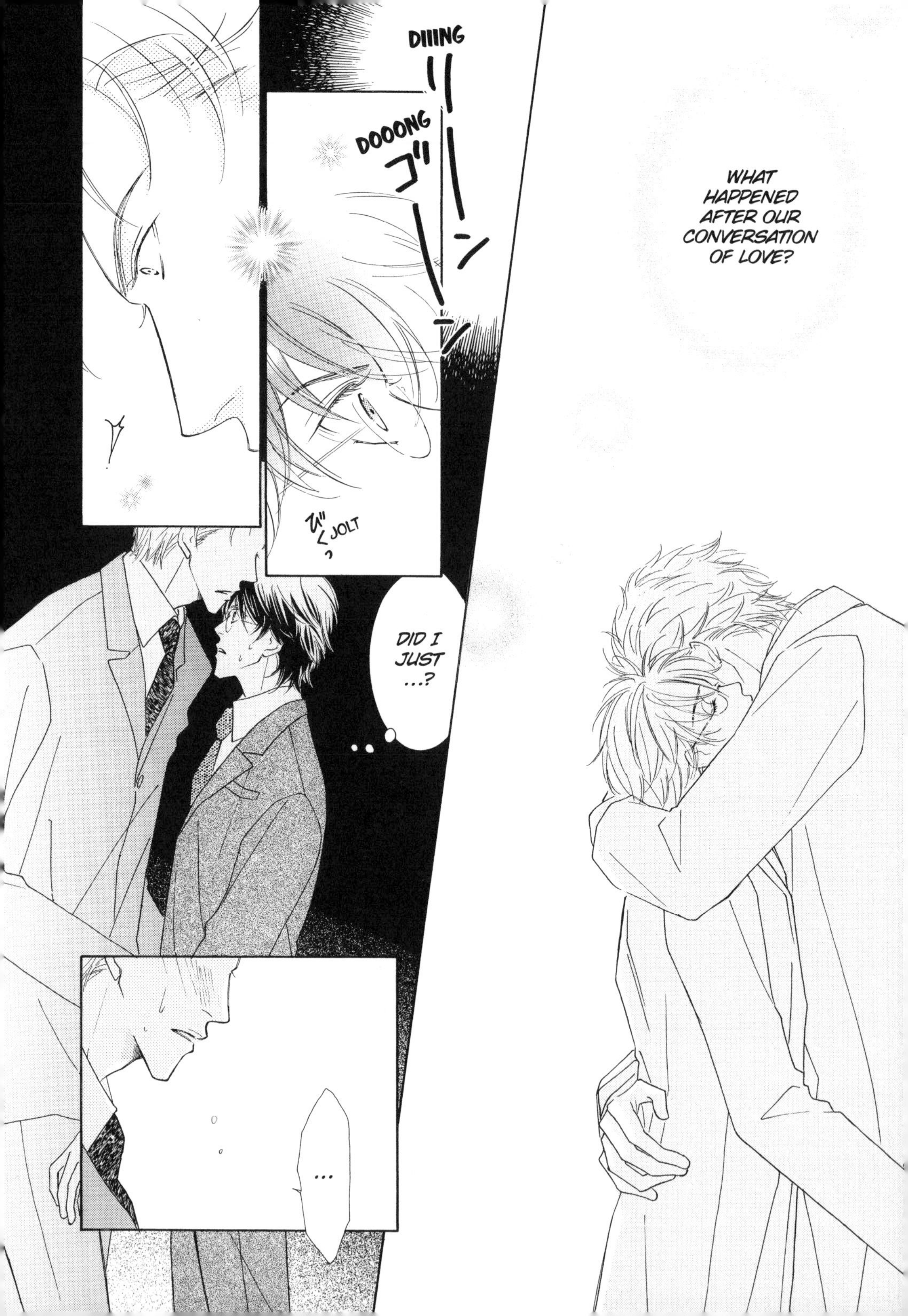
WHAT HAPPENED AFTER OUR CONVERSATION OF LOVE?
DIIING
リーン
DOOONG
ゴーン
びくっ
JOLT
DID I JUST ...?
...

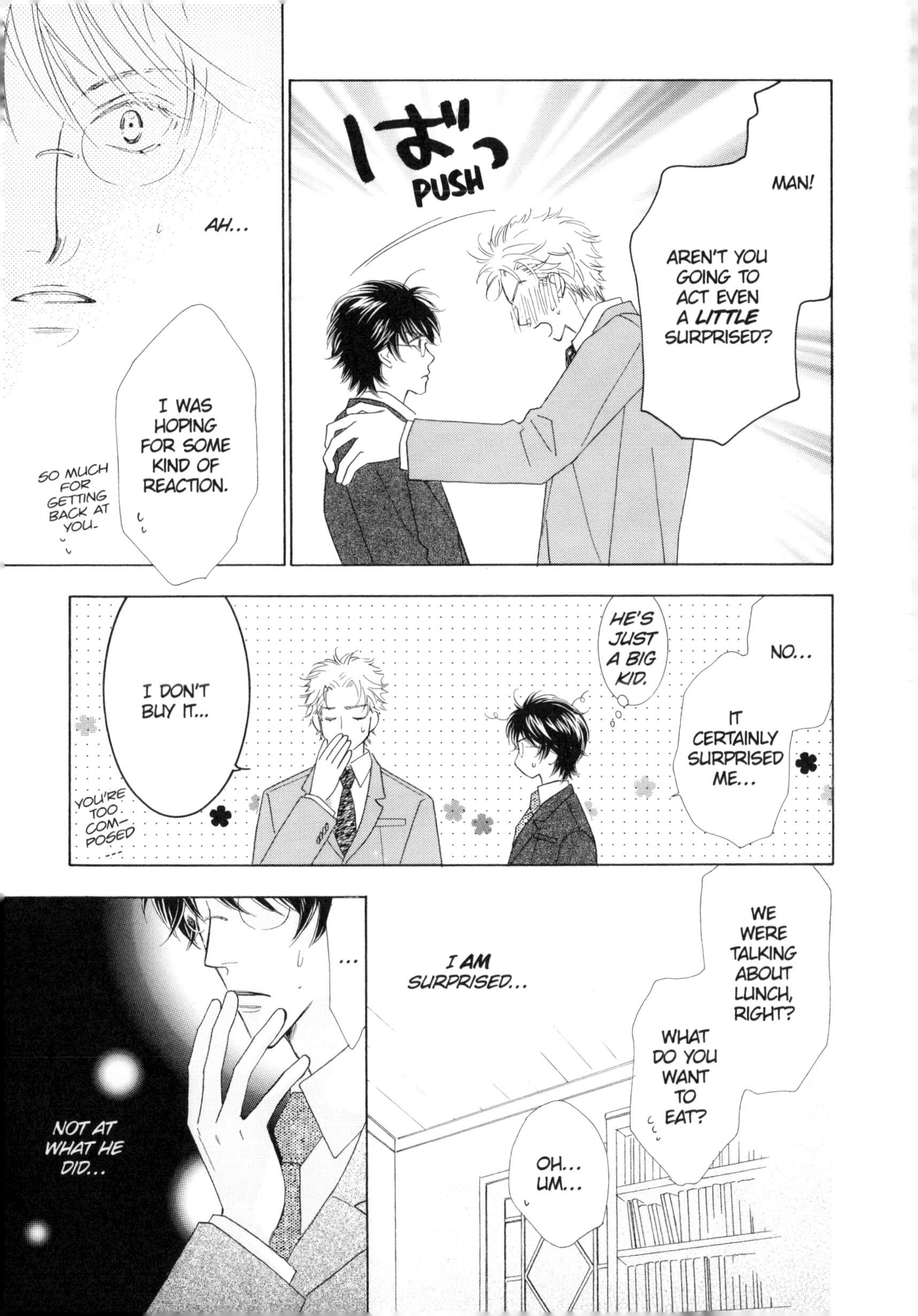
ばっ
PUSH
MAN!
AREN'T YOU GOING TO ACT EVEN A *LITTLE* SURPRISED?
AH...
I WAS HOPING FOR SOME KIND OF REACTION.
SO MUCH FOR GETTING BACK AT YOU...
NO...
IT CERTAINLY SURPRISED ME...
HE'S JUST A BIG KID.
I DON'T BUY IT...
YOU'RE TOO COM-POSED...
WE WERE TALKING ABOUT LUNCH, RIGHT?
WHAT DO YOU WANT TO EAT?
I *AM* SURPRISED...
OH... UM...
...
NOT AT WHAT HE DID...

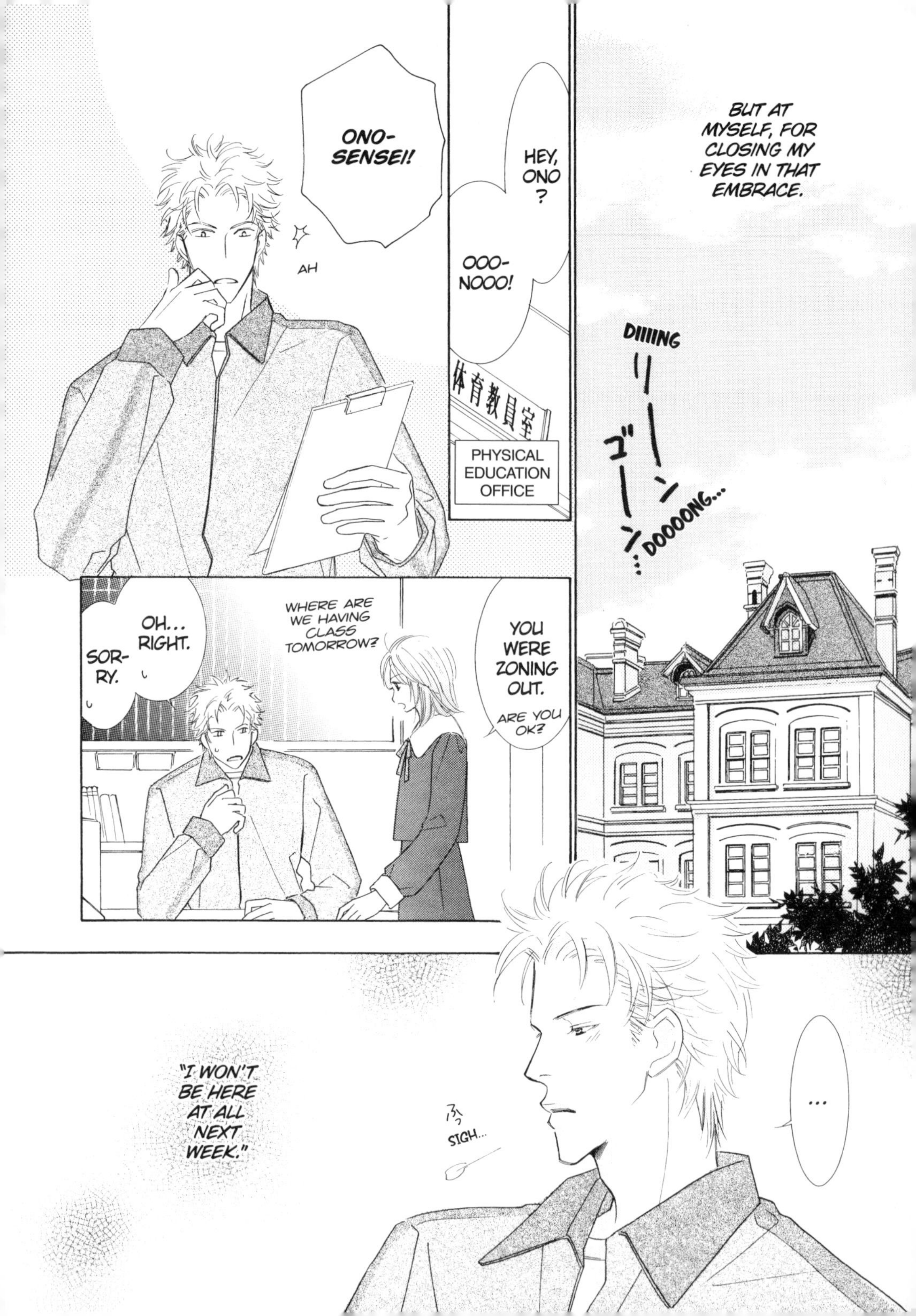
BUT AT MYSELF, FOR CLOSING MY EYES IN THAT EMBRACE.
リーン
DIIING
ゴーン…
DOOOONG...
HEY, ONO?
OOO-NOOO!
体育教員室
PHYSICAL EDUCATION OFFICE
ONO-SENSEI!
AH
YOU WERE ZONING OUT.
ARE YOU OK?
WHERE ARE WE HAVING CLASS TOMORROW?
OH... RIGHT.
SORRY.
...
ふっ
SIGH...
"I WON'T BE HERE AT ALL NEXT WEEK."

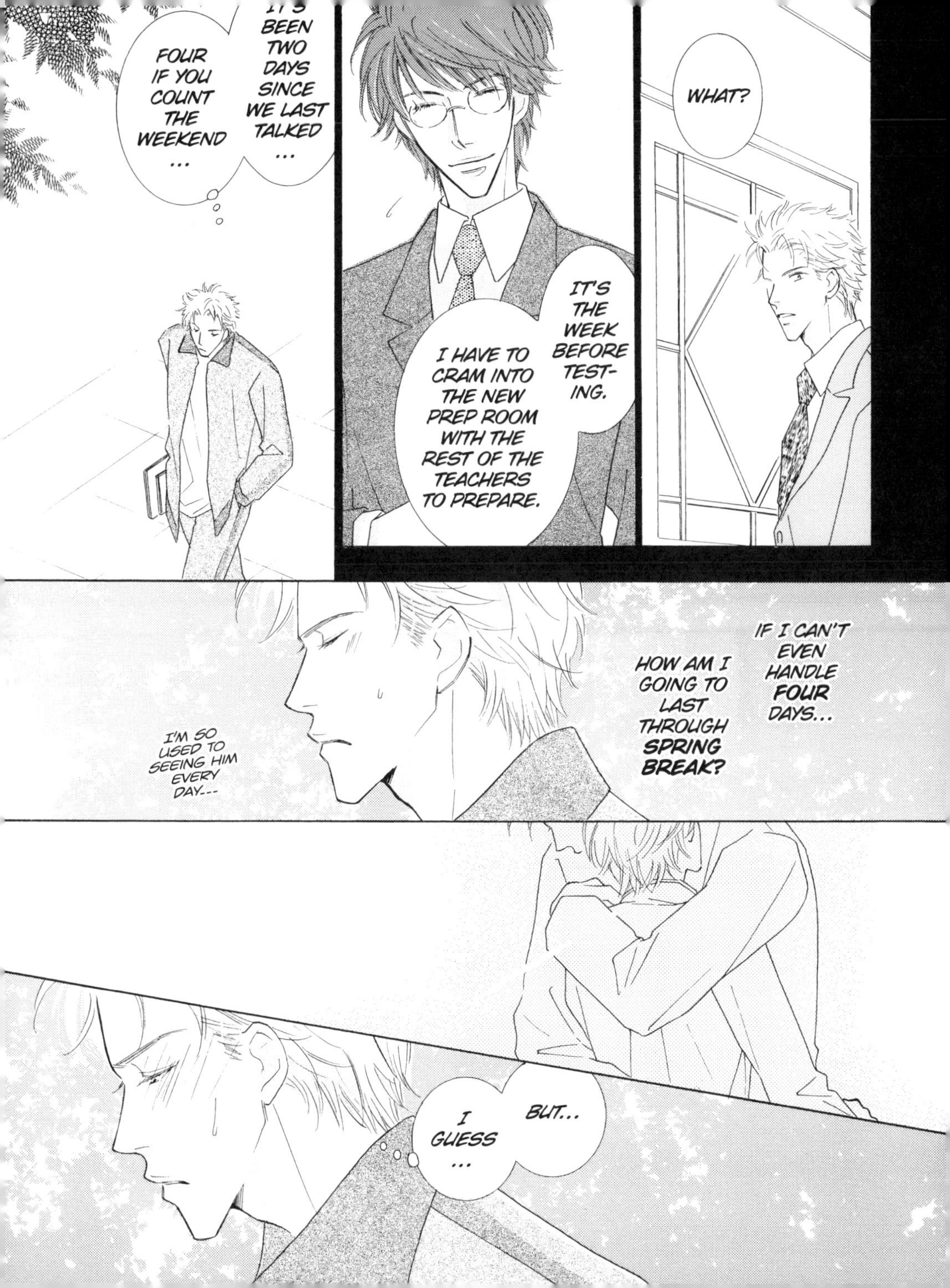
WHAT?
IT'S THE WEEK BEFORE TESTING.
I HAVE TO CRAM INTO THE NEW PREP ROOM WITH THE REST OF THE TEACHERS TO PREPARE.
IT'S BEEN TWO DAYS SINCE WE LAST TALKED...
FOUR IF YOU COUNT THE WEEKEND...
IF I CAN'T EVEN HANDLE FOUR DAYS...
HOW AM I GOING TO LAST THROUGH SPRING BREAK?
I'M SO USED TO SEEING HIM EVERY DAY---
BUT...
I GUESS...

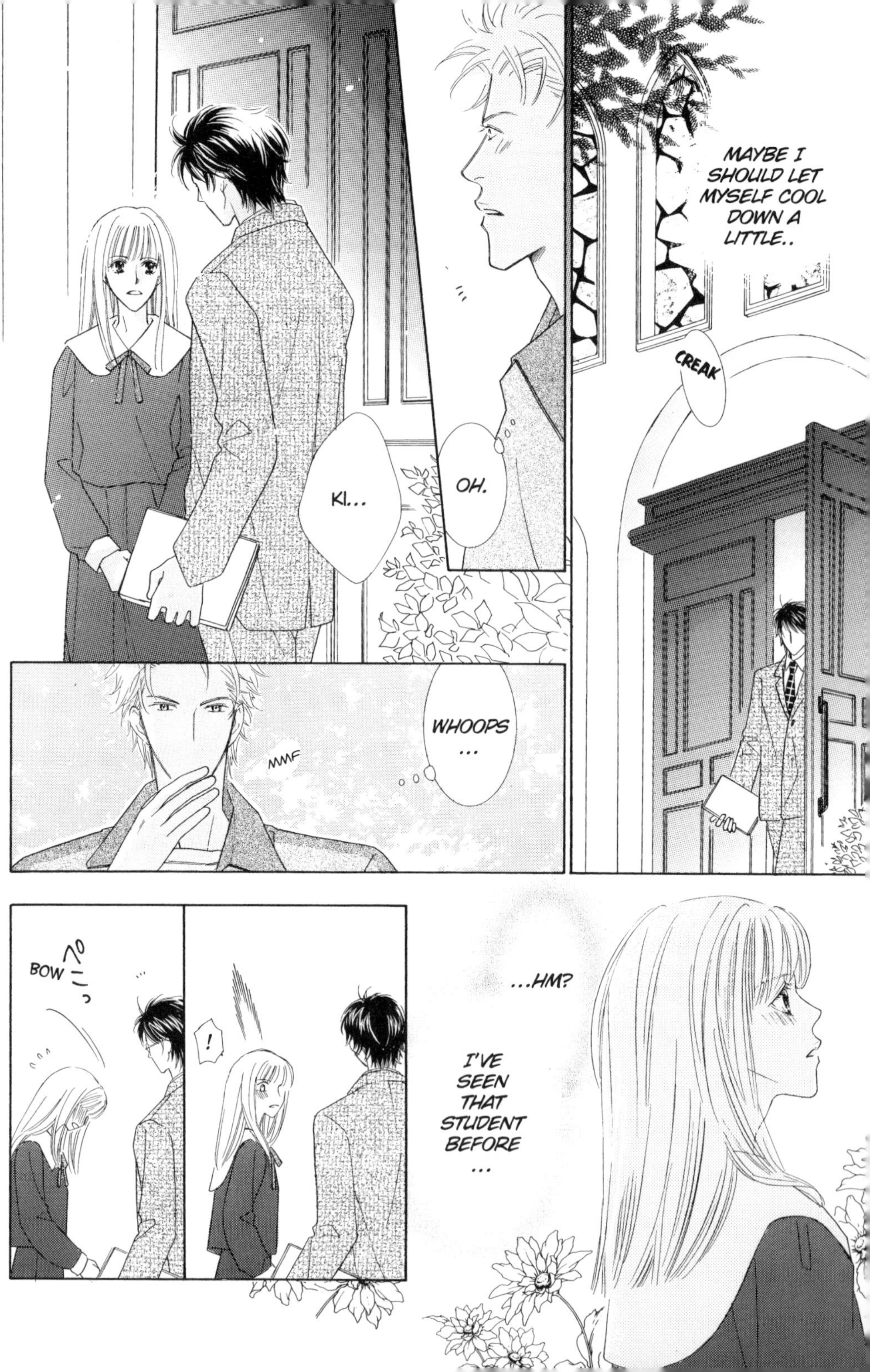
MAYBE I SHOULD LET MYSELF COOL DOWN A LITTLE..
CREAK
OH.
KI...
WHOOPS ...
MMF
...HM?
I'VE SEEN THAT STUDENT BEFORE ...
!
BOW

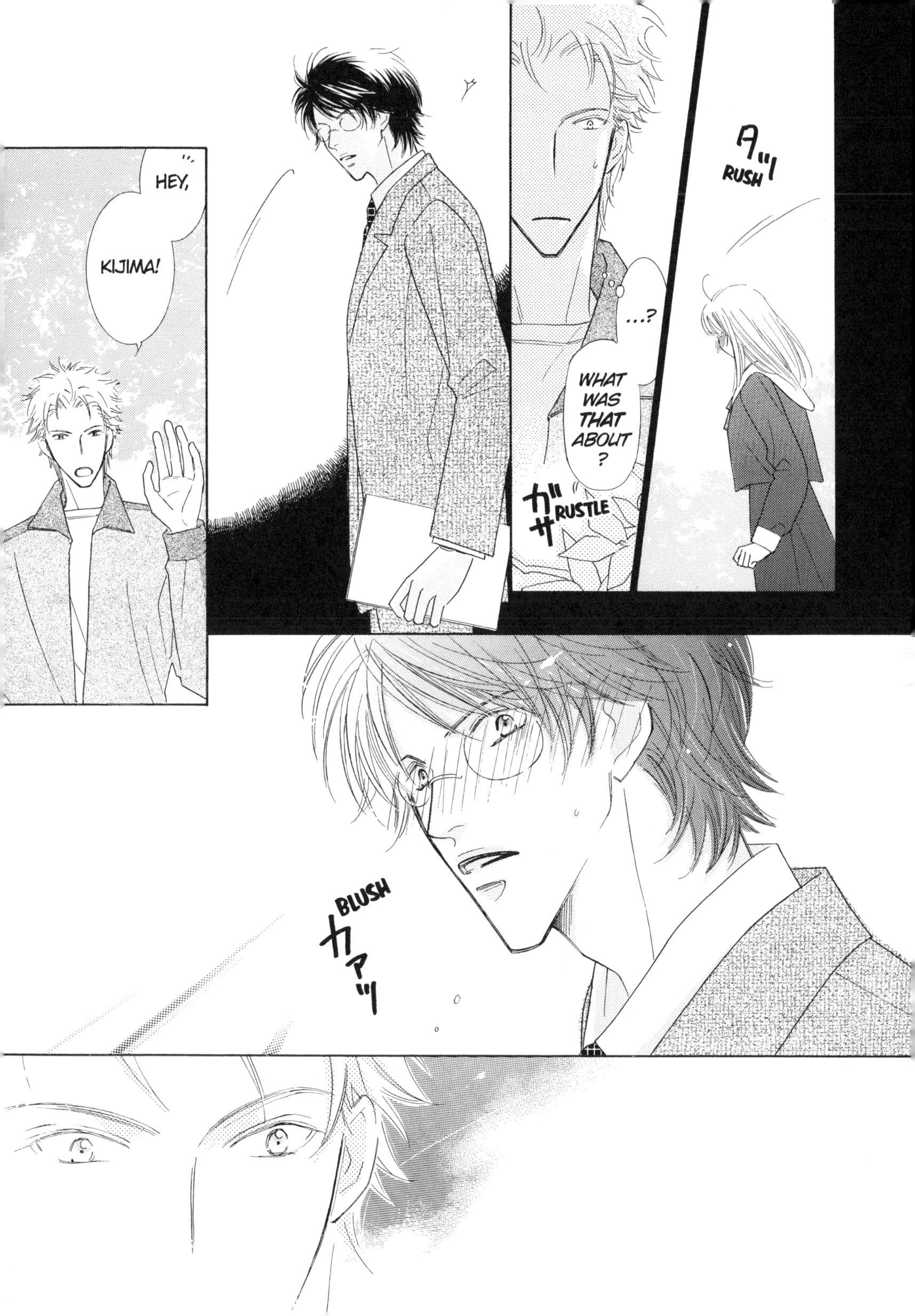
タッ
RUSH
...?
WHAT WAS THAT ABOUT?
ガサ
RUSTLE
HEY,
KIJIMA!
BLUSH
カァッ

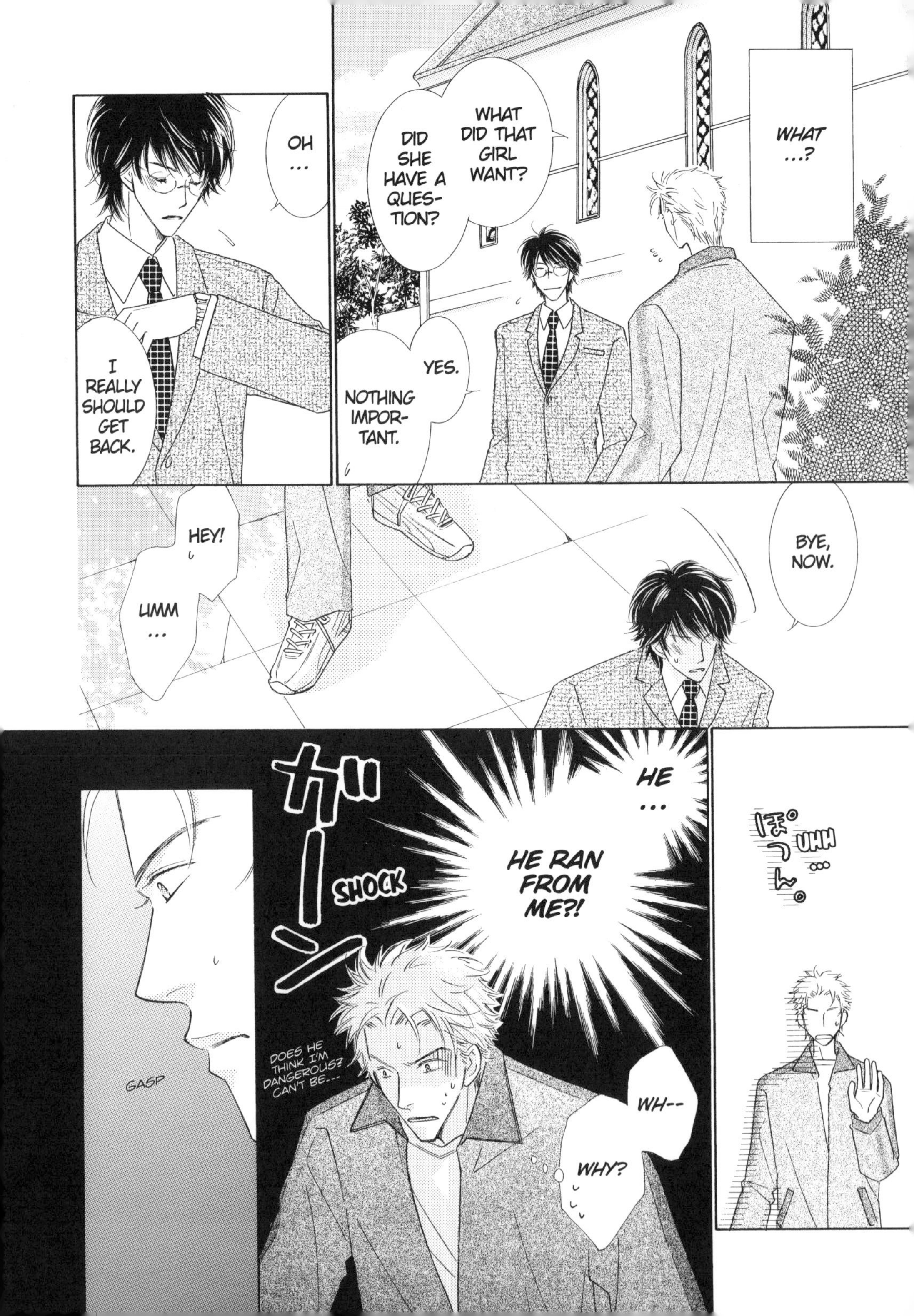
WHAT ...?
WHAT DID THAT GIRL WANT?
DID SHE HAVE A QUES-TION?
YES.
NOTHING IMPOR-TANT.
OH ...
I REALLY SHOULD GET BACK.
BYE, NOW.
HEY!
UMM ...
ぽつん。
UHH ...
HE ...
HE RAN FROM ME?!
ガーン
SHOCK
DOES HE THINK I'M DANGEROUS? CAN'T BE...
WH--
WHY?
GASP

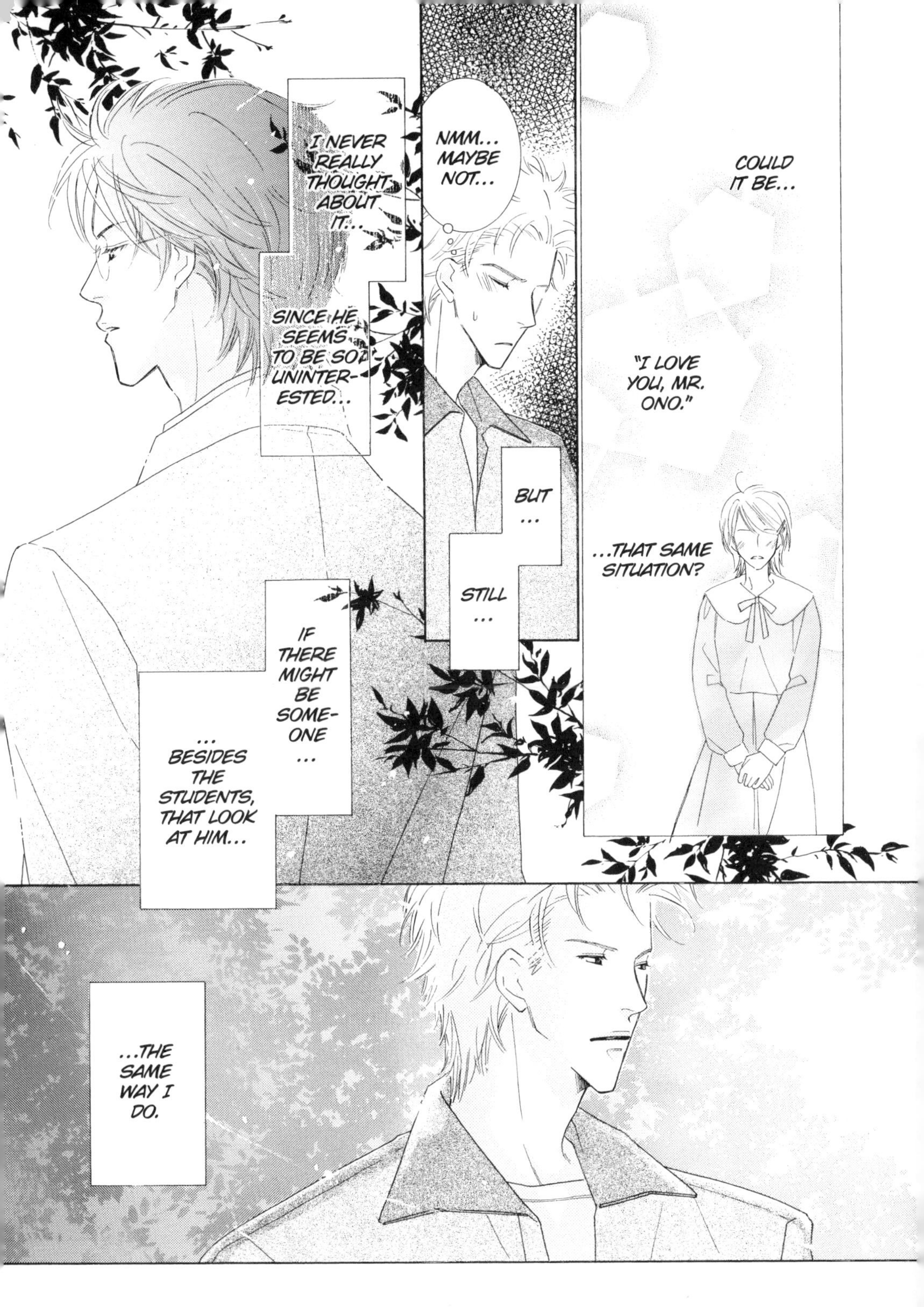
COULD IT BE...
"I LOVE YOU, MR. ONO."
...THAT SAME SITUATION?
NMM... MAYBE NOT...
I NEVER REALLY THOUGHT ABOUT IT...
SINCE HE SEEMS TO BE SO UNINTER-ESTED...
BUT ...
STILL ...
IF THERE MIGHT BE SOME-ONE ...
... BESIDES THE STUDENTS, THAT LOOK AT HIM...
...THE SAME WAY I DO.

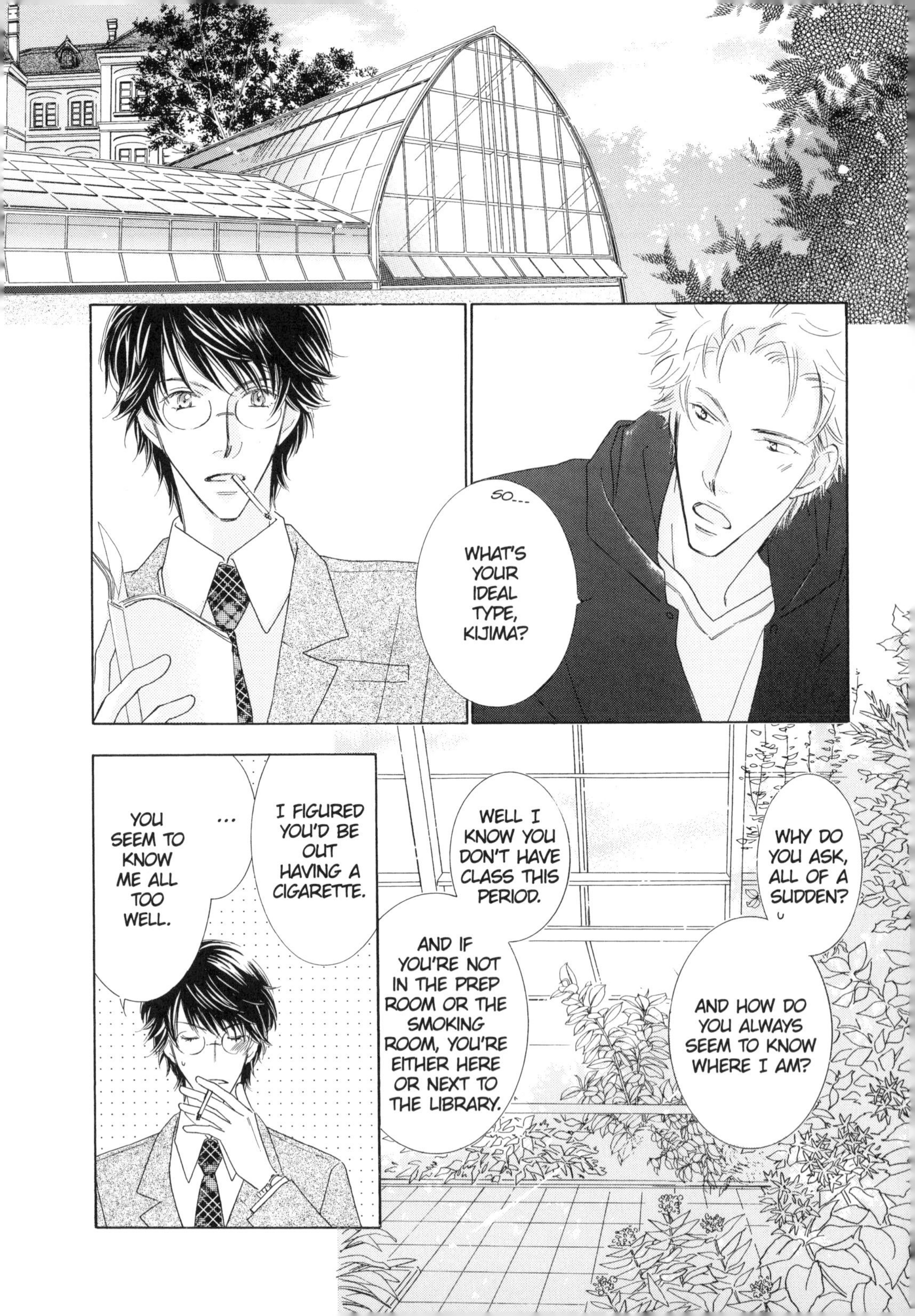
SO...
WHAT'S YOUR IDEAL TYPE, KIJIMA?
WHY DO YOU ASK, ALL OF A SUDDEN?
AND HOW DO YOU ALWAYS SEEM TO KNOW WHERE I AM?
WELL I KNOW YOU DON'T HAVE CLASS THIS PERIOD.
AND IF YOU'RE NOT IN THE PREP ROOM OR THE SMOKING ROOM, YOU'RE EITHER HERE OR NEXT TO THE LIBRARY.
I FIGURED YOU'D BE OUT HAVING A CIGARETTE.
...
YOU SEEM TO KNOW ME ALL TOO WELL.

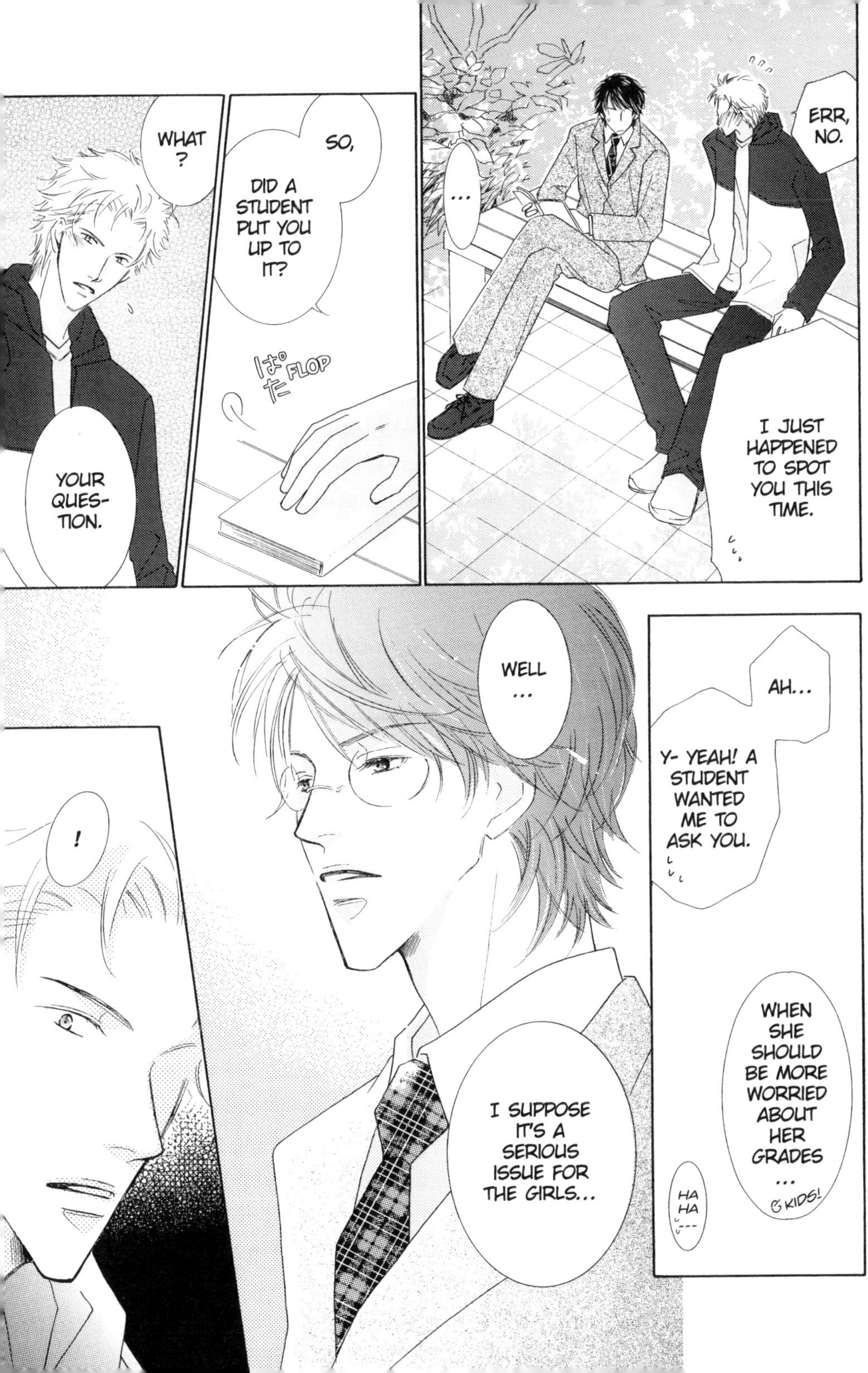
ERR, NO.
...
I JUST HAPPENED TO SPOT YOU THIS TIME.
SO,
DID A STUDENT PUT YOU UP TO IT?
ぱた FLOP
WHAT?
YOUR QUESTION.
AH...
Y- YEAH! A STUDENT WANTED ME TO ASK YOU.
WHEN SHE SHOULD BE MORE WORRIED ABOUT HER GRADES...
KIDS!
HA HA
WELL...
I SUPPOSE IT'S A SERIOUS ISSUE FOR THE GIRLS...
!

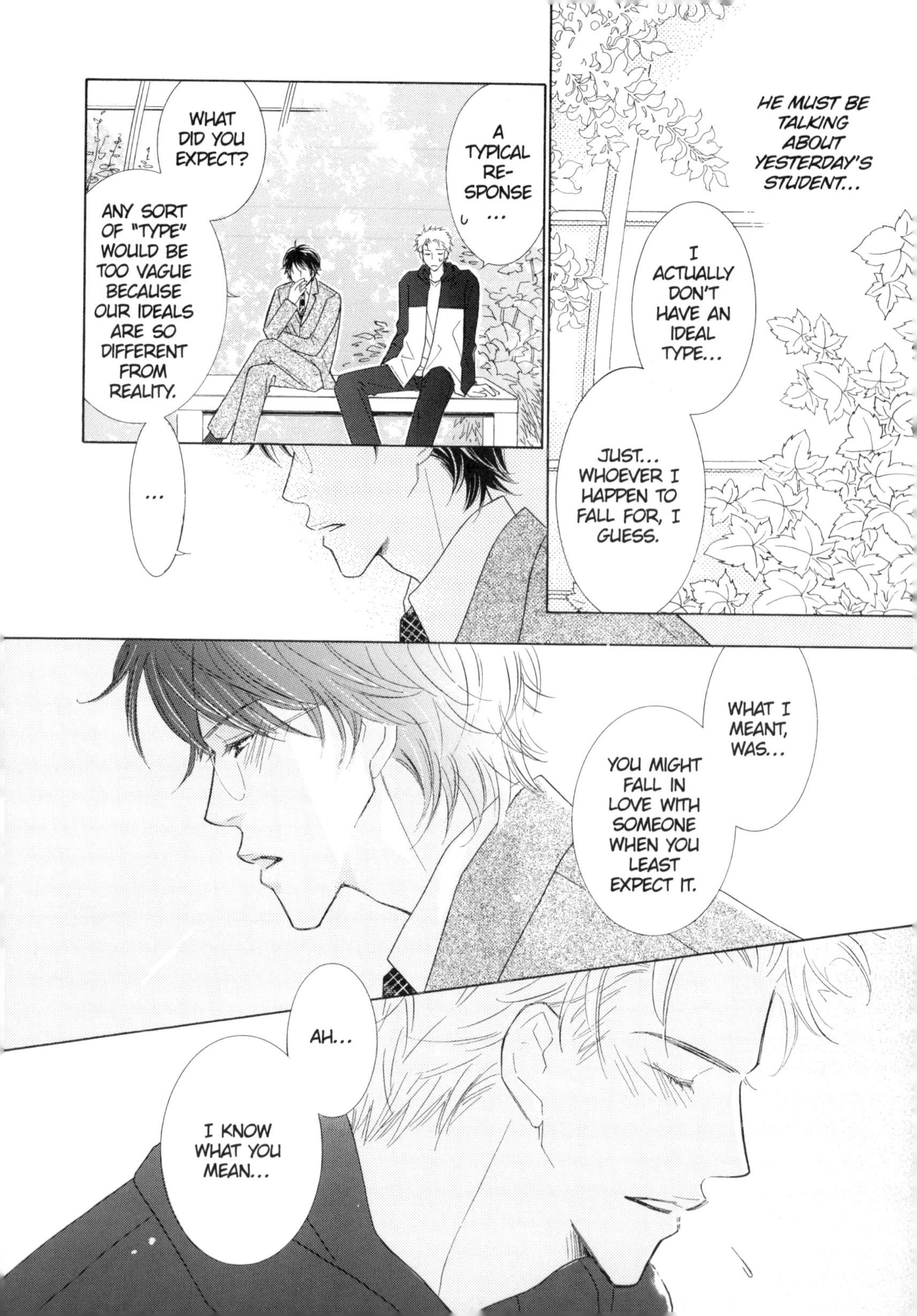
HE MUST BE TALKING ABOUT YESTERDAY'S STUDENT...
I ACTUALLY DON'T HAVE AN IDEAL TYPE...
JUST... WHOEVER I HAPPEN TO FALL FOR, I GUESS.
A TYPICAL RE-SPONSE...
WHAT DID YOU EXPECT?
ANY SORT OF "TYPE" WOULD BE TOO VAGUE BECAUSE OUR IDEALS ARE SO DIFFERENT FROM REALITY.
...
WHAT I MEANT, WAS...
YOU MIGHT FALL IN LOVE WITH SOMEONE WHEN YOU LEAST EXPECT IT.
AH...
I KNOW WHAT YOU MEAN...

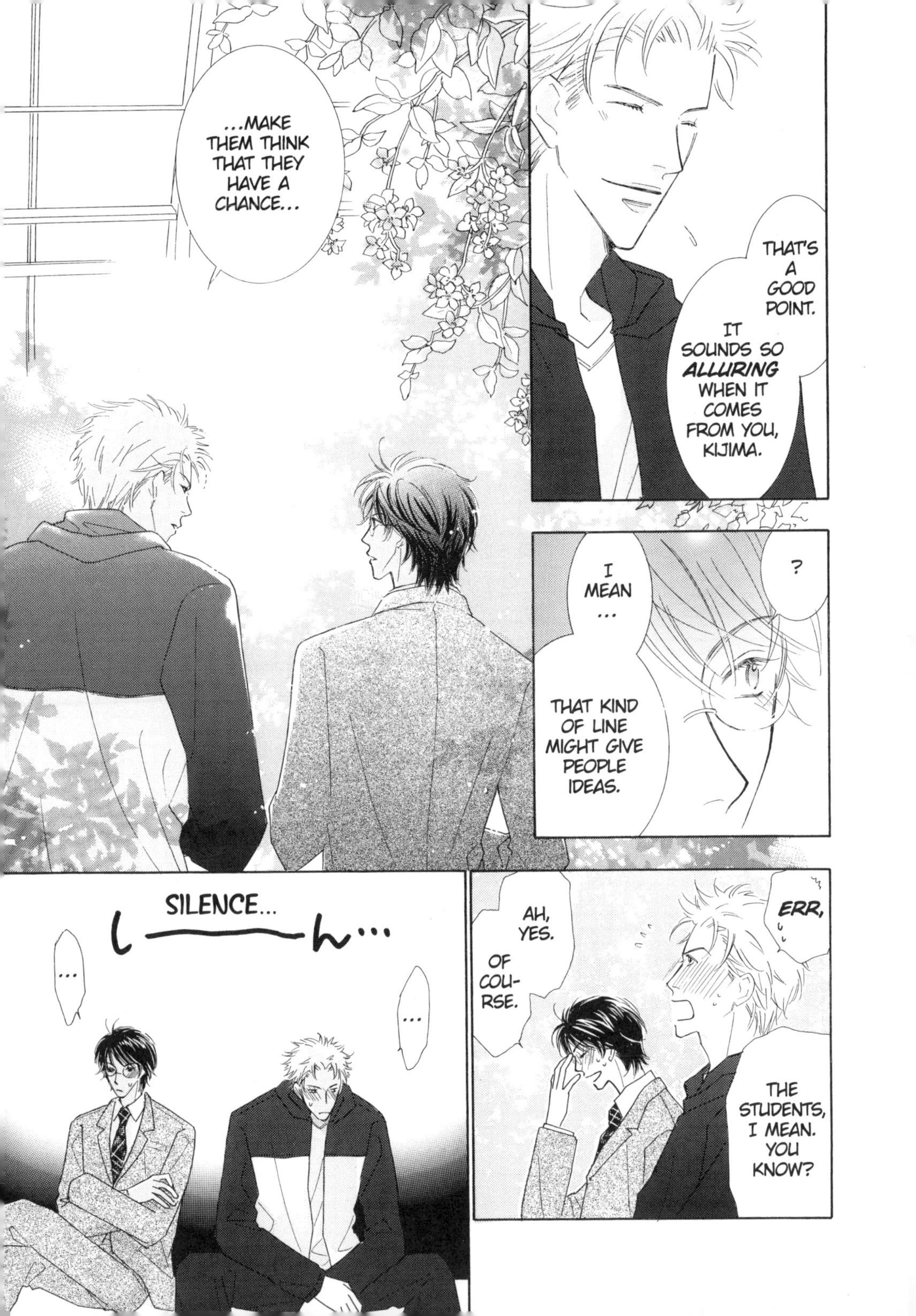
THAT'S A GOOD POINT.
IT SOUNDS SO ***ALLURING*** WHEN IT COMES FROM YOU, KIJIMA.
?
I MEAN...
THAT KIND OF LINE MIGHT GIVE PEOPLE IDEAS.
...MAKE THEM THINK THAT THEY HAVE A CHANCE...
ERR,
AH, YES. OF COU-RSE.
THE STUDENTS, I MEAN. YOU KNOW?
SILENCE...
し——ん…
...
...

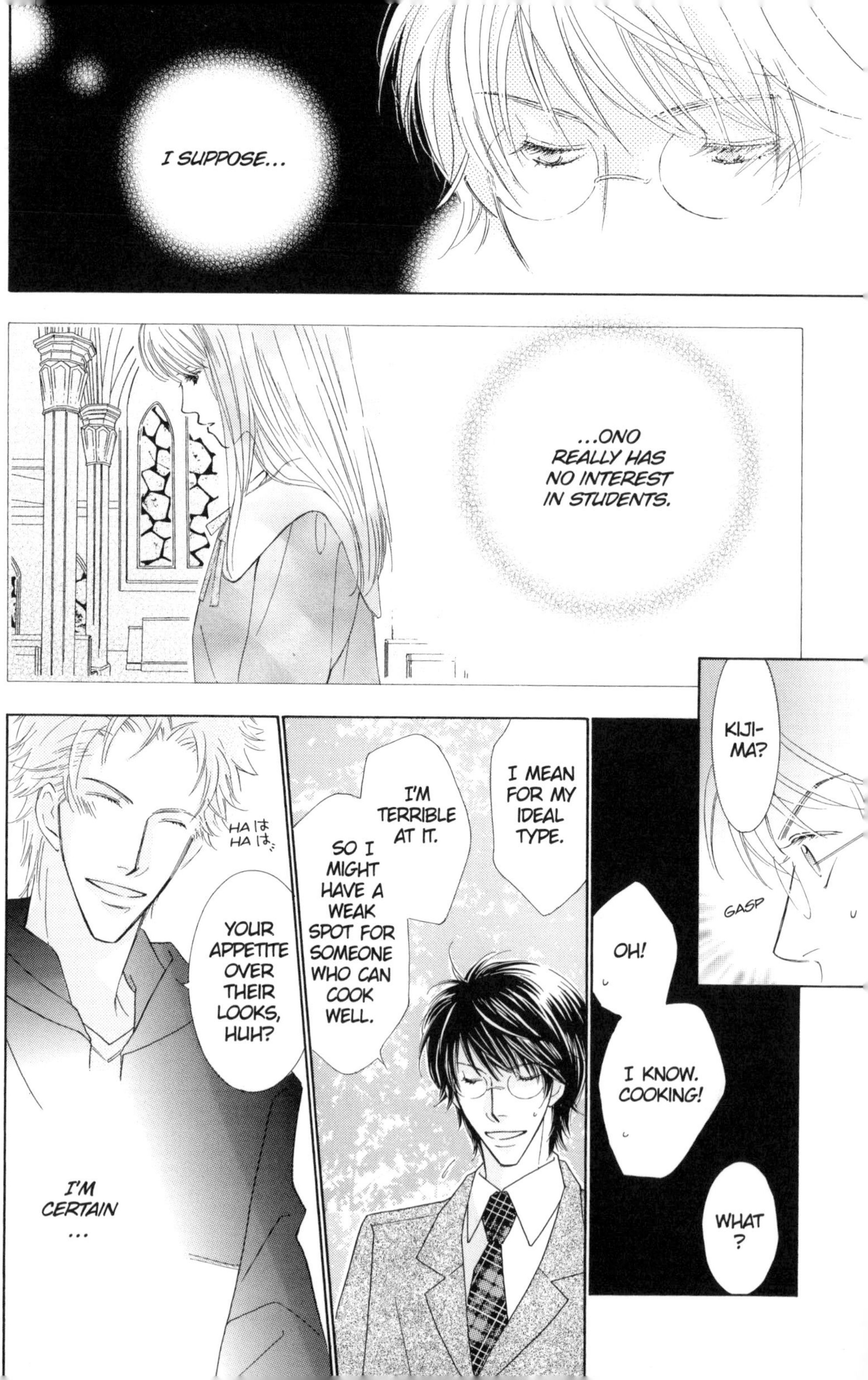
I SUPPOSE...
...ONO REALLY HAS NO INTEREST IN STUDENTS.
KIJI-MA?
GASP
OH!
I KNOW. COOKING!
WHAT?
I MEAN FOR MY IDEAL TYPE.
I'M TERRIBLE AT IT.
SO I MIGHT HAVE A WEAK SPOT FOR SOMEONE WHO CAN COOK WELL.
HA は HA は
YOUR APPETITE OVER THEIR LOOKS, HUH?
I'M CERTAIN...

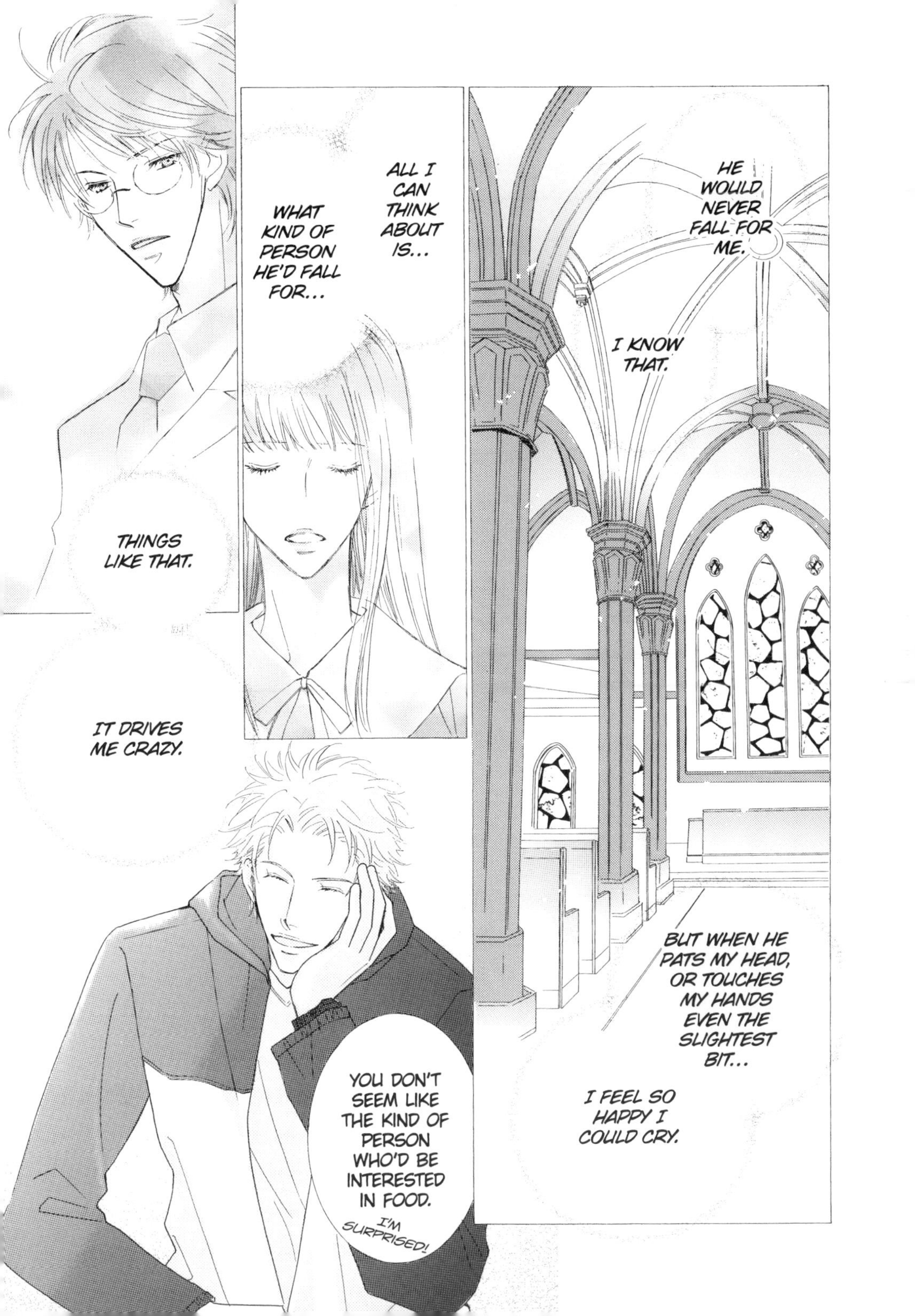

HE WOULD NEVER FALL FOR ME.
I KNOW THAT.
BUT WHEN HE PATS MY HEAD, OR TOUCHES MY HANDS EVEN THE SLIGHTEST BIT...
I FEEL SO HAPPY I COULD CRY.
ALL I CAN THINK ABOUT IS...
WHAT KIND OF PERSON HE'D FALL FOR...
THINGS LIKE THAT.
IT DRIVES ME CRAZY.
YOU DON'T SEEM LIKE THE KIND OF PERSON WHO'D BE INTERESTED IN FOOD.
I'M SURPRISED!

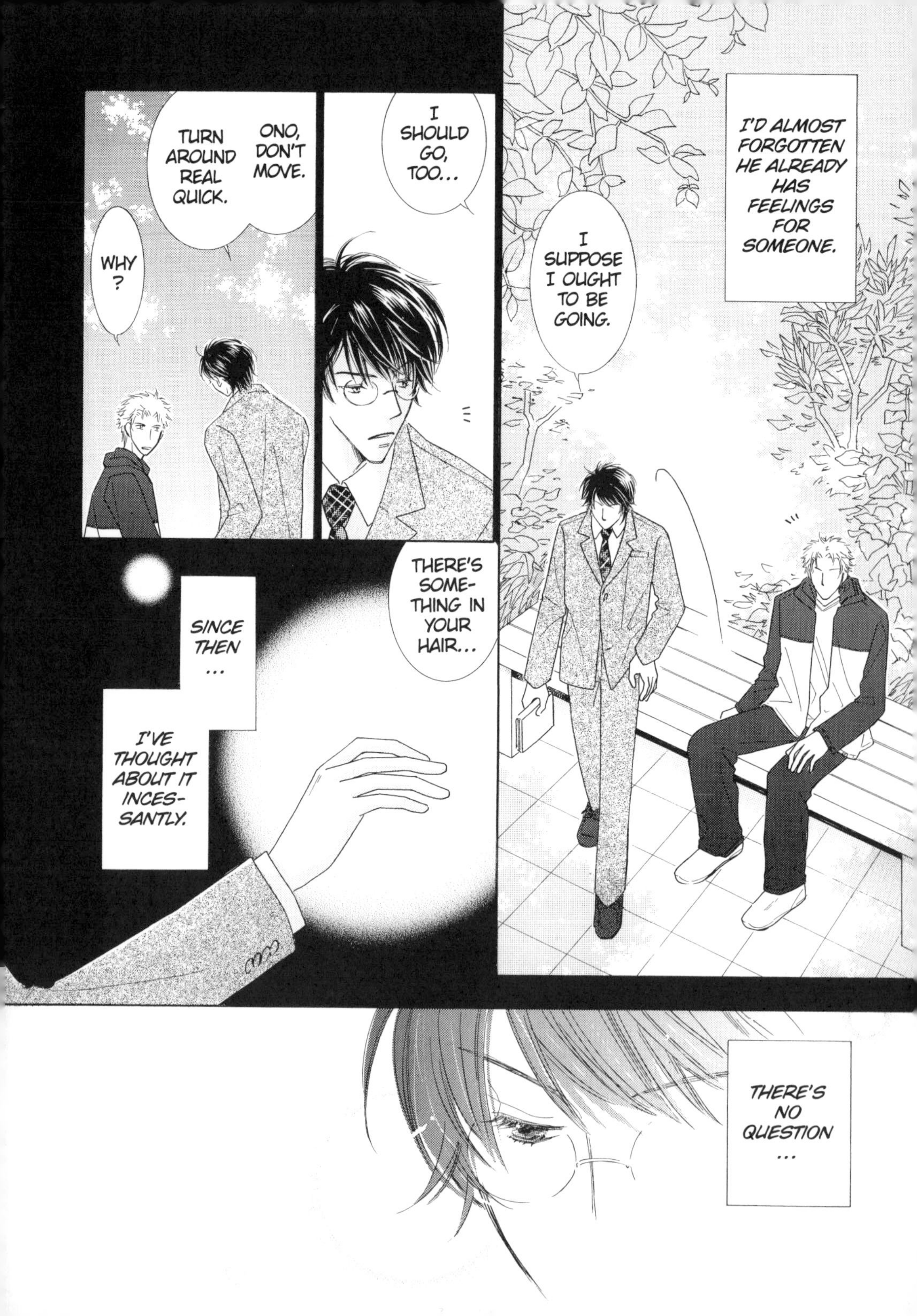
I'D ALMOST FORGOTTEN HE ALREADY HAS FEELINGS FOR SOMEONE.
I SUPPOSE I OUGHT TO BE GOING.
I SHOULD GO, TOO...
ONO, DON'T MOVE.
TURN AROUND REAL QUICK.
WHY?
THERE'S SOME-THING IN YOUR HAIR...
SINCE THEN...
I'VE THOUGHT ABOUT IT INCES-SANTLY.
THERE'S NO QUESTION...

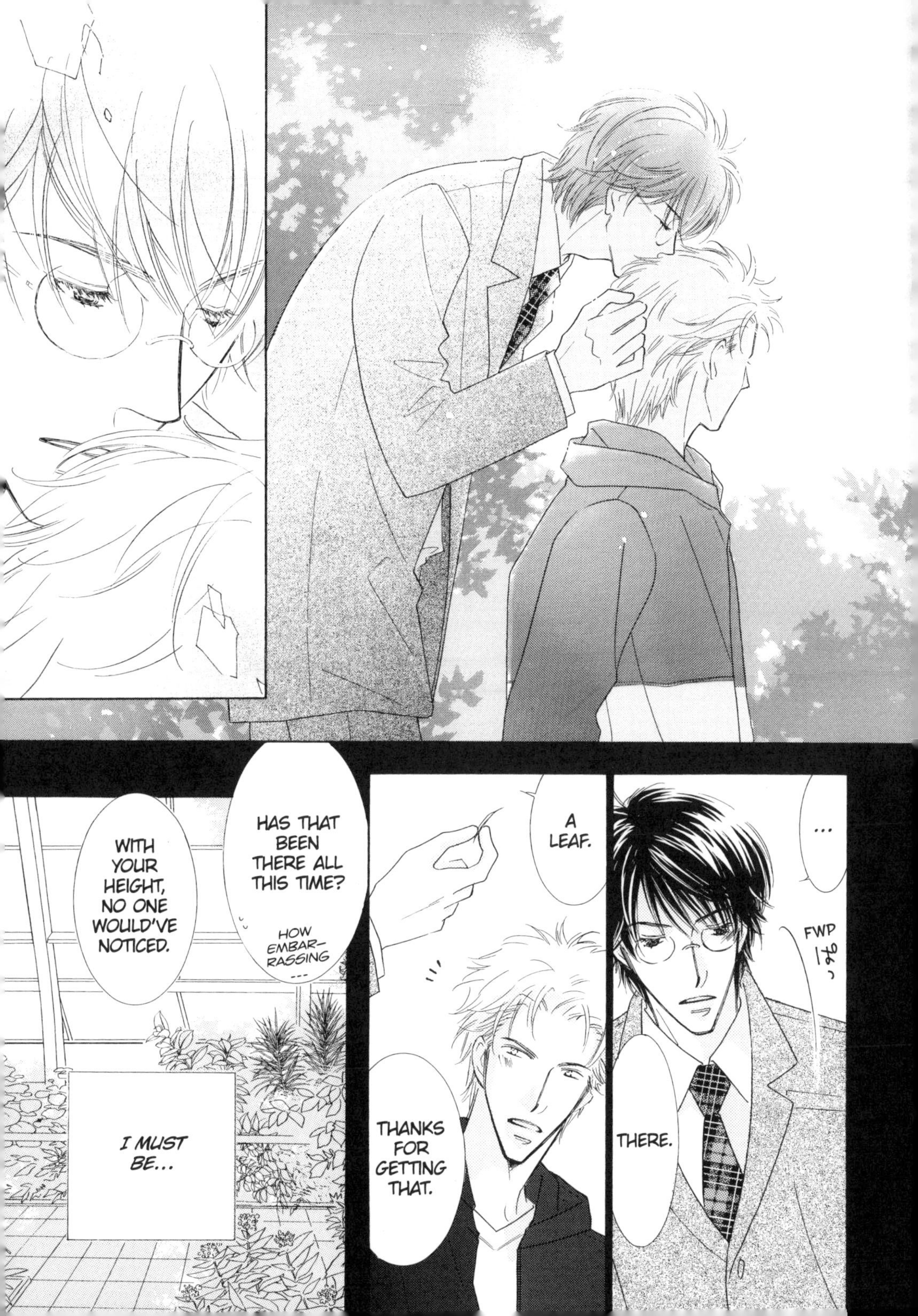
...
FWP
THERE.
A LEAF.
THANKS FOR GETTING THAT.
HAS THAT BEEN THERE ALL THIS TIME?
HOW EMBAR-RASSING...
WITH YOUR HEIGHT, NO ONE WOULD'VE NOTICED.
I MUST BE...

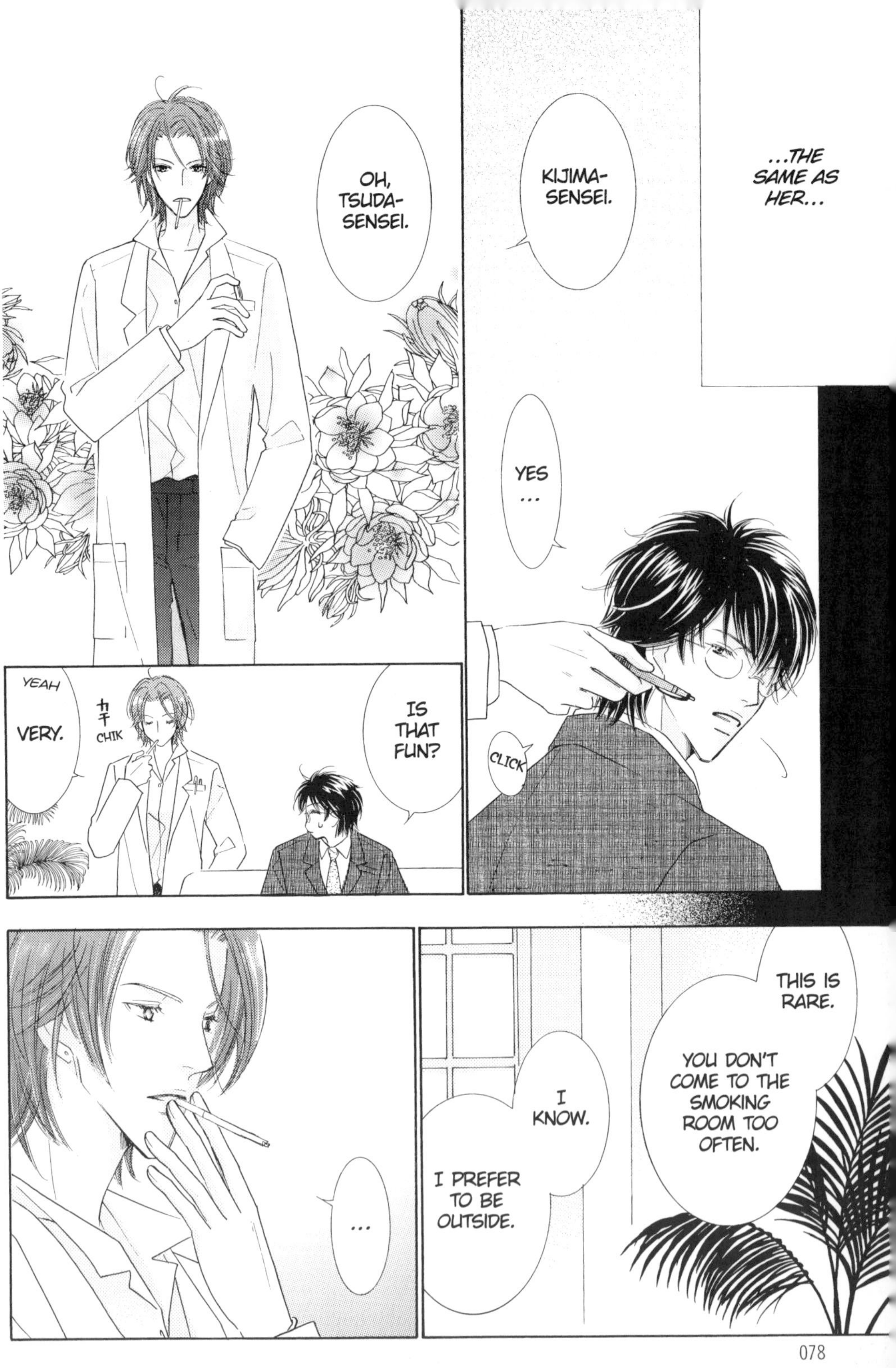
...THE SAME AS HER...
KIJIMA-SENSEI.
YES...
CLICK
OH, TSUDA-SENSEI.
IS THAT FUN?
カチ
CHIK
YEAH
VERY.
THIS IS RARE.
YOU DON'T COME TO THE SMOKING ROOM TOO OFTEN.
I KNOW.
I PREFER TO BE OUTSIDE.
...

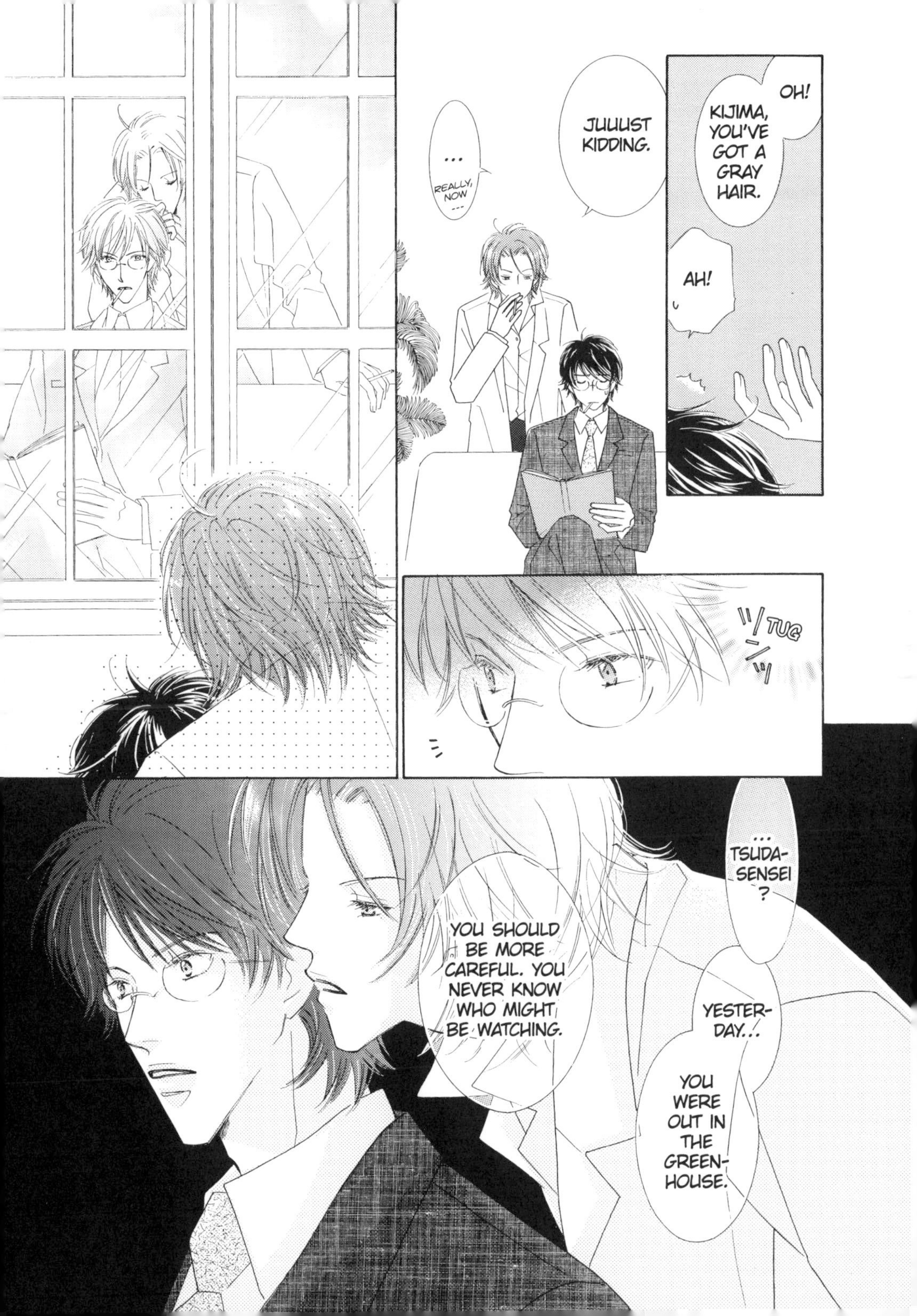
OH!
KIJIMA, YOU'VE GOT A GRAY HAIR.
AH!
JUUUST KIDDING.
...
REALLY, NOW ...
TUG
... TSUDA-SENSEI?
YESTER-DAY...
YOU WERE OUT IN THE GREEN-HOUSE.
YOU SHOULD BE MORE CAREFUL. YOU NEVER KNOW WHO MIGHT BE WATCHING.

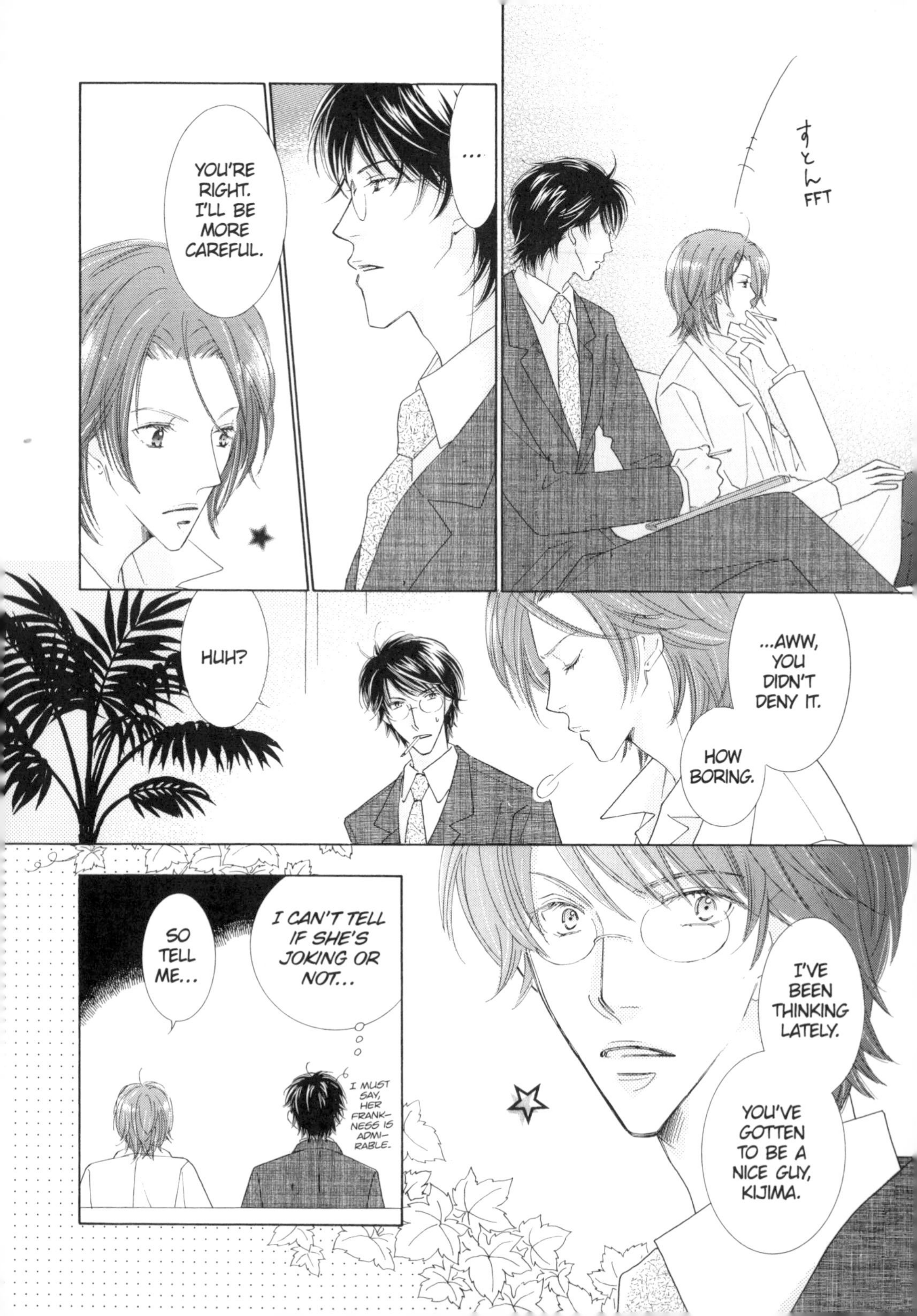
すとん
FFT
...
YOU'RE RIGHT. I'LL BE MORE CAREFUL.
...AWW, YOU DIDN'T DENY IT.
HOW BORING.
HUH?
I'VE BEEN THINKING LATELY.
YOU'VE GOTTEN TO BE A NICE GUY, KIJIMA.
I CAN'T TELL IF SHE'S JOKING OR NOT...
SO TELL ME...
I MUST SAY, HER FRANKNESS IS ADMIRABLE.

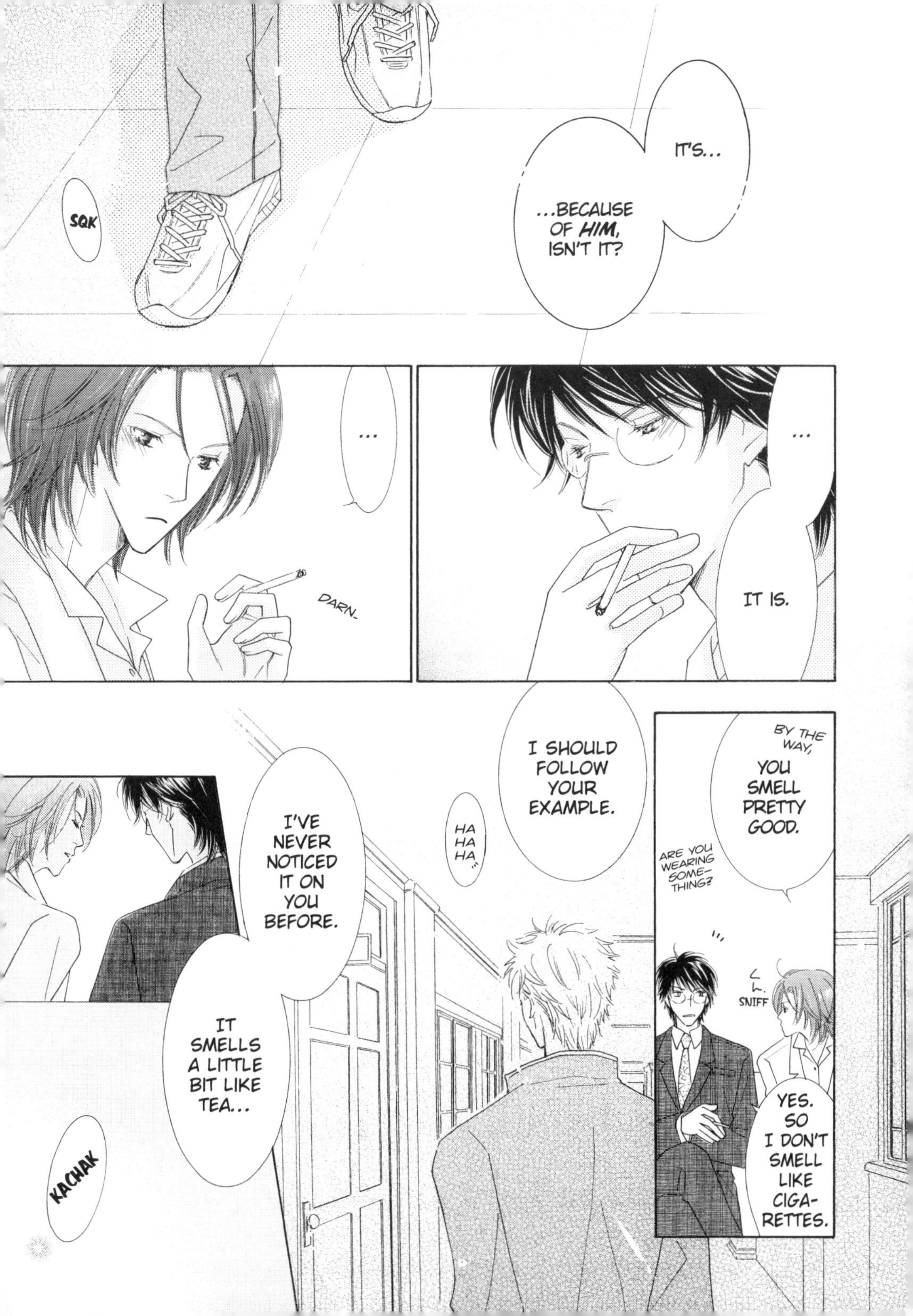
IT'S...
...BECAUSE OF *HIM*, ISN'T IT?
SQK
...
IT IS.
...
DARN.
BY THE WAY,
YOU SMELL PRETTY GOOD.
ARE YOU WEARING SOME-THING?
SNIFF
YES. SO I DON'T SMELL LIKE CIGA-RETTES.
I SHOULD FOLLOW YOUR EXAMPLE.
HA HA HA...
I'VE NEVER NOTICED IT ON YOU BEFORE.
IT SMELLS A LITTLE BIT LIKE TEA...
KACHAK

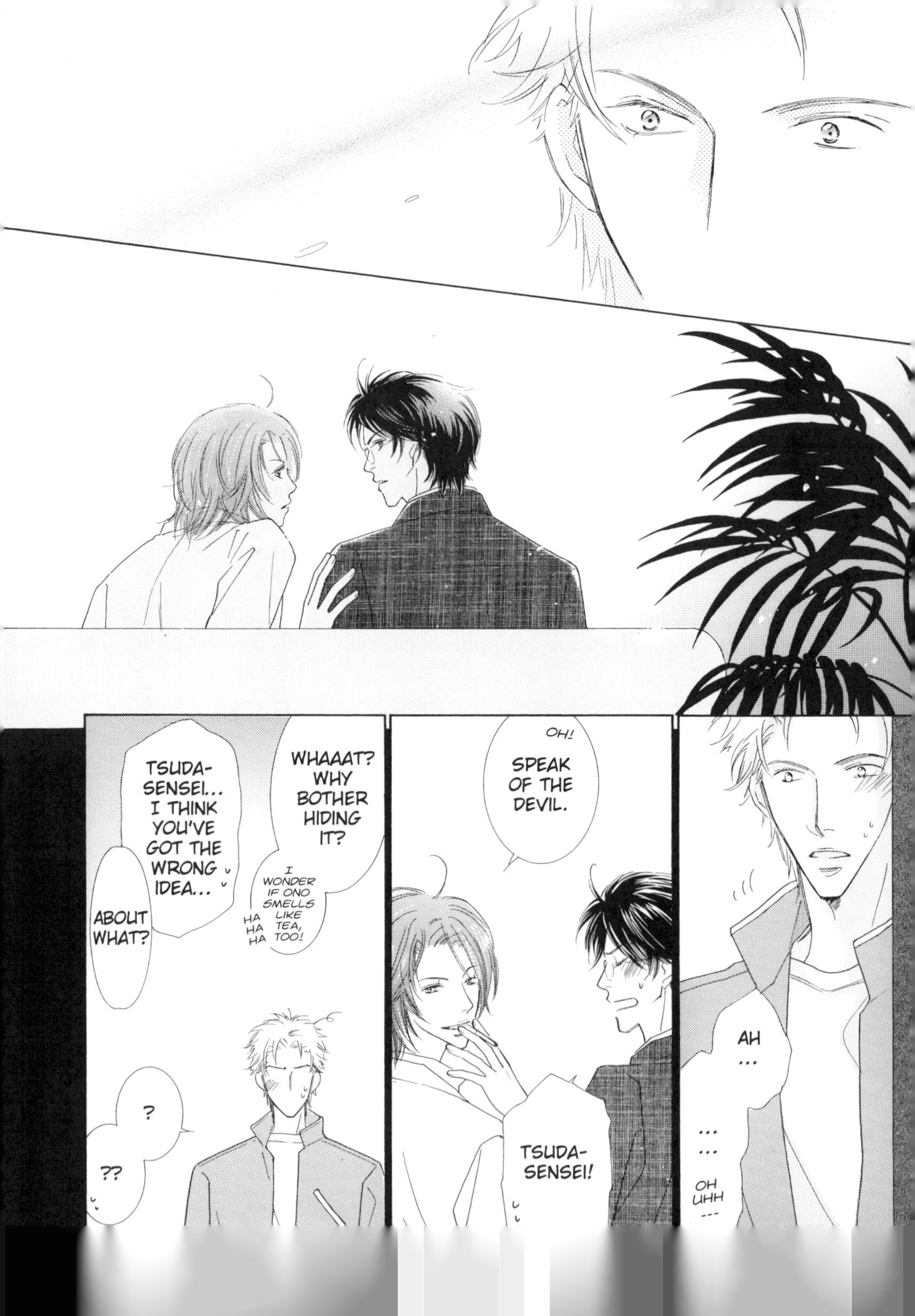
TSUDA-SENSEI... I THINK YOU'VE GOT THE WRONG IDEA...
ABOUT WHAT?
WHAAAT? WHY BOTHER HIDING IT?
I WONDER IF ONO SMELLS LIKE TEA, TOO!
HA HA HA
?
??
OH!
SPEAK OF THE DEVIL.
TSUDA-SENSEI!
AH ...
... ...
OH UHH ---

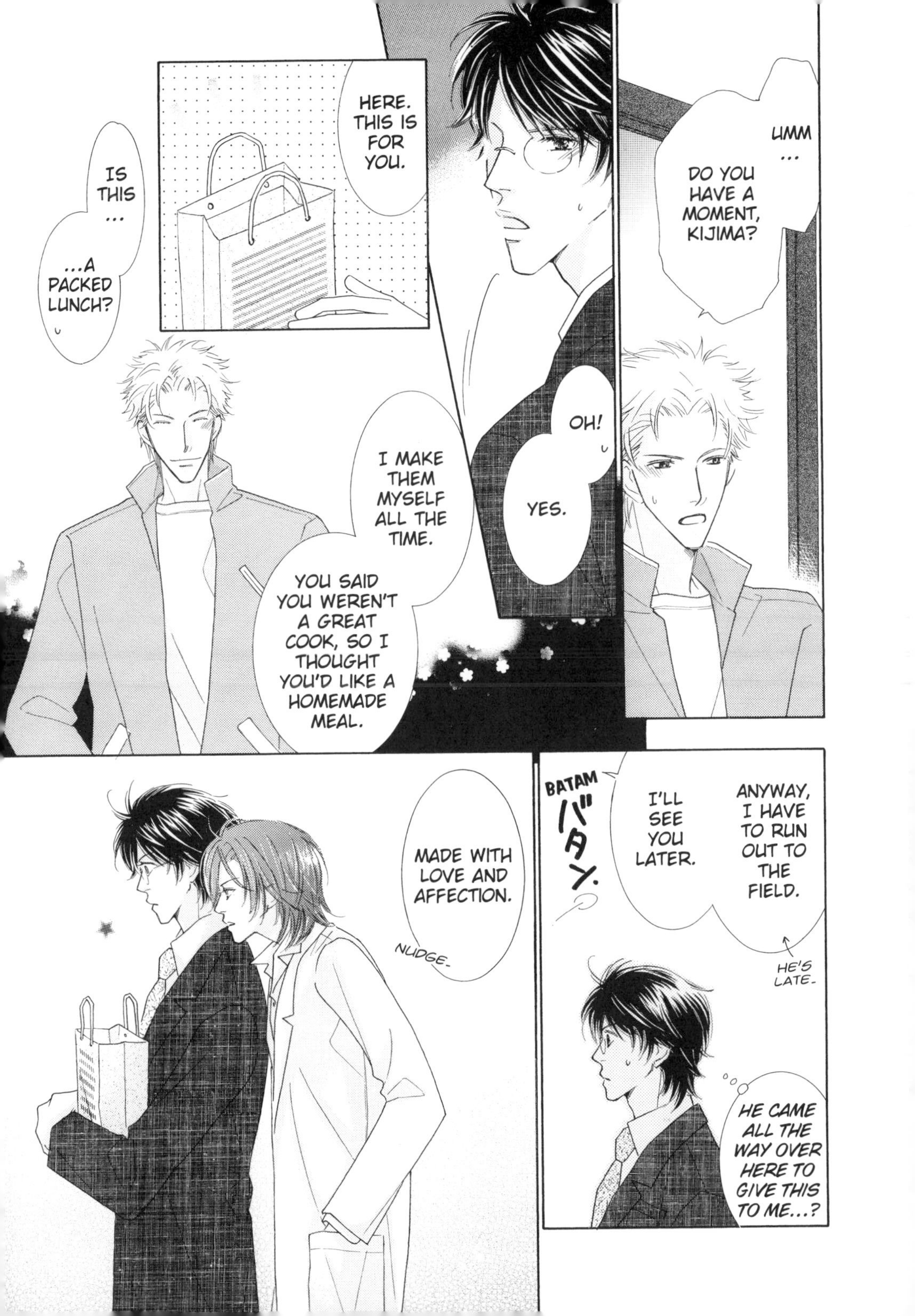
UMM ...
DO YOU HAVE A MOMENT, KIJIMA?
OH!
YES.
HERE. THIS IS FOR YOU.
IS THIS ...
...A PACKED LUNCH?
I MAKE THEM MYSELF ALL THE TIME.
YOU SAID YOU WEREN'T A GREAT COOK, SO I THOUGHT YOU'D LIKE A HOMEMADE MEAL.
ANYWAY, I HAVE TO RUN OUT TO THE FIELD.
I'LL SEE YOU LATER.
BATAM
バタン
HE'S LATE
HE CAME ALL THE WAY OVER HERE TO GIVE THIS TO ME...?
MADE WITH LOVE AND AFFECTION.
NUDGE

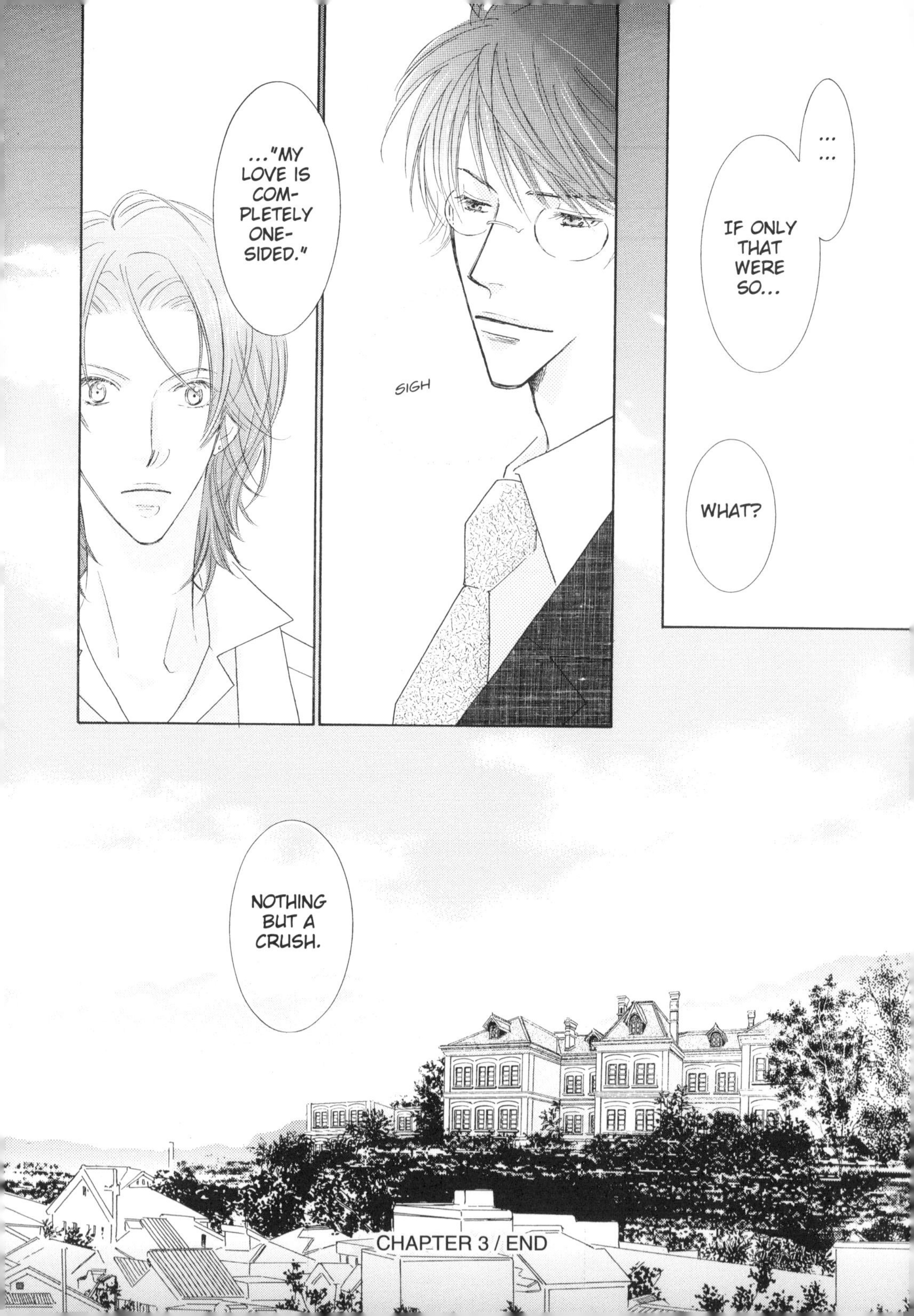
......
IF ONLY THAT WERE SO...
WHAT?
SIGH
..."MY LOVE IS COMPLETELY ONE-SIDED."
NOTHING BUT A CRUSH.
CHAPTER 3 / END

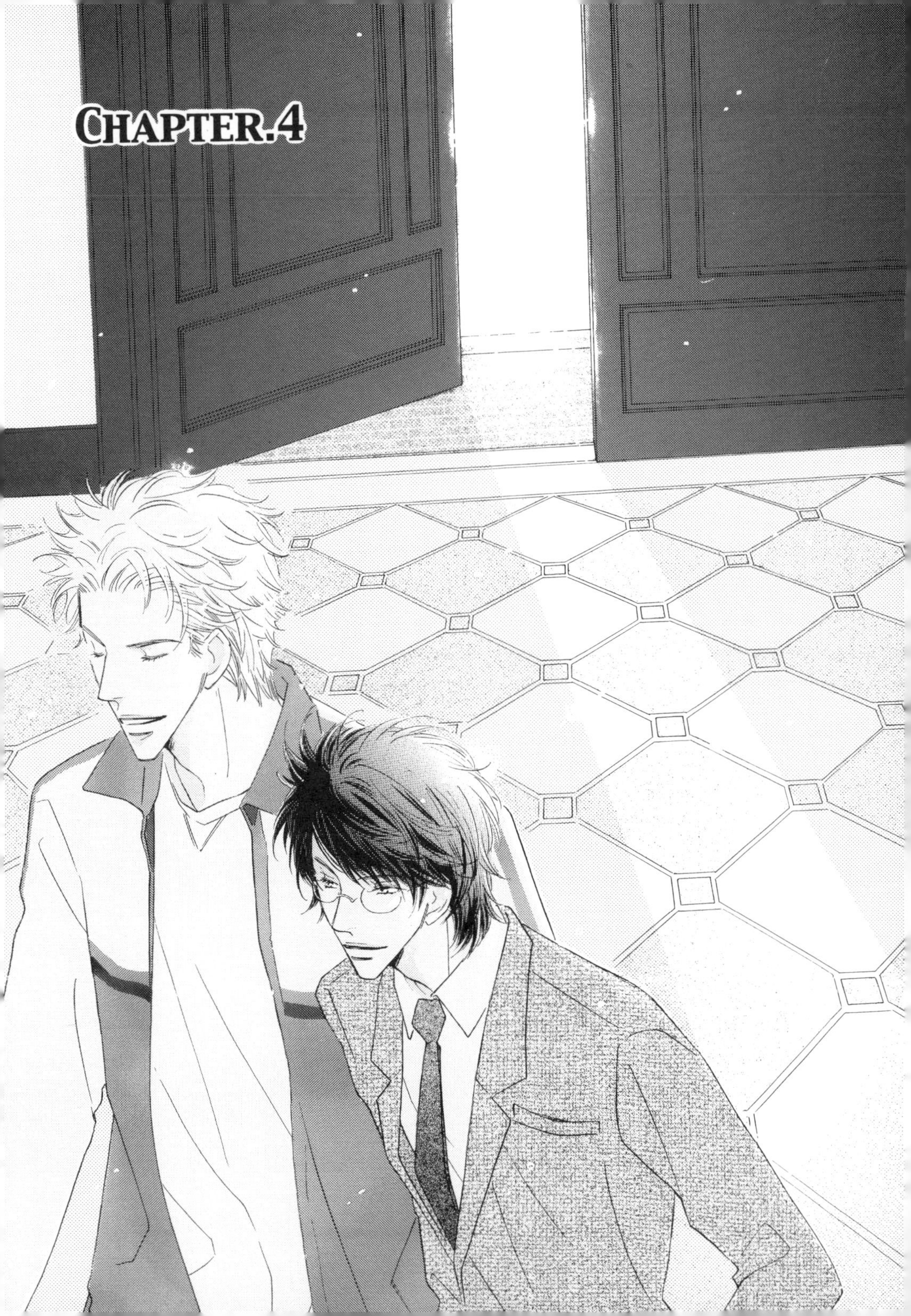
CHAPTER.4

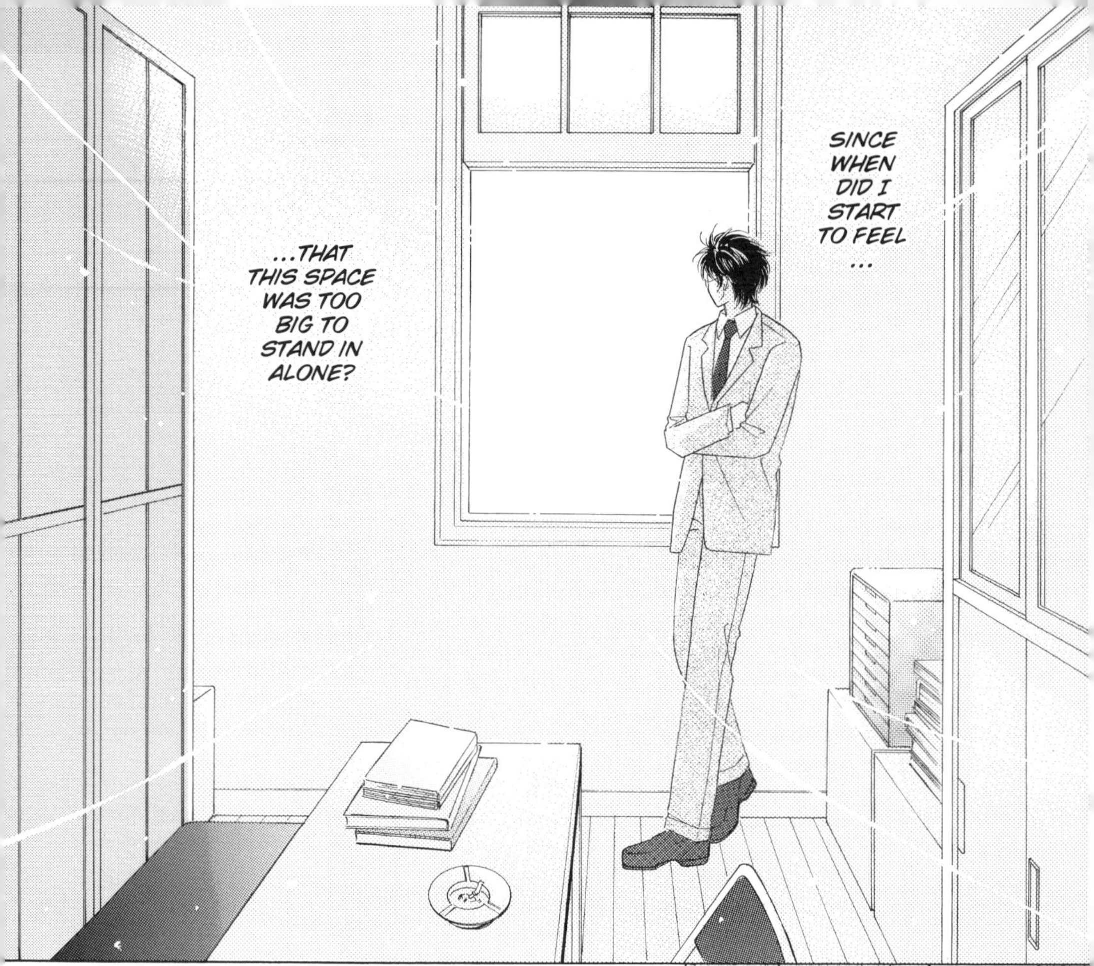
SINCE WHEN DID I START TO FEEL ...
...THAT THIS SPACE WAS TOO BIG TO STAND IN ALONE?
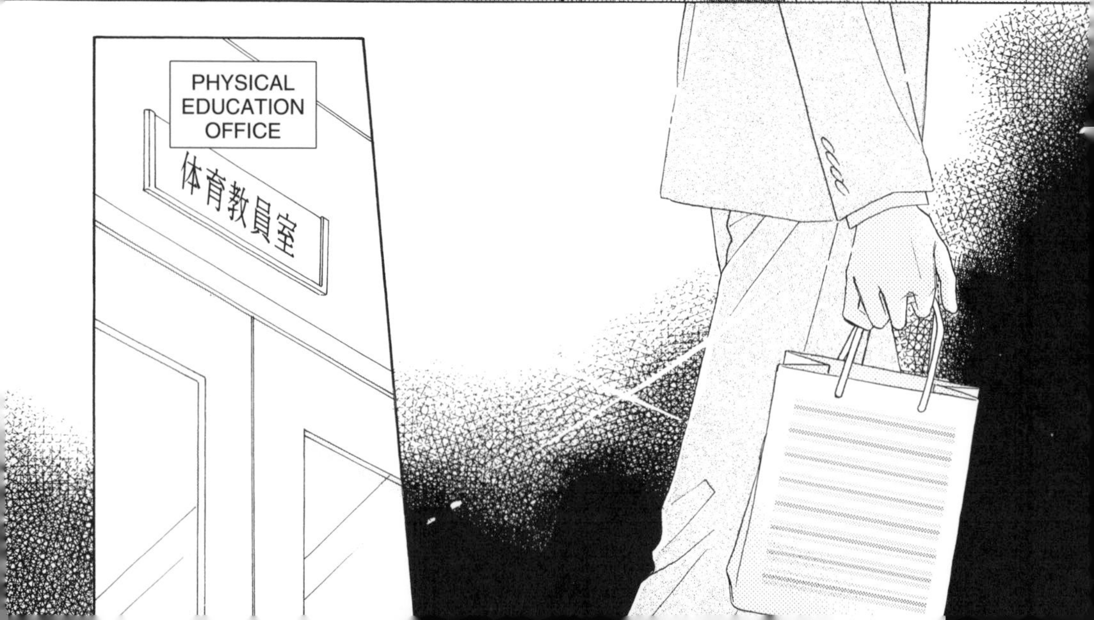
PHYSICAL EDUCATION OFFICE
体育教員室

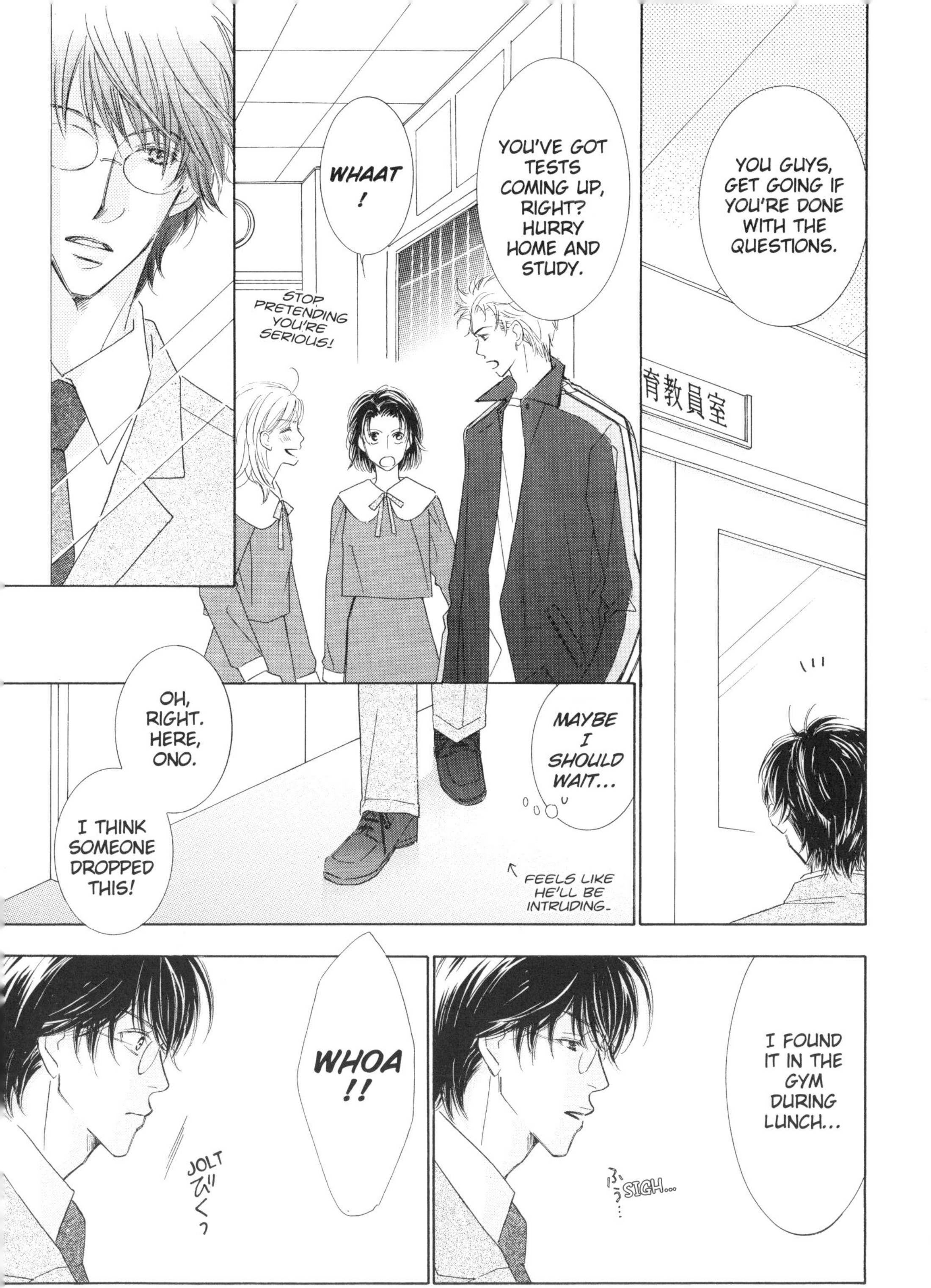

YOU GUYS, GET GOING IF YOU'RE DONE WITH THE QUESTIONS.
育教員室
YOU'VE GOT TESTS COMING UP, RIGHT? HURRY HOME AND STUDY.
WHAAT!
STOP PRETENDING YOU'RE SERIOUS!
MAYBE I SHOULD WAIT...
FEELS LIKE HE'LL BE INTRUDING.
OH, RIGHT. HERE, ONO.
I THINK SOMEONE DROPPED THIS!
I FOUND IT IN THE GYM DURING LUNCH...
ふぅ…
SIGH...
WHOA!!
JOLT
びくっ

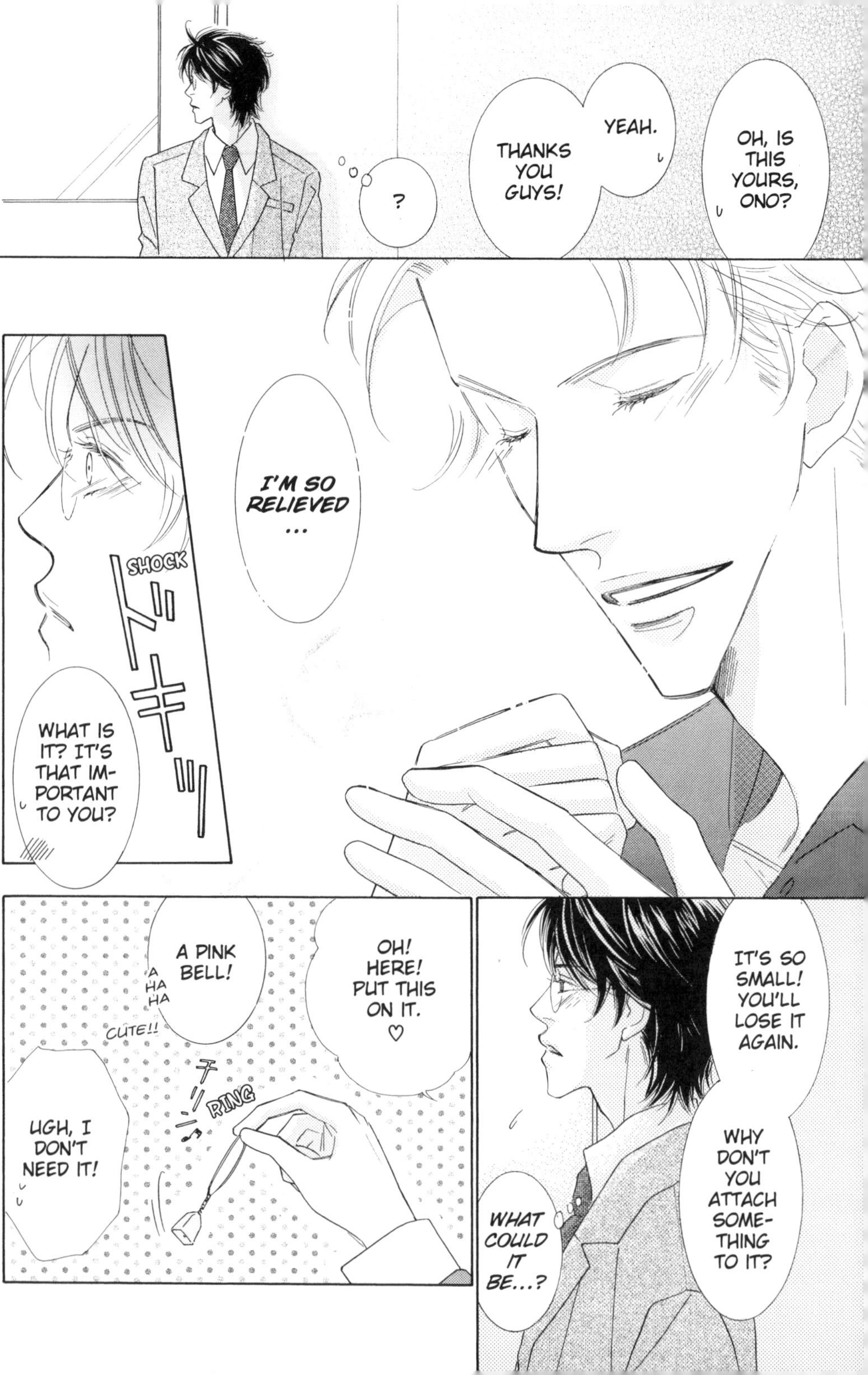
OH, IS THIS YOURS, ONO?
YEAH.
THANKS YOU GUYS!
?
I'M SO RELIEVED ...
WHAT IS IT? IT'S THAT IM-PORTANT TO YOU?
SHOCK
IT'S SO SMALL! YOU'LL LOSE IT AGAIN.
WHY DON'T YOU ATTACH SOME-THING TO IT?
WHAT COULD IT BE...?
OH! HERE! PUT THIS ON IT. ♡
A PINK BELL!
A HA HA
CUTE!!
RING
UGH, I DON'T NEED IT!

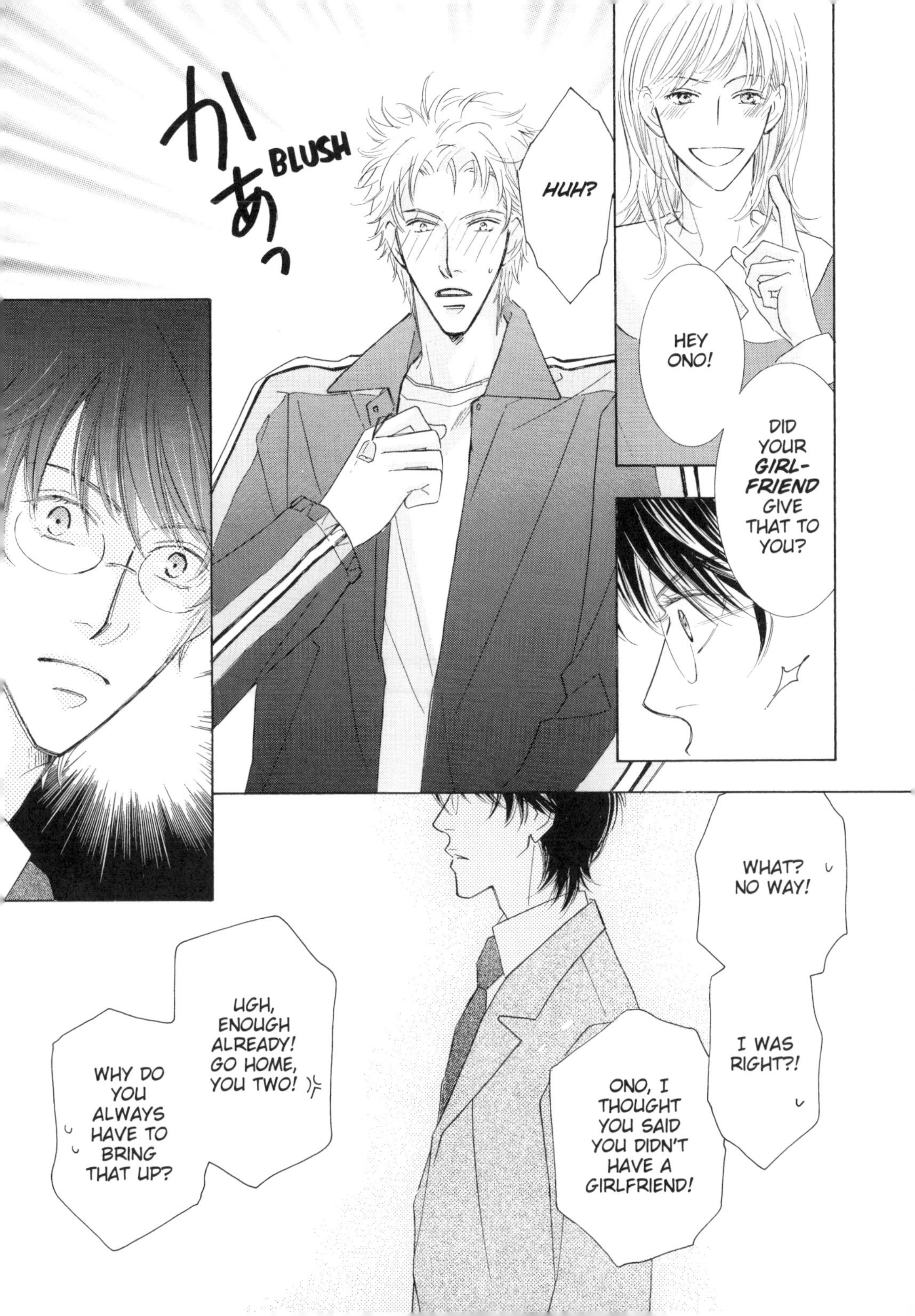
HEY ONO!
DID YOUR GIRLFRIEND GIVE THAT TO YOU?
HUH?
かあっ
BLUSH
WHAT? NO WAY!
I WAS RIGHT?!
ONO, I THOUGHT YOU SAID YOU DIDN'T HAVE A GIRLFRIEND!
UGH, ENOUGH ALREADY! GO HOME, YOU TWO!
WHY DO YOU ALWAYS HAVE TO BRING THAT UP?

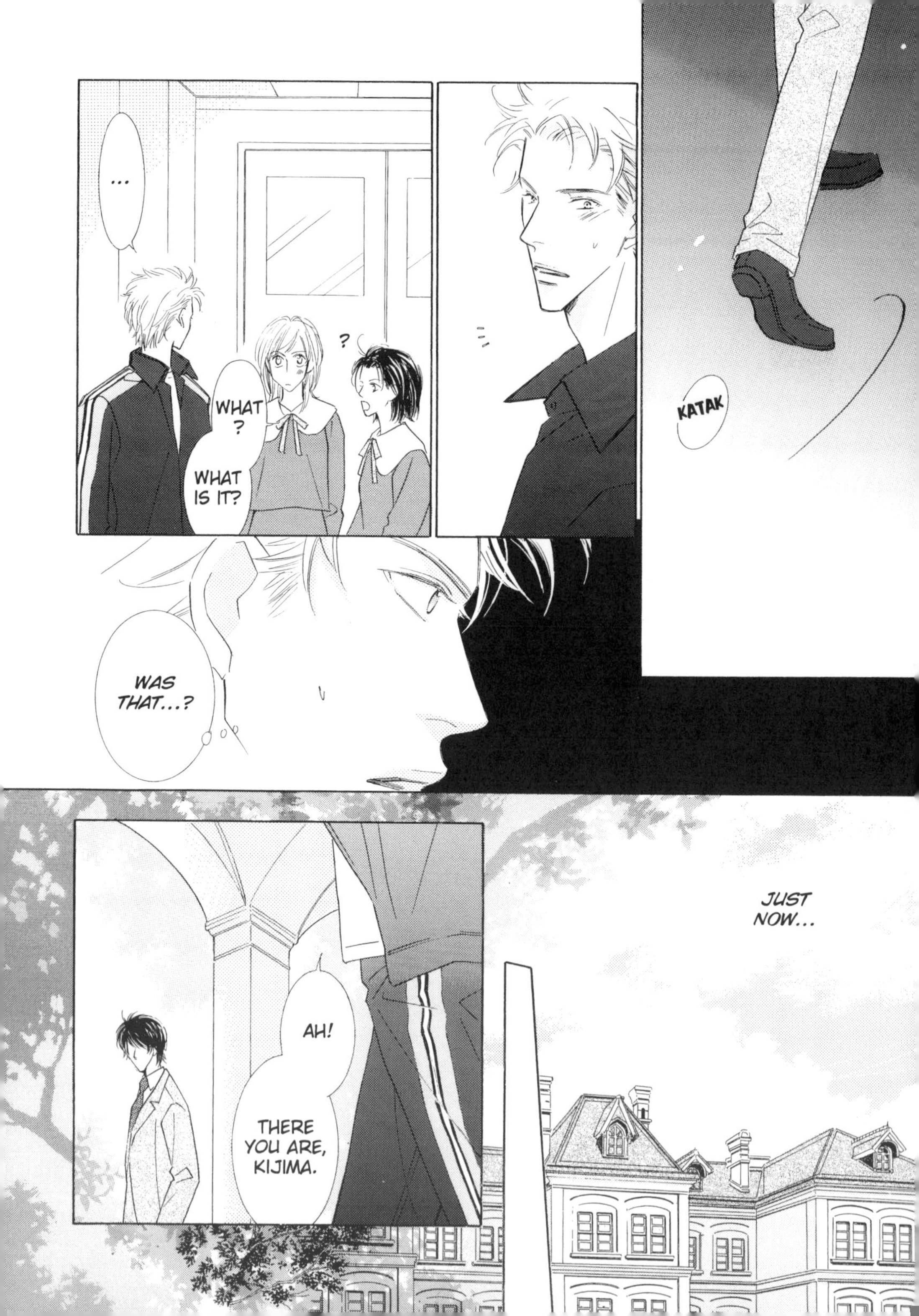
KATAK
...
?
WHAT ?
WHAT IS IT?
WAS THAT...?
JUST NOW...
AH!
THERE YOU ARE, KIJIMA.

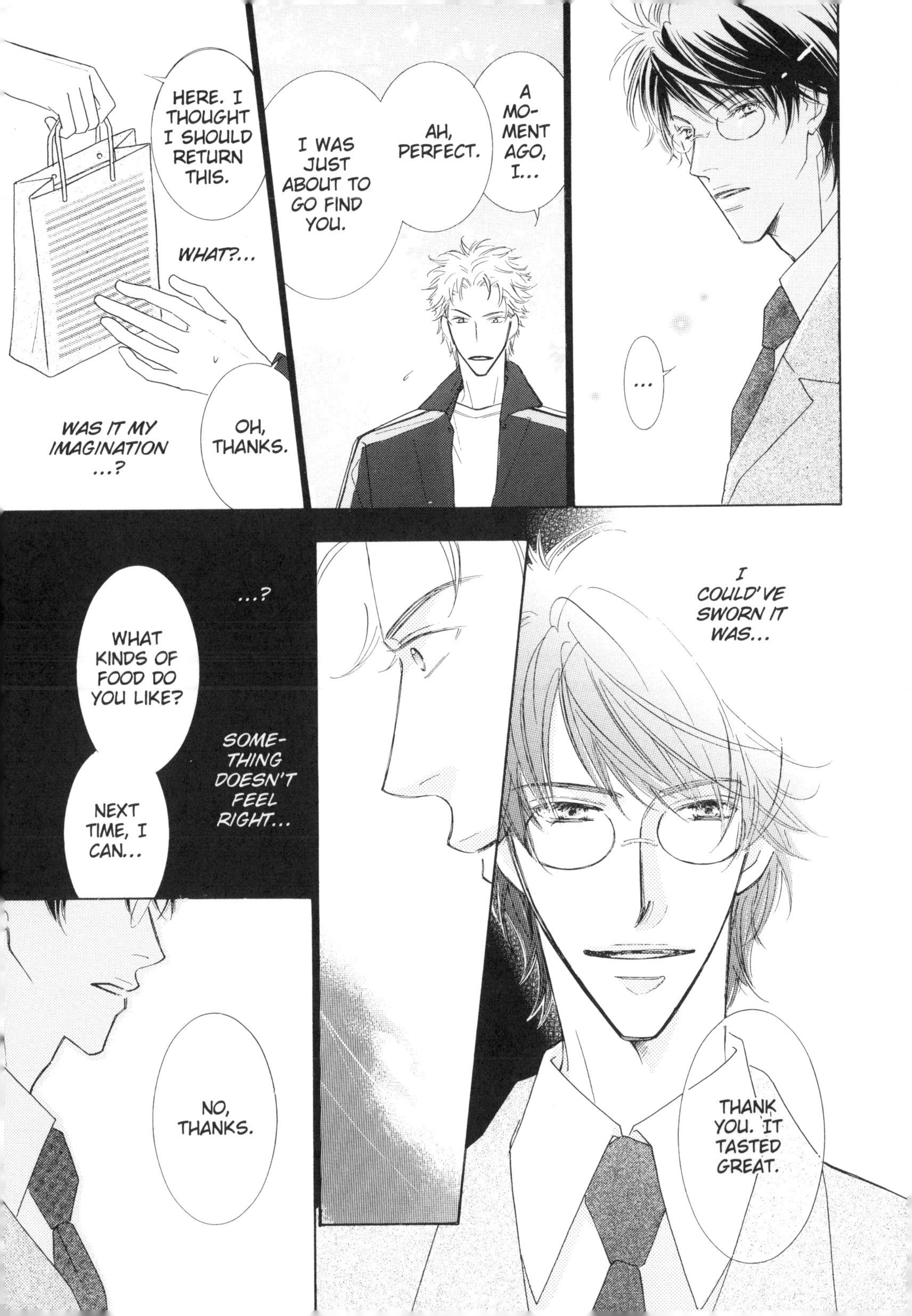
...
A MO-MENT AGO, I...
AH, PERFECT.
I WAS JUST ABOUT TO GO FIND YOU.
HERE. I THOUGHT I SHOULD RETURN THIS.
WHAT?...
OH, THANKS.
WAS IT MY IMAGINATION ...?
I COULD'VE SWORN IT WAS...
THANK YOU. IT TASTED GREAT.
...?
WHAT KINDS OF FOOD DO YOU LIKE?
SOME-THING DOESN'T FEEL RIGHT...
NEXT TIME, I CAN...
NO, THANKS.

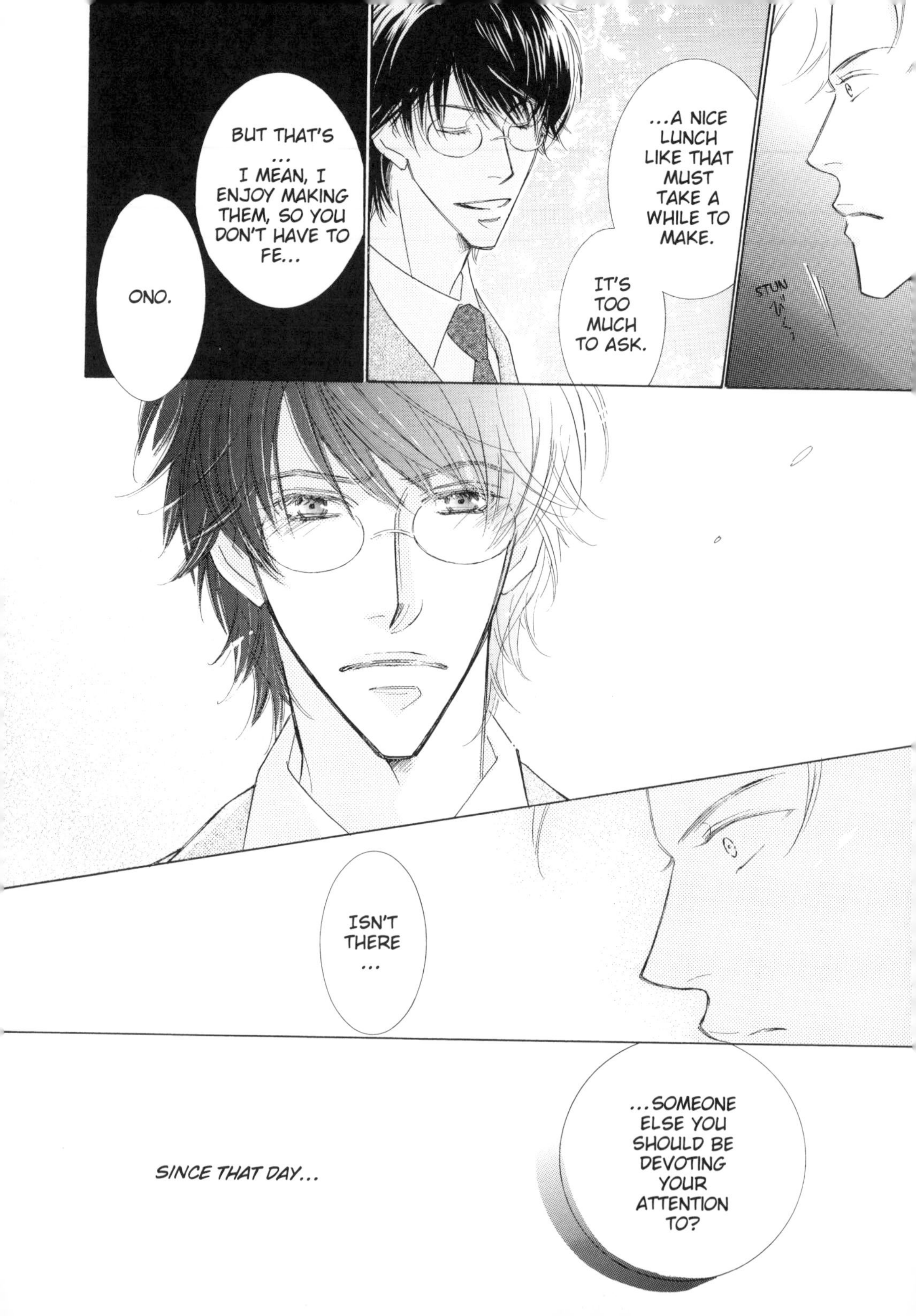
STUN
...A NICE LUNCH LIKE THAT MUST TAKE A WHILE TO MAKE.
IT'S TOO MUCH TO ASK.
BUT THAT'S ... I MEAN, I ENJOY MAKING THEM, SO YOU DON'T HAVE TO FE...
ONO.
ISN'T THERE ...
...SOMEONE ELSE YOU SHOULD BE DEVOTING YOUR ATTENTION TO?
SINCE THAT DAY...

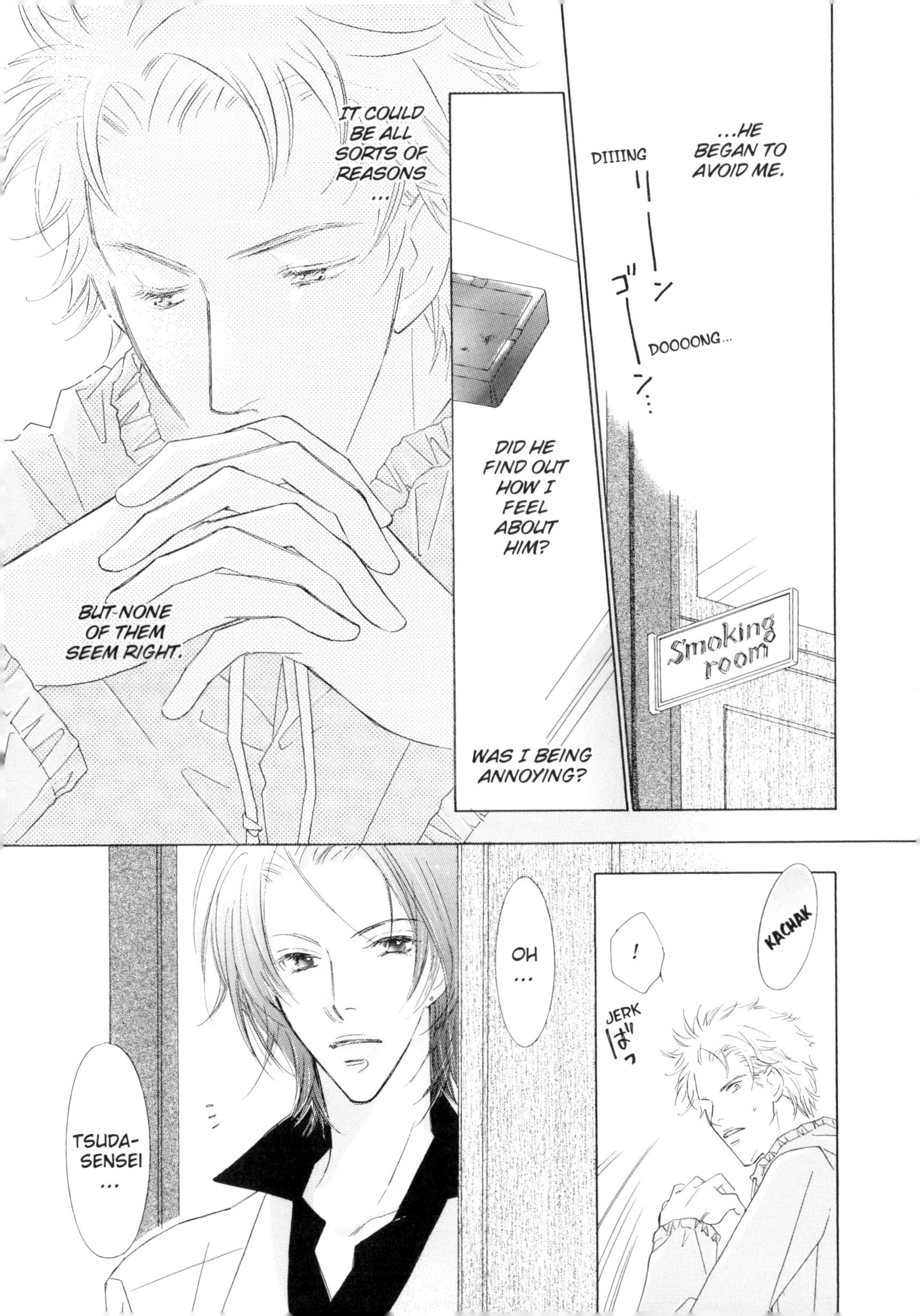
...HE BEGAN TO AVOID ME.
DIIIING
リーン
ゴーン…
DOOOONG...
Smoking room
DID HE FIND OUT HOW I FEEL ABOUT HIM?
WAS I BEING ANNOYING?
IT COULD BE ALL SORTS OF REASONS...
BUT-NONE OF THEM SEEM RIGHT.
KACHAK
!
JERK
ばっ
OH...
TSUDA-SENSEI...

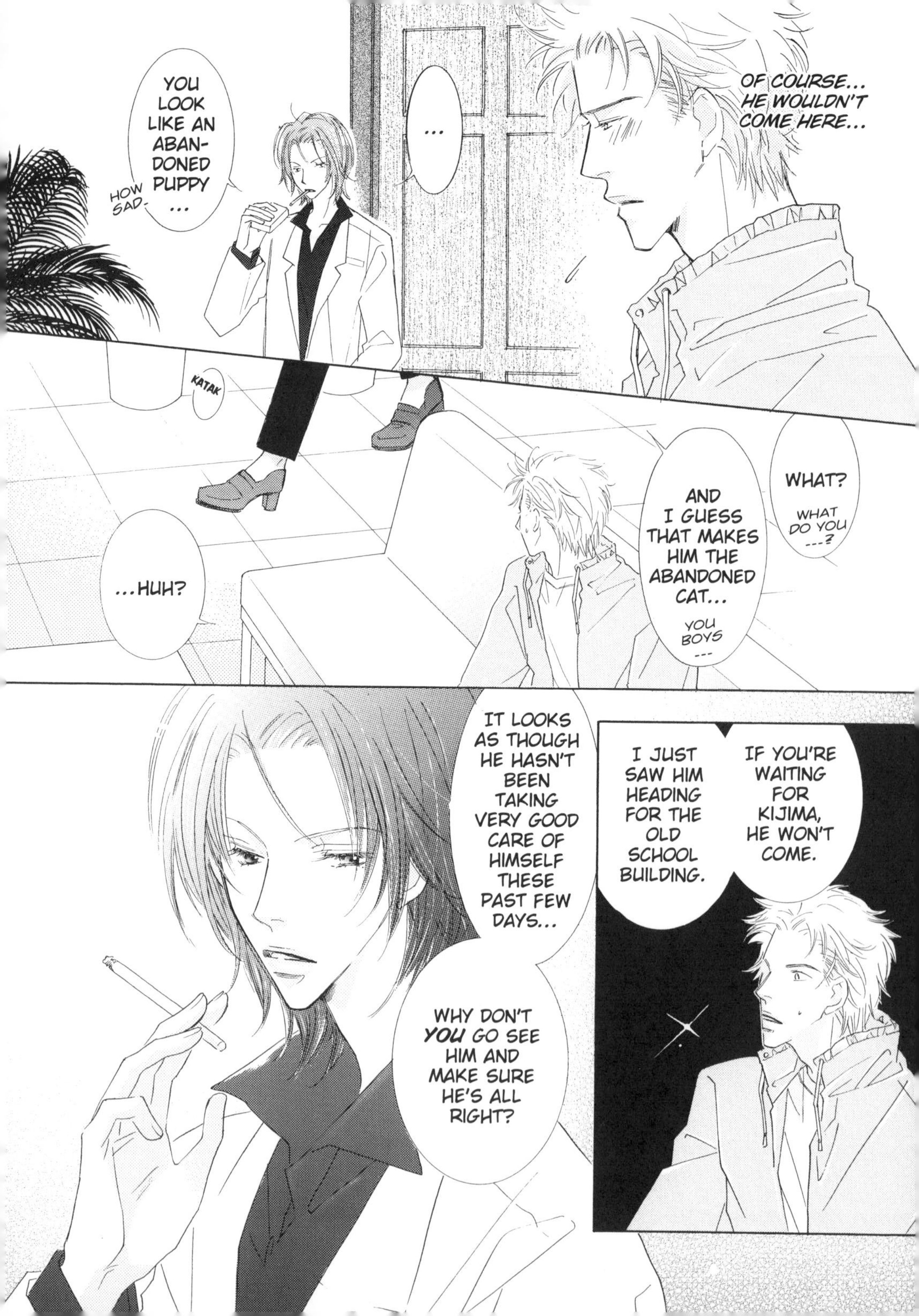
OF COURSE... HE WOULDN'T COME HERE...
...
YOU LOOK LIKE AN ABAN-DONED PUPPY...
HOW SAD...
KATAK
WHAT?
WHAT DO YOU---?
AND I GUESS THAT MAKES HIM THE ABANDONED CAT...
YOU BOYS---
...HUH?
IF YOU'RE WAITING FOR KIJIMA, HE WON'T COME.
I JUST SAW HIM HEADING FOR THE OLD SCHOOL BUILDING.
IT LOOKS AS THOUGH HE HASN'T BEEN TAKING VERY GOOD CARE OF HIMSELF THESE PAST FEW DAYS...
WHY DON'T *YOU* GO SEE HIM AND MAKE SURE HE'S ALL RIGHT?

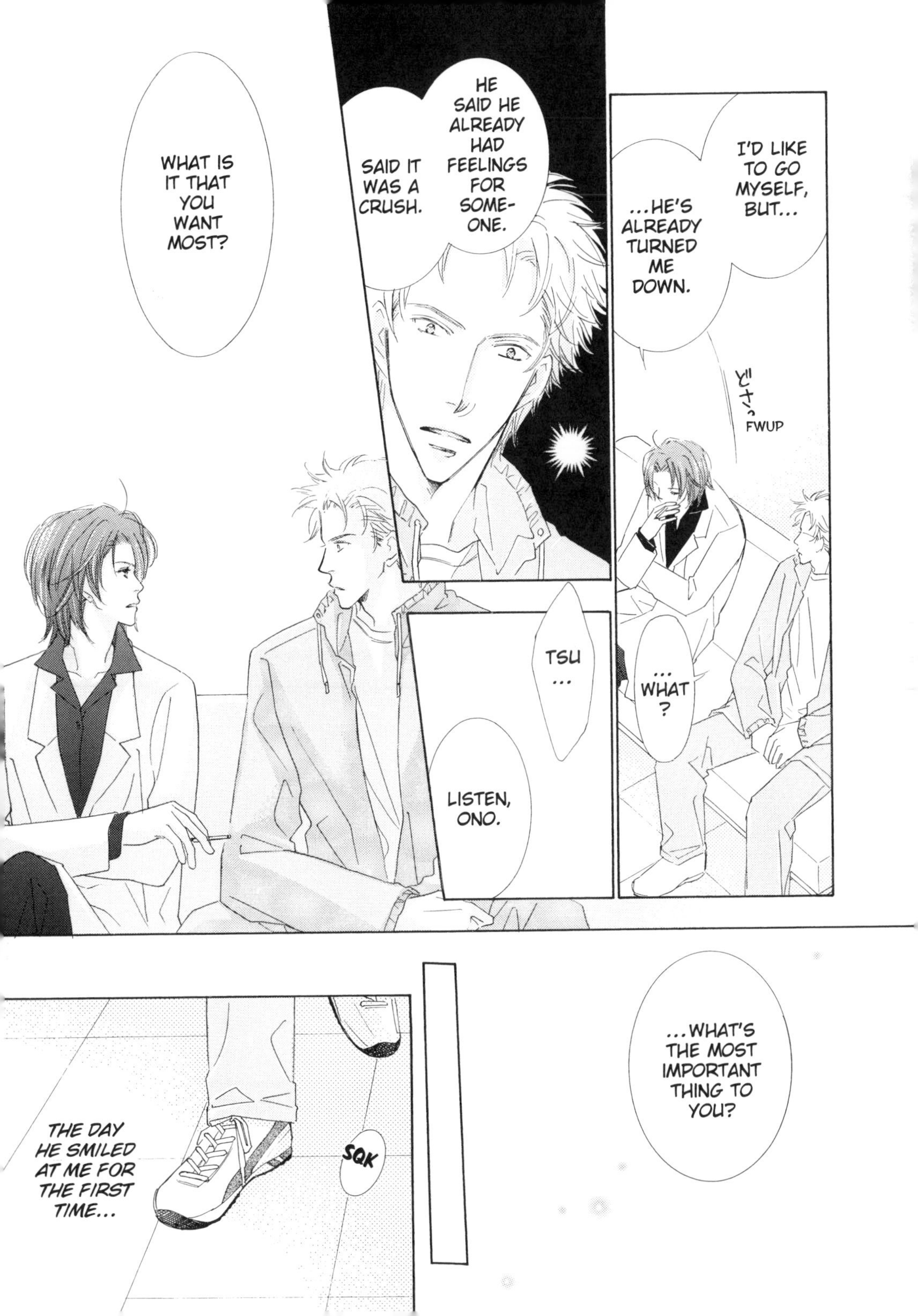
I'D LIKE TO GO MYSELF, BUT...
...HE'S ALREADY TURNED ME DOWN.
どさっ
FWUP
...WHAT?
HE SAID HE ALREADY HAD FEELINGS FOR SOME-ONE.
SAID IT WAS A CRUSH.
TSU...
LISTEN, ONO.
WHAT IS IT THAT YOU WANT MOST?
...WHAT'S THE MOST IMPORTANT THING TO YOU?
SQK
THE DAY HE SMILED AT ME FOR THE FIRST TIME...

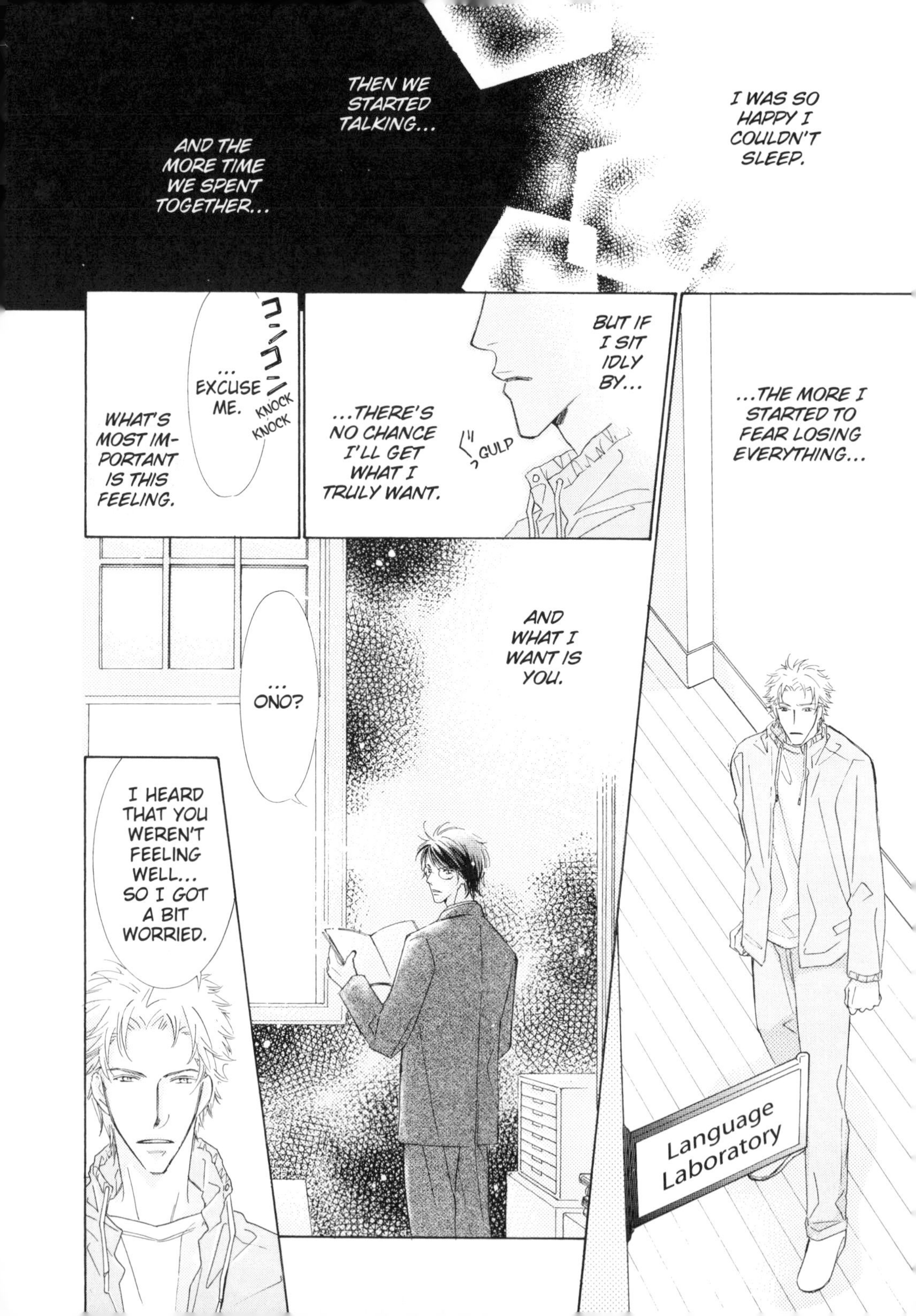

I WAS SO HAPPY I COULDN'T SLEEP.
THEN WE STARTED TALKING...
AND THE MORE TIME WE SPENT TOGETHER...
...THE MORE I STARTED TO FEAR LOSING EVERYTHING...
Language Laboratory
BUT IF I SIT IDLY BY...
GULP
...THERE'S NO CHANCE I'LL GET WHAT I TRULY WANT.
コンコン
KNOCK KNOCK
...EXCUSE ME.
WHAT'S MOST IMPORTANT IS THIS FEELING.
AND WHAT I WANT IS YOU.
...ONO?
I HEARD THAT YOU WEREN'T FEELING WELL... SO I GOT A BIT WORRIED.

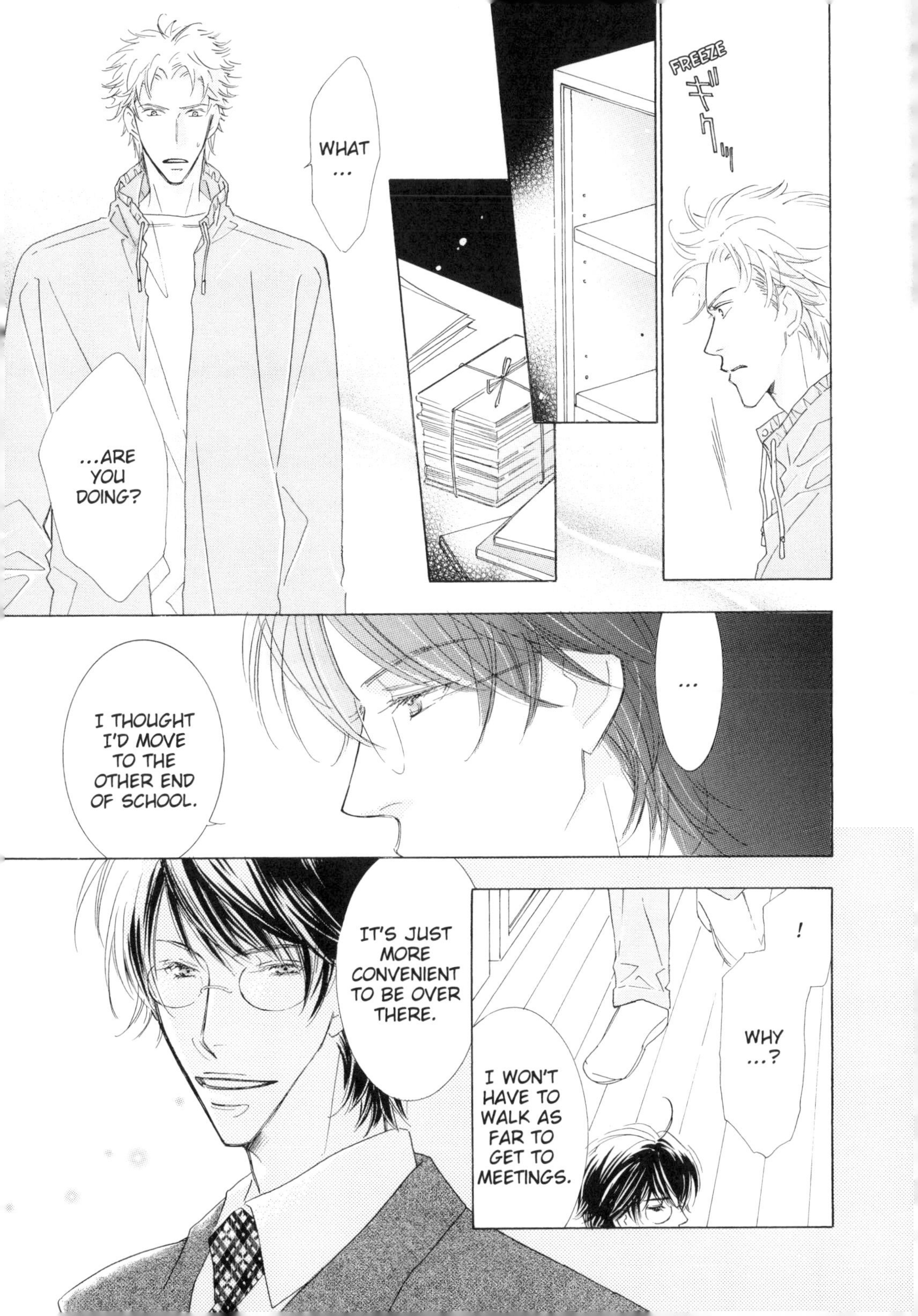
FREEZE
ギクッ
WHAT...
...ARE YOU DOING?
...
I THOUGHT I'D MOVE TO THE OTHER END OF SCHOOL.
!
WHY...?
I WON'T HAVE TO WALK AS FAR TO GET TO MEETINGS.
IT'S JUST MORE CONVENIENT TO BE OVER THERE.

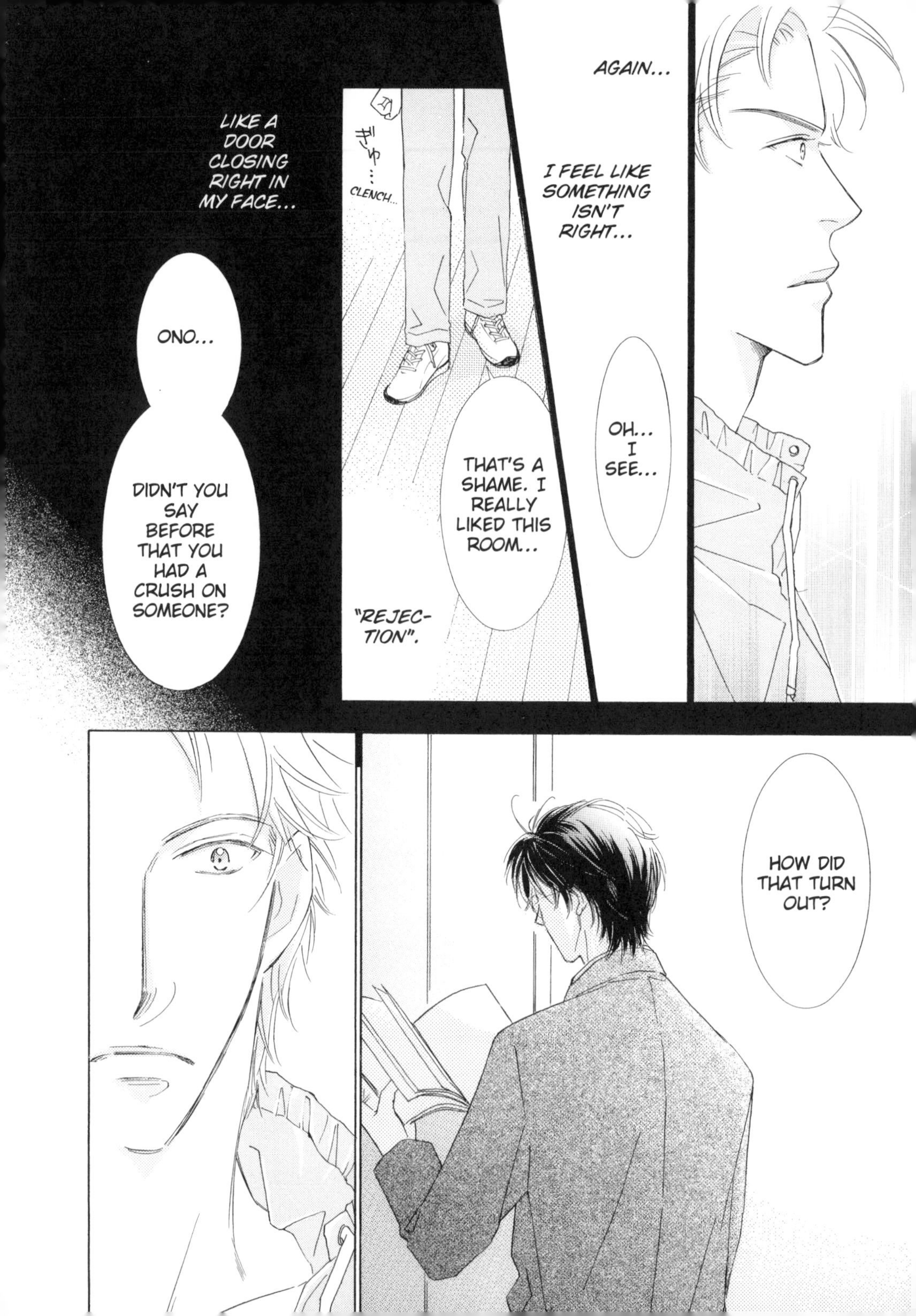
AGAIN...
I FEEL LIKE SOMETHING ISN'T RIGHT...
OH... I SEE...
THAT'S A SHAME. I REALLY LIKED THIS ROOM...
ぎゅ…
CLENCH...
"REJECTION".
LIKE A DOOR CLOSING RIGHT IN MY FACE...
ONO...
DIDN'T YOU SAY BEFORE THAT YOU HAD A CRUSH ON SOMEONE?
HOW DID THAT TURN OUT?

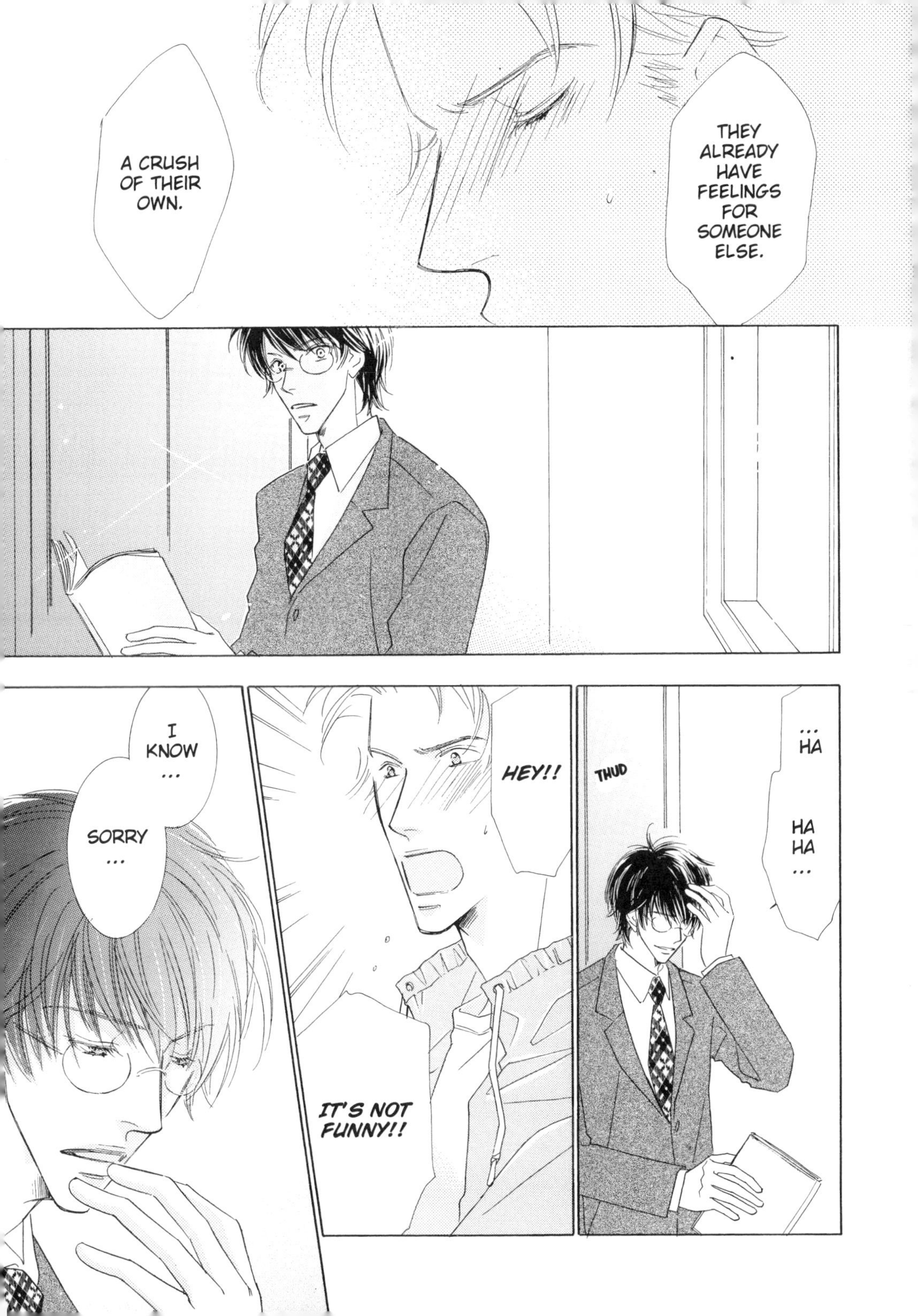
THEY ALREADY HAVE FEELINGS FOR SOMEONE ELSE.
A CRUSH OF THEIR OWN.
... HA HA HA ...
THUD
HEY!!
IT'S NOT FUNNY!!
I KNOW ...
SORRY ...

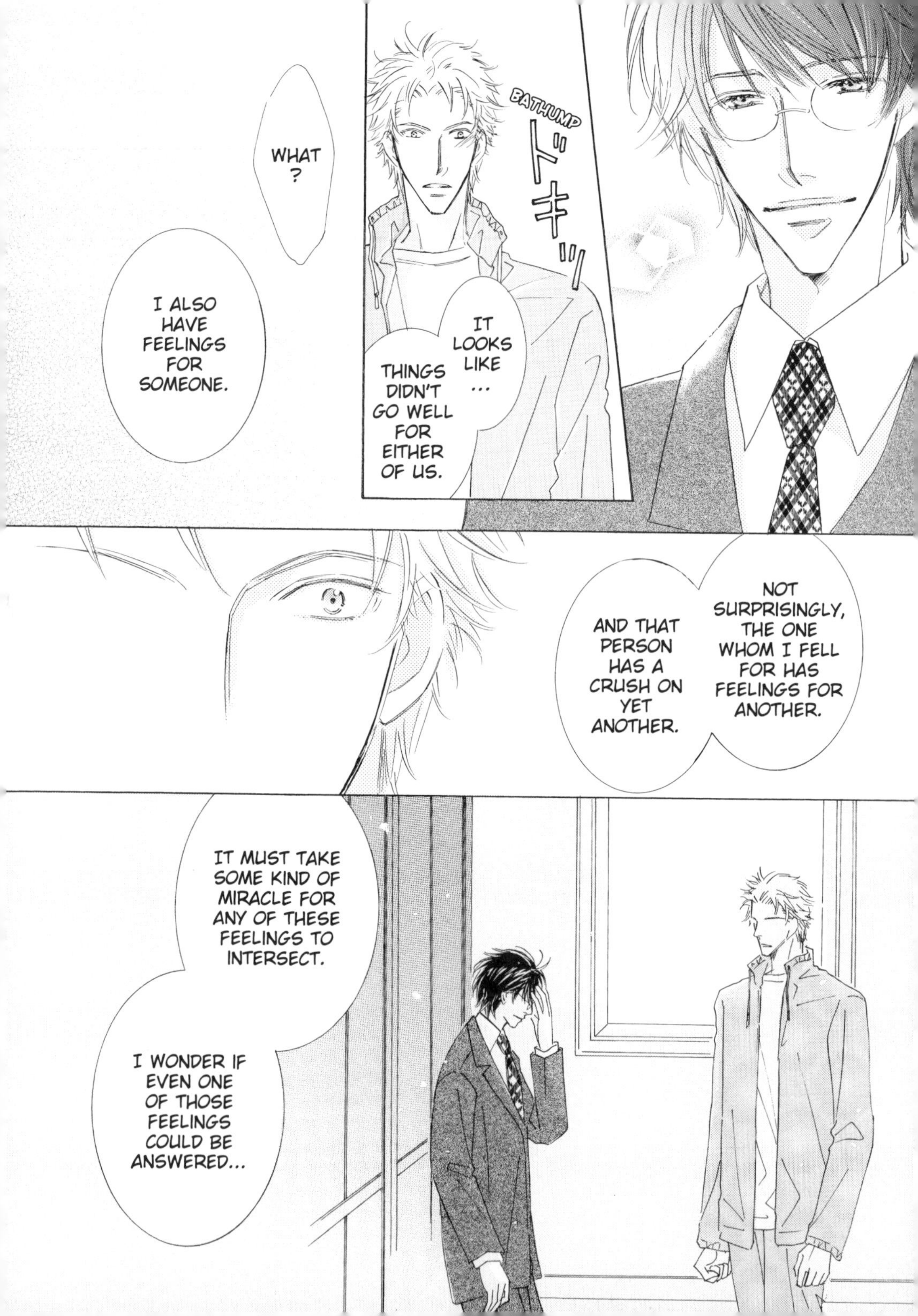
BATHUMP
ドキッ
IT LOOKS LIKE...
THINGS DIDN'T GO WELL FOR EITHER OF US.
WHAT ?
I ALSO HAVE FEELINGS FOR SOMEONE.
NOT SURPRISINGLY, THE ONE WHOM I FELL FOR HAS FEELINGS FOR ANOTHER.
AND THAT PERSON HAS A CRUSH ON YET ANOTHER.
IT MUST TAKE SOME KIND OF MIRACLE FOR ANY OF THESE FEELINGS TO INTERSECT.
I WONDER IF EVEN ONE OF THOSE FEELINGS COULD BE ANSWERED...

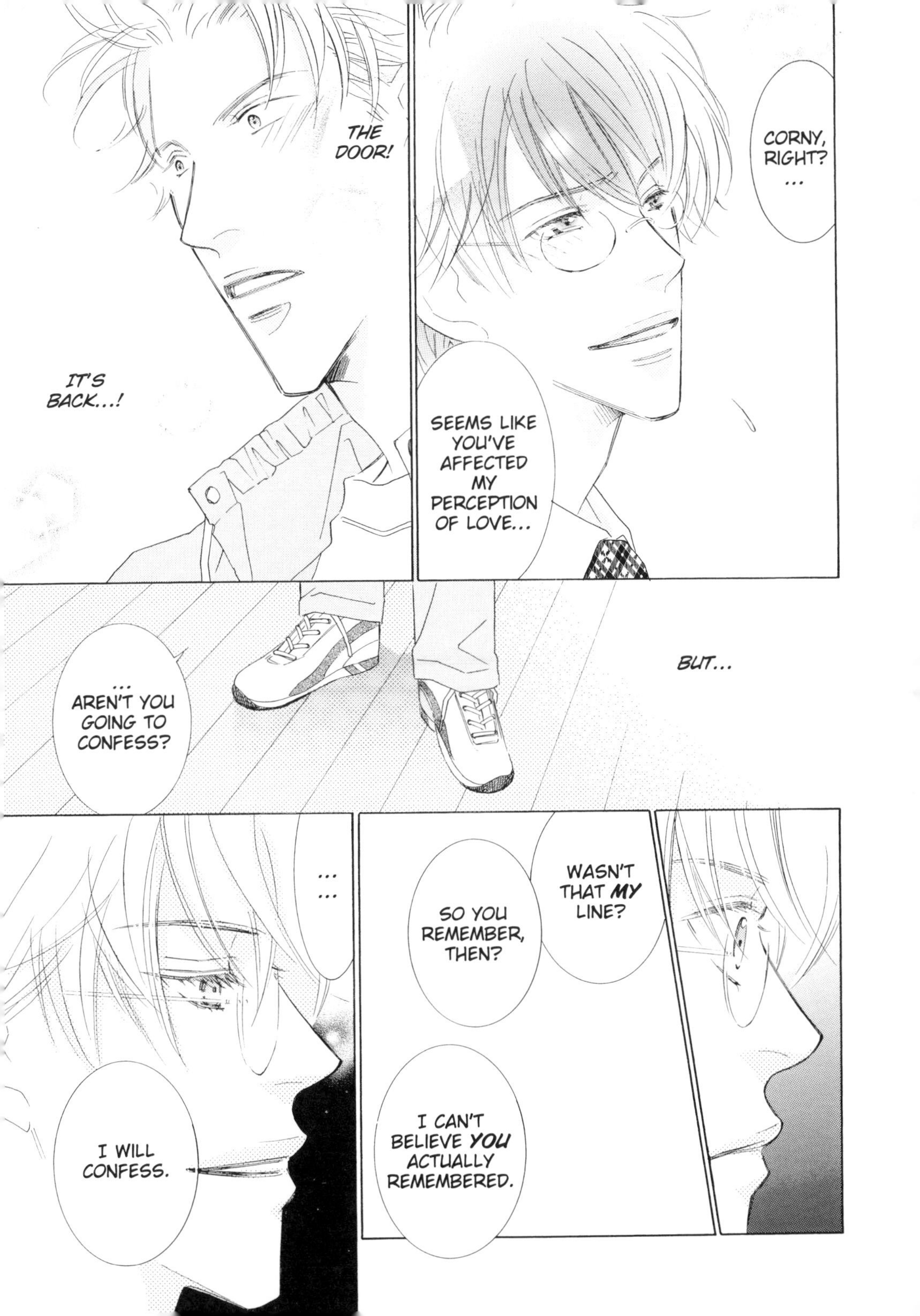
CORNY, RIGHT? ...
SEEMS LIKE YOU'VE AFFECTED MY PERCEPTION OF LOVE...
THE DOOR!
IT'S BACK...!
BUT...
... AREN'T YOU GOING TO CONFESS?
WASN'T THAT MY LINE?
SO YOU REMEMBER, THEN?
I CAN'T BELIEVE YOU ACTUALLY REMEMBERED.
... ...
I WILL CONFESS.

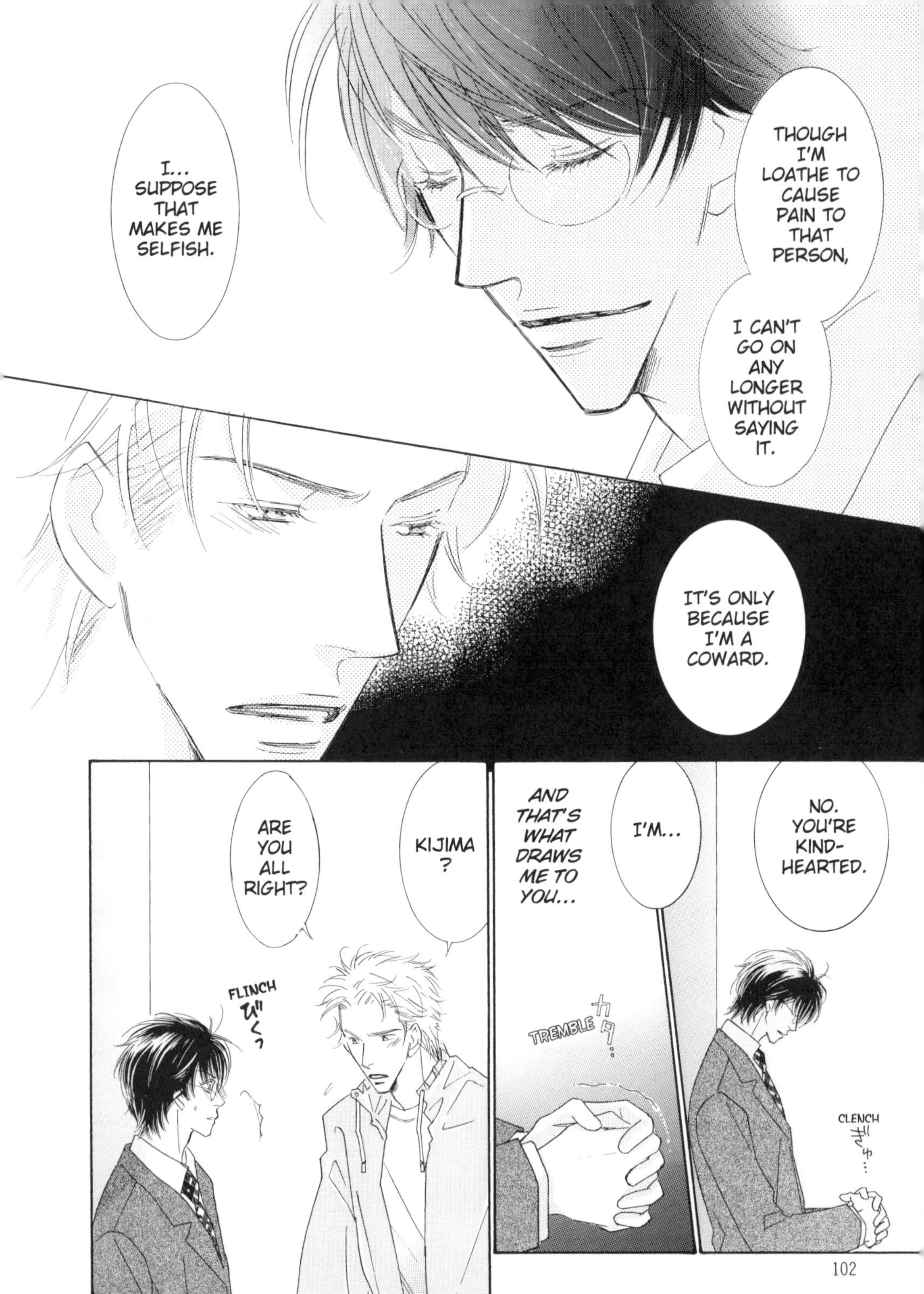
THOUGH I'M LOATHE TO CAUSE PAIN TO THAT PERSON,
I CAN'T GO ON ANY LONGER WITHOUT SAYING IT.
I... SUPPOSE THAT MAKES ME SELFISH.
IT'S ONLY BECAUSE I'M A COWARD.
NO. YOU'RE KIND-HEARTED.
CLENCH ぎゅ…
I'M...
AND THAT'S WHAT DRAWS ME TO YOU...
TREMBLE カタ…
KIJIMA ?
ARE YOU ALL RIGHT?
FLINCH びくっ

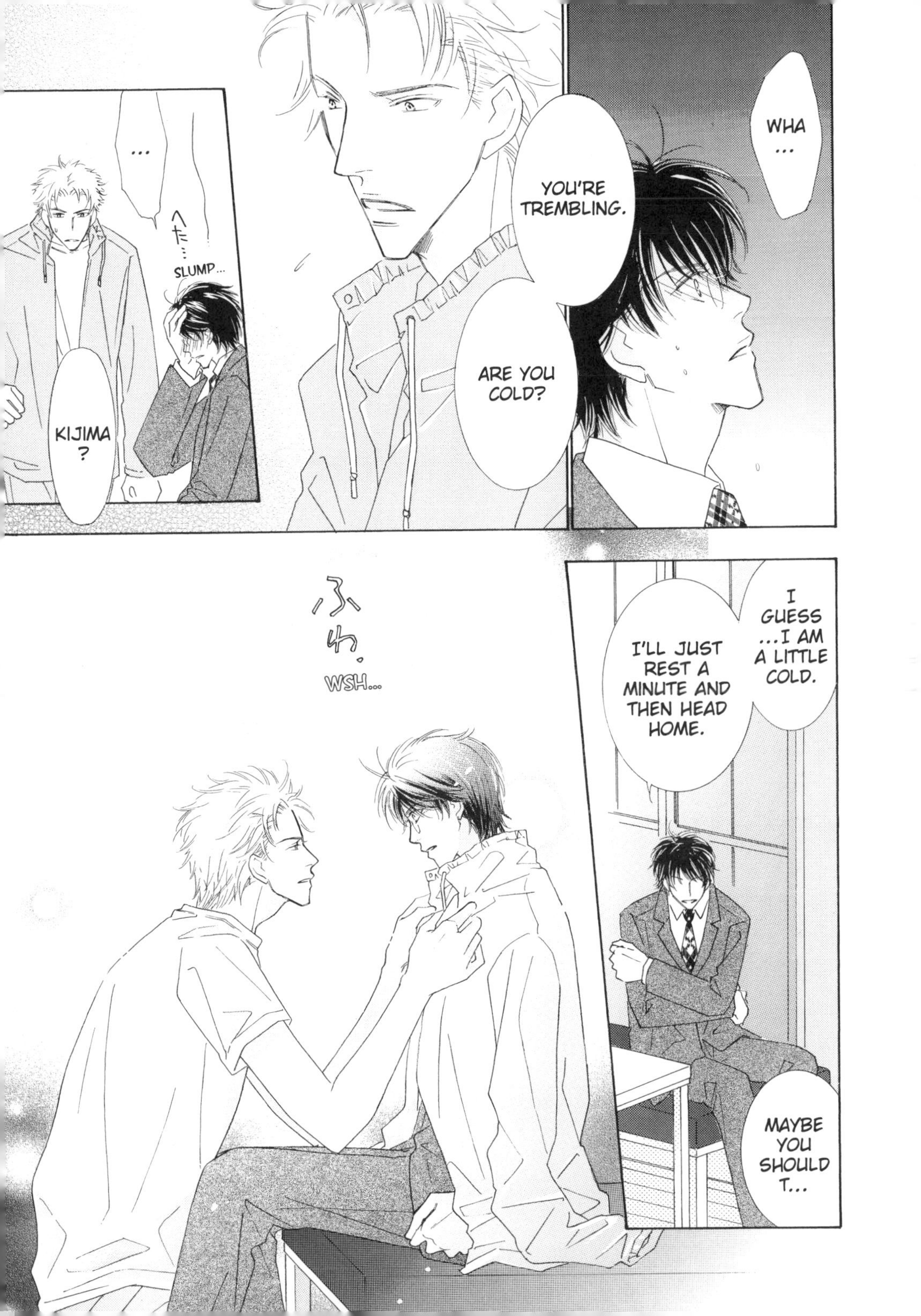
WHA...
YOU'RE TREMBLING.
ARE YOU COLD?
...
へた…
SLUMP...
KIJIMA?
I GUESS ...I AM A LITTLE COLD.
I'LL JUST REST A MINUTE AND THEN HEAD HOME.
MAYBE YOU SHOULD T...
ふわ。
WSH...

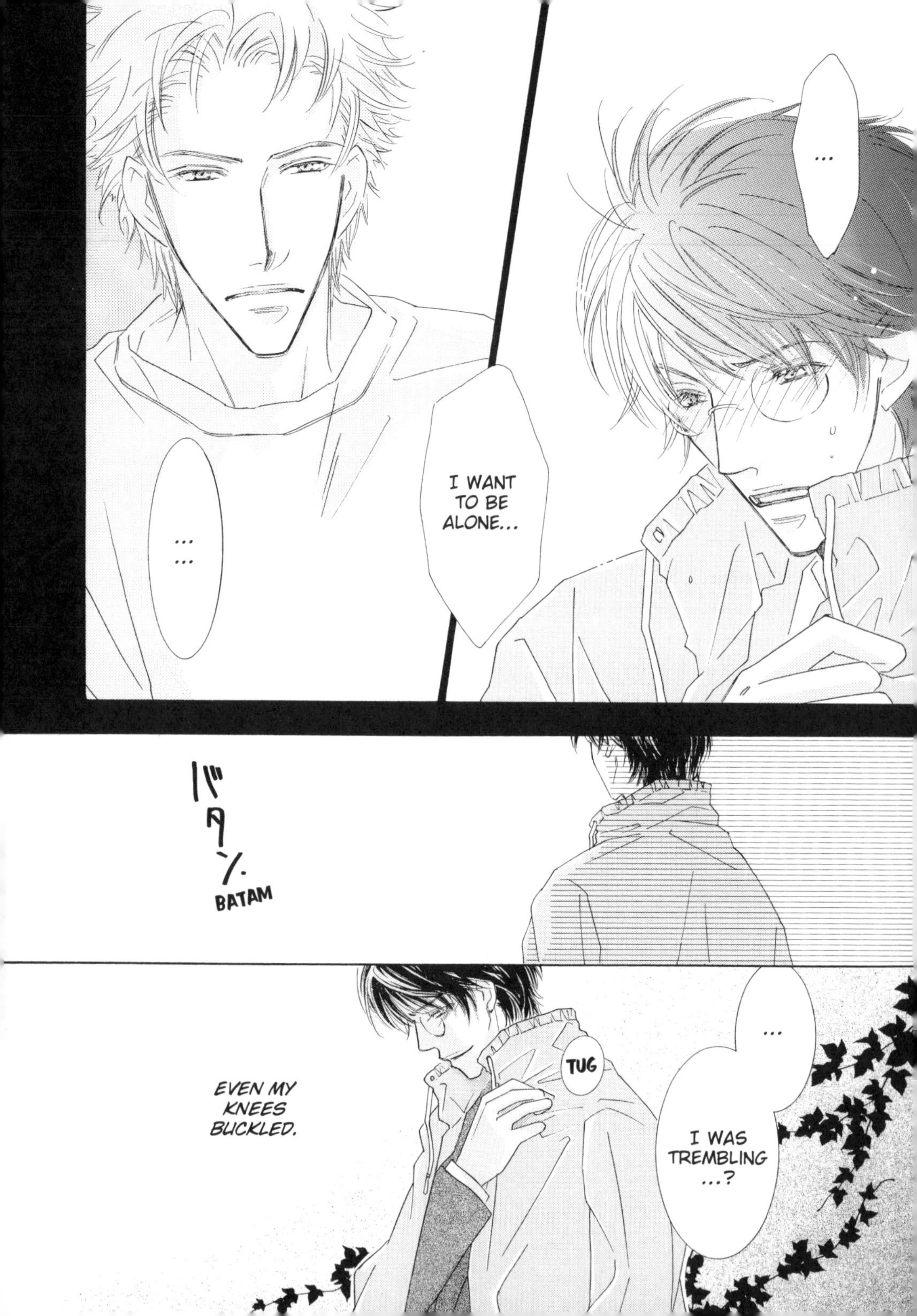
...
I WANT TO BE ALONE...
... ...
バタン.
BATAM
...
I WAS TREMBLING ...?
TUG
EVEN MY KNEES BUCKLED.

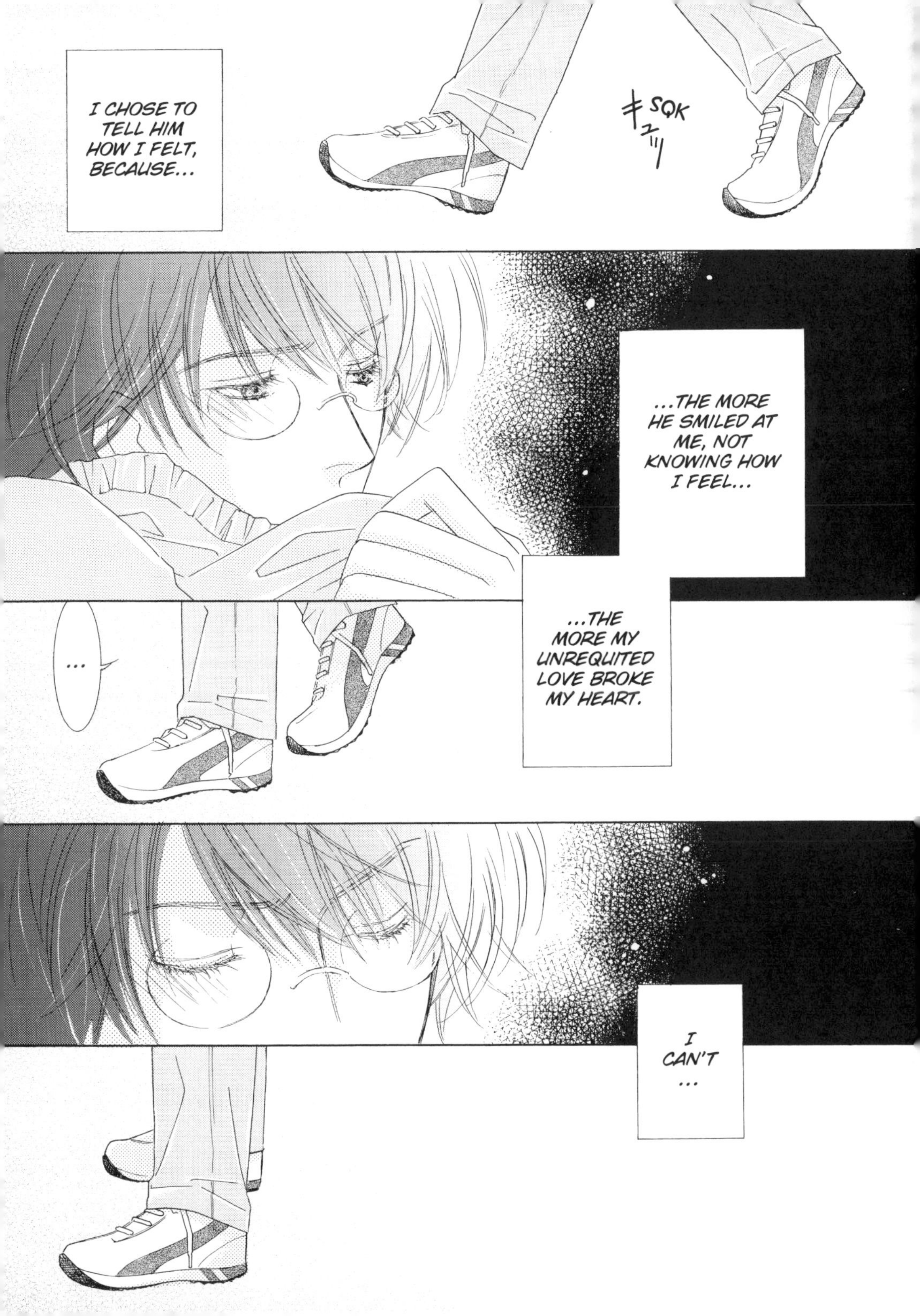
SQK
キュッ
I CHOSE TO TELL HIM HOW I FELT, BECAUSE...
...THE MORE HE SMILED AT ME, NOT KNOWING HOW I FEEL...
...THE MORE MY UNREQUITED LOVE BROKE MY HEART.
...
I CAN'T ...

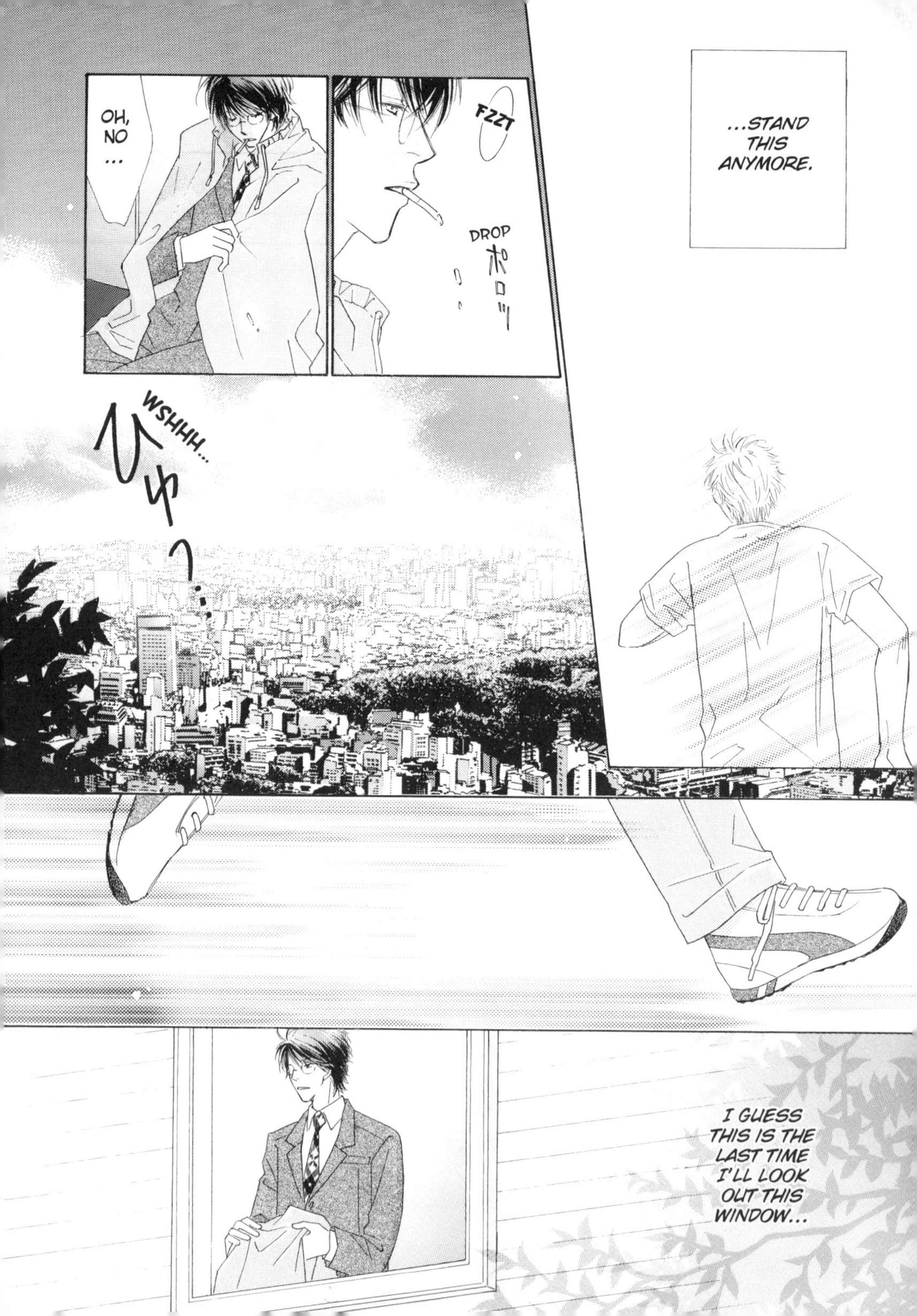
...STAND THIS ANYMORE.
FZZT
DROP
ポロッ
OH, NO ...
WSHHH...
ひゅっ
I GUESS THIS IS THE LAST TIME I'LL LOOK OUT THIS WINDOW...

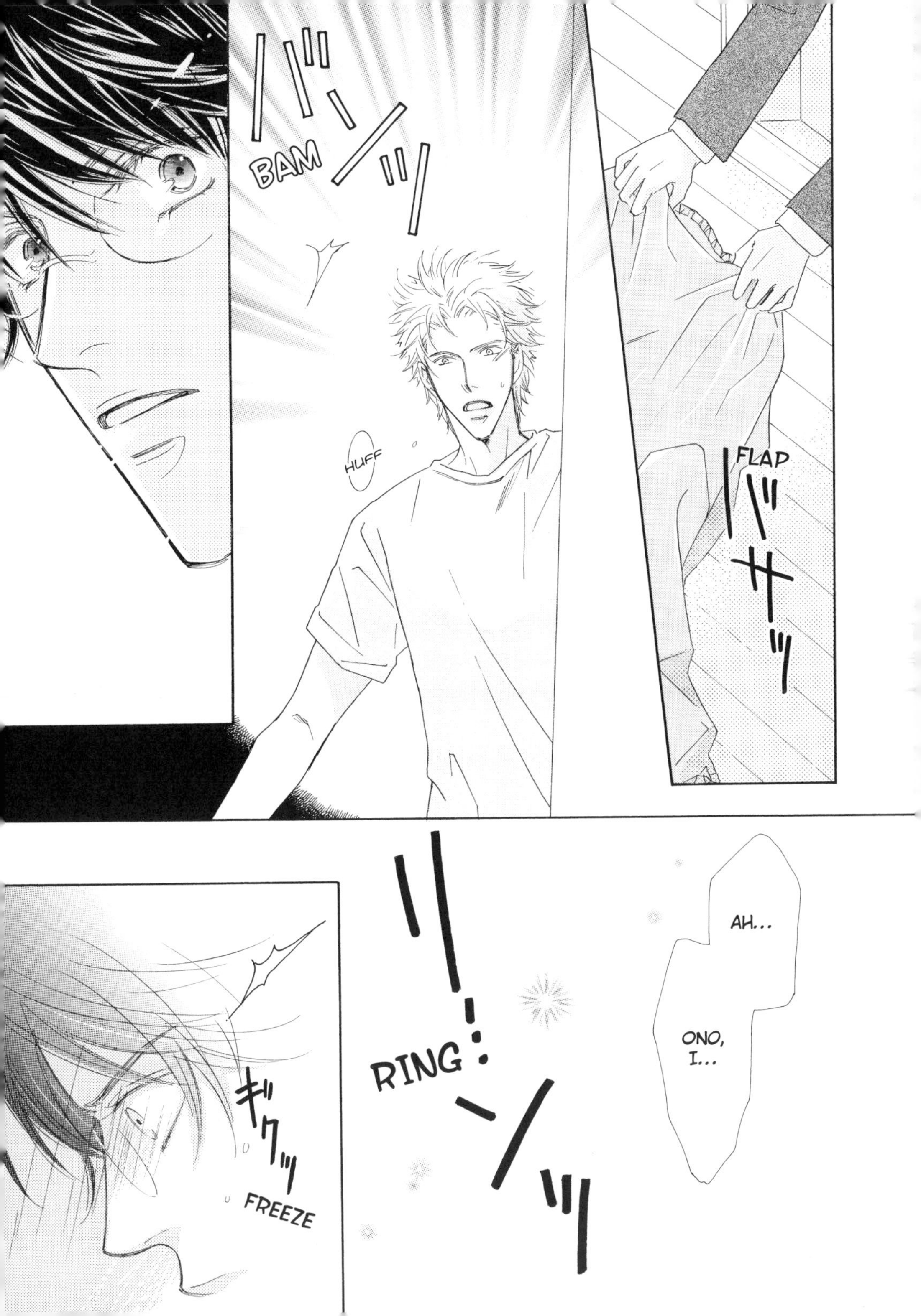
バサッ
FLAP
バンッ
BAM
HUFF
AH...
ONO, I...
リーンッ
RING
ギクッ
FREEZE

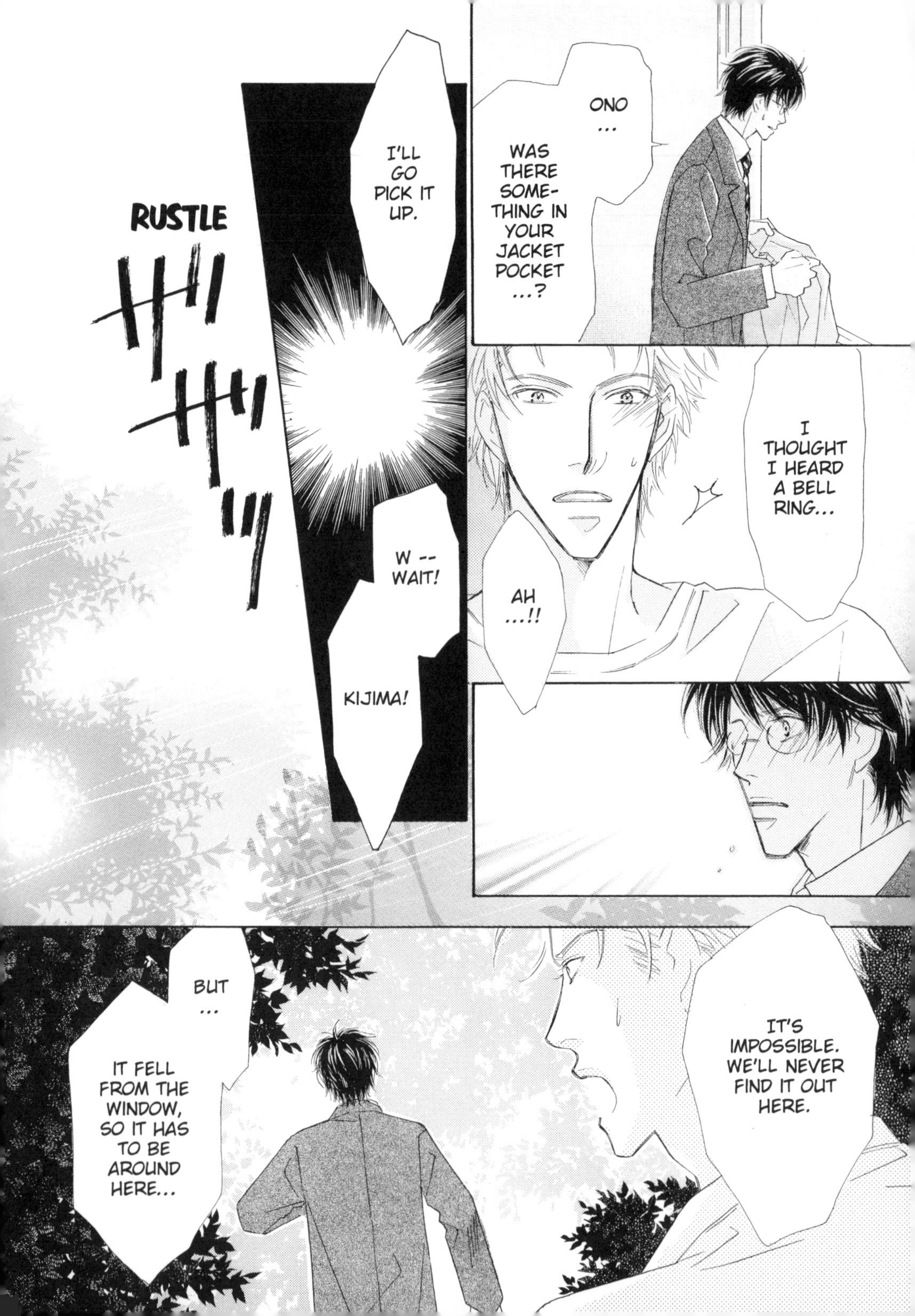
ONO ... WAS THERE SOMETHING IN YOUR JACKET POCKET ...?
I THOUGHT I HEARD A BELL RING...
AH ...!!
I'LL GO PICK IT UP.
RUSTLE
W -- WAIT!
KIJIMA!
IT'S IMPOSSIBLE. WE'LL NEVER FIND IT OUT HERE.
BUT ...
IT FELL FROM THE WINDOW, SO IT HAS TO BE AROUND HERE...

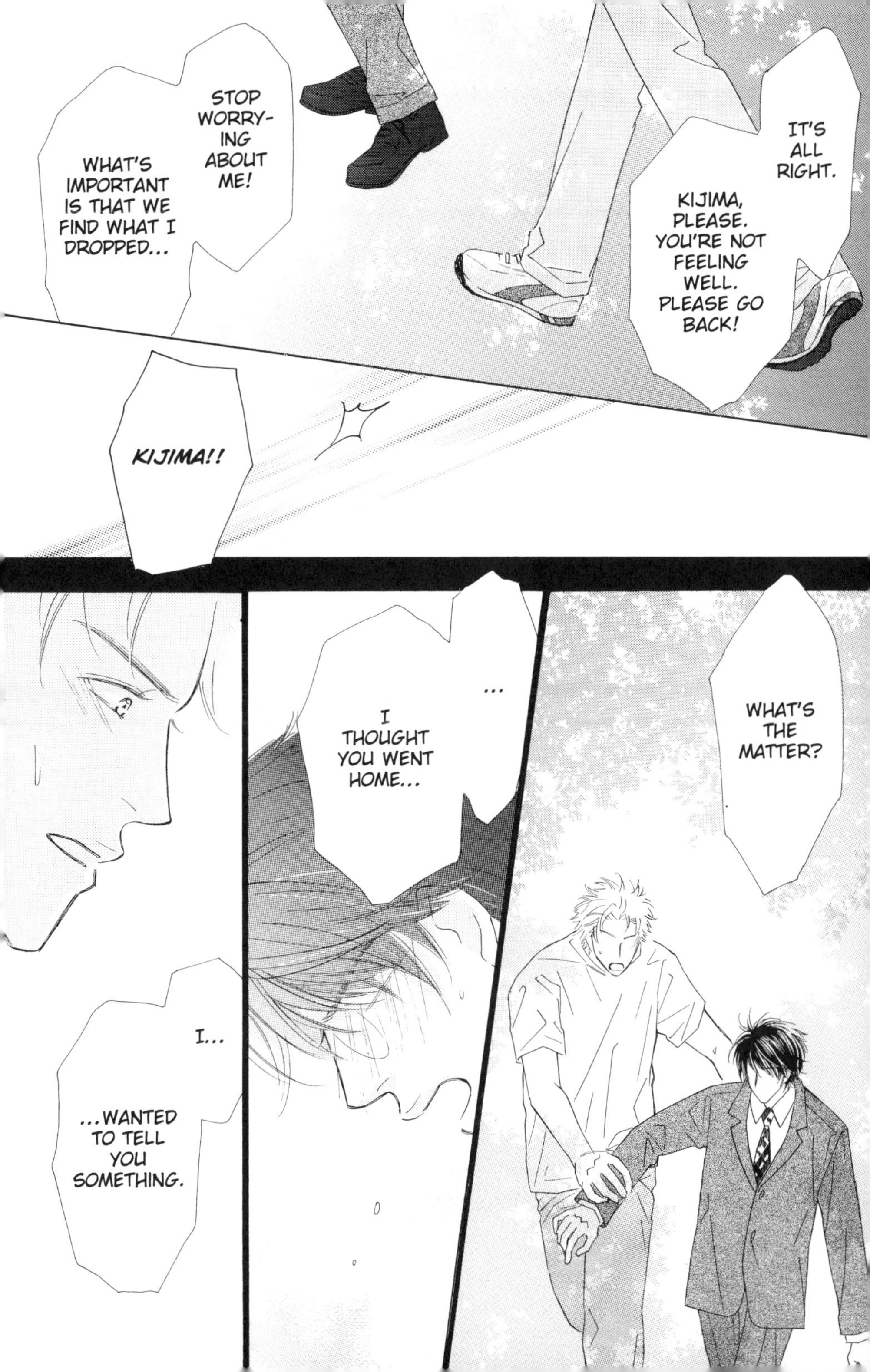
IT'S ALL RIGHT.
KIJIMA, PLEASE. YOU'RE NOT FEELING WELL. PLEASE GO BACK!
STOP WORRY-ING ABOUT ME!
WHAT'S IMPORTANT IS THAT WE FIND WHAT I DROPPED...
KIJIMA!!
WHAT'S THE MATTER?
...
I THOUGHT YOU WENT HOME...
I...
...WANTED TO TELL YOU SOMETHING.

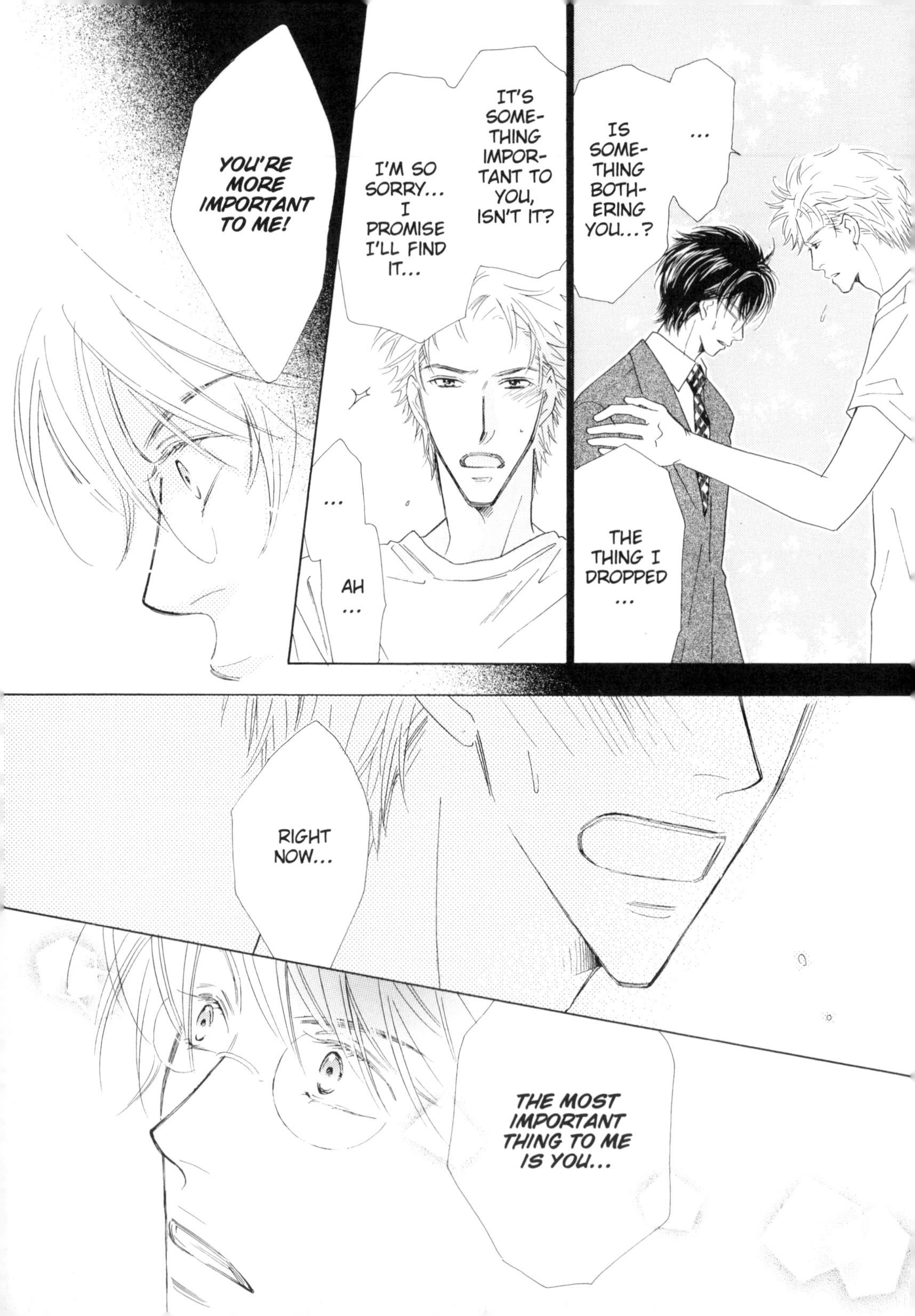
...
IS SOMETHING BOTHERING YOU...?
THE THING I DROPPED ...
IT'S SOMETHING IMPORTANT TO YOU, ISN'T IT?
I'M SO SORRY... I PROMISE I'LL FIND IT...
...
AH ...
YOU'RE MORE IMPORTANT TO ME!
RIGHT NOW...
THE MOST IMPORTANT THING TO ME IS YOU...

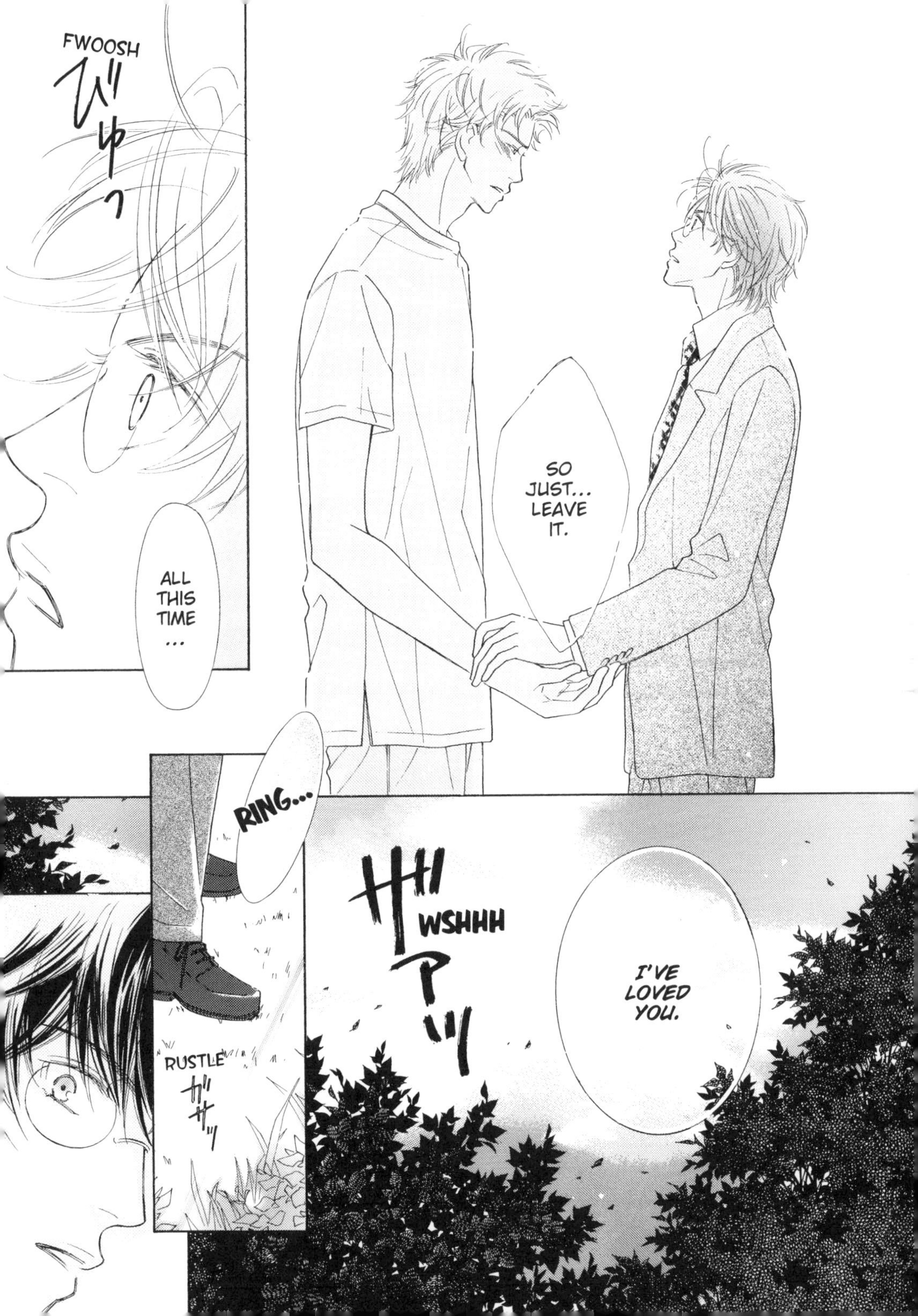
SO JUST... LEAVE IT.
FWOOSH
びゅっ
ALL THIS TIME...
ザアッ
WSHHH
I'VE LOVED YOU.
RING...
RUSTLE
ガサッ

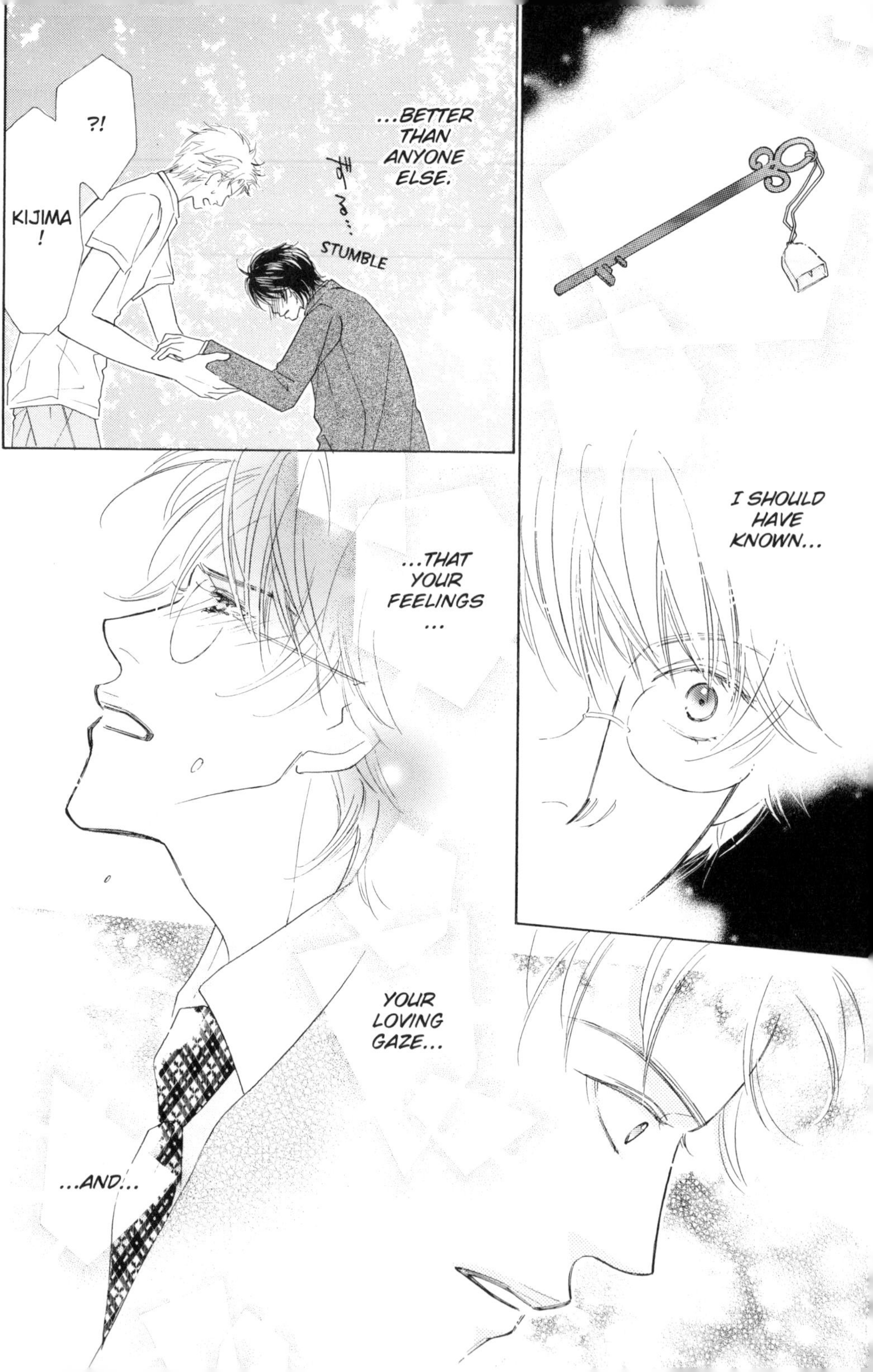
...BETTER THAN ANYONE ELSE.
STUMBLE
?!
KIJIMA!
I SHOULD HAVE KNOWN...
...THAT YOUR FEELINGS...
YOUR LOVING GAZE...
...AND...

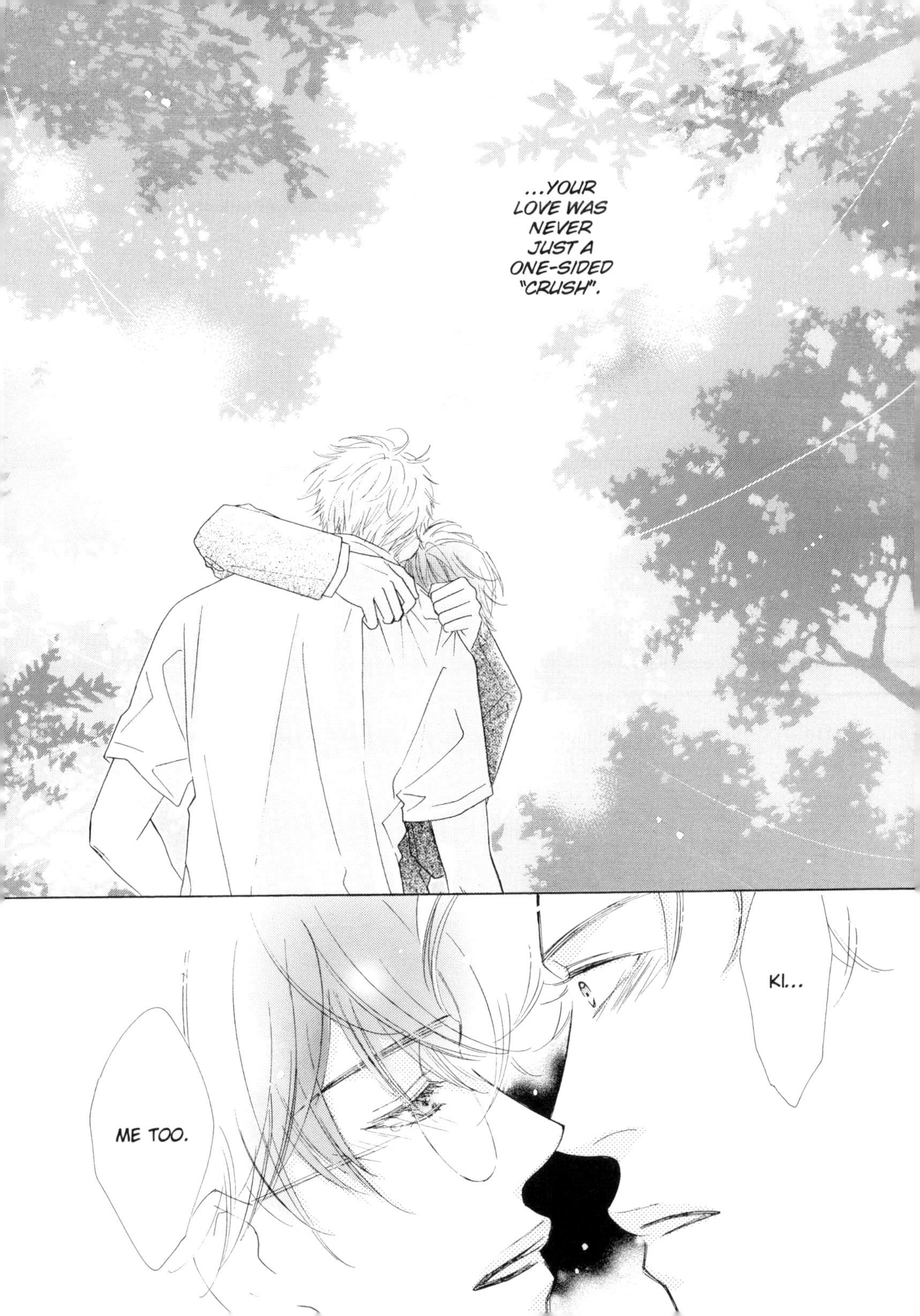
...YOUR LOVE WAS NEVER JUST A ONE-SIDED "CRUSH".
KI...
ME TOO.

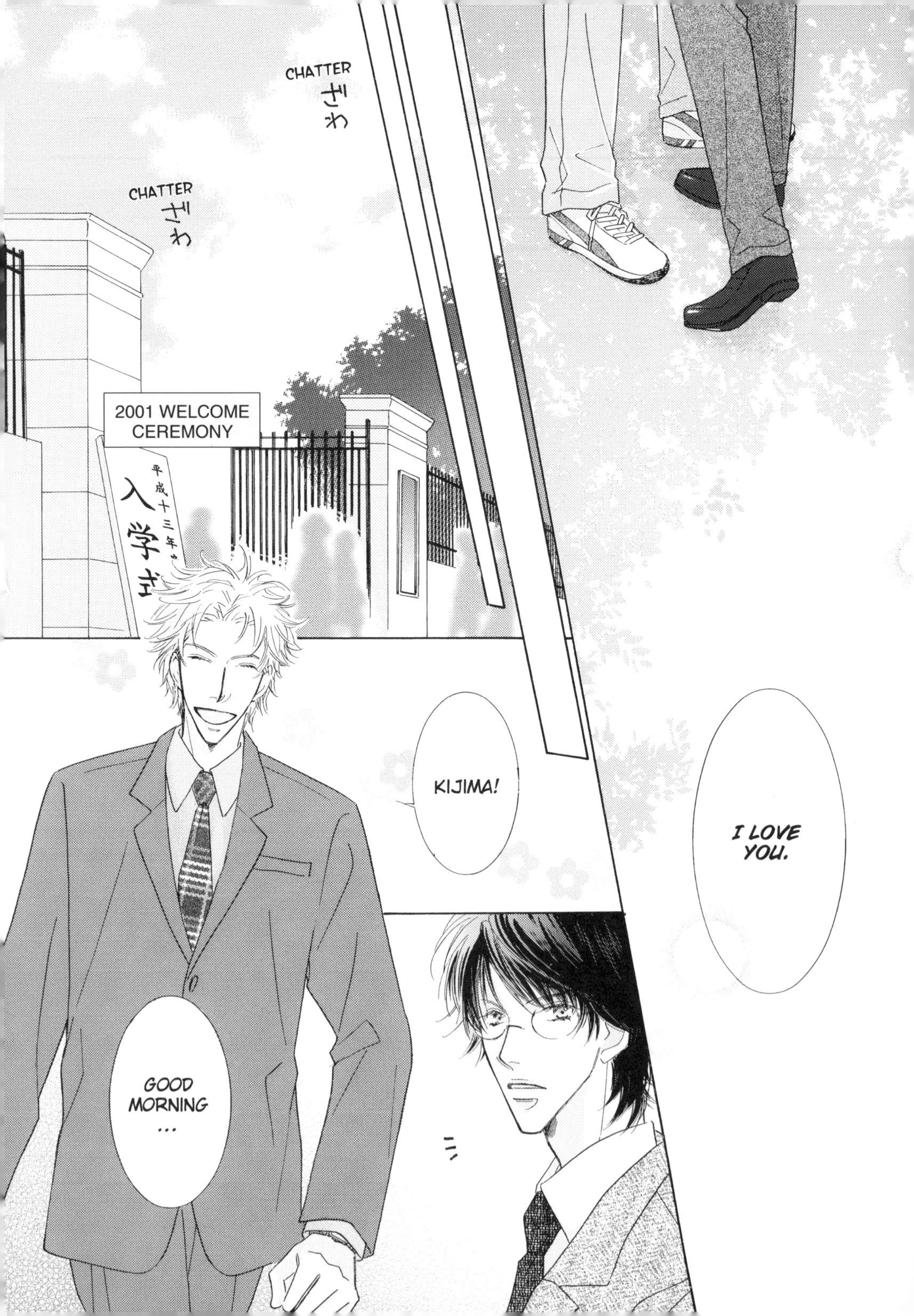
CHATTER
ざわ
CHATTER
ざわ
2001 WELCOME CEREMONY
I LOVE YOU.
KIJIMA!
GOOD MORNING ...

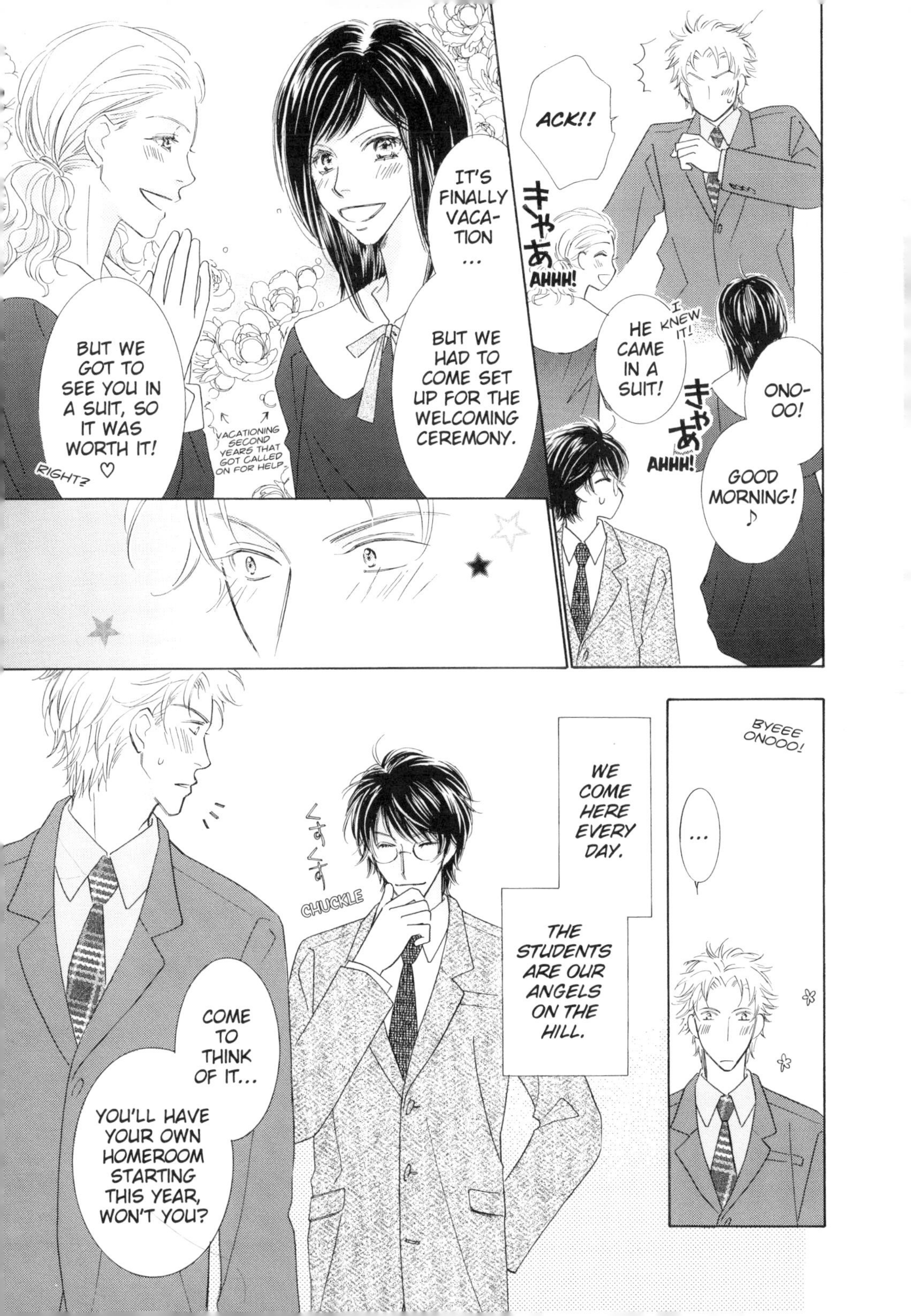
ACK!!
きゃあ AHHH!
ONO-OO!
GOOD MORNING! ♪
きゃあ AHHH!
I KNEW IT!
HE CAME IN A SUIT!
IT'S FINALLY VACATION...
BUT WE HAD TO COME SET UP FOR THE WELCOMING CEREMONY.
VACATIONING SECOND YEARS THAT GOT CALLED ON FOR HELP
BUT WE GOT TO SEE YOU IN A SUIT, SO IT WAS WORTH IT! ♡
RIGHT?
BYEEE ONOOO!
...
WE COME HERE EVERY DAY.
THE STUDENTS ARE OUR ANGELS ON THE HILL.
くすくす CHUCKLE
COME TO THINK OF IT...
YOU'LL HAVE YOUR OWN HOMEROOM STARTING THIS YEAR, WON'T YOU?

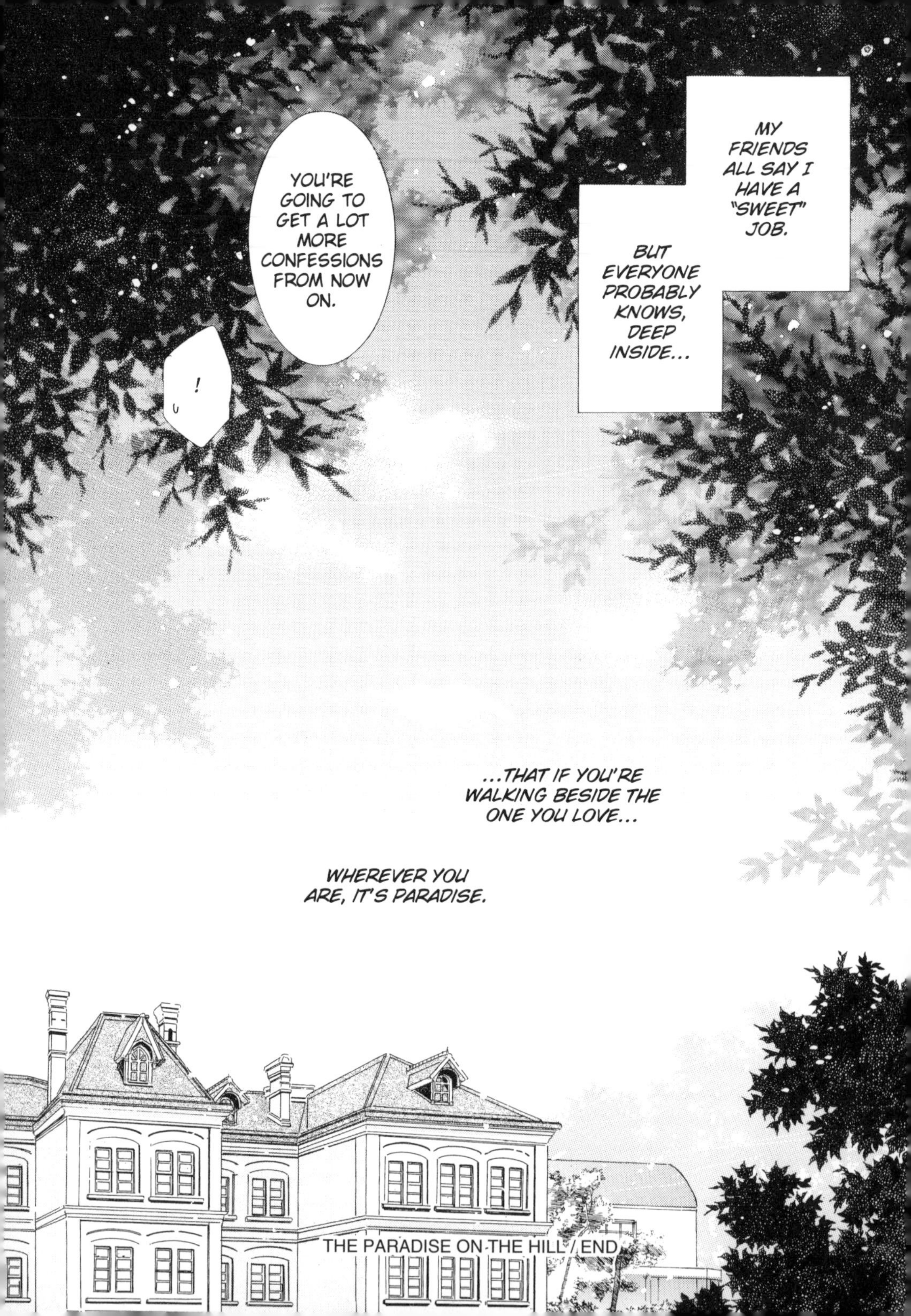
MY FRIENDS ALL SAY I HAVE A "SWEET" JOB.
BUT EVERYONE PROBABLY KNOWS, DEEP INSIDE...
YOU'RE GOING TO GET A LOT MORE CONFESSIONS FROM NOW ON.
!
...THAT IF YOU'RE WALKING BESIDE THE ONE YOU LOVE...
WHEREVER YOU ARE, IT'S PARADISE.
THE PARADISE ON THE HILL / END

DATE

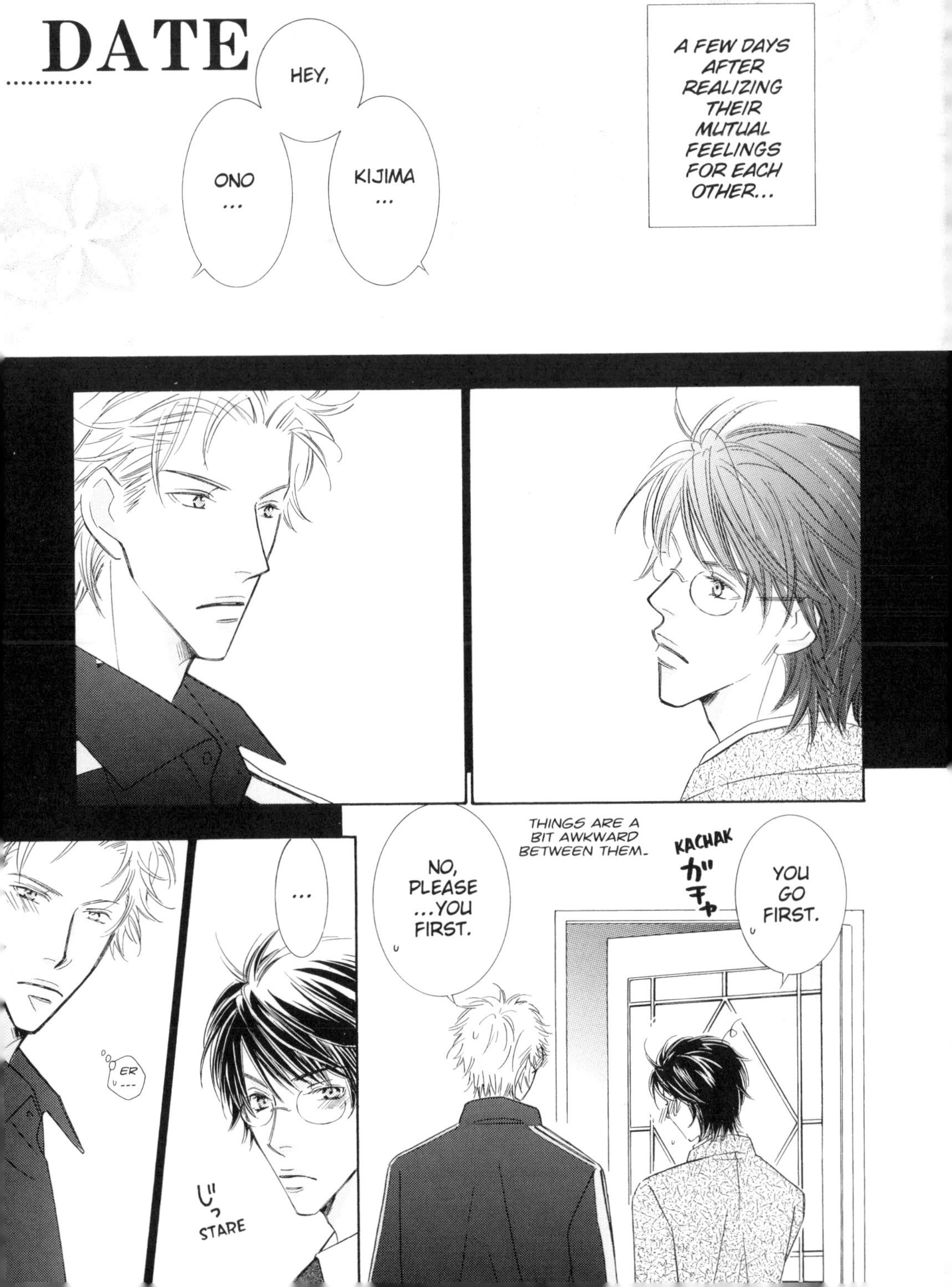
A FEW DAYS AFTER REALIZING THEIR MUTUAL FEELINGS FOR EACH OTHER...
HEY,
KIJIMA ...
ONO ...
YOU GO FIRST.
KACHAK
ガチャ
THINGS ARE A BIT AWKWARD BETWEEN THEM.
NO, PLEASE ...YOU FIRST.
...
ER ---
じっ
STARE

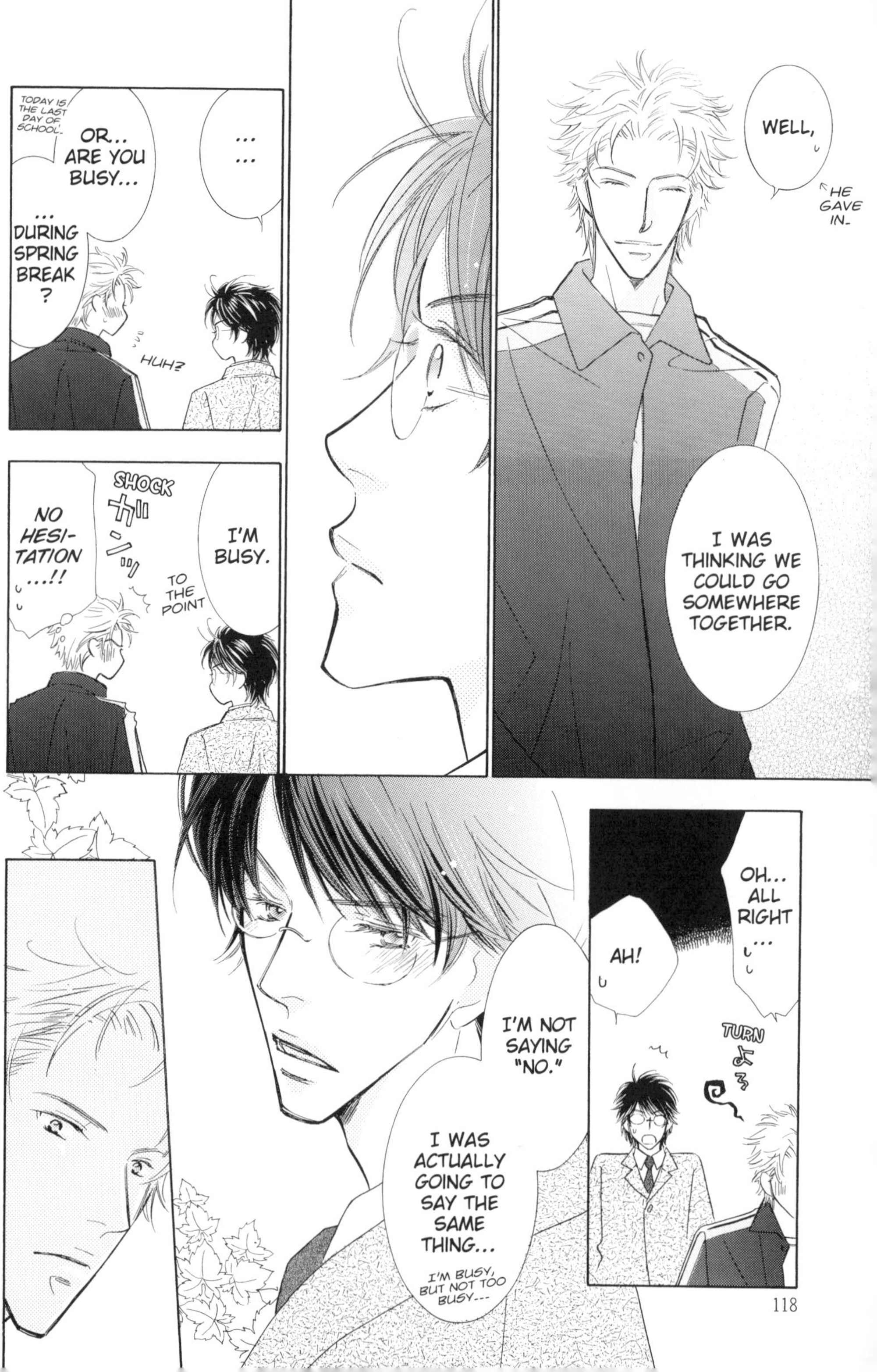
WELL,
HE GAVE IN.
I WAS THINKING WE COULD GO SOMEWHERE TOGETHER.
... ...
OR... ARE YOU BUSY...
TODAY IS THE LAST DAY OF SCHOOL.
... DURING SPRING BREAK?
HUH?
I'M BUSY.
TO THE POINT
SHOCK
NO HESITATION ...!!
OH... ALL RIGHT...
AH!
TURN
I'M NOT SAYING "NO."
I WAS ACTUALLY GOING TO SAY THE SAME THING...
I'M BUSY, BUT NOT TOO BUSY...

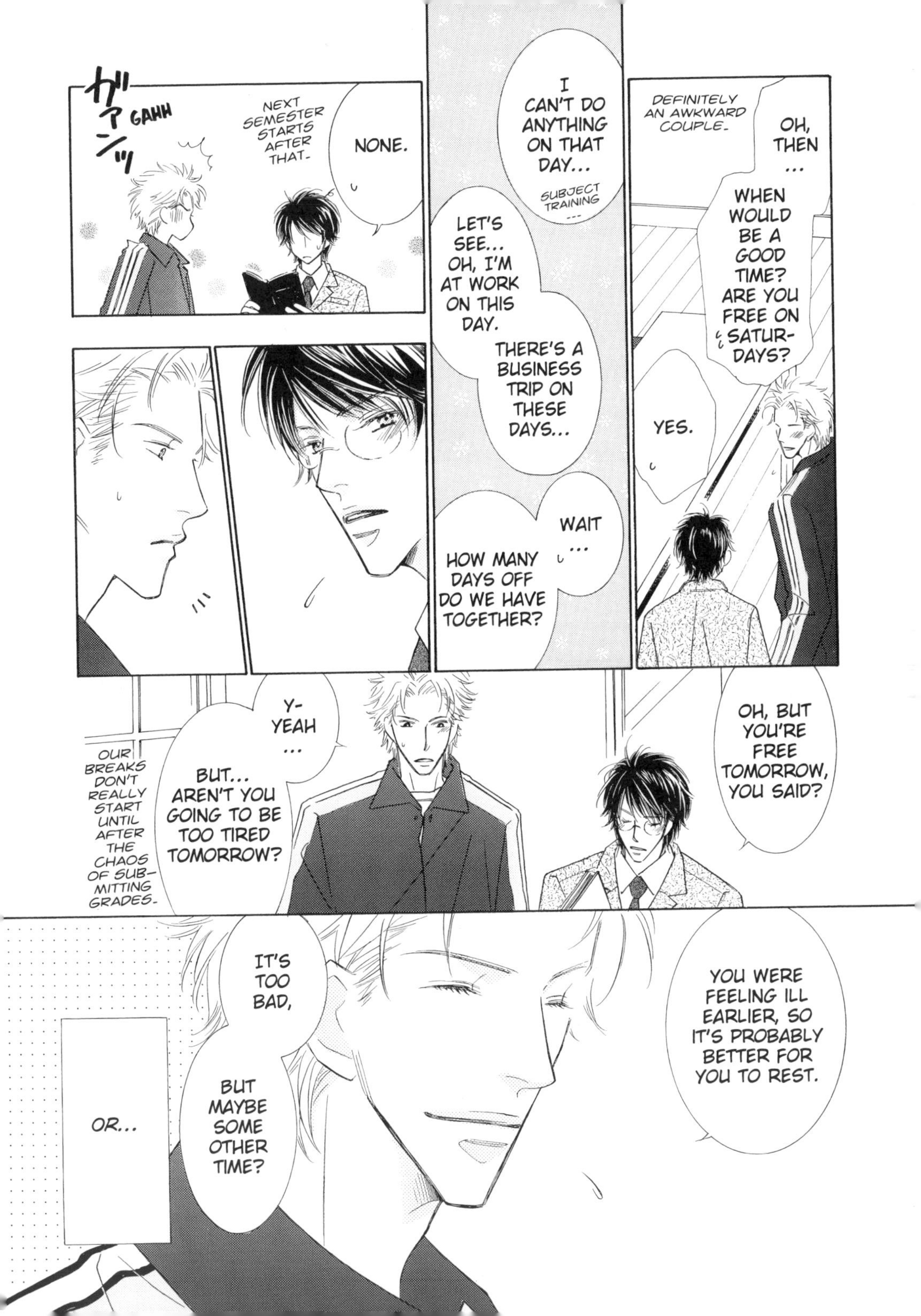
DEFINITELY AN AWKWARD COUPLE.
OH, THEN ...
WHEN WOULD BE A GOOD TIME? ARE YOU FREE ON SATURDAYS?
YES.
I CAN'T DO ANYTHING ON THAT DAY...
SUBJECT TRAINING ...
LET'S SEE... OH, I'M AT WORK ON THIS DAY.
THERE'S A BUSINESS TRIP ON THESE DAYS...
WAIT ...
HOW MANY DAYS OFF DO WE HAVE TOGETHER?
NONE.
NEXT SEMESTER STARTS AFTER THAT.
GAHH
OH, BUT YOU'RE FREE TOMORROW, YOU SAID?
Y-YEAH ...
BUT... AREN'T YOU GOING TO BE TOO TIRED TOMORROW?
OUR BREAKS DON'T REALLY START UNTIL AFTER THE CHAOS OF SUBMITTING GRADES.
YOU WERE FEELING ILL EARLIER, SO IT'S PROBABLY BETTER FOR YOU TO REST.
IT'S TOO BAD,
BUT MAYBE SOME OTHER TIME?
OR...

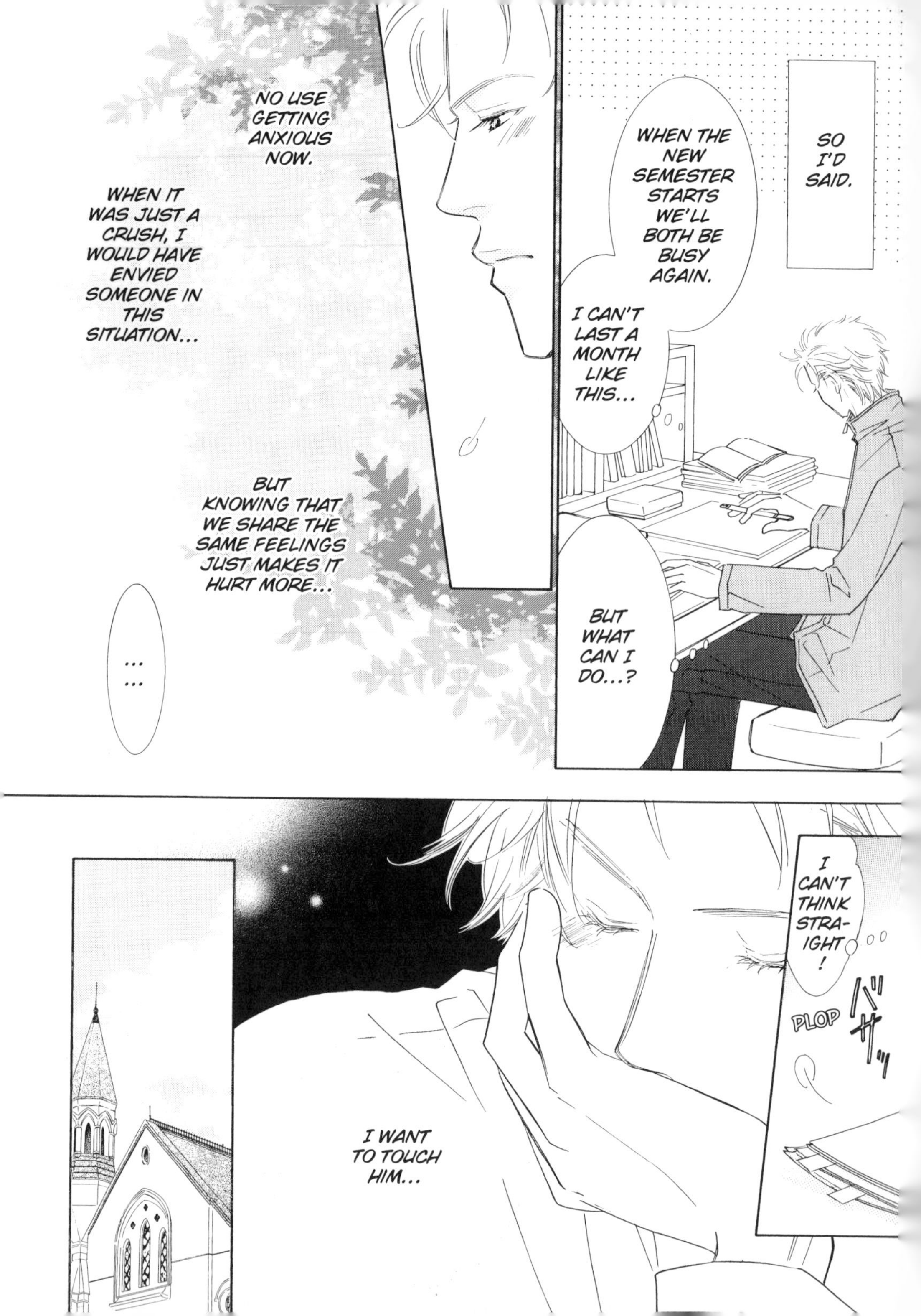
SO I'D SAID.
WHEN THE NEW SEMESTER STARTS WE'LL BOTH BE BUSY AGAIN.
I CAN'T LAST A MONTH LIKE THIS...
BUT WHAT CAN I DO...?
NO USE GETTING ANXIOUS NOW.
WHEN IT WAS JUST A CRUSH, I WOULD HAVE ENVIED SOMEONE IN THIS SITUATION...
BUT KNOWING THAT WE SHARE THE SAME FEELINGS JUST MAKES IT HURT MORE...
......
I CAN'T THINK STRAIGHT!
バサッ
PLOP
I WANT TO TOUCH HIM...

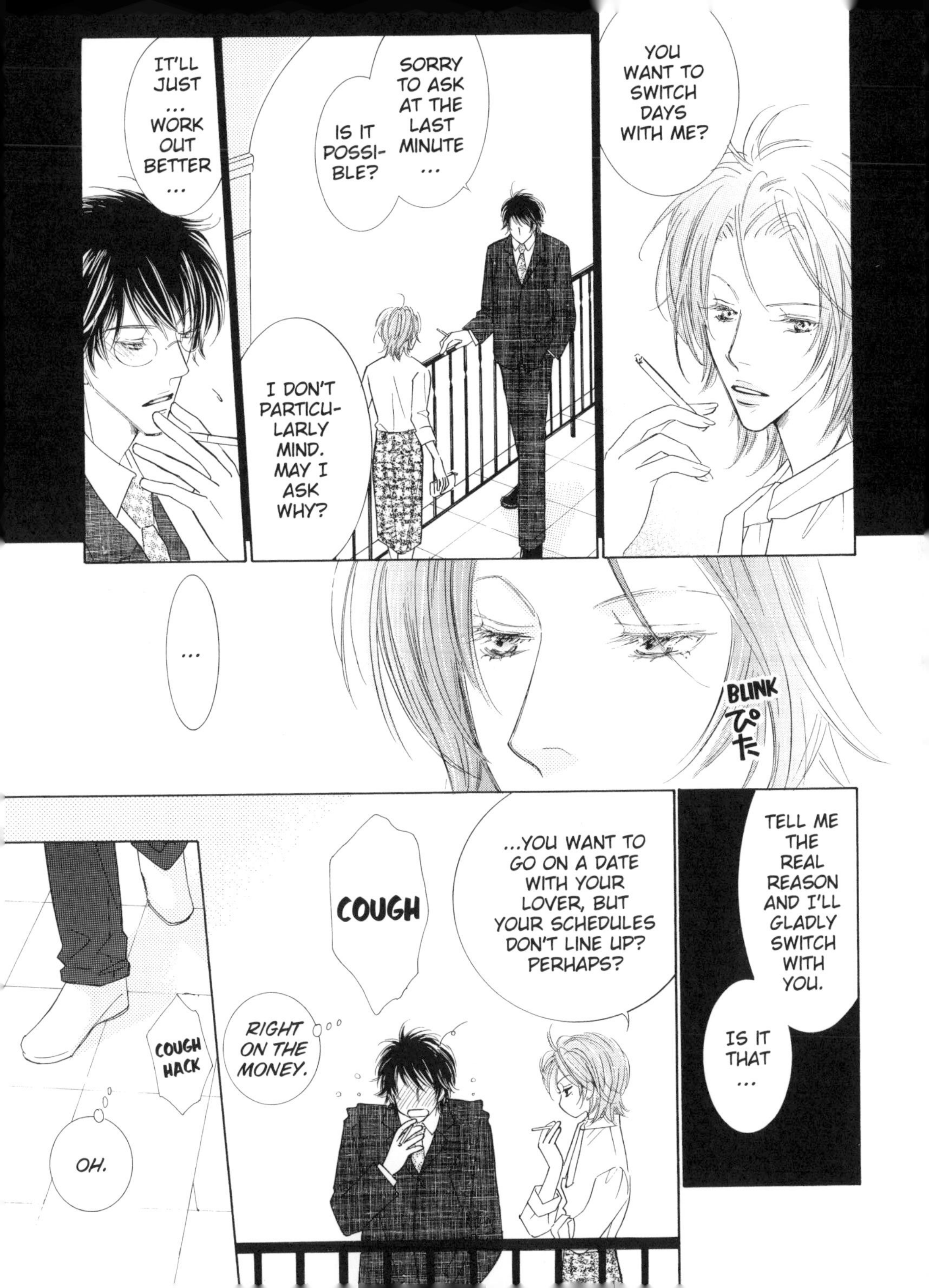
YOU WANT TO SWITCH DAYS WITH ME?
SORRY TO ASK AT THE LAST MINUTE ...
IS IT POSSIBLE?
I DON'T PARTICULARLY MIND. MAY I ASK WHY?
IT'LL JUST ... WORK OUT BETTER ...
BLINK
ぴた
...
TELL ME THE REAL REASON AND I'LL GLADLY SWITCH WITH YOU.
IS IT THAT ...
...YOU WANT TO GO ON A DATE WITH YOUR LOVER, BUT YOUR SCHEDULES DON'T LINE UP? PERHAPS?
COUGH
RIGHT ON THE MONEY.
COUGH HACK
OH.

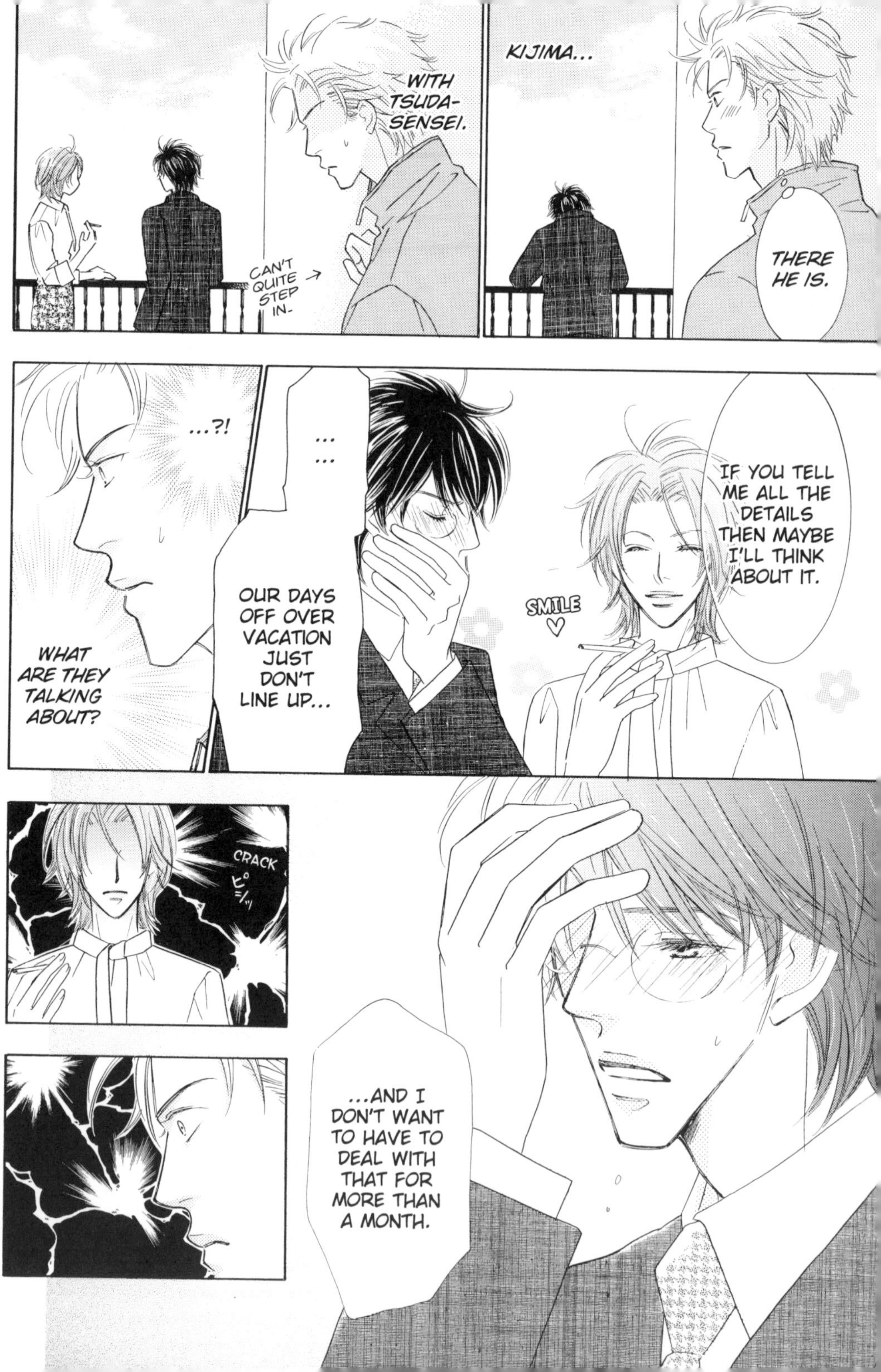
KIJIMA...
THERE HE IS.
WITH TSUDA-SENSEI.
CAN'T QUITE STEP IN.
IF YOU TELL ME ALL THE DETAILS THEN MAYBE I'LL THINK ABOUT IT.
SMILE ♥
... ...
OUR DAYS OFF OVER VACATION JUST DON'T LINE UP...
...?!
WHAT ARE THEY TALKING ABOUT?
...AND I DON'T WANT TO HAVE TO DEAL WITH THAT FOR MORE THAN A MONTH.
CRACK
ピシッ

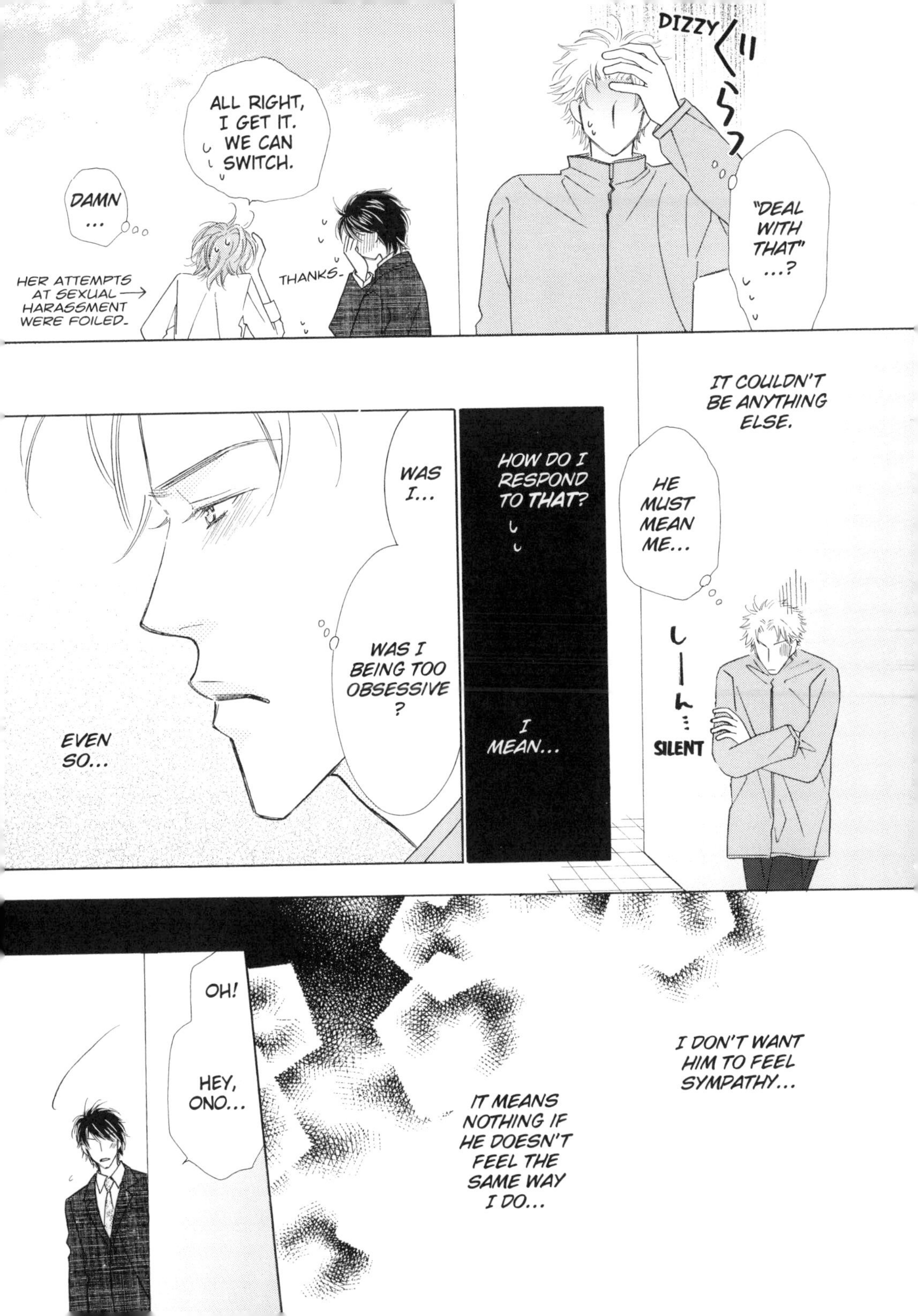
DIZZY
ぐらっ
"DEAL WITH THAT" ...?
ALL RIGHT, I GET IT. WE CAN SWITCH.
DAMN ...
THANKS.
HER ATTEMPTS AT SEXUAL HARASSMENT WERE FOILED.
IT COULDN'T BE ANYTHING ELSE.
HE MUST MEAN ME...
しーん
SILENT
HOW DO I RESPOND TO THAT?
I MEAN...
WAS I...
WAS I BEING TOO OBSESSIVE ?
EVEN SO...
I DON'T WANT HIM TO FEEL SYMPATHY...
IT MEANS NOTHING IF HE DOESN'T FEEL THE SAME WAY I DO...
OH!
HEY, ONO...

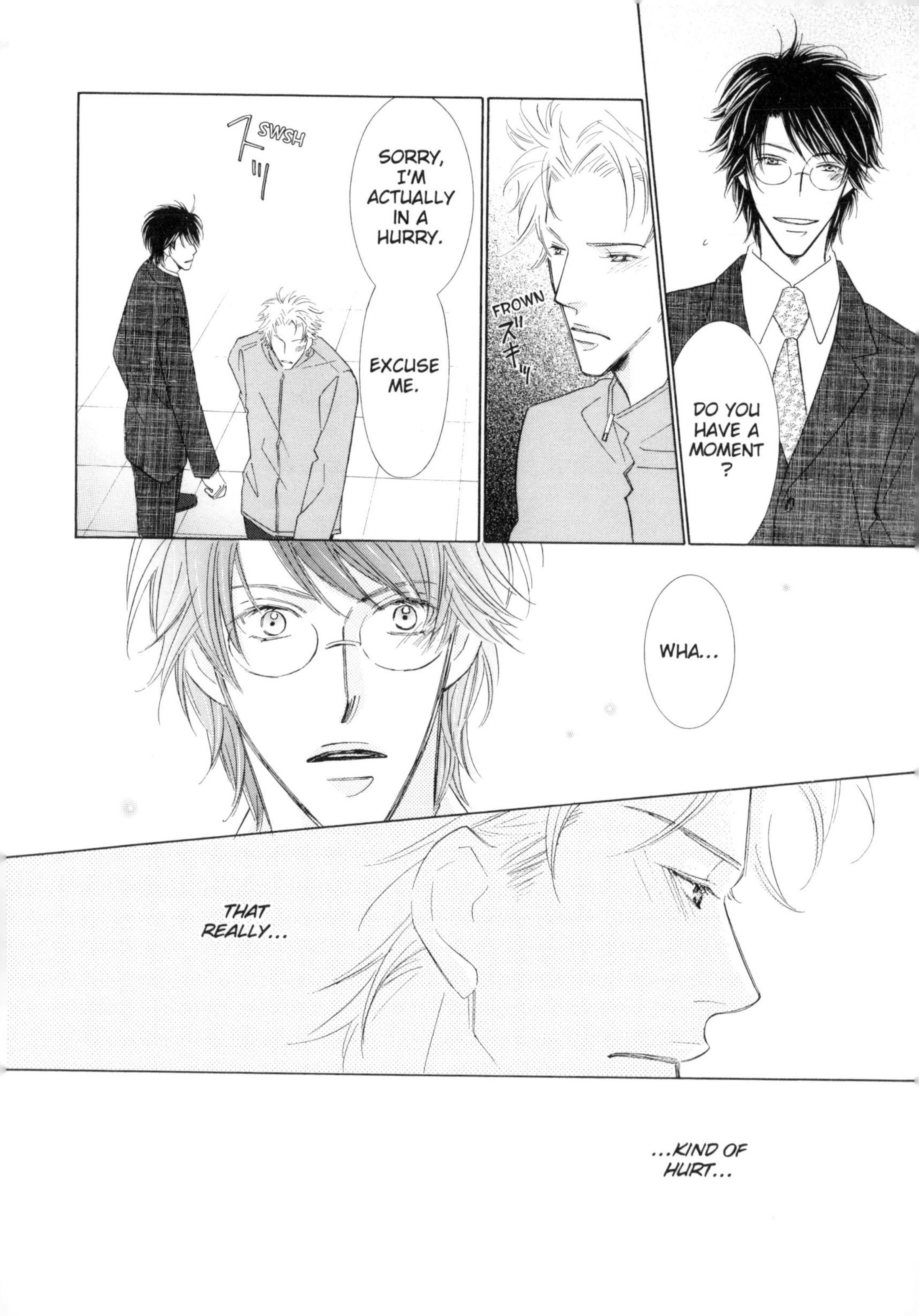

DO YOU HAVE A MOMENT ?
FROWN
ズキッ
SWSH
スッ
SORRY, I'M ACTUALLY IN A HURRY.
EXCUSE ME.
WHA...
THAT REALLY...
...KIND OF HURT...

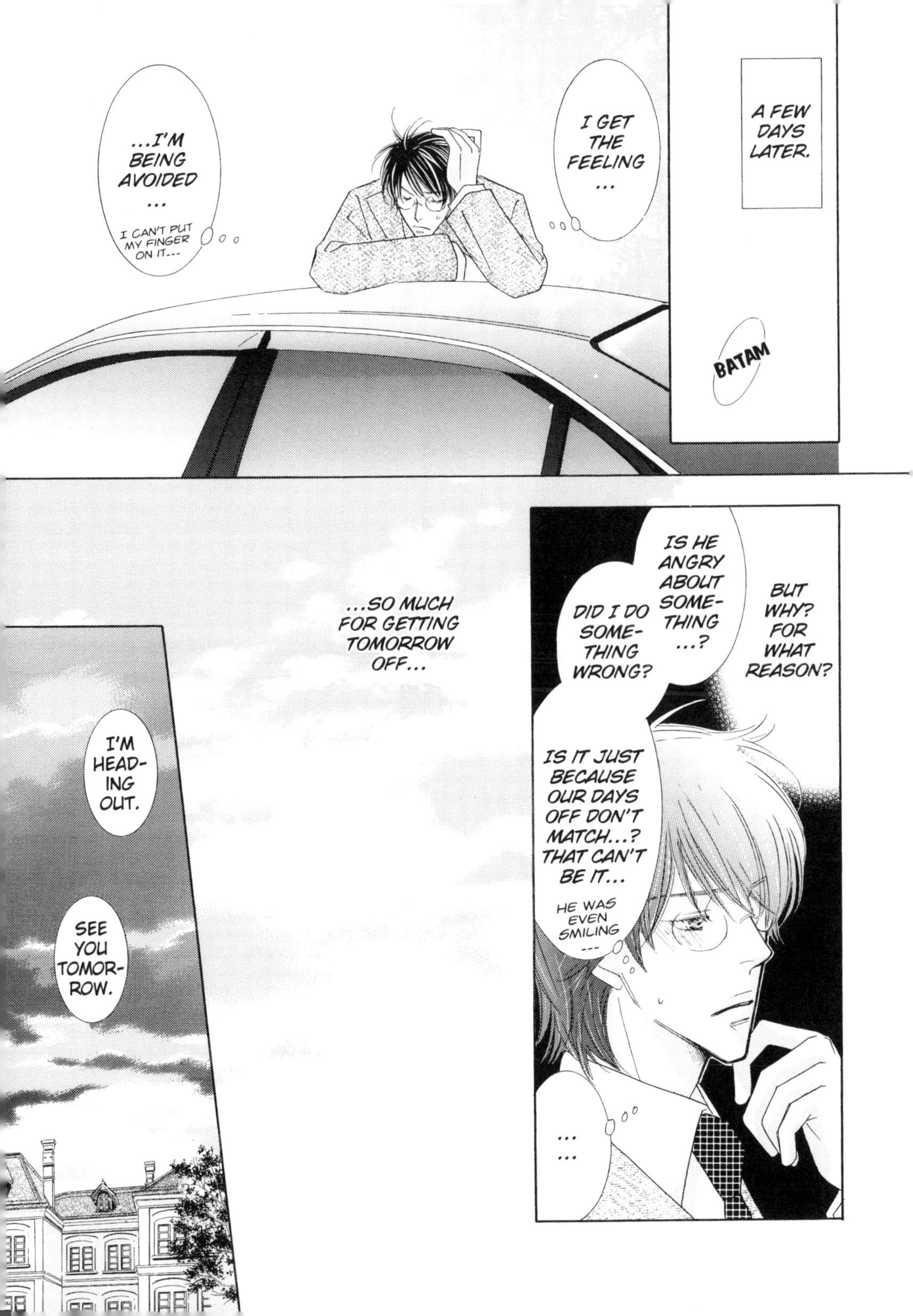

A FEW DAYS LATER.
BATAM
I GET THE FEELING ...
...I'M BEING AVOIDED ...
I CAN'T PUT MY FINGER ON IT---
BUT WHY? FOR WHAT REASON?
IS HE ANGRY ABOUT SOMETHING ...?
DID I DO SOMETHING WRONG?
IS IT JUST BECAUSE OUR DAYS OFF DON'T MATCH...? THAT CAN'T BE IT...
HE WAS EVEN SMILING ---
... ...
...SO MUCH FOR GETTING TOMORROW OFF...
I'M HEADING OUT.
SEE YOU TOMORROW.

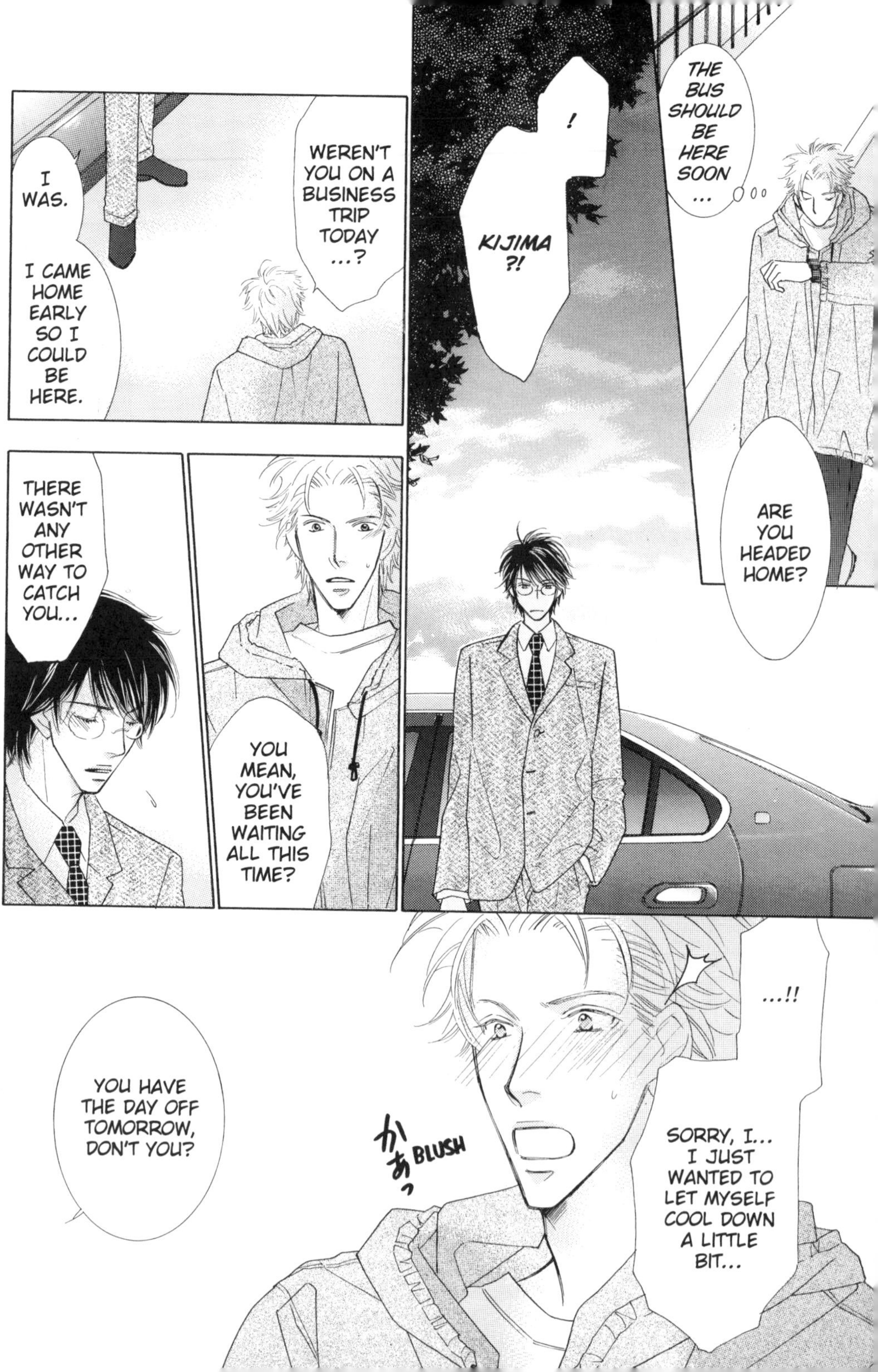
THE BUS SHOULD BE HERE SOON ...
ARE YOU HEADED HOME?
!
KIJIMA ?!
WEREN'T YOU ON A BUSINESS TRIP TODAY ...?
I WAS.
I CAME HOME EARLY SO I COULD BE HERE.
YOU MEAN, YOU'VE BEEN WAITING ALL THIS TIME?
THERE WASN'T ANY OTHER WAY TO CATCH YOU...
...!!
SORRY, I... I JUST WANTED TO LET MYSELF COOL DOWN A LITTLE BIT...
かあっ BLUSH
YOU HAVE THE DAY OFF TOMORROW, DON'T YOU?

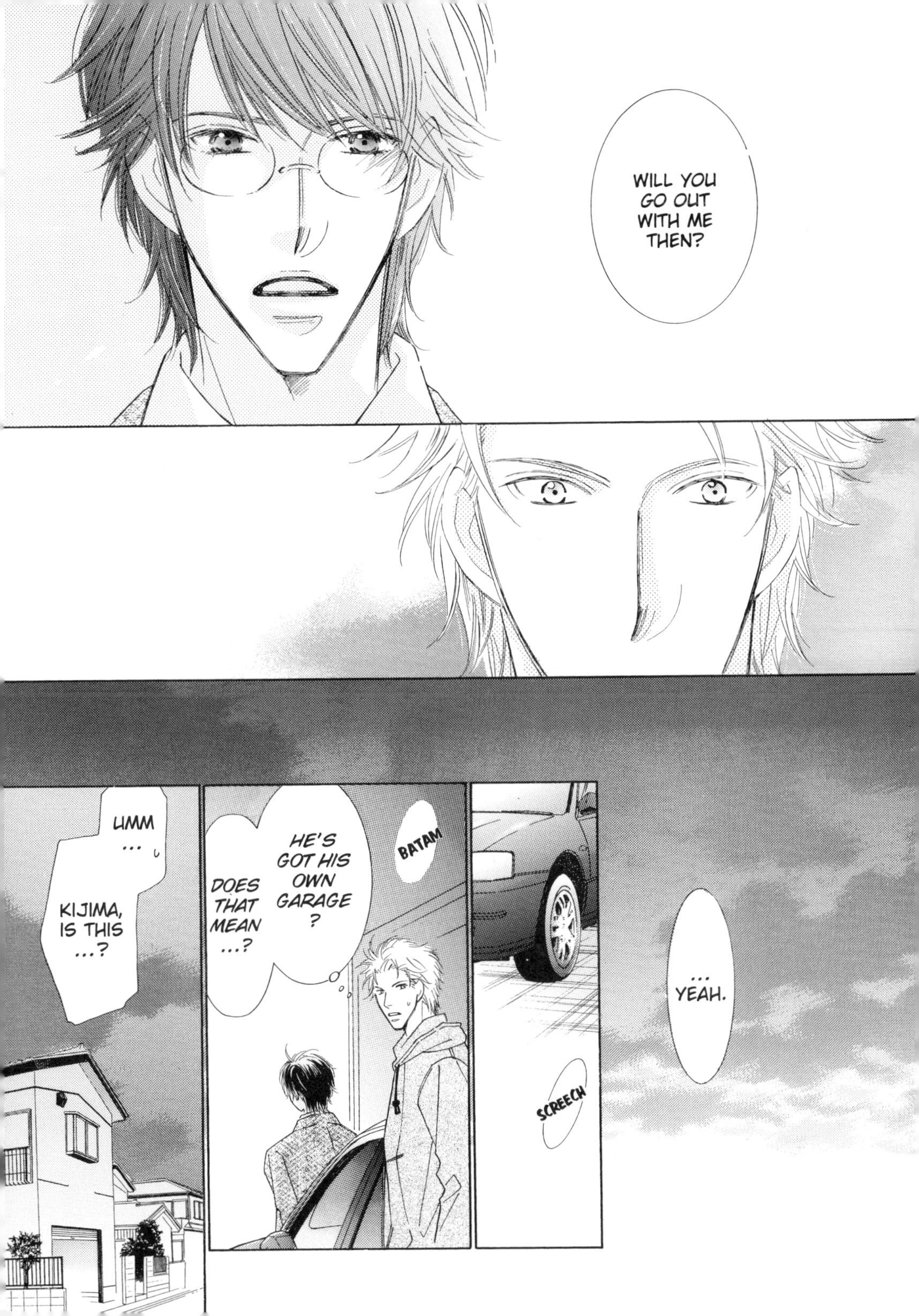
WILL YOU GO OUT WITH ME THEN?
... YEAH.
SCREECH
BATAM
HE'S GOT HIS OWN GARAGE?
DOES THAT MEAN ...?
UMM ...
KIJIMA, IS THIS ...?

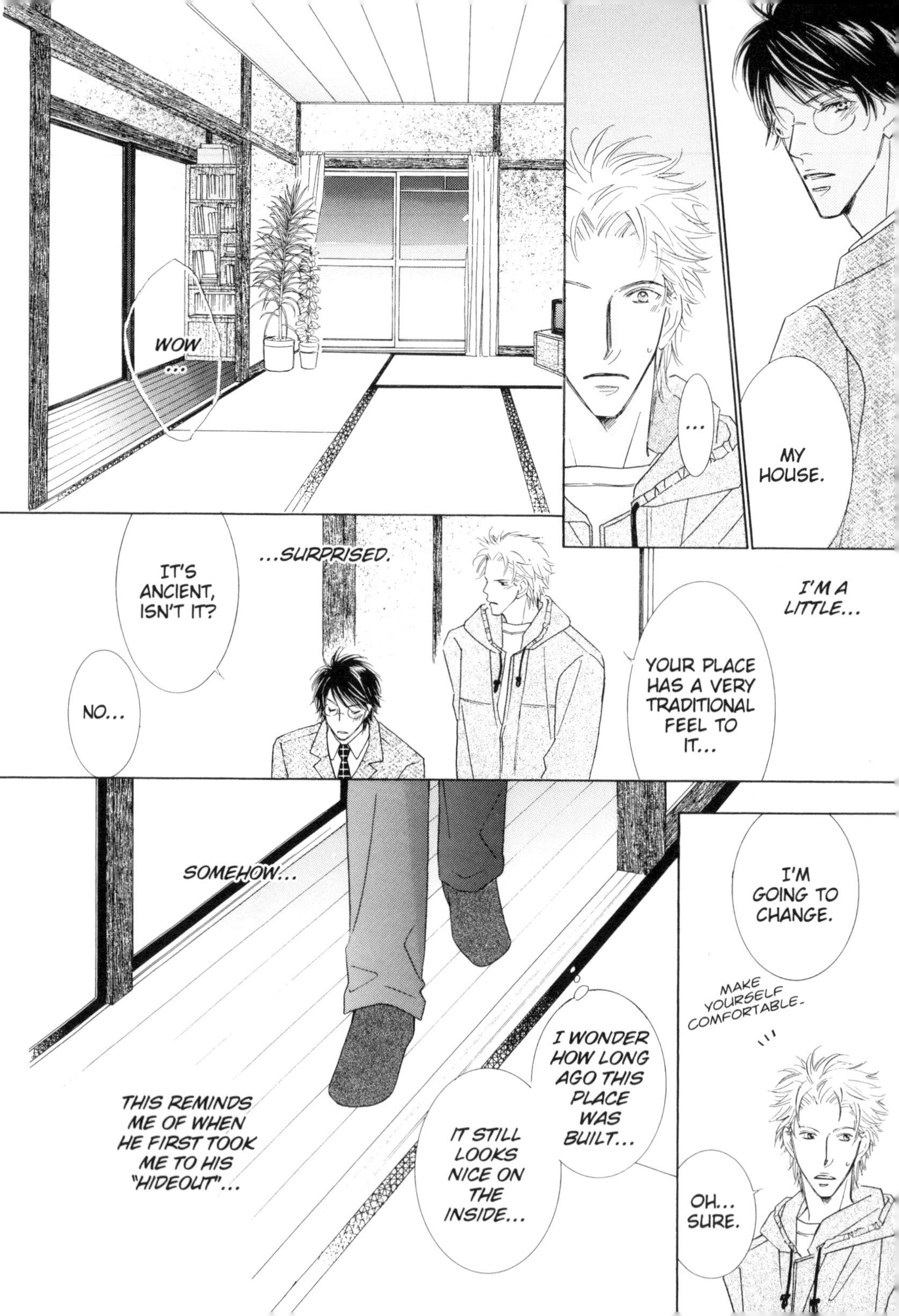
MY HOUSE.
...
WOW ...
I'M A LITTLE...
YOUR PLACE HAS A VERY TRADITIONAL FEEL TO IT...
...SURPRISED.
IT'S ANCIENT, ISN'T IT?
NO...
I'M GOING TO CHANGE.
MAKE YOURSELF COMFORTABLE.
OH... SURE.
SOMEHOW...
I WONDER HOW LONG AGO THIS PLACE WAS BUILT...
IT STILL LOOKS NICE ON THE INSIDE...
THIS REMINDS ME OF WHEN HE FIRST TOOK ME TO HIS "HIDEOUT"...

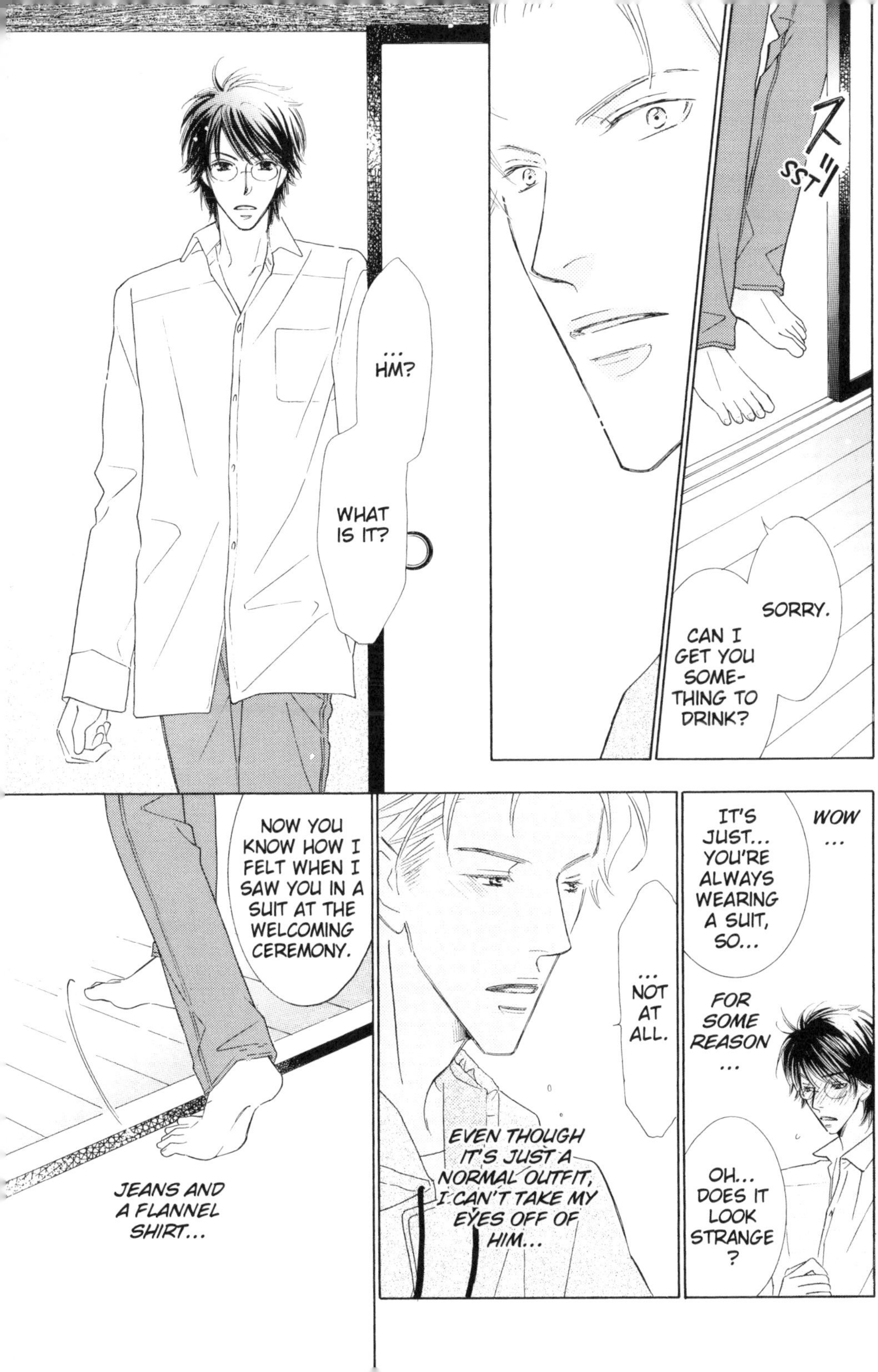
SST
SORRY.
CAN I GET YOU SOMETHING TO DRINK?
...HM?
WHAT IS IT?
WOW...
IT'S JUST... YOU'RE ALWAYS WEARING A SUIT, SO...
FOR SOME REASON...
OH... DOES IT LOOK STRANGE?
...NOT AT ALL.
EVEN THOUGH IT'S JUST A NORMAL OUTFIT, I CAN'T TAKE MY EYES OFF OF HIM...
NOW YOU KNOW HOW I FELT WHEN I SAW YOU IN A SUIT AT THE WELCOMING CEREMONY.
JEANS AND A FLANNEL SHIRT...

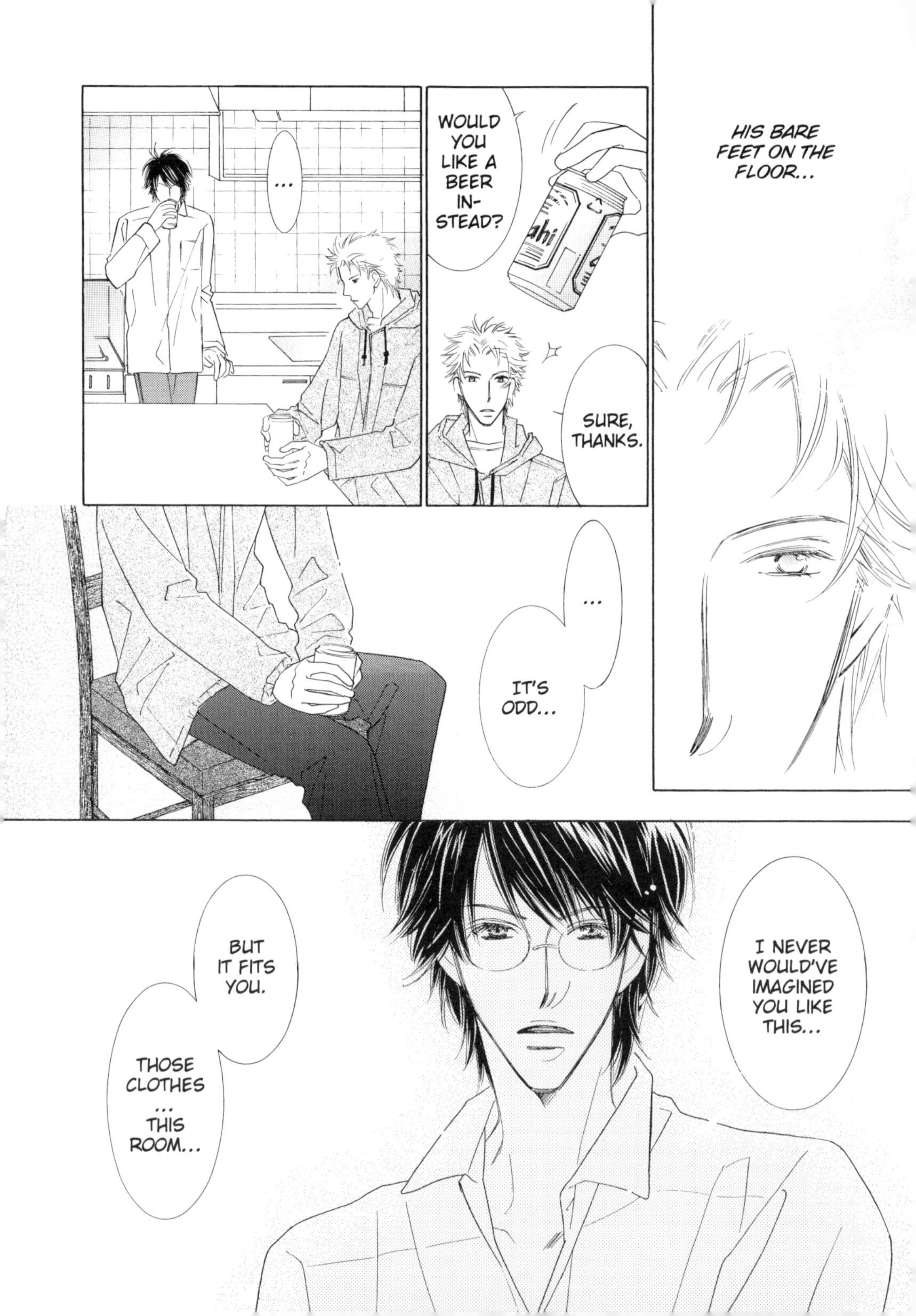
HIS BARE FEET ON THE FLOOR...
WOULD YOU LIKE A BEER IN-STEAD?
SURE, THANKS.
...
...
IT'S ODD...
I NEVER WOULD'VE IMAGINED YOU LIKE THIS...
BUT IT FITS YOU.
THOSE CLOTHES ... THIS ROOM...

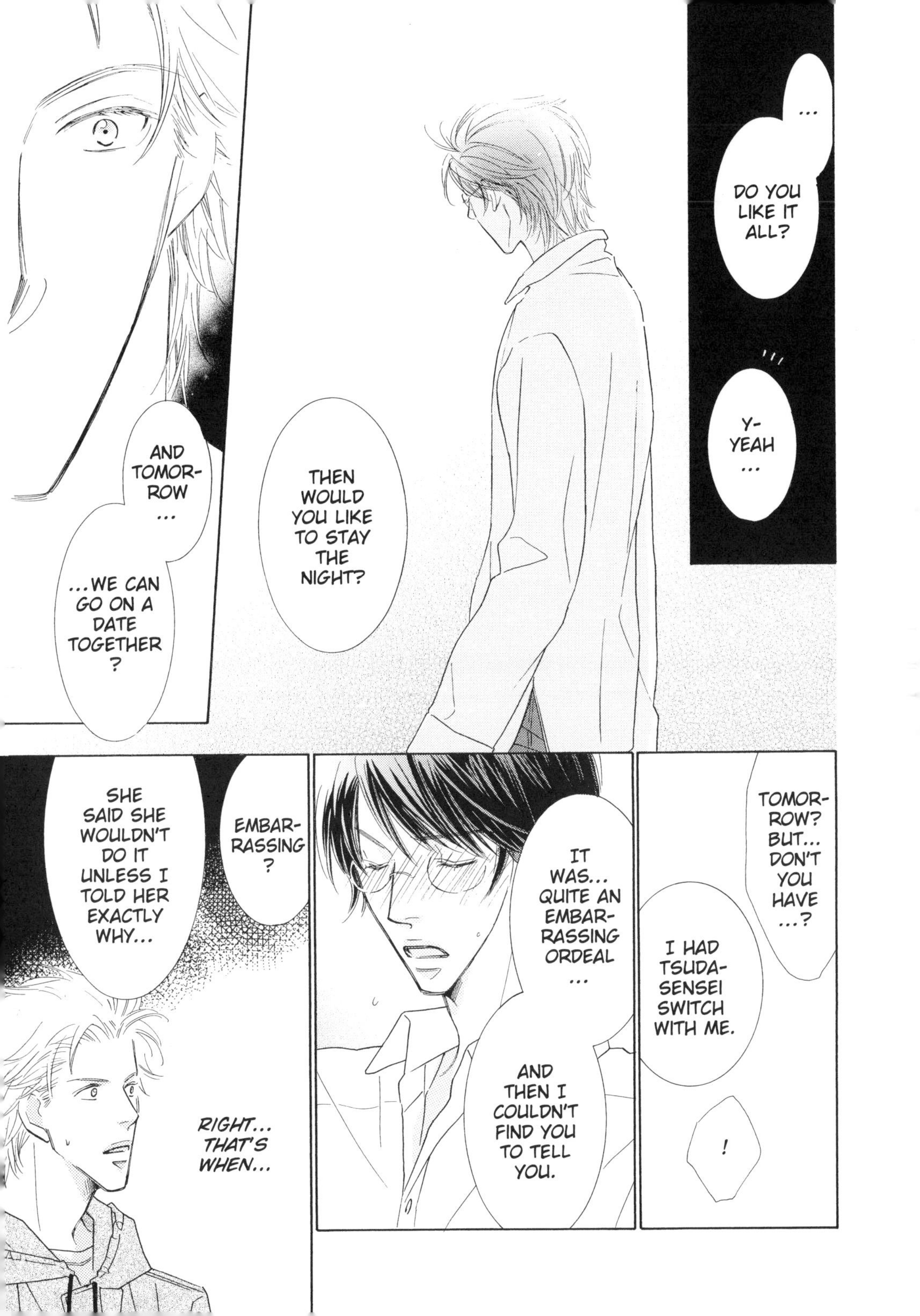
...
DO YOU LIKE IT ALL?
Y-YEAH...
THEN WOULD YOU LIKE TO STAY THE NIGHT?
AND TOMORROW...
...WE CAN GO ON A DATE TOGETHER?
TOMORROW? BUT... DON'T YOU HAVE...?
I HAD TSUDA-SENSEI SWITCH WITH ME.
!
IT WAS... QUITE AN EMBARRASSING ORDEAL...
AND THEN I COULDN'T FIND YOU TO TELL YOU.
EMBARRASSING?
SHE SAID SHE WOULDN'T DO IT UNLESS I TOLD HER EXACTLY WHY...
RIGHT... THAT'S WHEN...

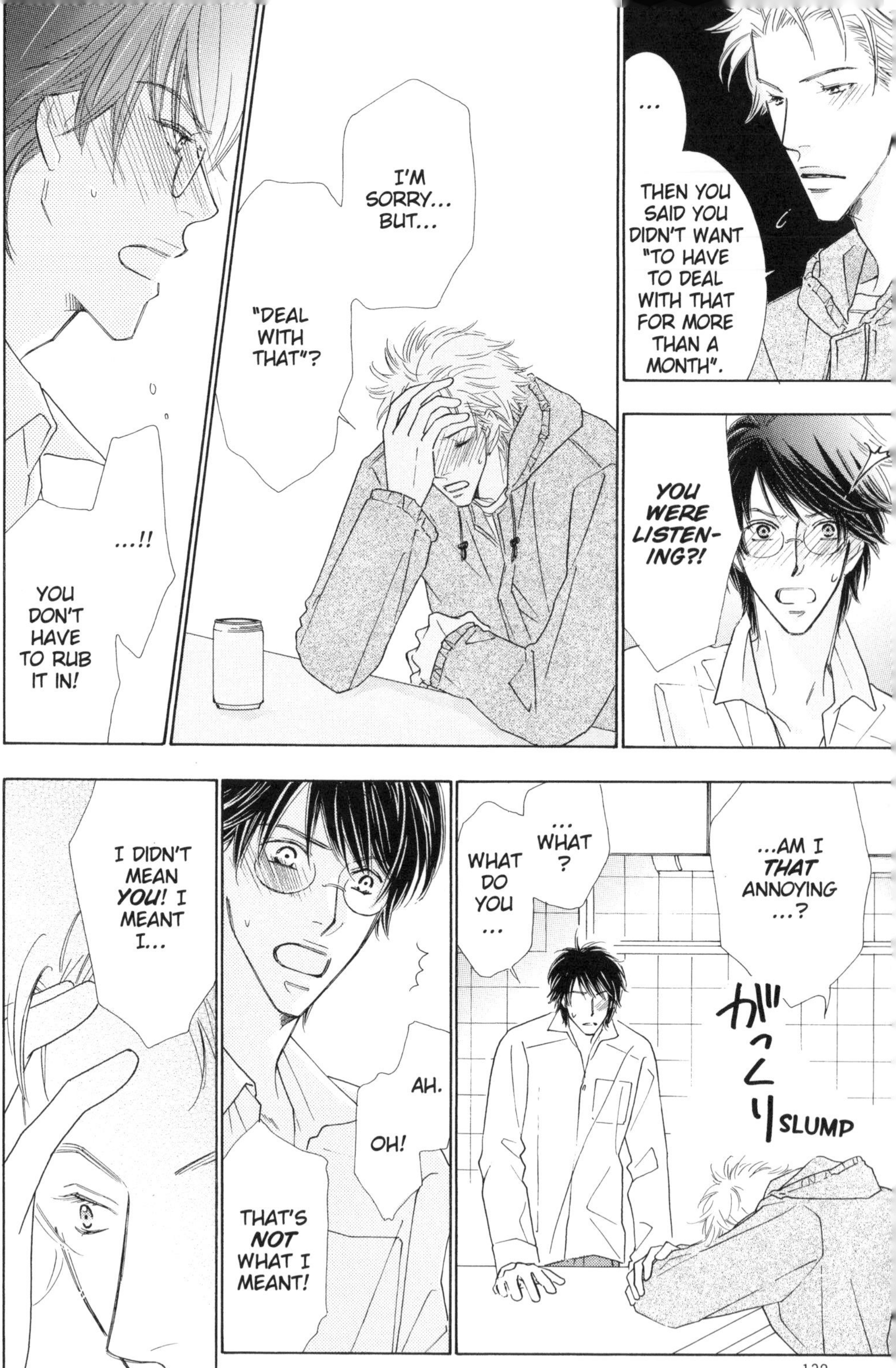
...
THEN YOU SAID YOU DIDN'T WANT "TO HAVE TO DEAL WITH THAT FOR MORE THAN A MONTH".
YOU WERE LISTENING?!
I'M SORRY... BUT...
"DEAL WITH THAT"?
...!!
YOU DON'T HAVE TO RUB IT IN!
...AM I THAT ANNOYING ...?
... WHAT ?
WHAT DO YOU ...
がっくり SLUMP
AH.
OH!
THAT'S NOT WHAT I MEANT!
I DIDN'T MEAN YOU! I MEANT I...

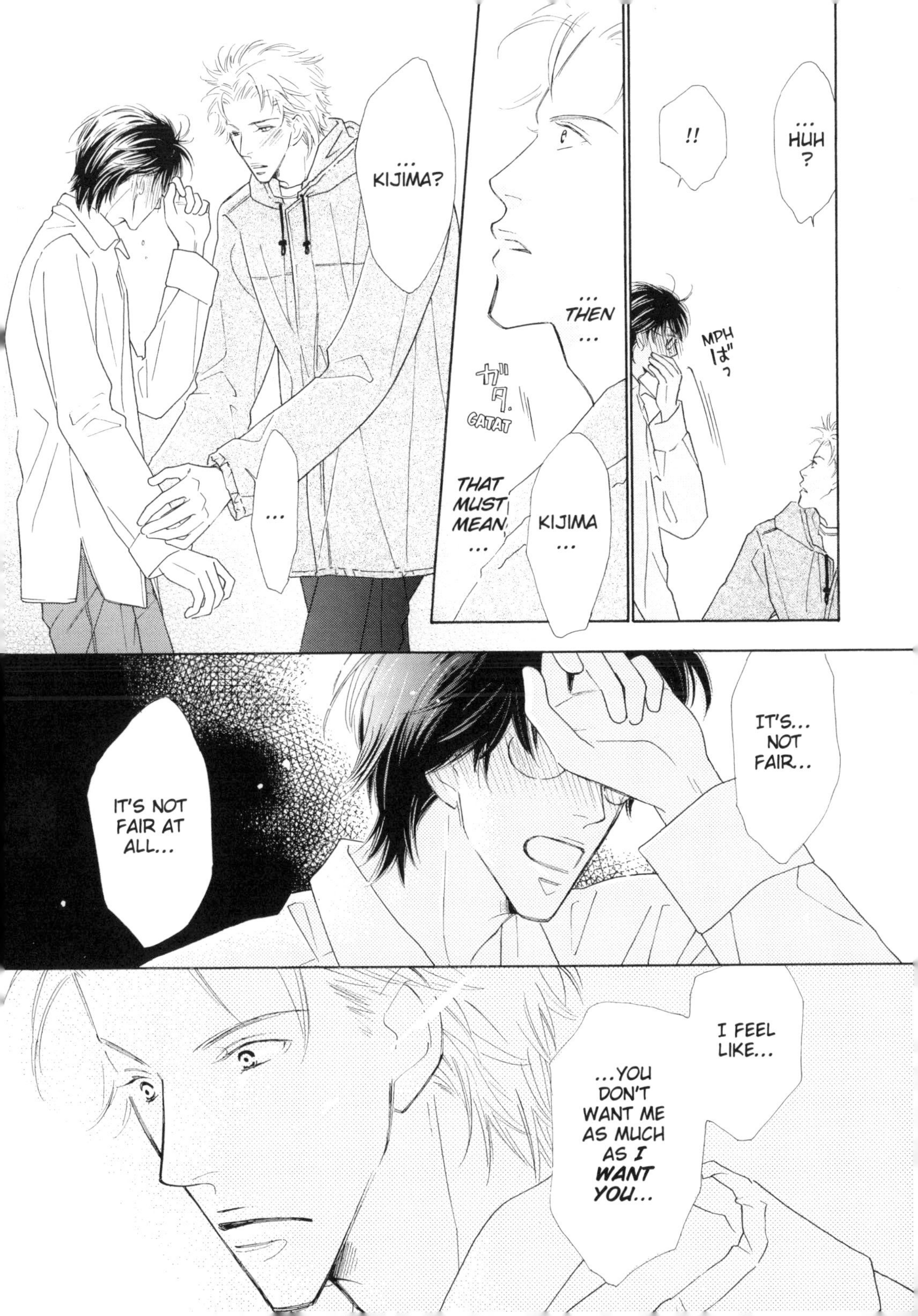
...HUH?
!!
MPH
ばっ
...THEN...
ガタ.
GATAT
KIJIMA...
THAT MUST MEAN...
...KIJIMA?
...
IT'S... NOT FAIR...
IT'S NOT FAIR AT ALL...
I FEEL LIKE...
...YOU DON'T WANT ME AS MUCH AS *I WANT YOU*...

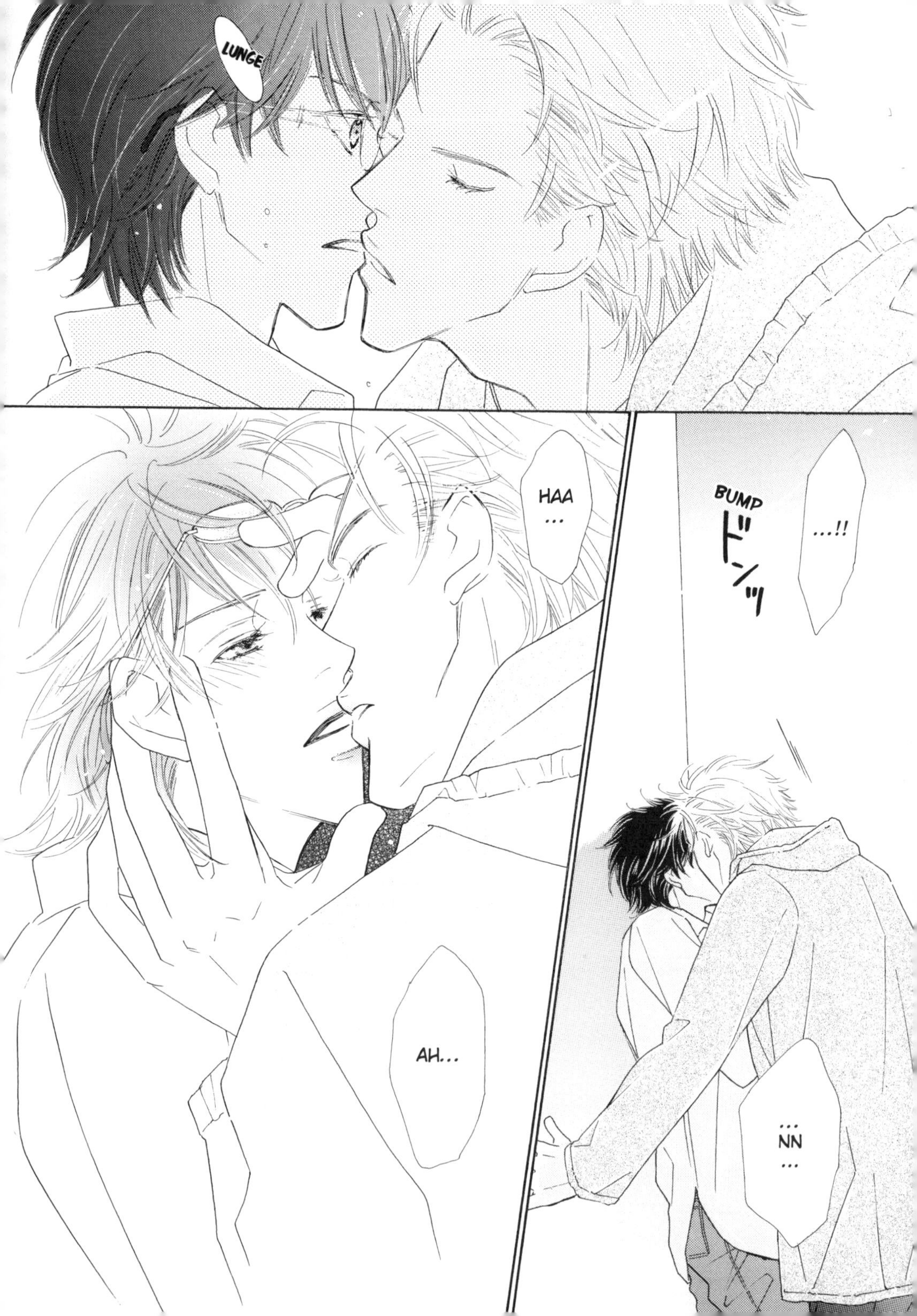
LUNGE
BUMP
ドーンッ
...!!
...NN...
HAA...
AH...

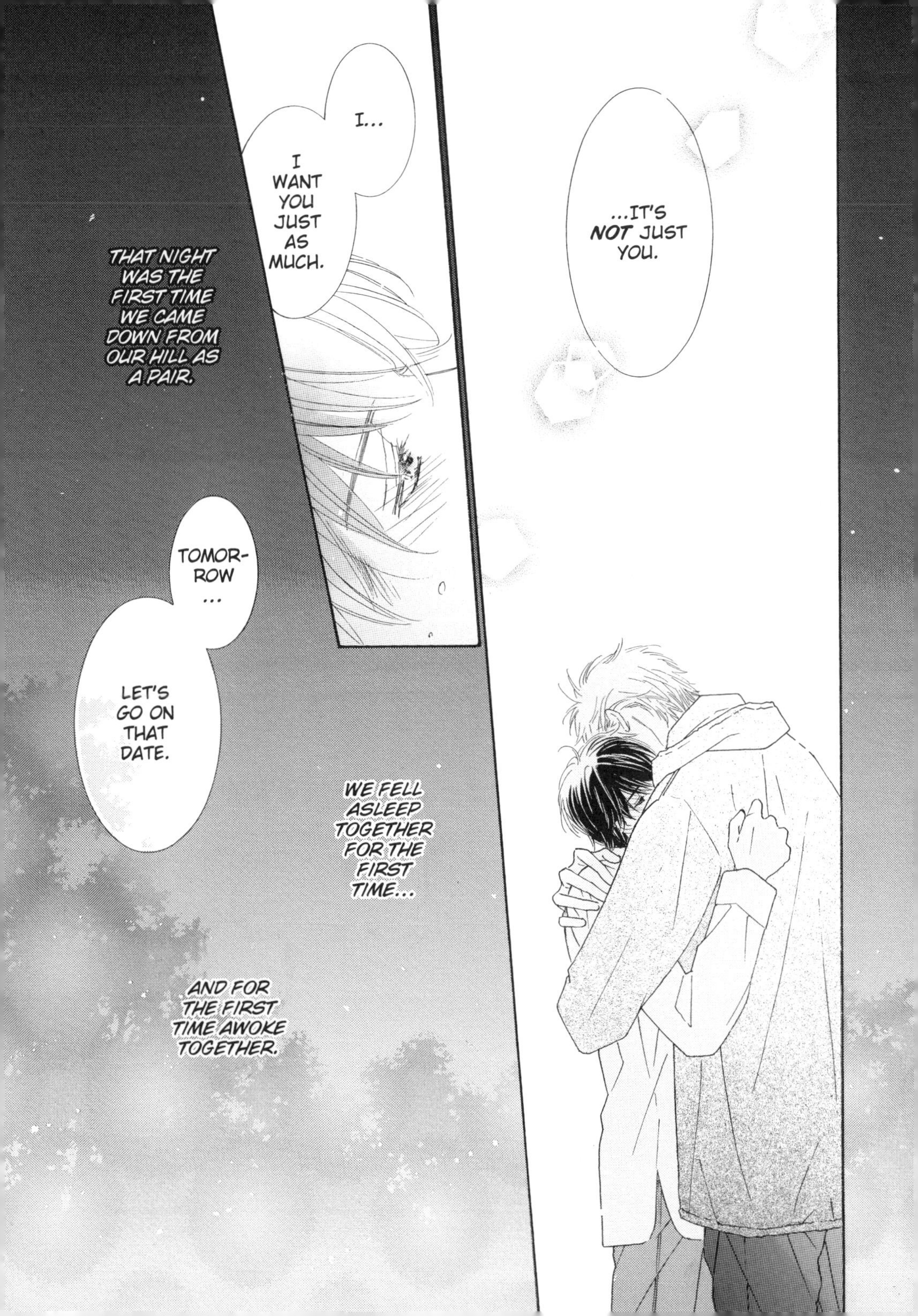
...IT'S *NOT* JUST YOU.
I...
I WANT YOU JUST AS MUCH.
THAT NIGHT WAS THE FIRST TIME WE CAME DOWN FROM OUR HILL AS A PAIR.
TOMOR-ROW...
LET'S GO ON THAT DATE.
WE FELL ASLEEP TOGETHER FOR THE FIRST TIME...
AND FOR THE FIRST TIME AWOKE TOGETHER.

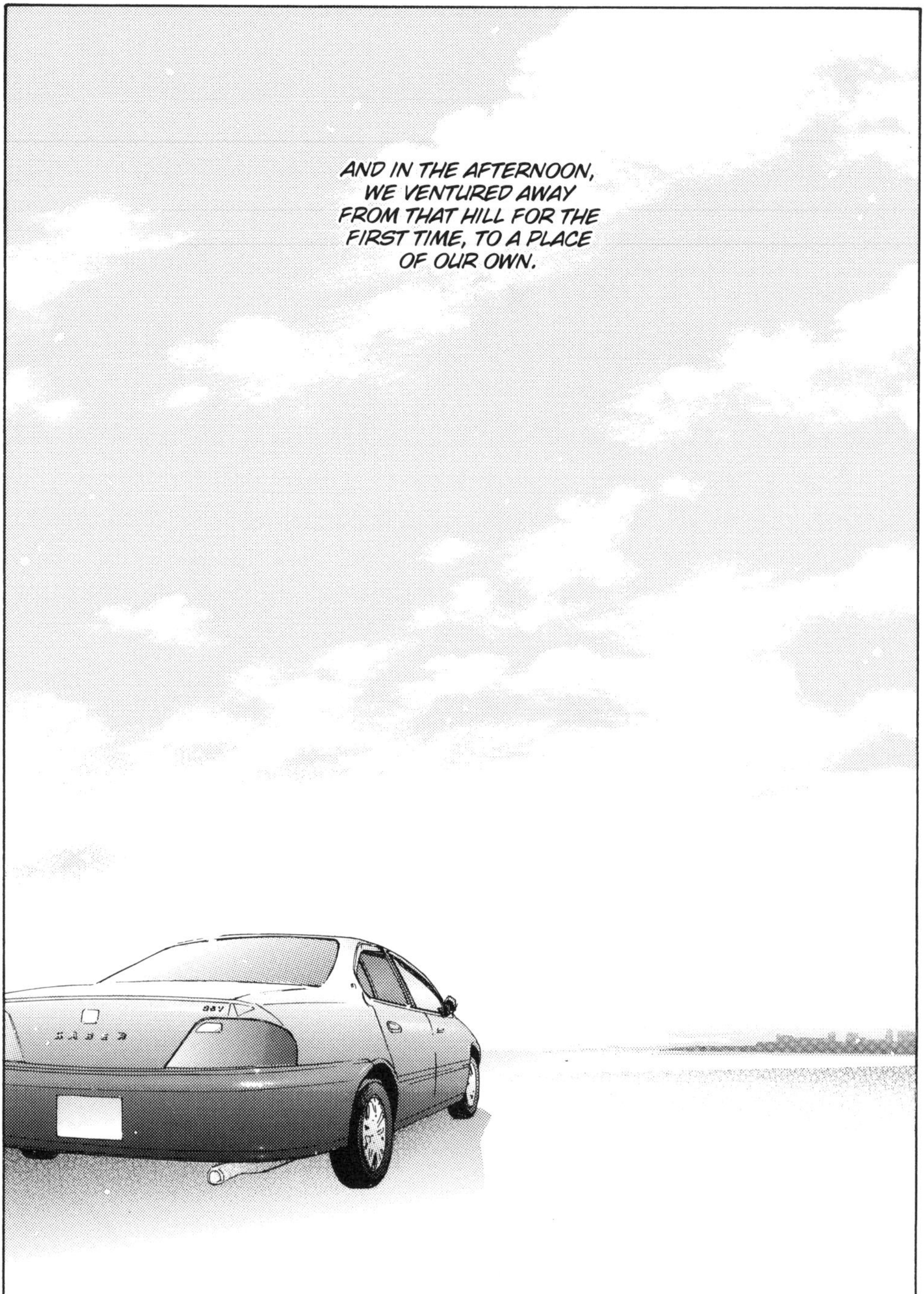
AND IN THE AFTERNOON, WE VENTURED AWAY FROM THAT HILL FOR THE FIRST TIME, TO A PLACE OF OUR OWN.

DATE / END

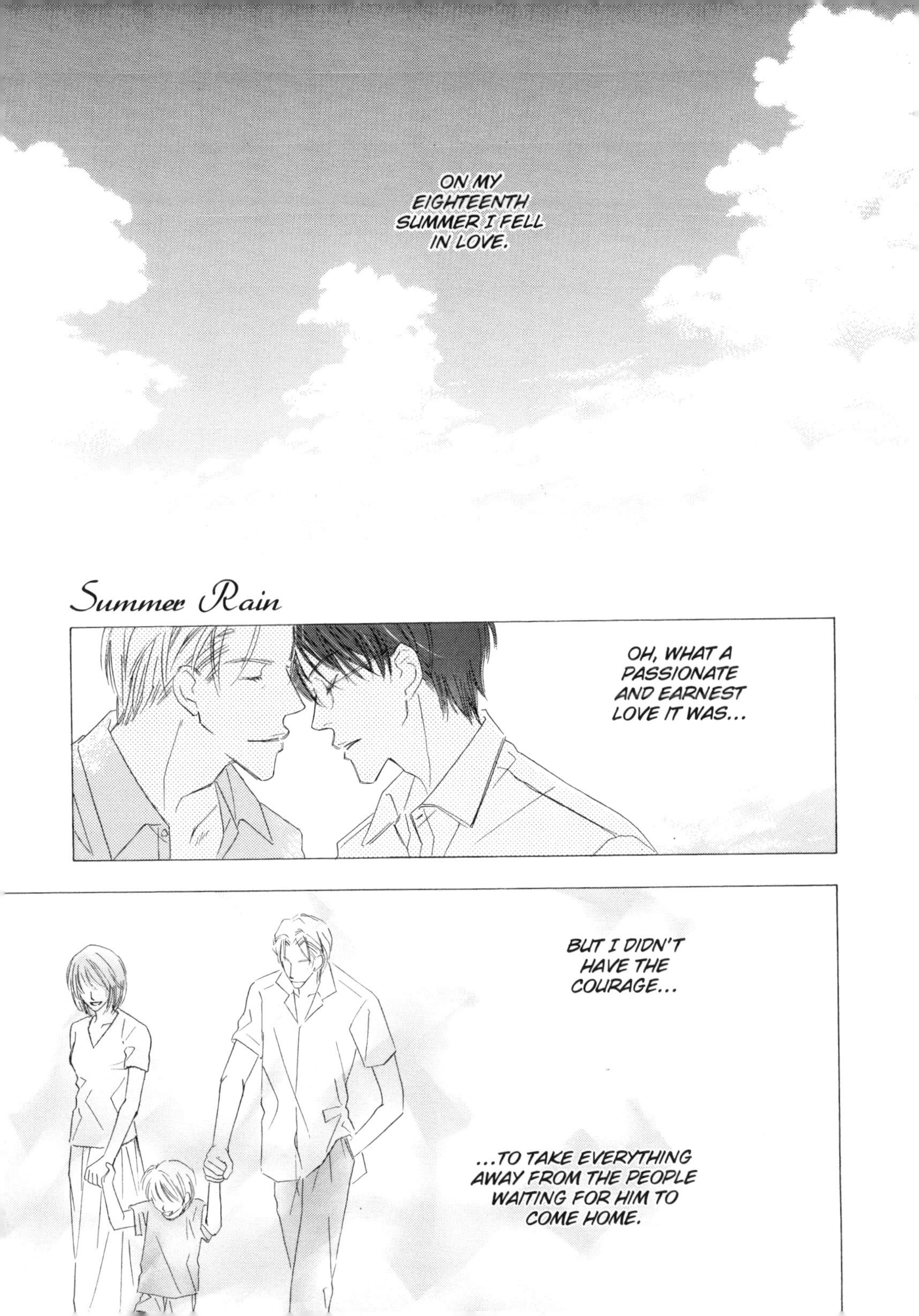
ON MY EIGHTEENTH SUMMER I FELL IN LOVE.
Summer Rain
OH, WHAT A PASSIONATE AND EARNEST LOVE IT WAS...
BUT I DIDN'T HAVE THE COURAGE...
...TO TAKE EVERYTHING AWAY FROM THE PEOPLE WAITING FOR HIM TO COME HOME.

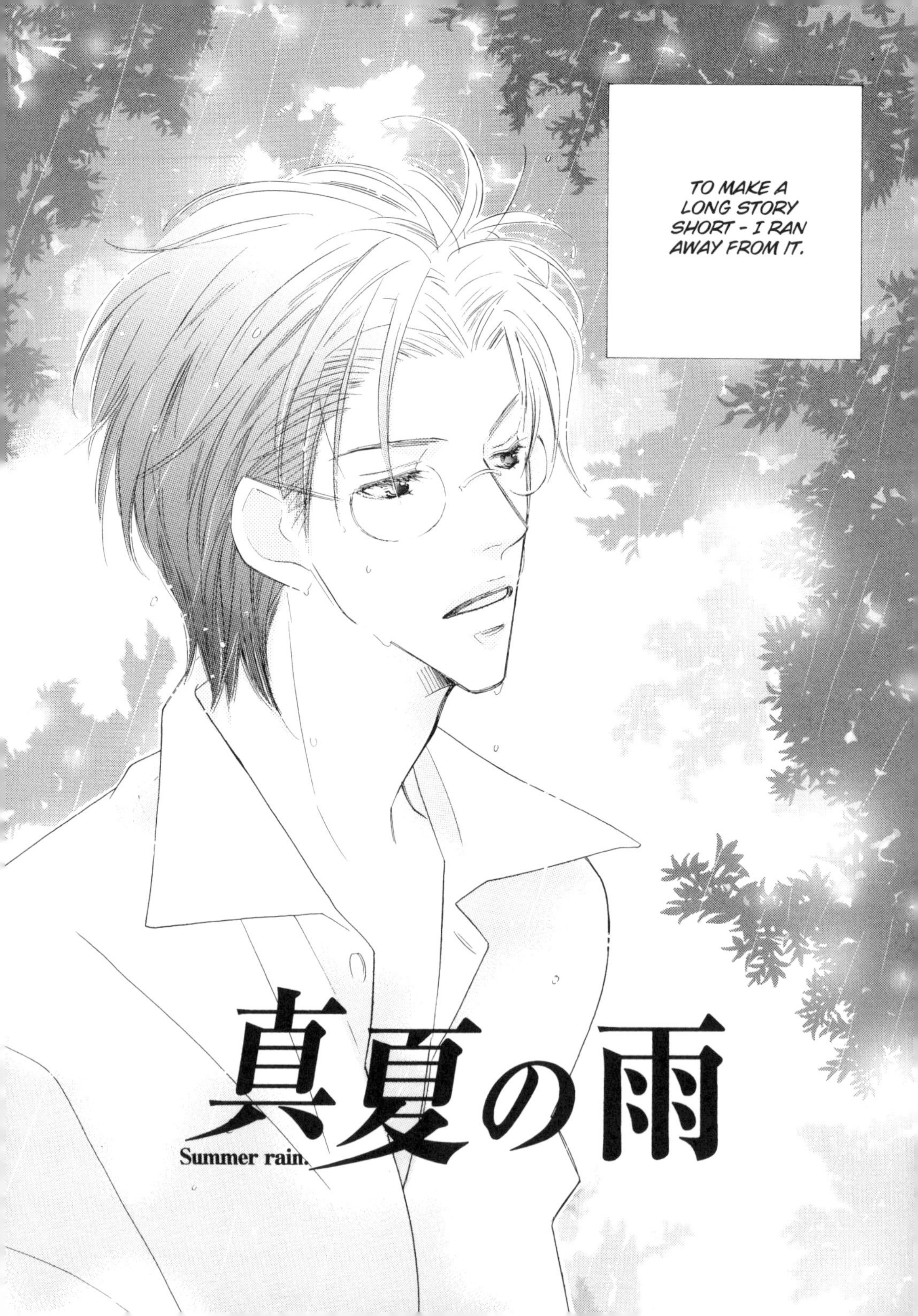
TO MAKE A LONG STORY SHORT - I RAN AWAY FROM IT.
真夏の雨
Summer rain.

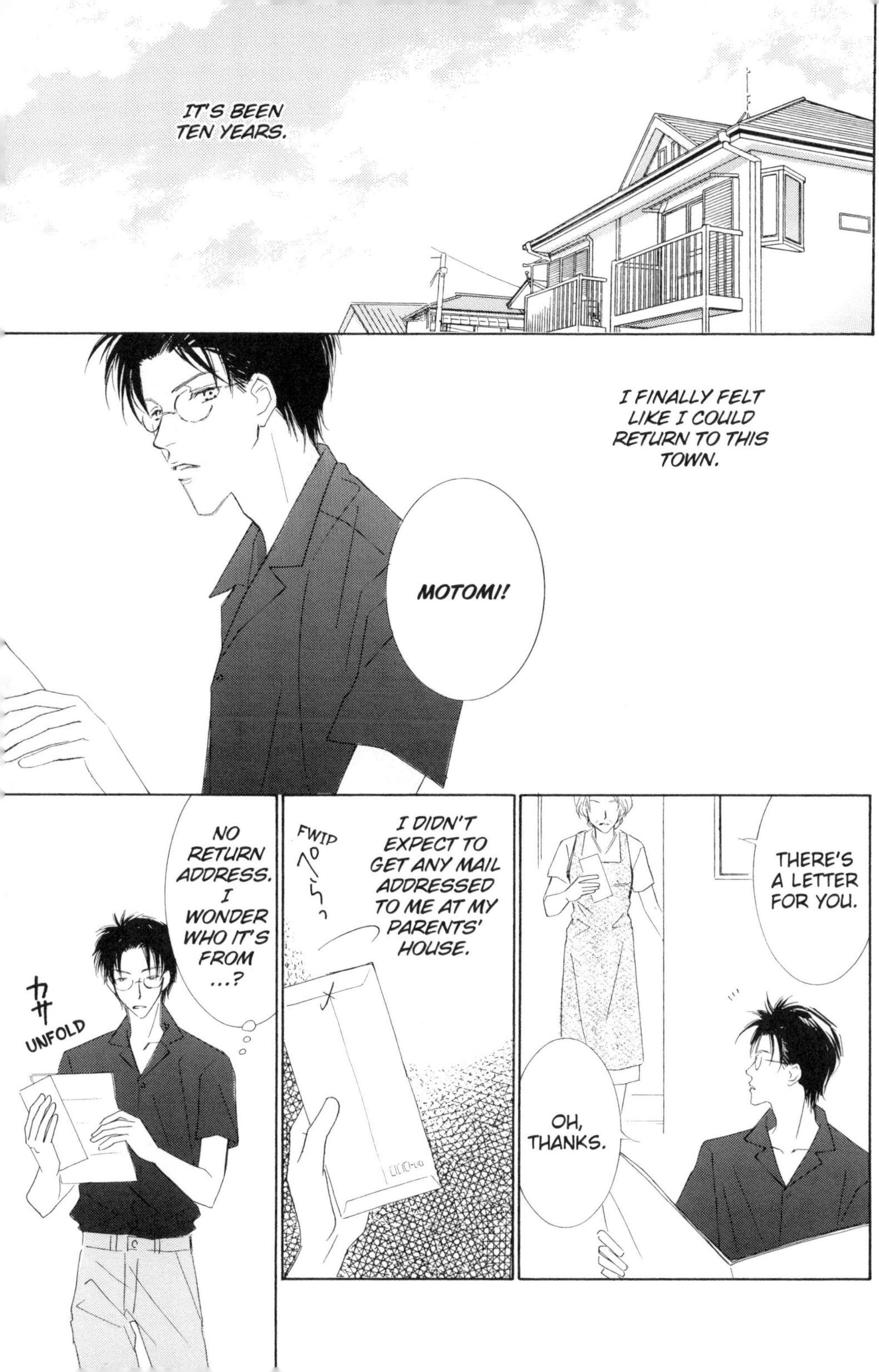
IT'S BEEN TEN YEARS.
I FINALLY FELT LIKE I COULD RETURN TO THIS TOWN.
MOTOMI!
THERE'S A LETTER FOR YOU.
OH, THANKS.
I DIDN'T EXPECT TO GET ANY MAIL ADDRESSED TO ME AT MY PARENTS' HOUSE.
FWIP
NO RETURN ADDRESS. I WONDER WHO IT'S FROM ...?
カサ
UNFOLD

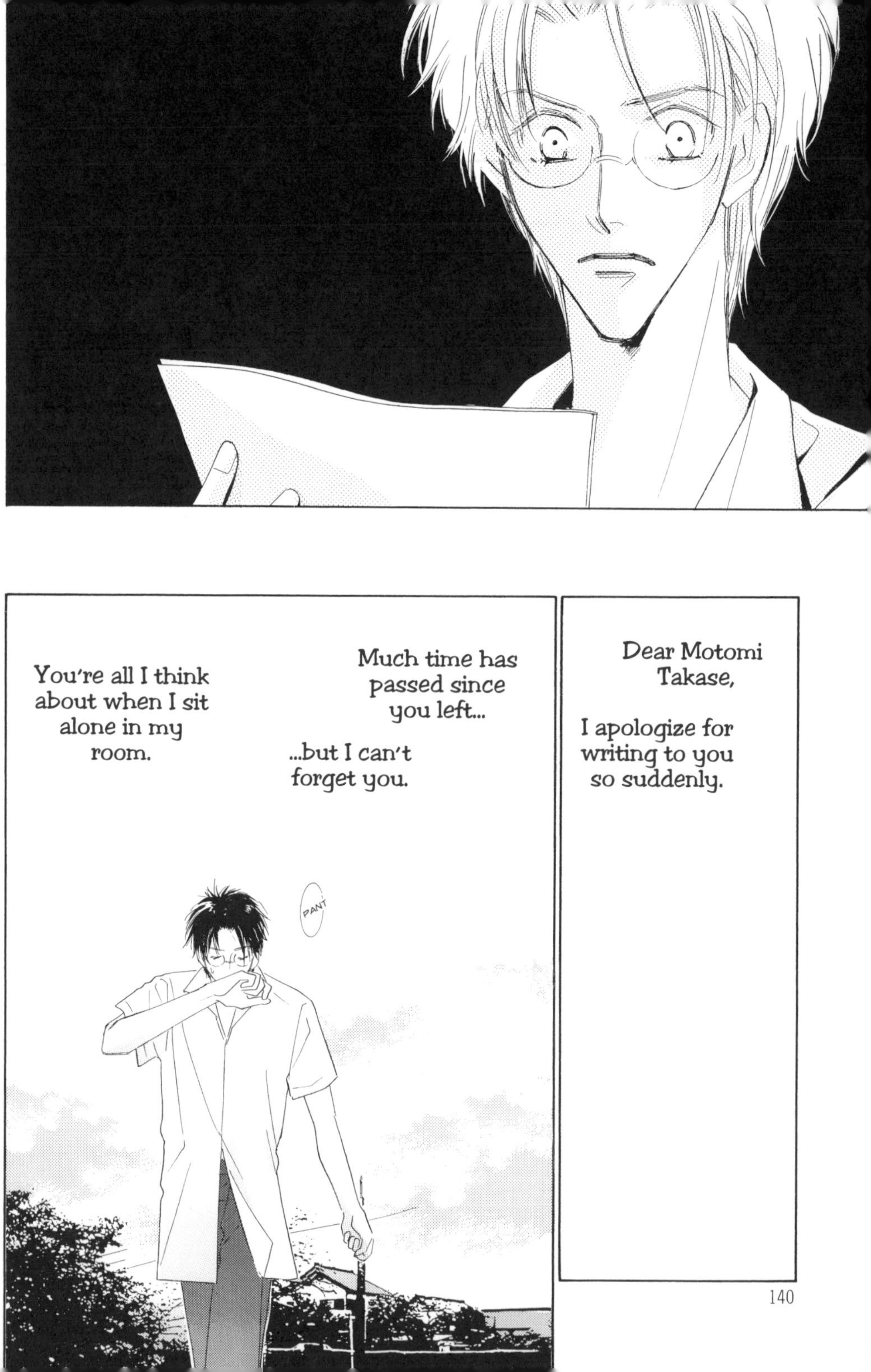
Dear Motomi Takase,
I apologize for writing to you so suddenly.
Much time has passed since you left...
...but I can't forget you.
You're all I think about when I sit alone in my room.
PANT

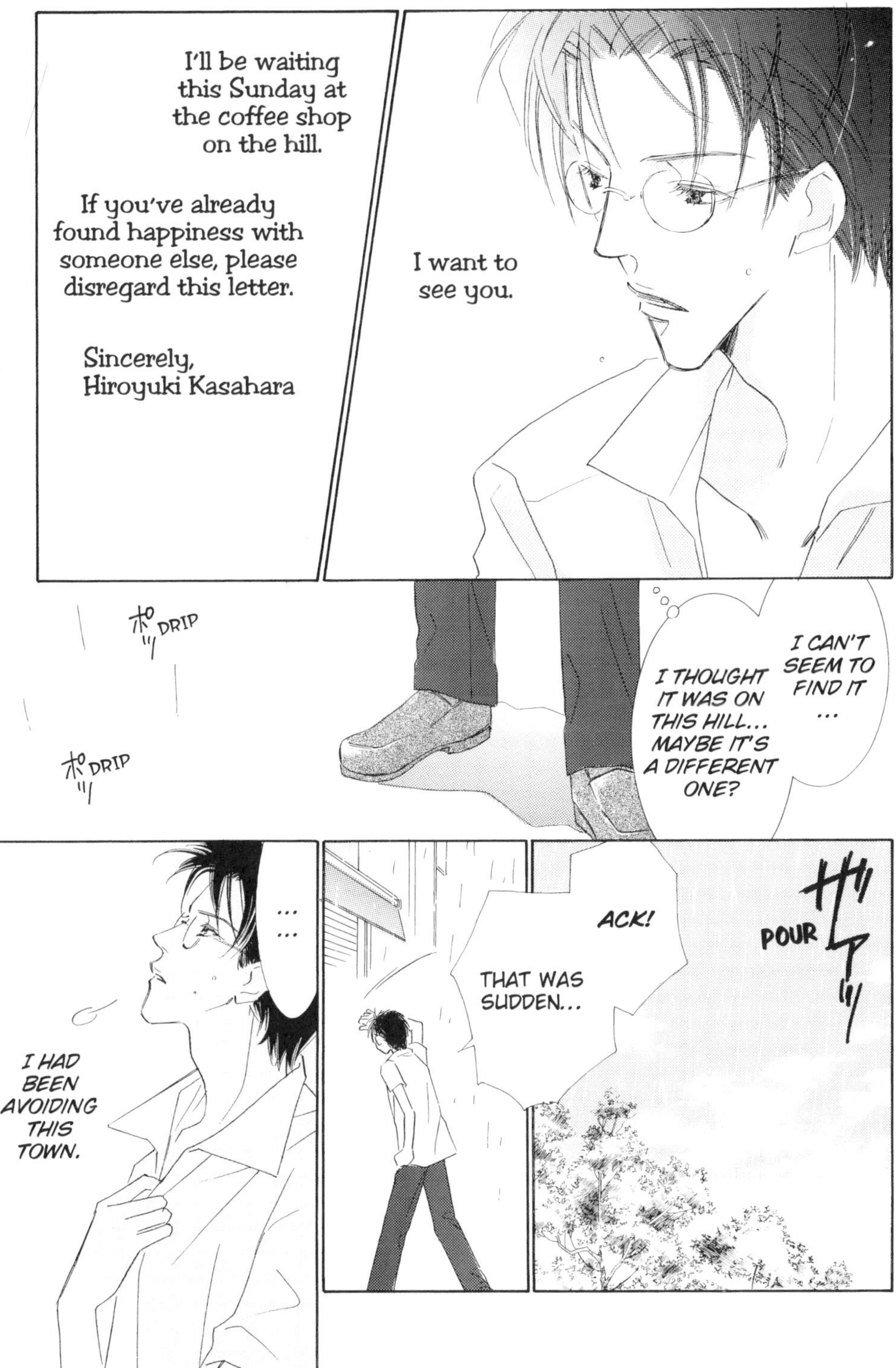

I want to see you.
I'll be waiting this Sunday at the coffee shop on the hill.
If you've already found happiness with someone else, please disregard this letter.
Sincerely,
Hiroyuki Kasahara
I CAN'T SEEM TO FIND IT ...
I THOUGHT IT WAS ON THIS HILL... MAYBE IT'S A DIFFERENT ONE?
ポツ DRIP
ポツ DRIP
ザァッ POUR
ACK!
THAT WAS SUDDEN...
......
I HAD BEEN AVOIDING THIS TOWN.

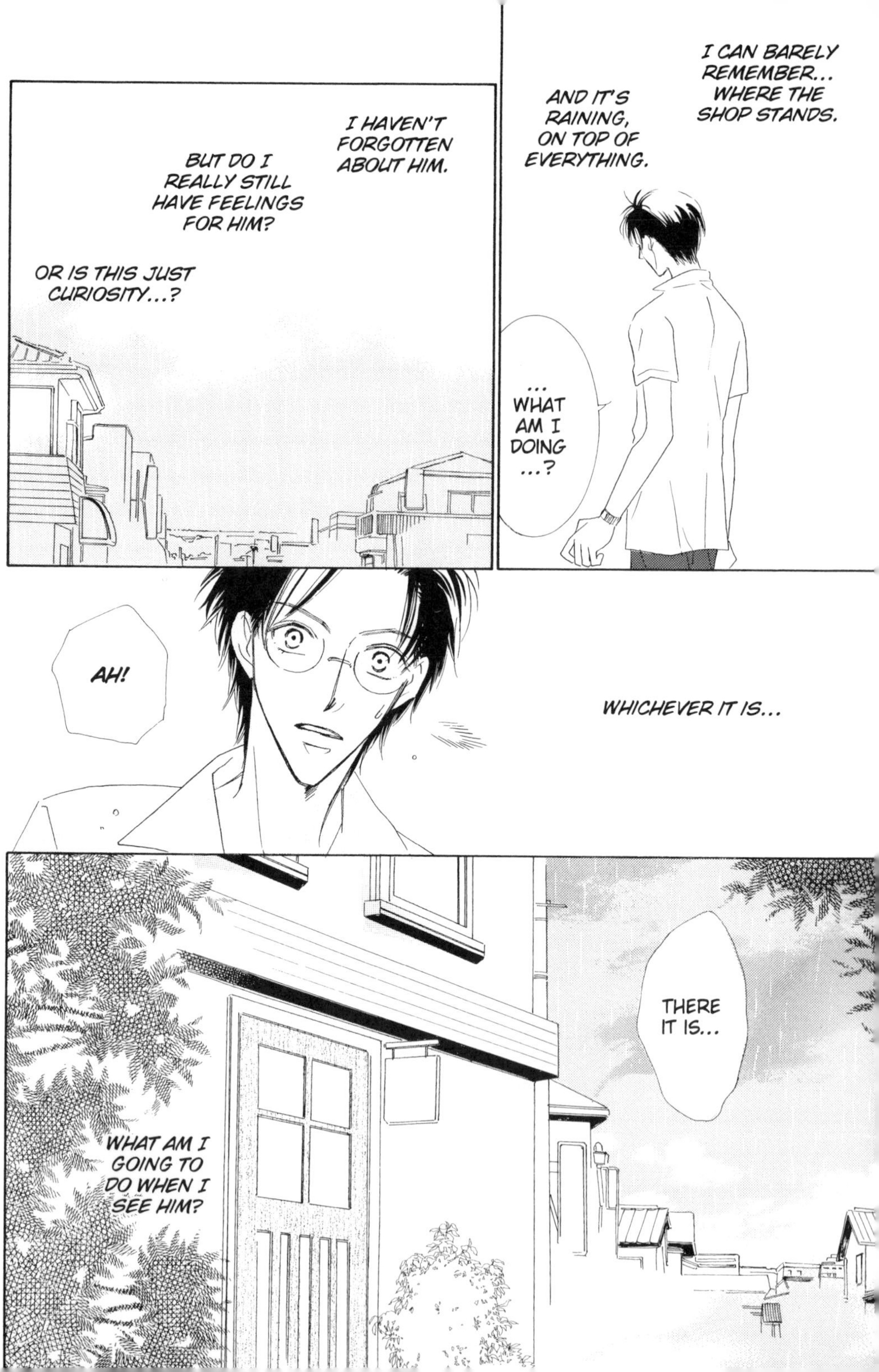
I CAN BARELY REMEMBER... WHERE THE SHOP STANDS.
AND IT'S RAINING, ON TOP OF EVERYTHING.
...WHAT AM I DOING...?
I HAVEN'T FORGOTTEN ABOUT HIM.
BUT DO I REALLY STILL HAVE FEELINGS FOR HIM?
OR IS THIS JUST CURIOSITY...?
WHICHEVER IT IS...
AH!
THERE IT IS...
WHAT AM I GOING TO DO WHEN I SEE HIM?

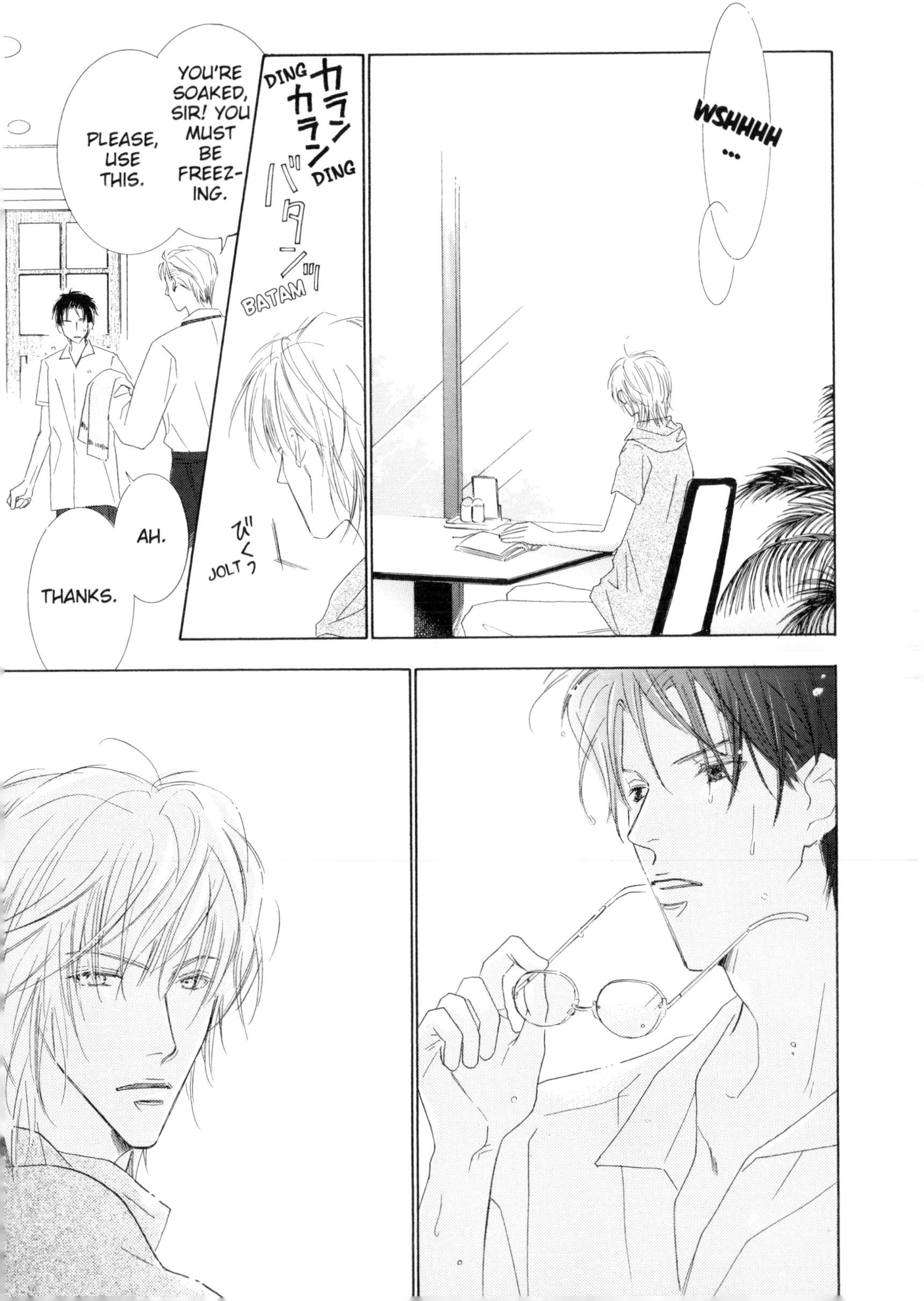
WSHHHH...
DING カランカラン DING
バタンッ
BATAM
びくっ
JOLT
YOU'RE SOAKED, SIR! YOU MUST BE FREEZ-ING.
PLEASE, USE THIS.
AH.
THANKS.

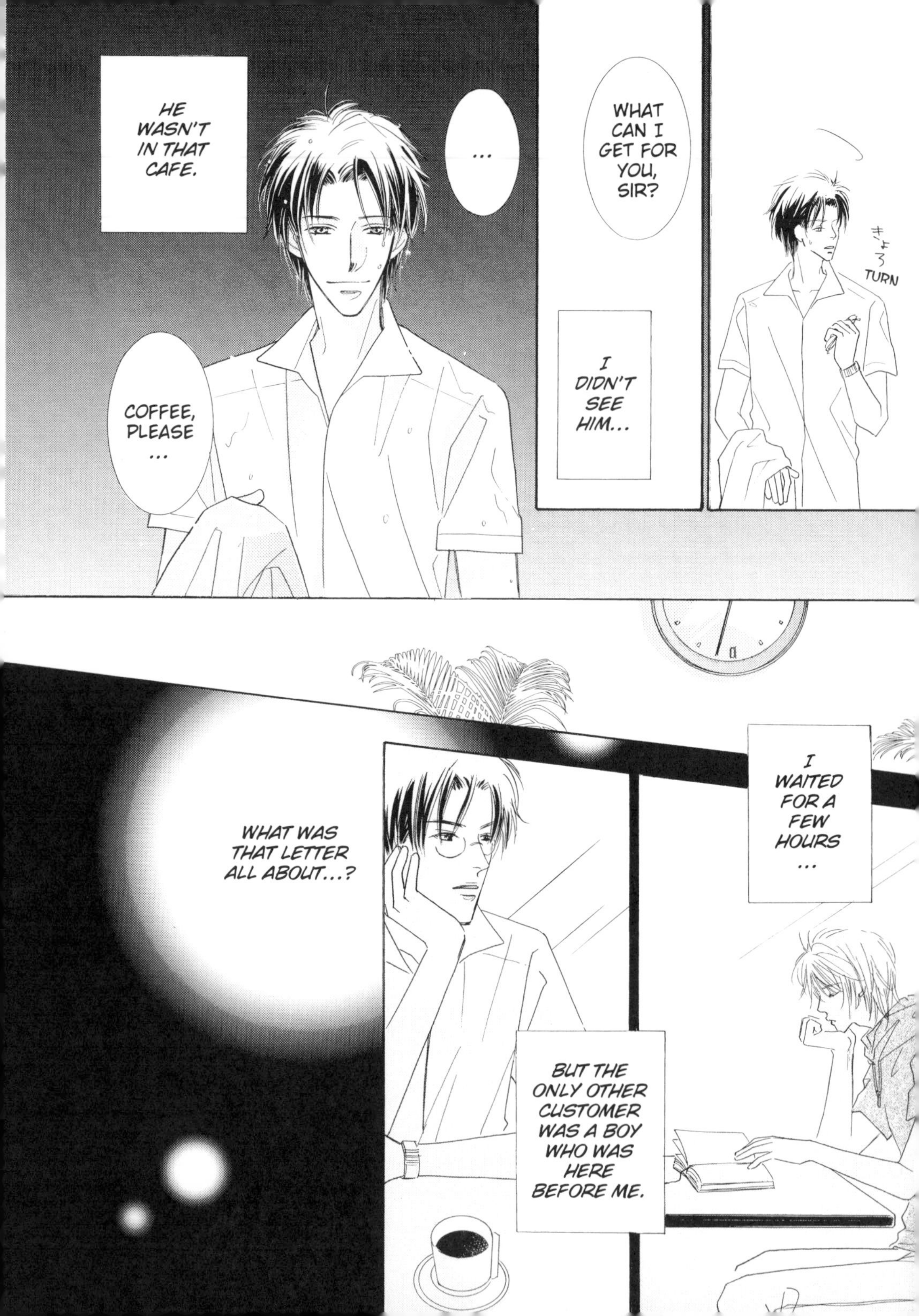
きょろ
TURN
WHAT CAN I GET FOR YOU, SIR?
I DIDN'T SEE HIM...
...
HE WASN'T IN THAT CAFE.
COFFEE, PLEASE ...
I WAITED FOR A FEW HOURS ...
WHAT WAS THAT LETTER ALL ABOUT...?
BUT THE ONLY OTHER CUSTOMER WAS A BOY WHO WAS HERE BEFORE ME.

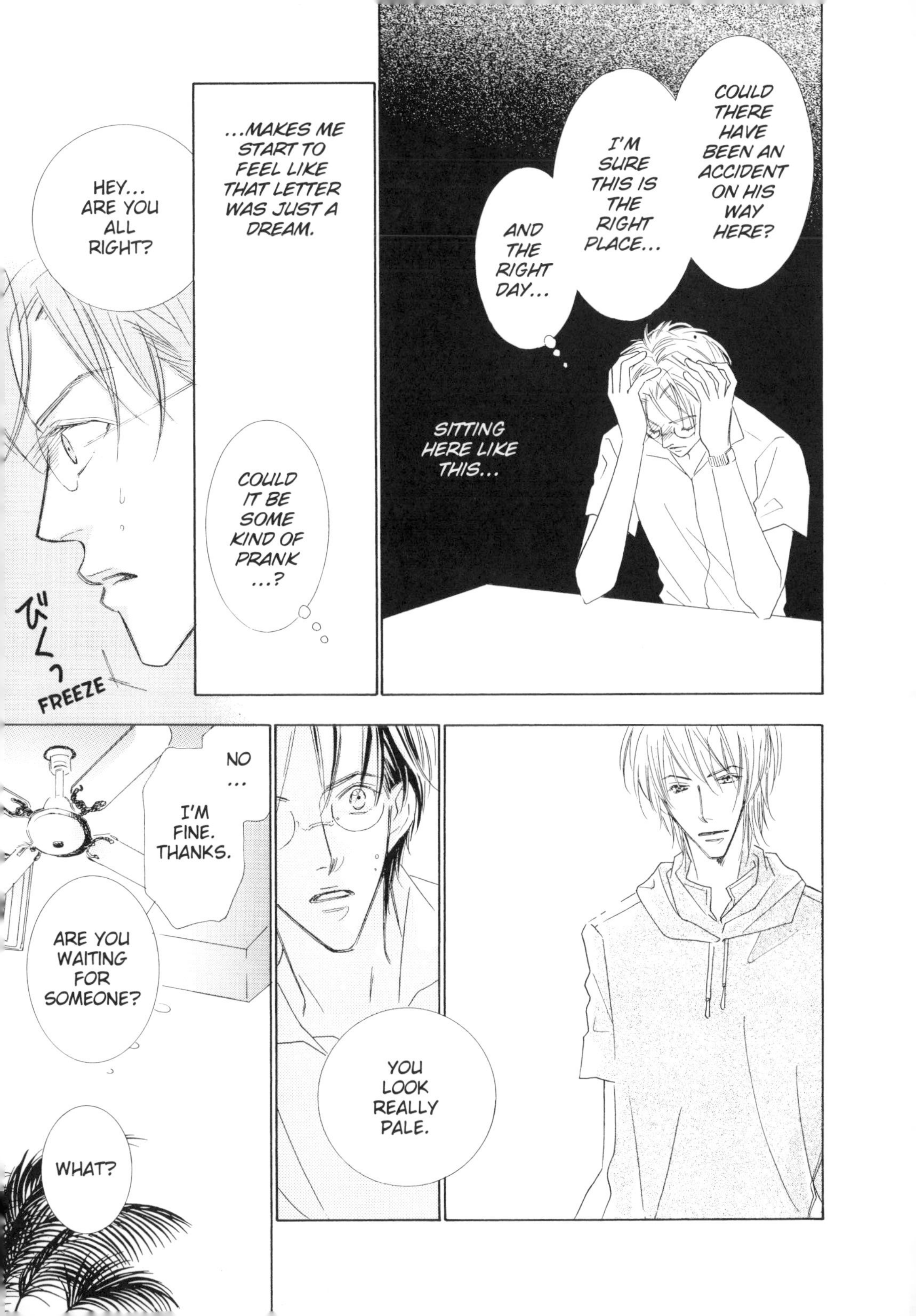
COULD THERE HAVE BEEN AN ACCIDENT ON HIS WAY HERE?
I'M SURE THIS IS THE RIGHT PLACE...
AND THE RIGHT DAY...
SITTING HERE LIKE THIS...
...MAKES ME START TO FEEL LIKE THAT LETTER WAS JUST A DREAM.
COULD IT BE SOME KIND OF PRANK...?
HEY... ARE YOU ALL RIGHT?
びくっ
FREEZE
YOU LOOK REALLY PALE.
NO... I'M FINE. THANKS.
ARE YOU WAITING FOR SOMEONE?
WHAT?

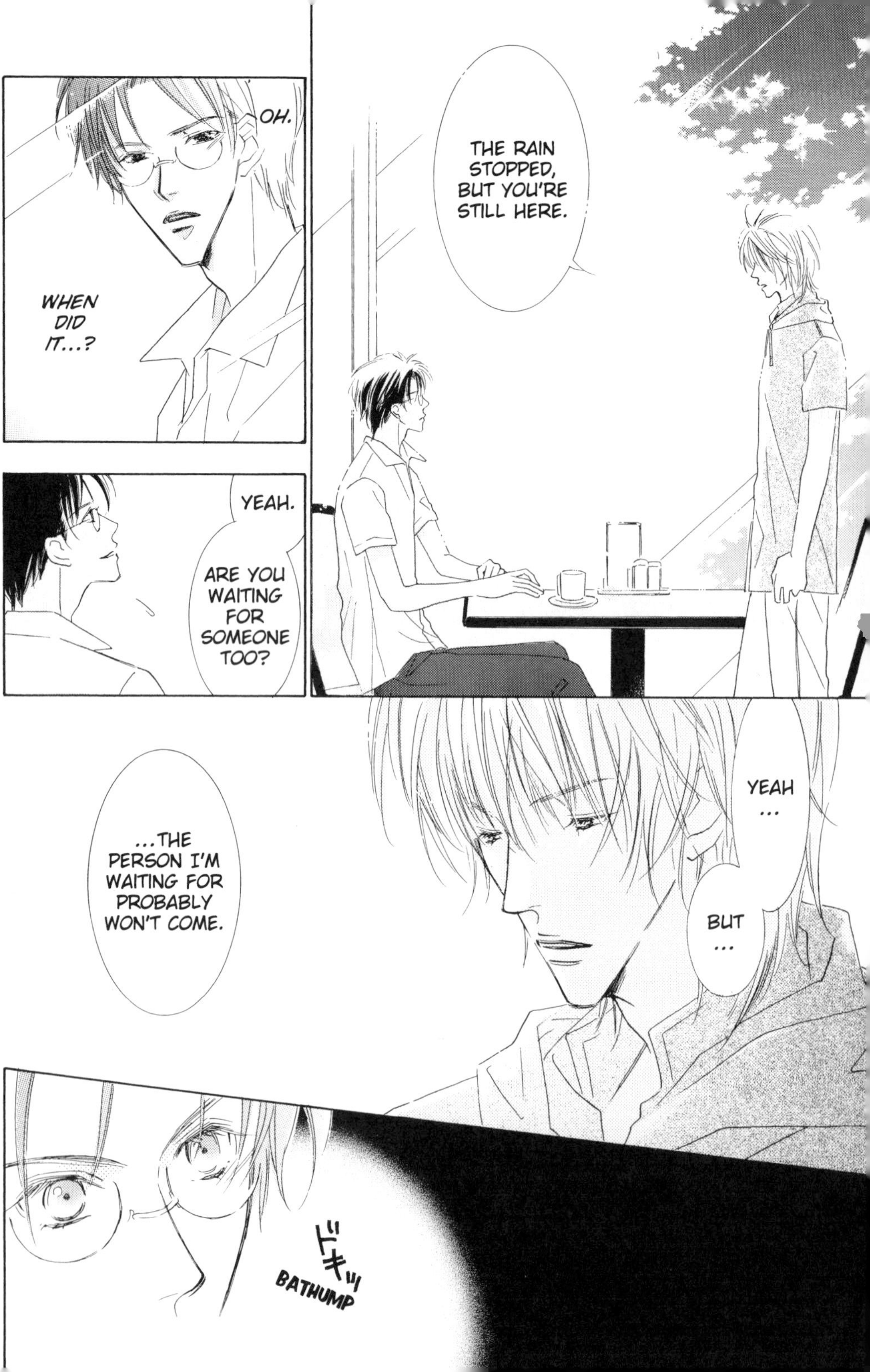
THE RAIN STOPPED, BUT YOU'RE STILL HERE.
OH.
WHEN DID IT...?
YEAH.
ARE YOU WAITING FOR SOMEONE TOO?
YEAH...
BUT...
...THE PERSON I'M WAITING FOR PROBABLY WON'T COME.
ドキッ
BATHUMP

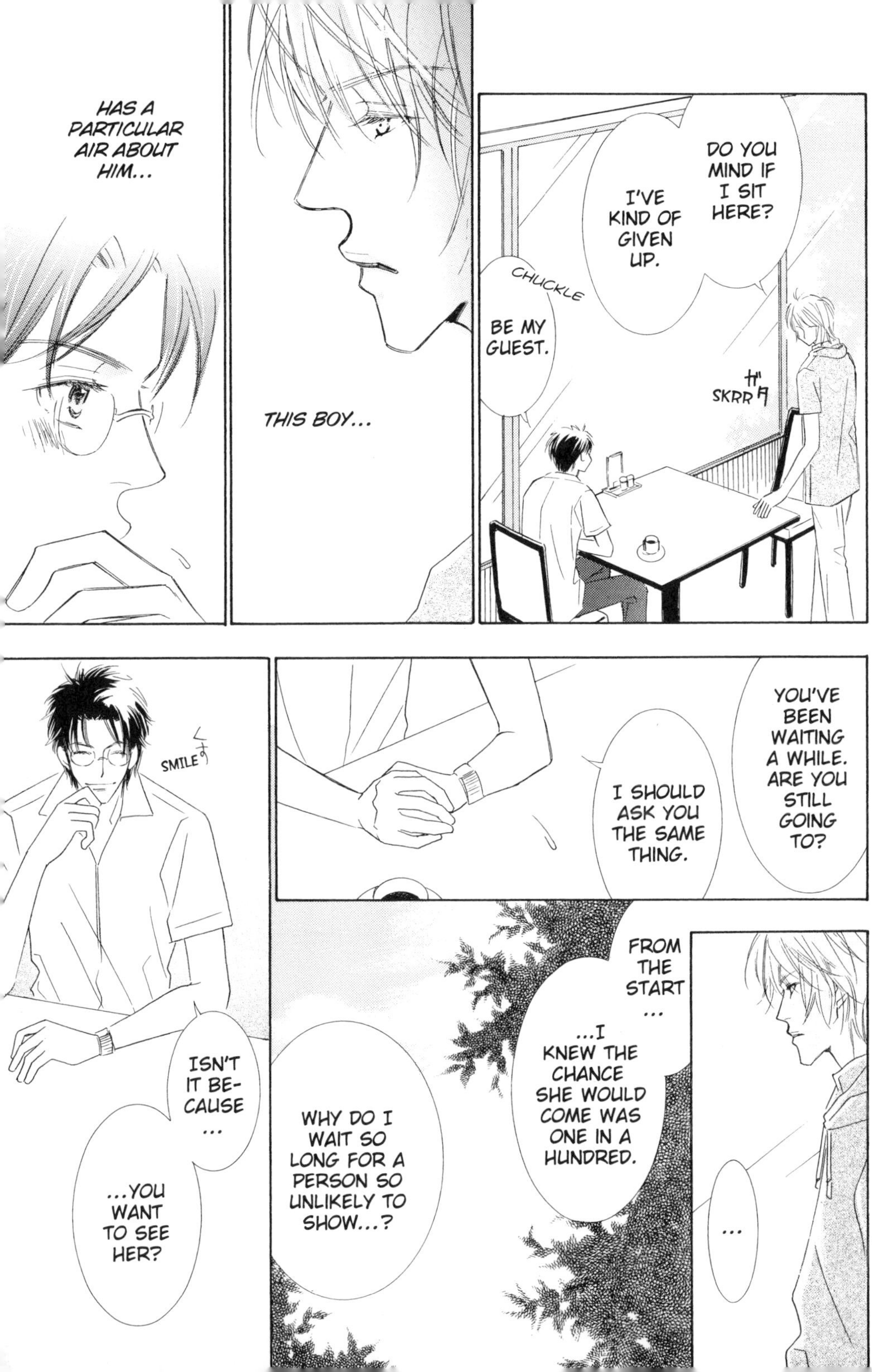
DO YOU MIND IF I SIT HERE?
I'VE KIND OF GIVEN UP.
CHUCKLE
BE MY GUEST.
SKRR ガタ
THIS BOY...
HAS A PARTICULAR AIR ABOUT HIM...
YOU'VE BEEN WAITING A WHILE. ARE YOU STILL GOING TO?
I SHOULD ASK YOU THE SAME THING.
FROM THE START...
...I KNEW THE CHANCE SHE WOULD COME WAS ONE IN A HUNDRED.
...
WHY DO I WAIT SO LONG FOR A PERSON SO UNLIKELY TO SHOW...?
SMILE くす
ISN'T IT BE-CAUSE...
...YOU WANT TO SEE HER?

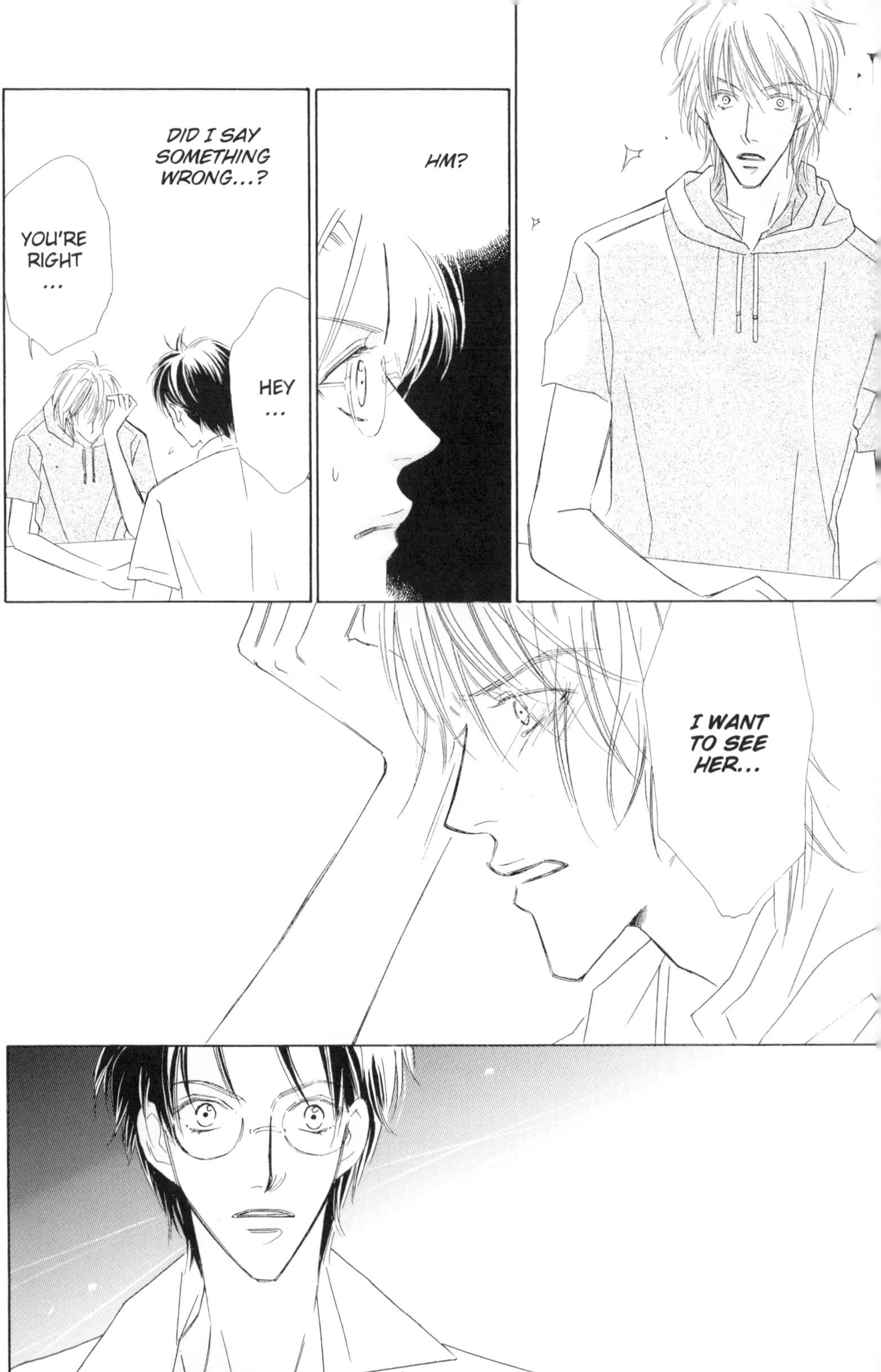
HM?
HEY...
DID I SAY SOMETHING WRONG...?
YOU'RE RIGHT...
I WANT TO SEE HER...

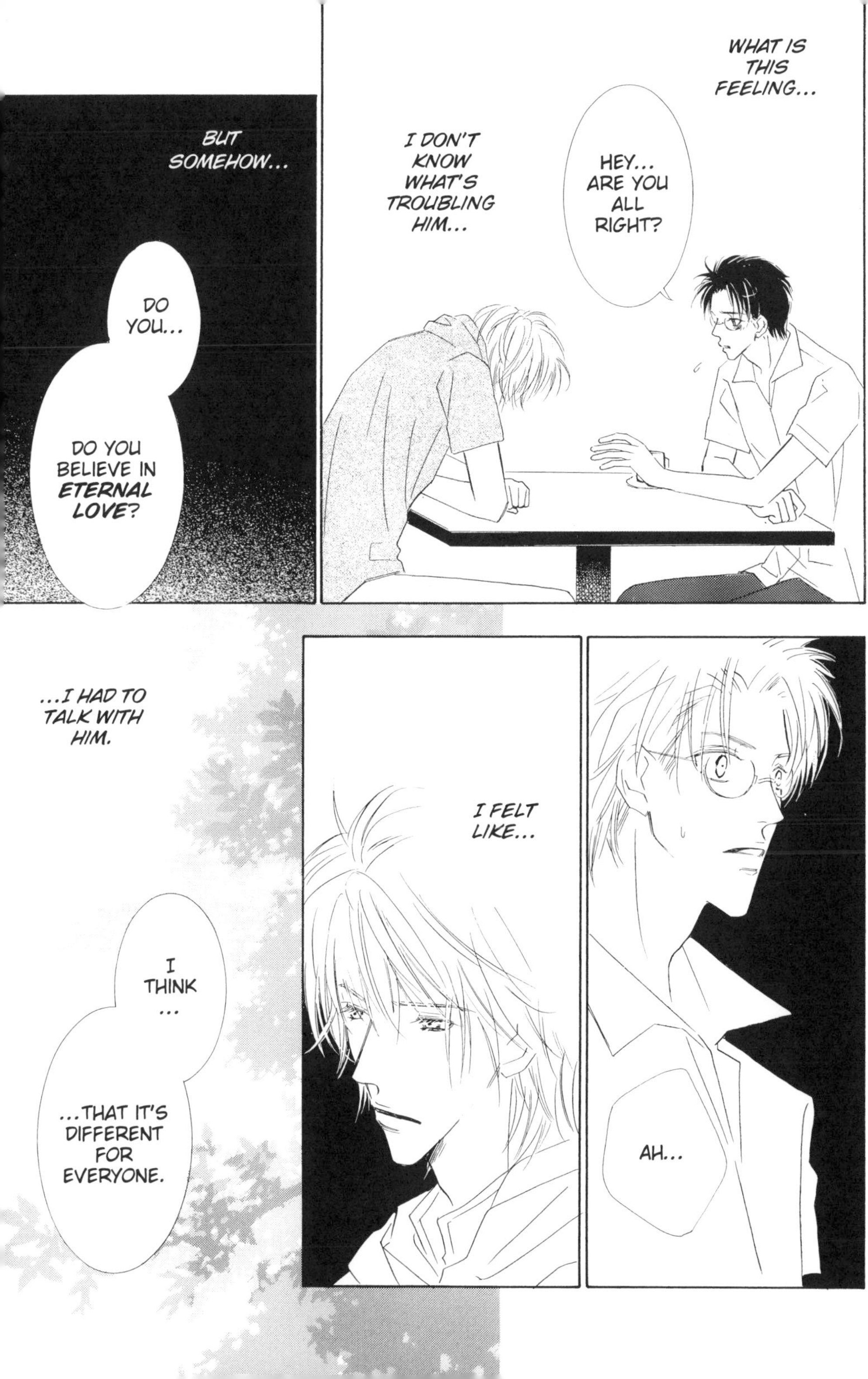
WHAT IS THIS FEELING...
HEY... ARE YOU ALL RIGHT?
I DON'T KNOW WHAT'S TROUBLING HIM...
BUT SOMEHOW...
DO YOU...
DO YOU BELIEVE IN ETERNAL LOVE?
AH...
I FELT LIKE...
...I HAD TO TALK WITH HIM.
I THINK...
...THAT IT'S DIFFERENT FOR EVERYONE.

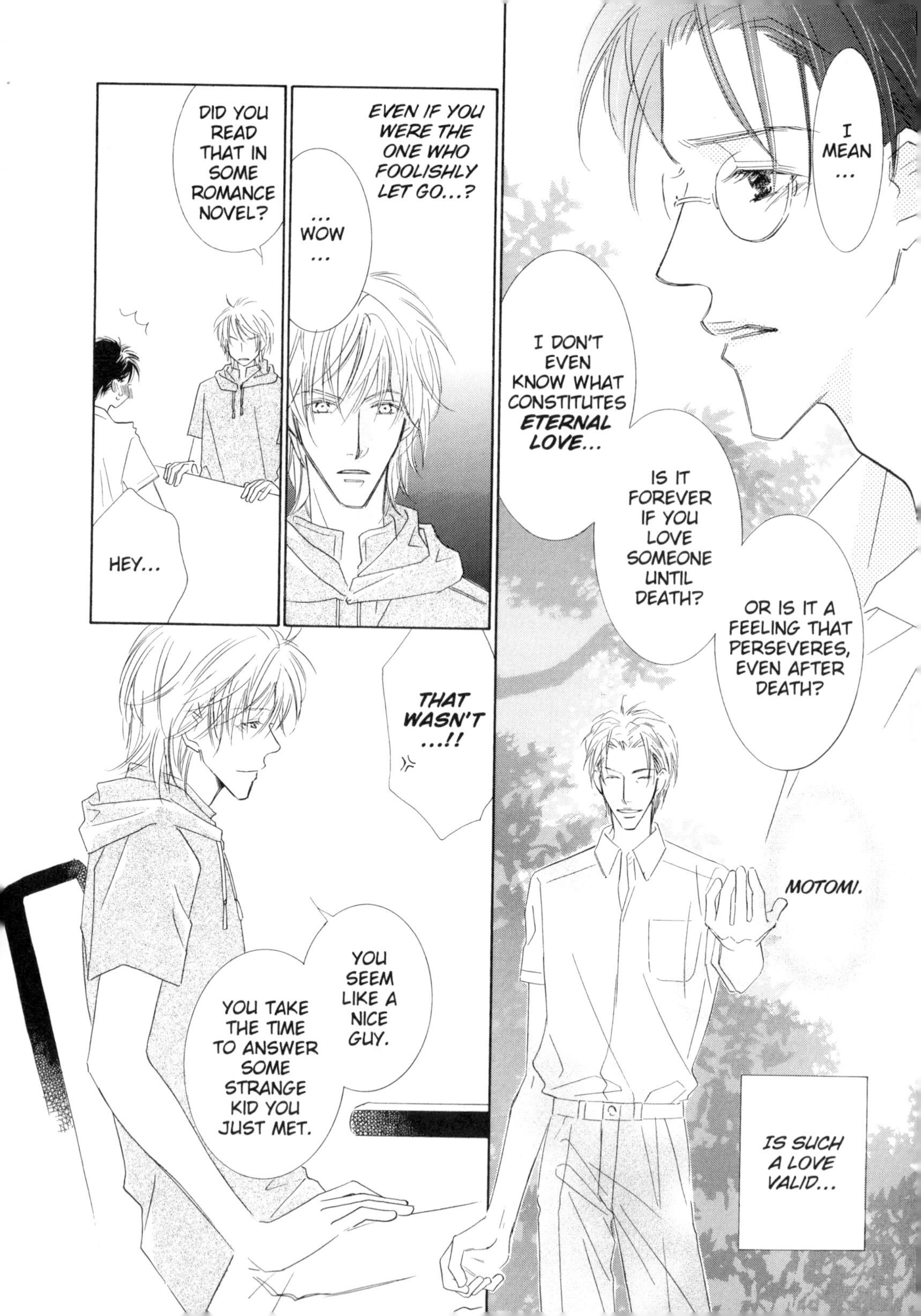
I MEAN...
I DON'T EVEN KNOW WHAT CONSTITUTES ETERNAL LOVE...
IS IT FOREVER IF YOU LOVE SOMEONE UNTIL DEATH?
OR IS IT A FEELING THAT PERSEVERES, EVEN AFTER DEATH?
MOTOMI.
IS SUCH A LOVE VALID...
EVEN IF YOU WERE THE ONE WHO FOOLISHLY LET GO...?
...WOW...
DID YOU READ THAT IN SOME ROMANCE NOVEL?
HEY...
THAT WASN'T...!!
YOU SEEM LIKE A NICE GUY.
YOU TAKE THE TIME TO ANSWER SOME STRANGE KID YOU JUST MET.

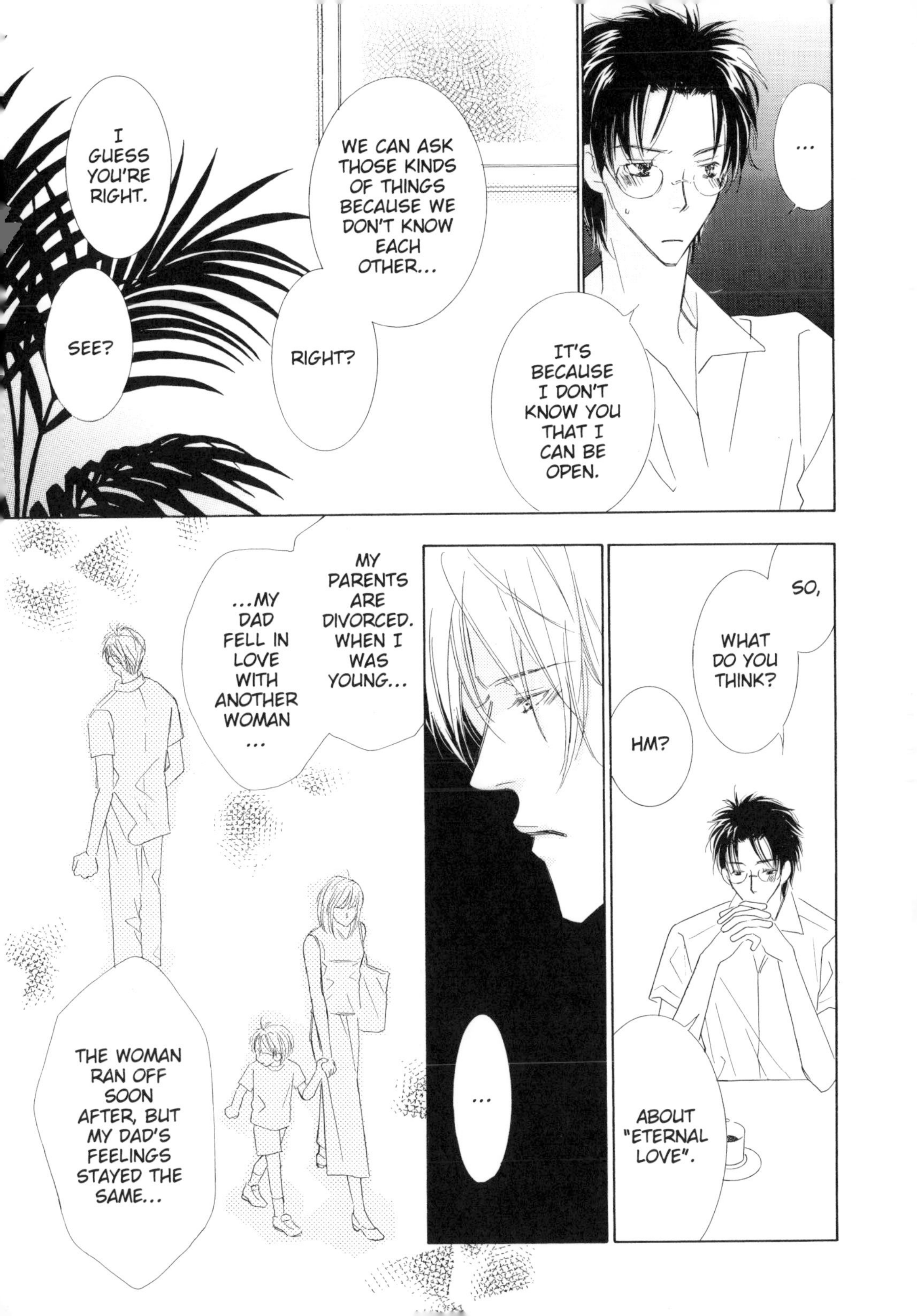
...
IT'S BECAUSE I DON'T KNOW YOU THAT I CAN BE OPEN.
WE CAN ASK THOSE KINDS OF THINGS BECAUSE WE DON'T KNOW EACH OTHER...
RIGHT?
I GUESS YOU'RE RIGHT.
SEE?
SO,
WHAT DO YOU THINK?
HM?
ABOUT "ETERNAL LOVE".
...
MY PARENTS ARE DIVORCED. WHEN I WAS YOUNG...
...MY DAD FELL IN LOVE WITH ANOTHER WOMAN...
THE WOMAN RAN OFF SOON AFTER, BUT MY DAD'S FEELINGS STAYED THE SAME...

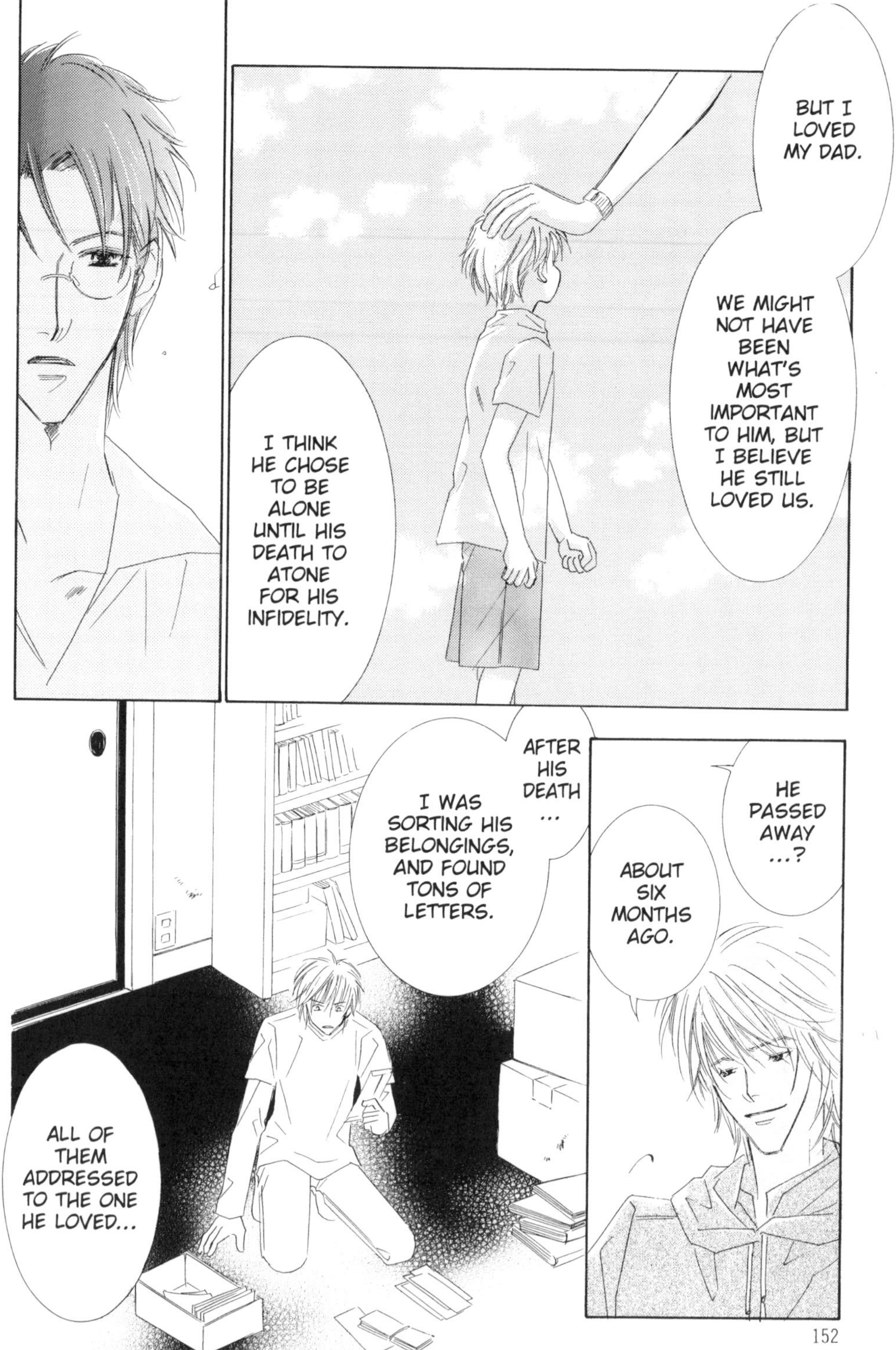
BUT I LOVED MY DAD.
WE MIGHT NOT HAVE BEEN WHAT'S MOST IMPORTANT TO HIM, BUT I BELIEVE HE STILL LOVED US.
I THINK HE CHOSE TO BE ALONE UNTIL HIS DEATH TO ATONE FOR HIS INFIDELITY.
HE PASSED AWAY ...?
ABOUT SIX MONTHS AGO.
AFTER HIS DEATH ...
I WAS SORTING HIS BELONGINGS, AND FOUND TONS OF LETTERS.
ALL OF THEM ADDRESSED TO THE ONE HE LOVED...

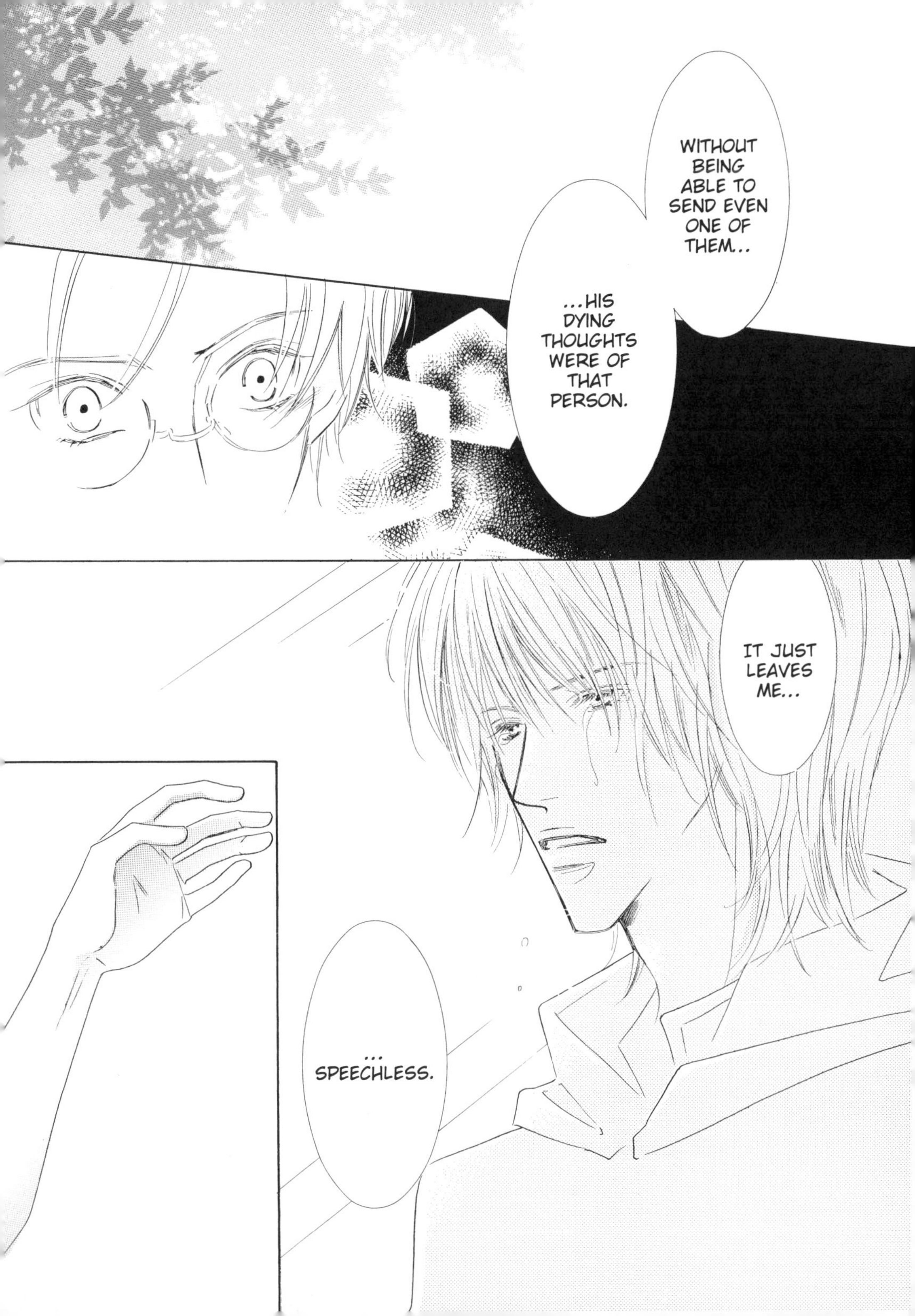
WITHOUT BEING ABLE TO SEND EVEN ONE OF THEM...
...HIS DYING THOUGHTS WERE OF THAT PERSON.
IT JUST LEAVES ME...
... SPEECHLESS.

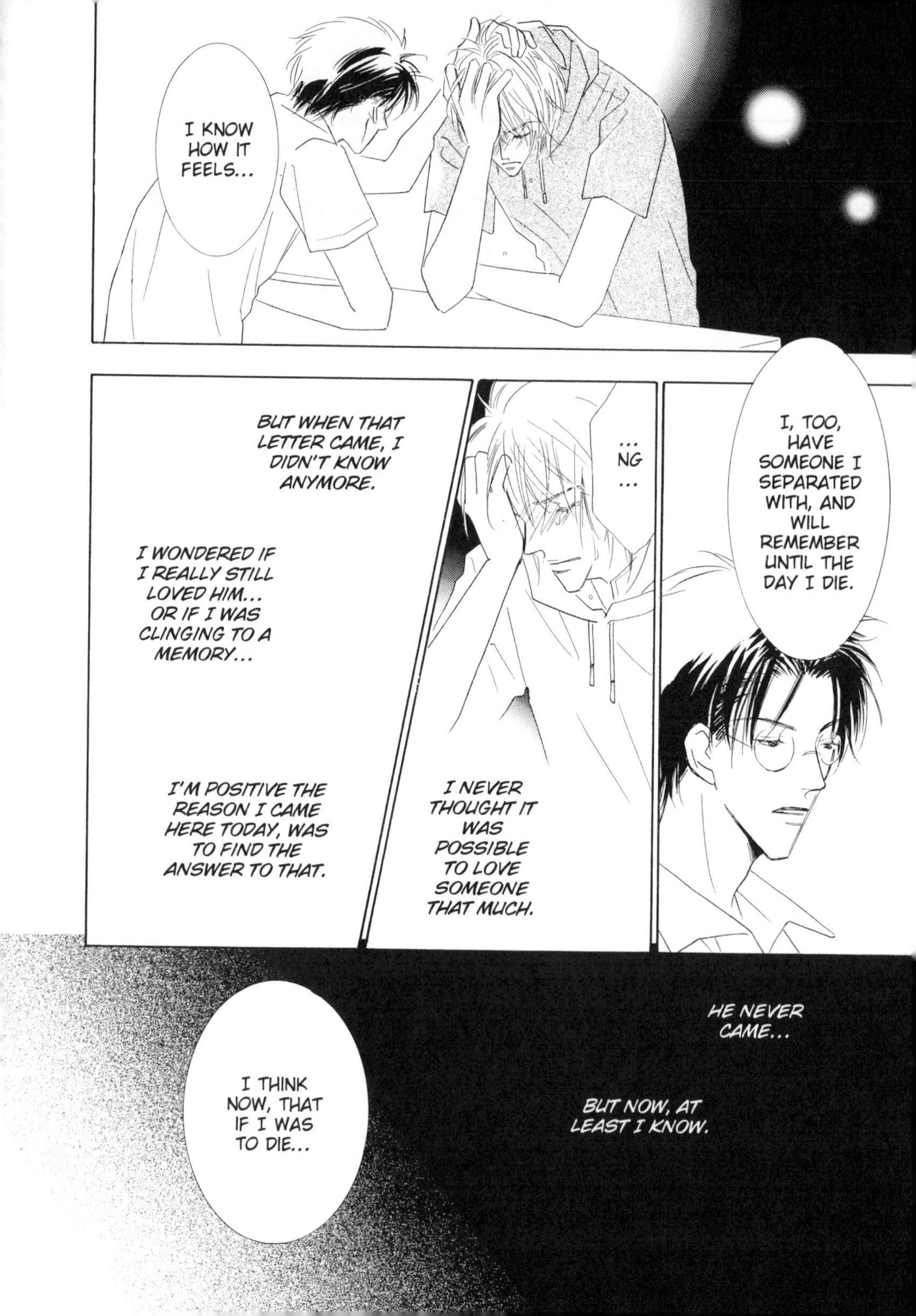
I KNOW HOW IT FEELS...
I, TOO, HAVE SOMEONE I SEPARATED WITH, AND WILL REMEMBER UNTIL THE DAY I DIE.
...NG...
I NEVER THOUGHT IT WAS POSSIBLE TO LOVE SOMEONE THAT MUCH.
BUT WHEN THAT LETTER CAME, I DIDN'T KNOW ANYMORE.
I WONDERED IF I REALLY STILL LOVED HIM... OR IF I WAS CLINGING TO A MEMORY...
I'M POSITIVE THE REASON I CAME HERE TODAY, WAS TO FIND THE ANSWER TO THAT.
HE NEVER CAME...
BUT NOW, AT LEAST I KNOW.
I THINK NOW, THAT IF I WAS TO DIE...

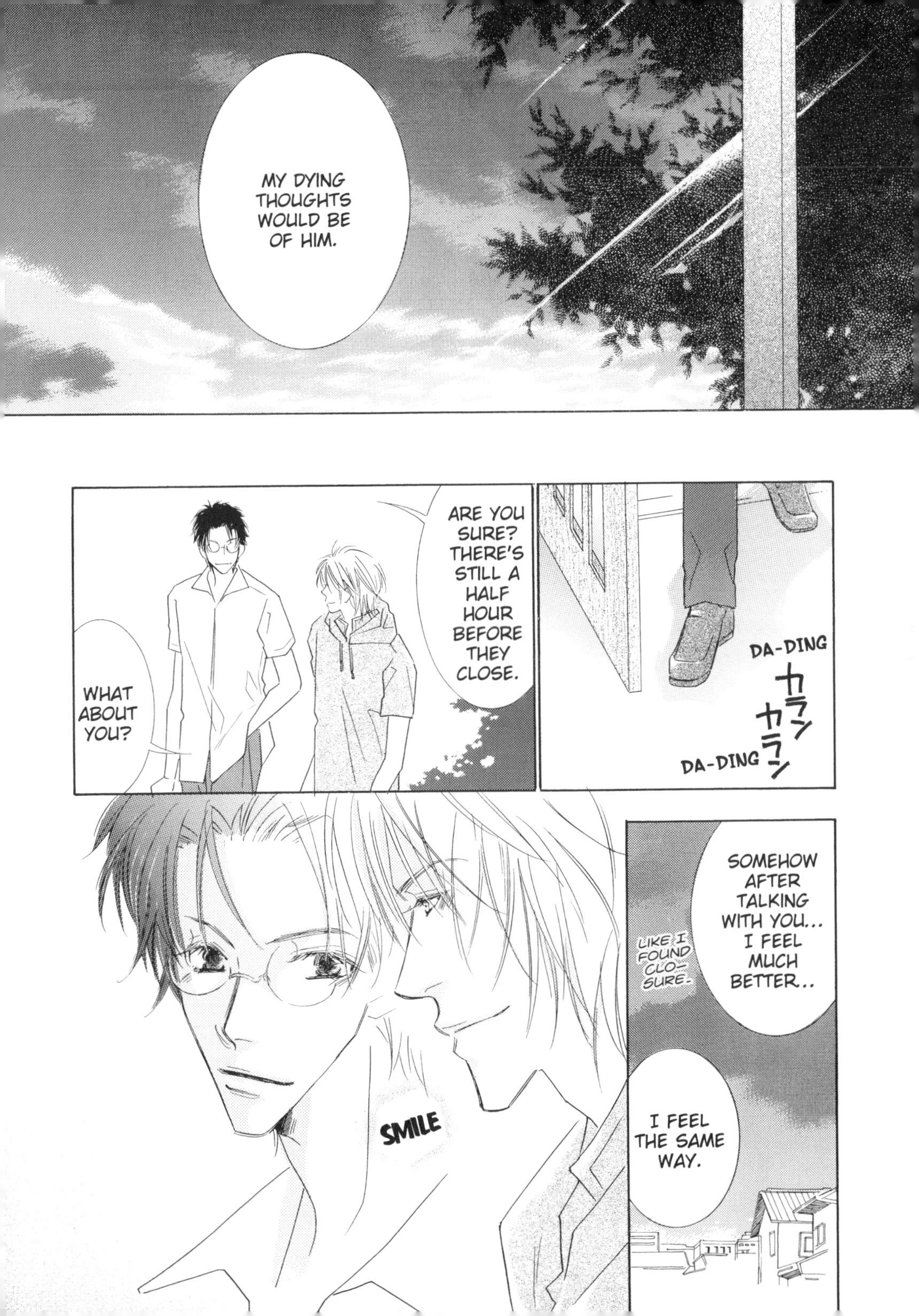
MY DYING THOUGHTS WOULD BE OF HIM.
DA-DING
カラン
カラン
DA-DING
ARE YOU SURE? THERE'S STILL A HALF HOUR BEFORE THEY CLOSE.
WHAT ABOUT YOU?
SOMEHOW AFTER TALKING WITH YOU... I FEEL MUCH BETTER..
LIKE I FOUND CLO-SURE.
I FEEL THE SAME WAY.
SMILE

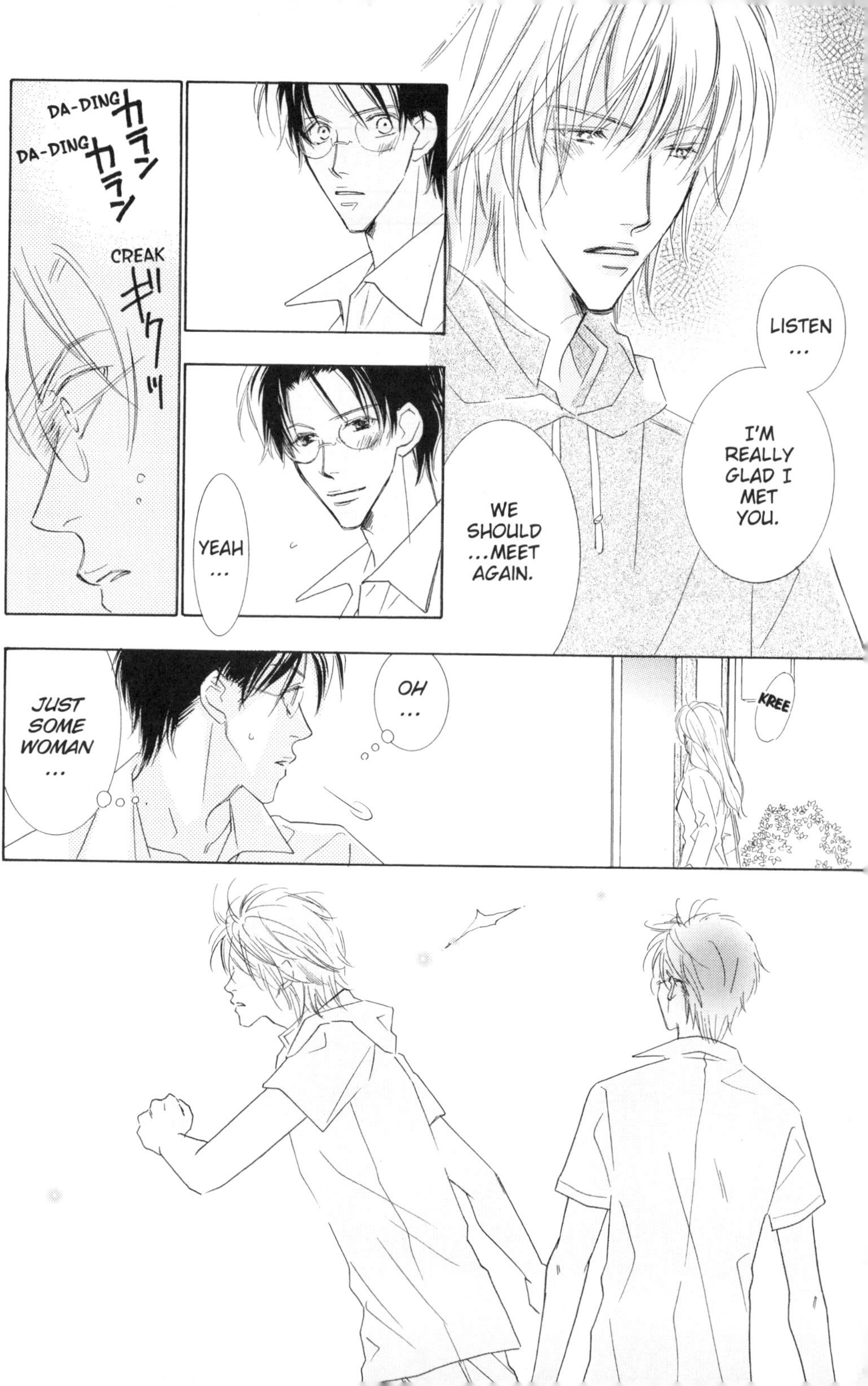
LISTEN ...
I'M REALLY GLAD I MET YOU.
WE SHOULD ...MEET AGAIN.
YEAH ...
DA-DING カラン
DA-DING カラン
CREAK ギクッ
KREE
OH ...
JUST SOME WOMAN ...

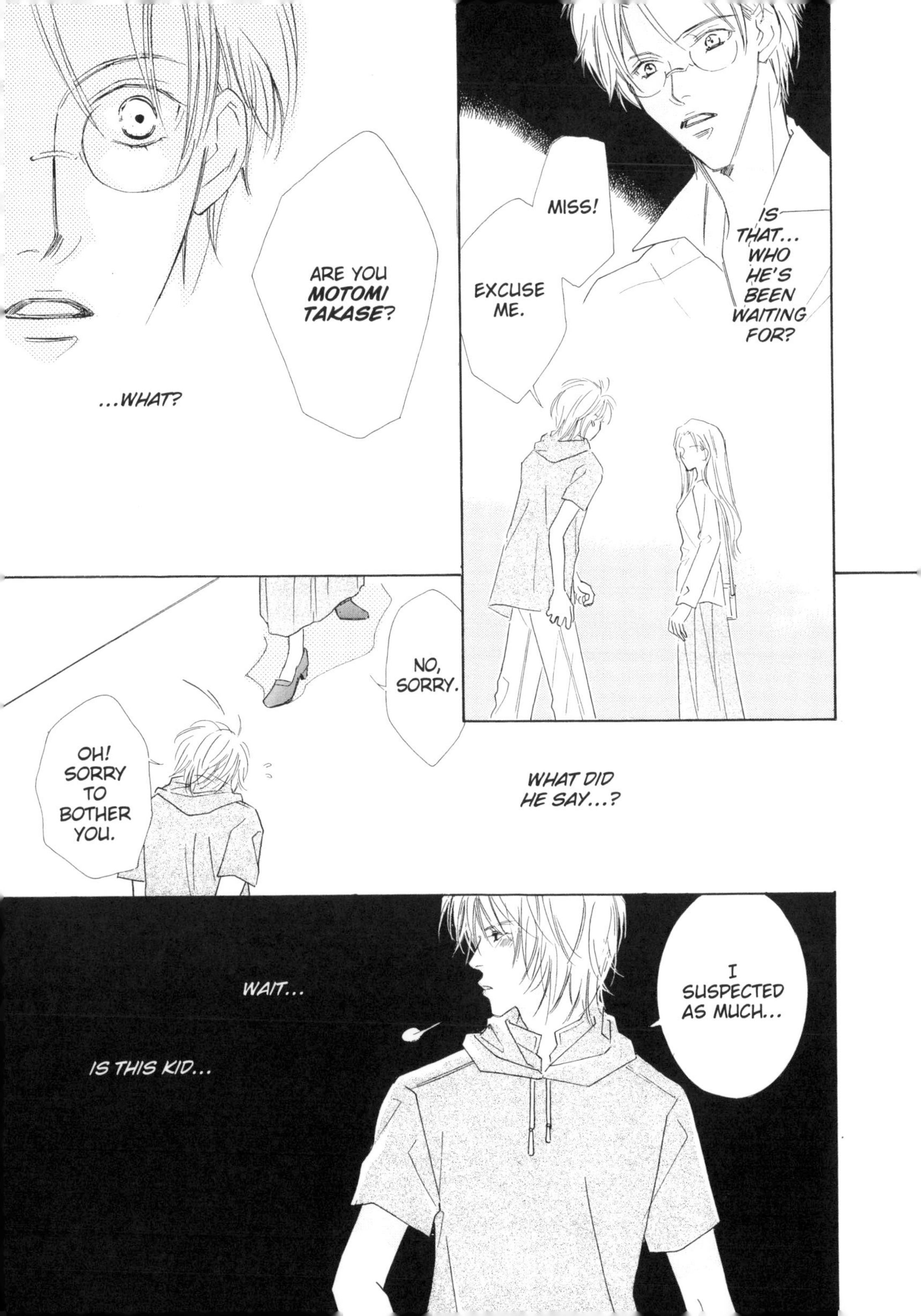
IS THAT... WHO HE'S BEEN WAITING FOR?
MISS!
EXCUSE ME.
ARE YOU MOTOMI TAKASE?
...WHAT?
NO, SORRY.
WHAT DID HE SAY...?
OH! SORRY TO BOTHER YOU.
I SUSPECTED AS MUCH...
WAIT...
IS THIS KID...

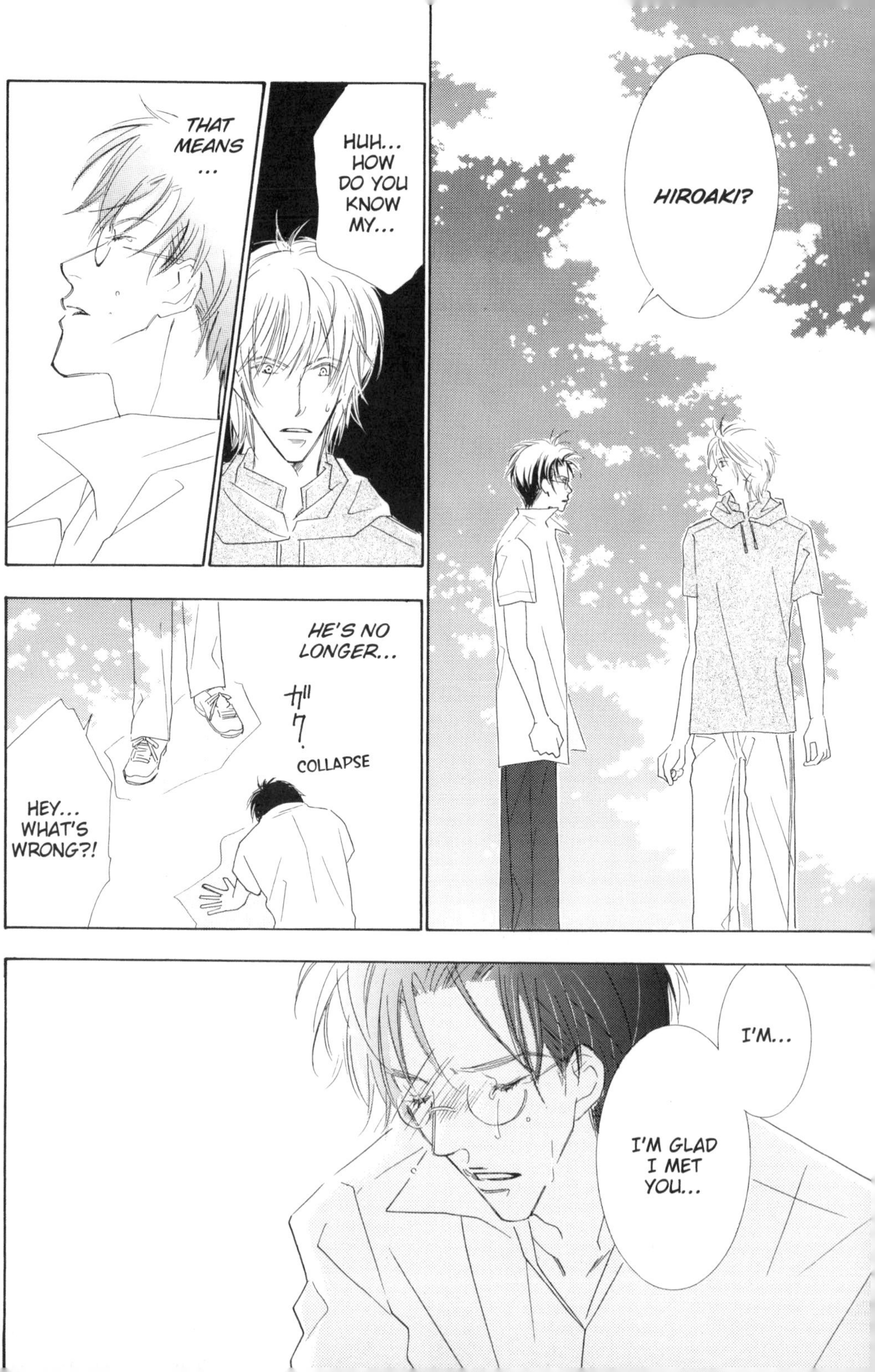
HIROAKI?
HUH... HOW DO YOU KNOW MY...
THAT MEANS ...
HE'S NO LONGER...
ガク
COLLAPSE
HEY... WHAT'S WRONG?!
I'M...
I'M GLAD I MET YOU...

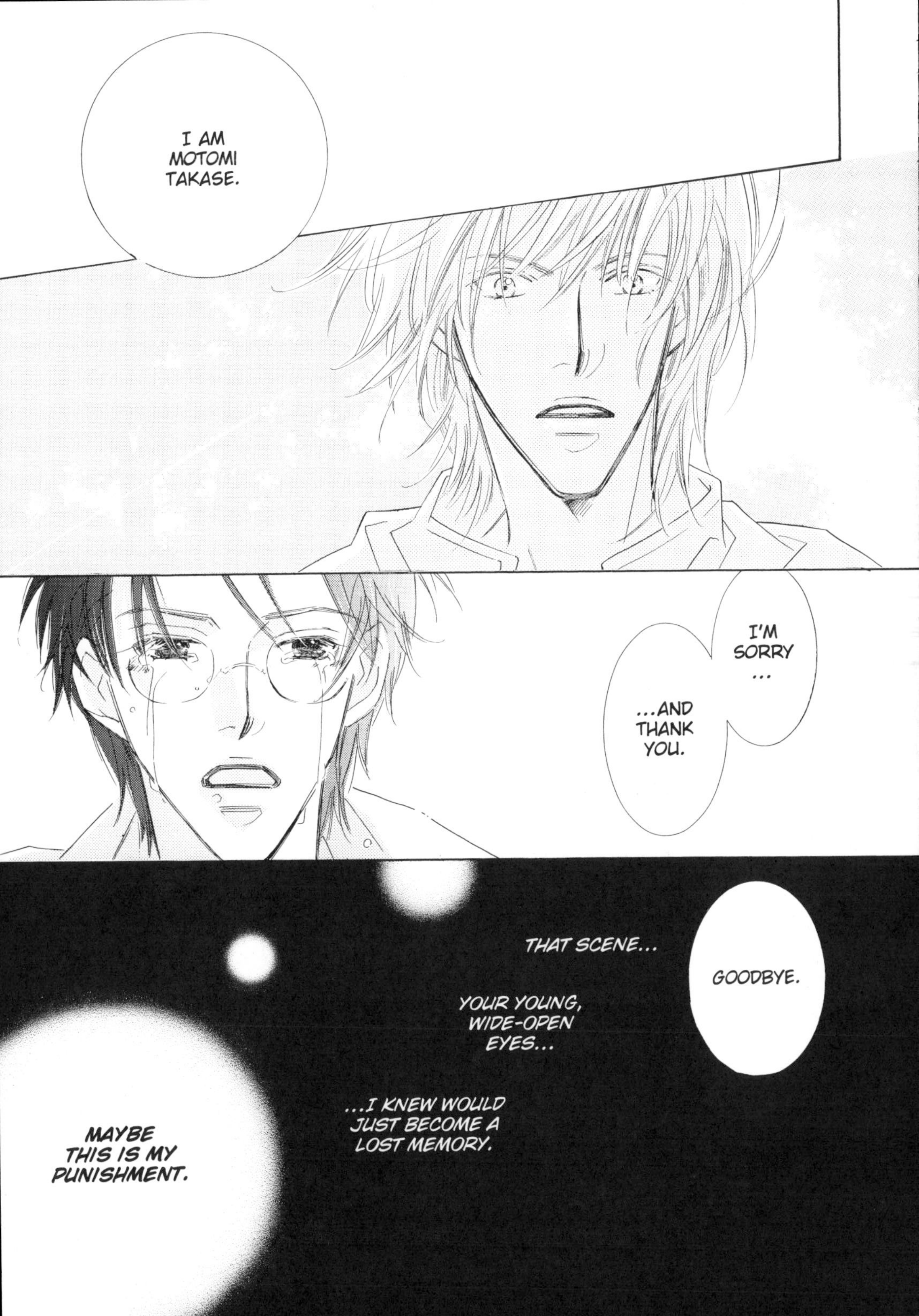
I AM MOTOMI TAKASE.
I'M SORRY...
...AND THANK YOU.
GOODBYE.
THAT SCENE...
YOUR YOUNG, WIDE-OPEN EYES...
...I KNEW WOULD JUST BECOME A LOST MEMORY.
MAYBE THIS IS MY PUNISHMENT.

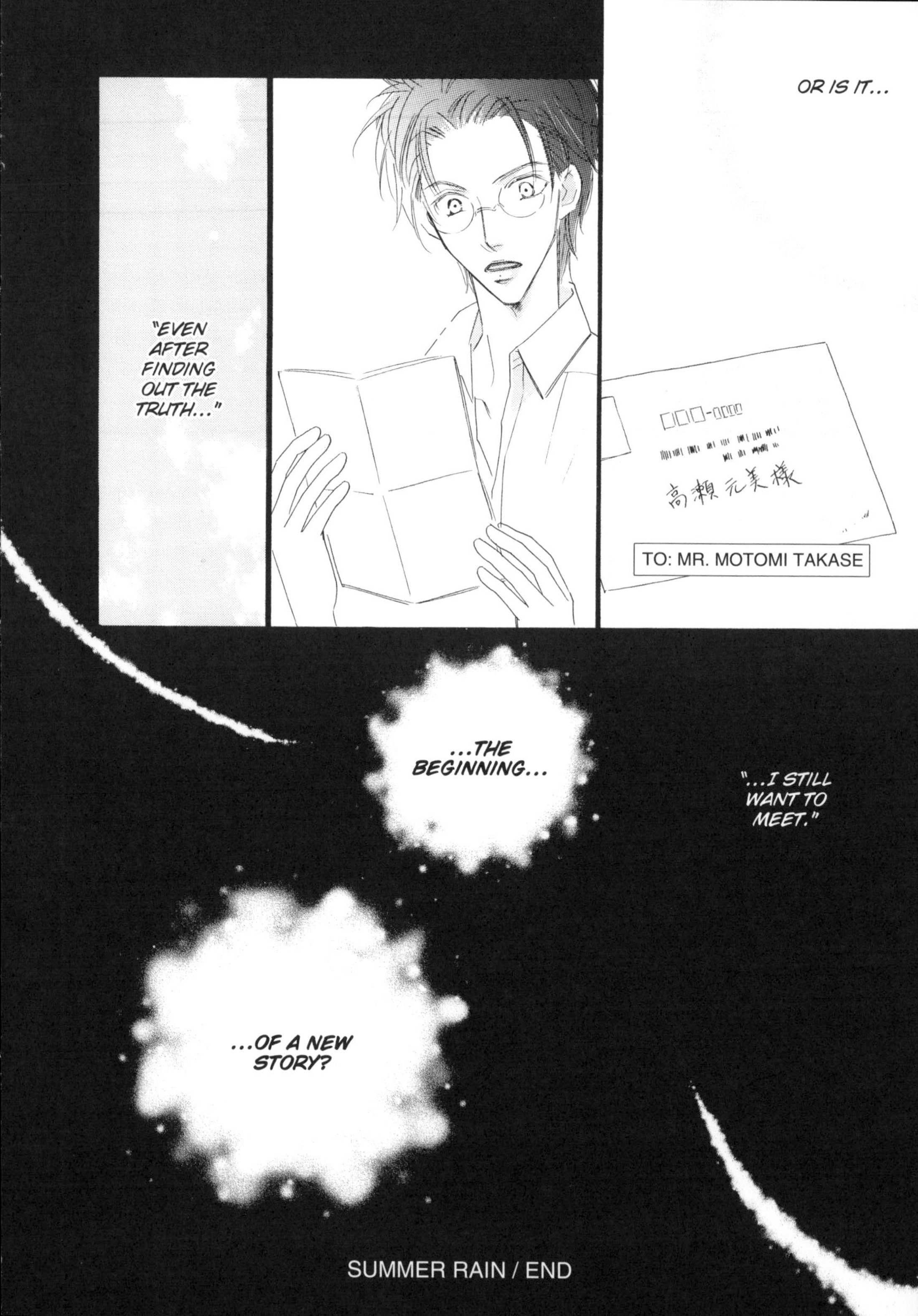
OR IS IT...
高瀬元美様
TO: MR. MOTOMI TAKASE
"EVEN AFTER FINDING OUT THE TRUTH..."
"...I STILL WANT TO MEET."
...THE BEGINNING...
...OF A NEW STORY?
SUMMER RAIN / END

✳ THANK YOU SO MUCH FOR READING MY
MANGA, DESPITE ALL ITS FLAWS. THIS
IS MY SECOND MANGA WITH CRAFT
COMICS, AND MY THIRD OVERALL
(SURPRISED).

✳ SOME COMMENTS ABOUT THE BOOK.

THE PARADISE ON THE HILL

THE THEME HERE WAS "GIRLY ROMANTIC."

THE MAIDEN KIJIMA — ONO THE STALKER —
THE GORGEOUS TSUDA... I'VE WANTED TO
DRAW THIS FOR A LONG TIME, BUT I DIDN'T
FEEL I WAS READY UNTIL NOW, SO I'M
REALLY HAPPY I WAS FINALLY ABLE TO
MAKE IT WORK (I'M GLAD I DIDN'T GIVE
UP!). KIJIMA WAS ORIGINALLY SUPPOSED
TO BE "COOL AND SUAVE," BUT SOMEHOW
HE ENDED UP GIRLY. I DO LIKE HIM,
THOUGH. AS FOR ONO, WHAT I REMEM-
BER MOST IS THAT MY EDITOR KEPT
TELLING ME "HE NEEDS TO BE COOLER!!"
LOL. (MY EDITOR AND I DON'T CARE TOO
MUCH FOR P.E. TEACHERS...). THEN
WHY DID I MAKE HIM A P.E. TEACHER,
YOU ASK? BECAUSE I WANTED TO DRAW
SWEATS — LOL. ACTUALLY, ONO REALLY
WANTED TO BECOME AN ELEMENTARY
SCHOOL TEACHER.

WHEN I GET TO WORK, I HAVE THIS
CHRONIC ILLNESS WHERE I FEEL I DON'T
EVER HAVE ENOUGH PAGES. SO THIS TIME
AROUND, MY GOAL WAS TO USE AS MANY
AS I COULD. THAT, IN TURN, CAUSED THE
STORY TO LAG IN PARTS... IT'S REALLY
HARD TO FIND A BALANCE!! (I'VE GOT A
LONG WAY TO GO). ALSO, THERE'S
SOMETHING I REGRET TERRIBLY ABOUT
CHAPTER 4. WHEN I FIRST COMPLETED IT,
I FELT I DEFINITELY NEEDED TO REDRAW,
BUT I COULDN'T DO IT (NOT ENOUGH
TIME). MAYBE IT'D BE SMARTER TO NOT
TELL YOU ALL THIS... BUT I WAS SO
STRESSED ABOUT IT, I THOUGHT I'D LOSE
MY MIND! HOPEFULLY I CAN USE THIS
EXTRA STRESS AS FUEL FOR MY FUTURE
PROJECTS! (IS THAT POSSIBLE?)

I GUESS THAT'S ALL I HAVE TO SAY
ABOUT IT — I PUT MY HEART INTO THIS
PIECE.

→
KIJIMA PROBABLY WEARS SWEATS
ON OCCASION. MAYBE AT THE
SPORTS FESTIVAL, OR A BASEBALL
MEET.
FOR EXAMPLE, IN THE TEACHER'S
VOLLEYBALL TOURNAMENT (IN WHICH
HE'S NO GOOD), ALL WILL PROBABLY
BE MESMERIZED BY TSUDA-SENSEI,
SO HE'D BE ABLE TO SCORE A FEW
POINTS THERE.
(WHAT HE'S REALLY GOOD AT IS
TENNIS. SO THESE ARE ACTUALLY HIS
TENNIS CLOTHES.)
(ONO USUALLY WEARS BASKETBALL
ATTIRE.)

THE PARADISE
ON THE HILL

AFTERWORD

DATE

LOOKING BACK AT CHAPTERS 1-4, I REALIZED THAT I DREW KIJIMA IN HIS SUIT FOR ALL OF THEM. IT KIND OF SURPRISED ME... (HE NEVER EVEN TAKES HIS BLAZER OFF!) I THOUGHT HE'D LOOK PRETTY HOT EVEN WITH JUST HIS SLEEVES ROLLED UP. AM I WRONG? OR MAYBE I'M JUST THE TYPE THAT LIKES ARMS. (OK, I **LOVE** ARMS.) SO I DREW THIS STORY WITH THAT IN MIND. THOUGH ARMS DON'T REALLY MAKE MUCH OF AN APPEARANCE. I THINK THESE TWO GUYS WILL ALWAYS BE THIS WAY AROUND EACH OTHER... THEY'LL NEVER GROW OUT OF PUPPY LOVE.

SUMMER RAIN

THIS ONE REALLY, REALLY HAD ME ON THE EDGE (EMOTIONALLY). THAT'S WHAT I REMEMBER ABOUT IT. (THOUGH THERE'S NEVER REALLY A TIME WHEN I'M **NOT** ON THE EDGE...) SO I COULDN'T RE-READ IT 'CUZ I WAS TOO SCARED. WHEN I LOOK AT IT NOW, THOUGH, I LIKE THE STORY A LOT... EVEN THOUGH MY ART IS PATHETIC. THE ONLY THING WRONG WITH IT IS THAT MOTOMI LOOKS A LITTLE BIT LIKE KIJIMA... AND TO THINK THE TWO STORIES GOT PUT INTO THE SAME BOOK. I GUESS I SHOULD'VE THOUGHT ABOUT THAT... HEH HEH...

❀PEOPLE I'D LIKE TO THANK❀

♥CATHERINE AND KUMIKO. SORRY ABOUT THE LAST-MINUTE DRAWINGS... AH, AND THANKS FOR CHAPTER 4, CATHERINE! (THAT'S WHAT HAPPENS WHEN YOU LIVE SO CLOSE TO ME...) THIS TIME I REALLY THOUGHT I WOULD BE DEAD WITHOUT THE HELP OF MY ASSISTANTS. BETTER SAY THAT BEFORE I FORGET (BAD ME!).

♥MY DEAR EDITOR UTSUNOMIYA. THANK YOU SO... SO... SO MUCH!! (I'M CONSTANTLY AMAZED AT HOW YOU KNOW WHAT I HAVE IN MIND, WHEN I'M COMPLETELY LACKING IN COMMUNICA- TION SKILLS). I LOOK FORWARD TO WORKING WITH YOU AGAIN!

♥IKEDA, WHO HELPED ME OUT WITH SUMMER RAIN.

♥EVERYONE INVOLVED IN THE PRODUCTION AND SALES OF THIS BOOK. THANK YOU VERY MUCH!

KIJIMA ALWAYS WEARS SUITS BECAUSE HE LIKES THEM. I'LL BET HE'LL HAVE LOADS OF FUN PLAYING "DRESS-UP" WITH ONO IF THEY GET TO A SUIT STORE ON A DATE. IN A DOUBLE-BUTTON SUIT WITH A PEAKED LAPEL LIKE THIS, IT'S SO OUT OF CHARACTER FOR HIM, IT'S LIKE, "WHO THE HELL ARE YOU? WHERE'S ONO?!"

THANK YOU SO MUCH FOR READING ALL OF THAT. IF YOU HAD EVEN A LITTLE BIT OF FUN, THEN I'M GRATEFUL.

UNTIL WE MEET AGAIN. WHEREVER THAT IS.

Jan. 2002.
momokolenzen.

He has no luck.
He has no name.

Sometimes letting go of the past...
requires finding love in the present.

SEVEN

BY MOMOKO TENZEN

June

junemanga.com

ISBN# 978-1-56970-849-1 $12.95

SEVEN © Momoko Tenzen 2004.
Originally published in Japan in 2004 by TAIYOH TOSHO Co., Ltd.

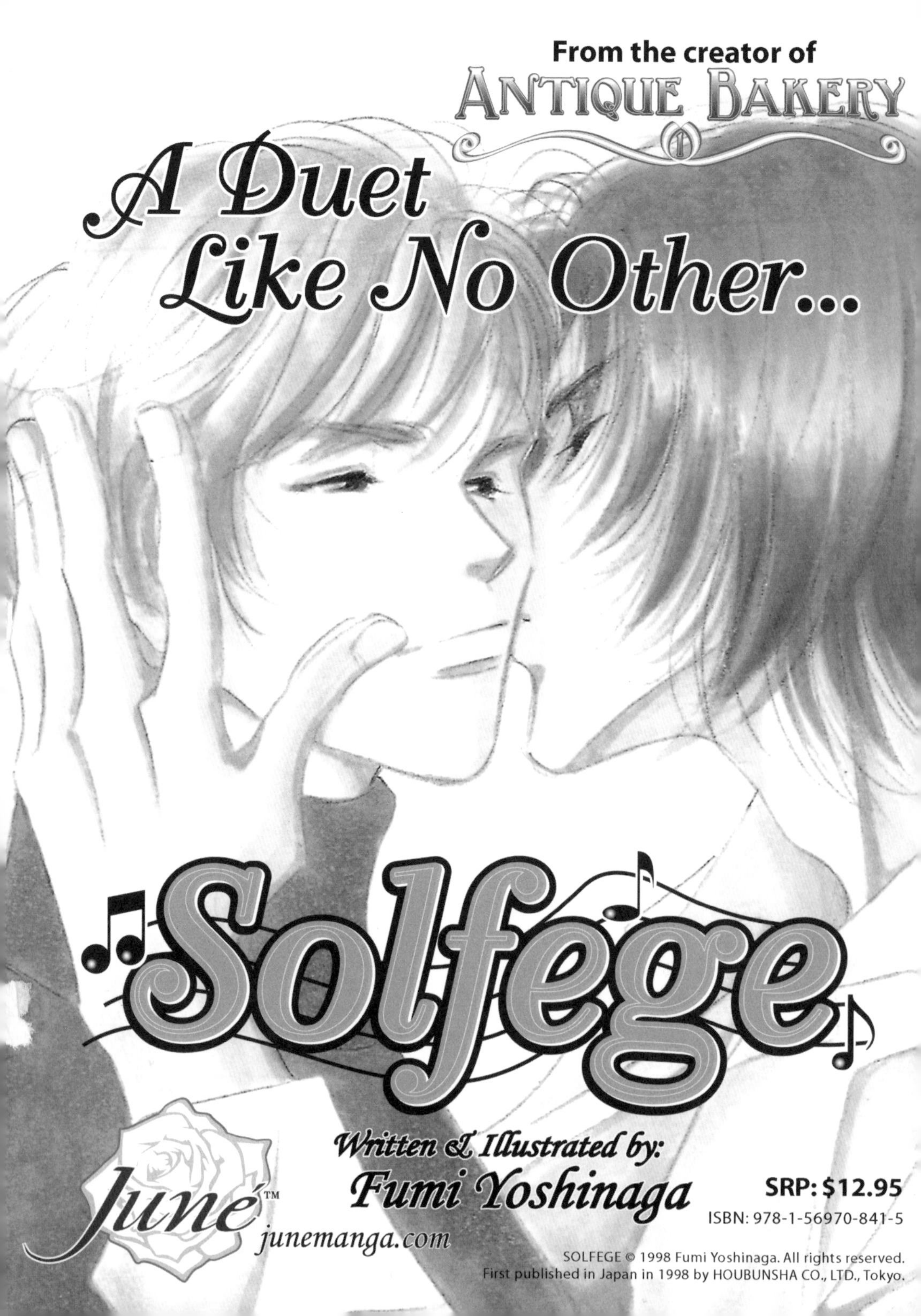
From the creator of
ANTIQUE BAKERY
A Duet Like No Other...
Solfege
Written & Illustrated by:
Fumi Yoshinaga
June™
junemanga.com
SRP: $12.95
ISBN: 978-1-56970-841-5
SOLFEGE © 1998 Fumi Yoshinaga. All rights reserved.
First published in Japan in 1998 by HOUBUNSHA CO., LTD., Tokyo.

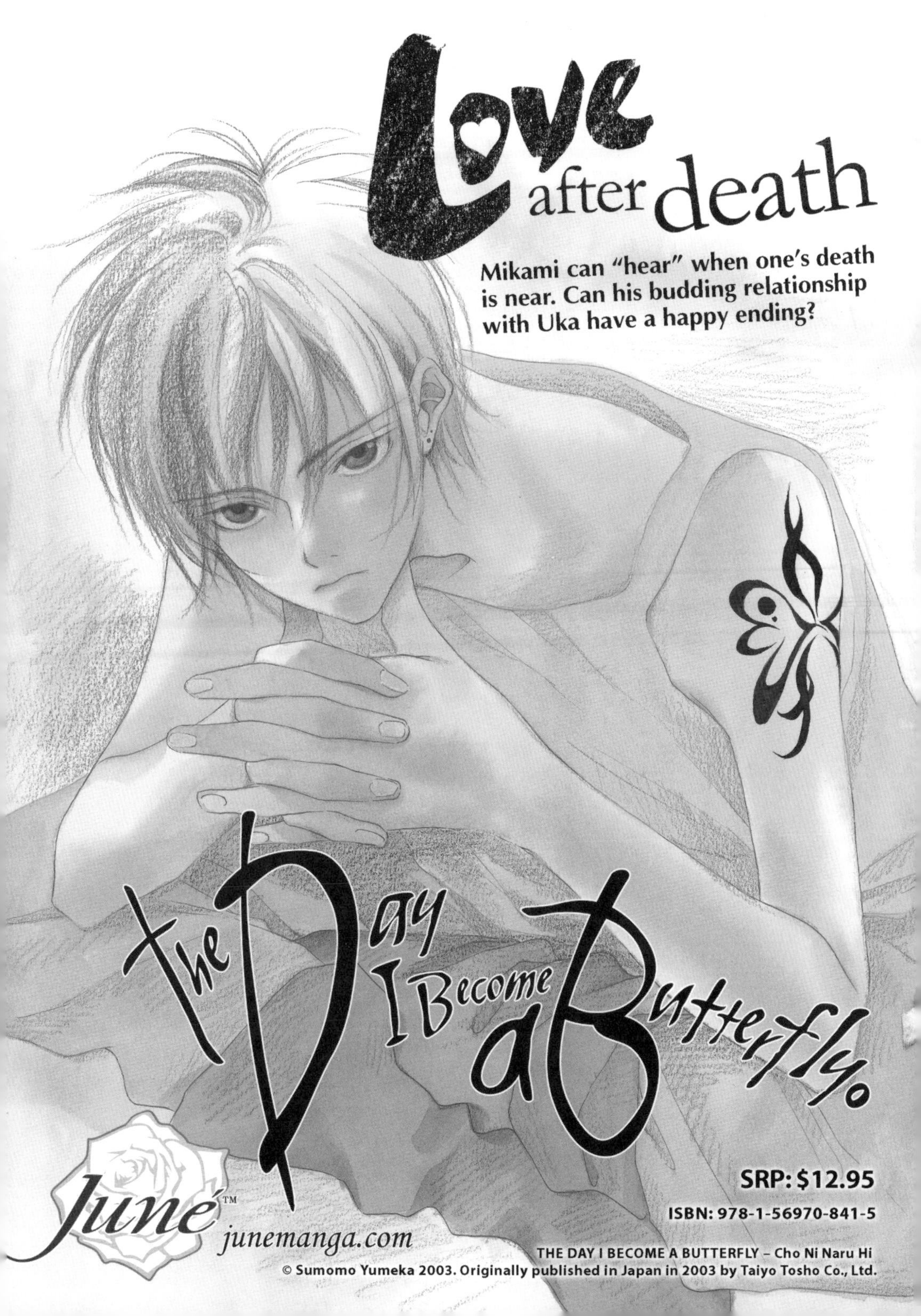
Love after death
Mikami can "hear" when one's death is near. Can his budding relationship with Uka have a happy ending?
The Day I Become a Butterfly
Juné™
junemanga.com
SRP: $12.95
ISBN: 978-1-56970-841-5
THE DAY I BECOME A BUTTERFLY – Cho Ni Naru Hi
© Sumomo Yumeka 2003. Originally published in Japan in 2003 by Taiyo Tosho Co., Ltd.

When love's on the rebound...
"friends with benefits" take a holiday.
PICNIC
YUGI YAMADA
"The Legend of Yaoi"
SRP: $12.95
ISBN: 978-1-56970-872-9
PICNIC © 2004 Yugi Yamada. All rights reserved.
First published in Japan in 2004 by HOUBUNSHA CO., LTD., Tokyo.
June™
junemanga.com

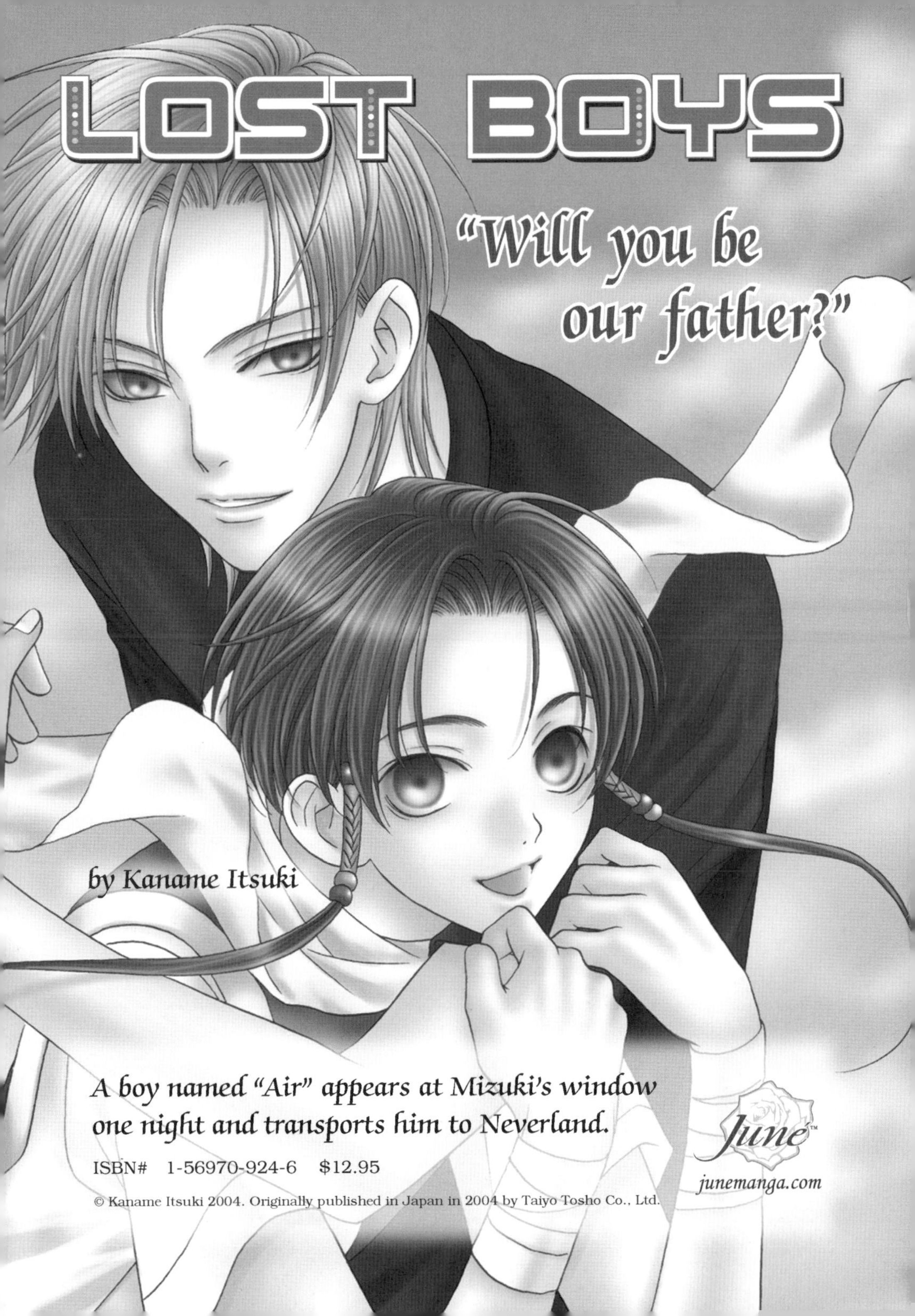

THE Moon AND Sandals Vol. 1

月とサンダル

SEE ME AFTER CLASS!

ISBN# 978-1-56970-802-9 SRP $12.95

june
by DMP

As a newly appointed high school teacher, Ida has yet to gain confidence in his abilities. His insecurity grows worse when he feels someone staring intensely at him during class. The piercing eyes belong to a tall, intimidating student – Koichi Kobayashi. What exactly should Ida do about it? Is it discontent that fuels Kobayashi's sultry gaze… or could it be something else?

Written and Illustrated by:
Fumi Yoshinaga

junemanga.com

STOP

This is the back of the book!
Start from the other side.

NATIVE MANGA readers read manga from *right to left*.

1
2
1
3
2
3
5
4
6
5
8
7
6

*If you run into our **Native Manga** logo on any of our books... you'll know that this manga is published in it's true original native Japanese right to left reading format, as it was intended. Turn to the other side of the book and start reading from right to left, top to bottom.*

Follow the diagram to see how its done.
Surf's Up!

NATIVE MANGA
READ RIGHT TO LEFT